Hammond's
Cooking Explained

Jill Davies

fourth edition

 **LONGMAN**

Contents

Part 1

1 Nutrition and health

Health promotion

Until recently, inconclusive evidence on the role of diet as a causal factor in the aetiology (origin) of 'diet-related' diseases has been a major barrier to preventive action. Fortunately, the tide has turned and this is primarily due to two publications.

1 The Committee on Medical Aspects of Food Policy (COMA) report on *Dietary Reference Values for Food Energy and Nutrients for the United Kingdom*.
2 *The Health of the Nation* White Paper.

Both of these publications acknowledge that diet is one of several lifestyle factors which can contribute to good health. The COMA report has made clear the changes required in the nutritional balance of the diet. The White Paper has set targets for diet and nutrition in the overall context of COMA.

The Health of the Nation White Paper has focused attention on the fact that many people die prematurely or suffer debilitating ill-health conditions which, to a large extent, are preventable. The White Paper strategy is about securing a continuing improvement in the general health of the population by 'adding years to life' and 'life to years' so that people not only live longer, but spend these additional years free from ill-health. The emergence of Western diseases in developing regions of the world and in populations migrating to westernised areas show that *The Health of the Nation* targets have potential for worldwide application.

Diet-related diseases

Obesity

Incidence
Obesity is the most common nutritional disorder in affluent societies and the prevalence of obesity in the UK has increased gradually during the last 50 years. Obesity is most common in middle age although it can occur at any stage of life.

Definition
Obesity is simply defined as a condition in which there is an excessive amount of body fat. If the intake of energy from the diet is greater than energy output, the excess is stored as adipose tissue and this is associated with an increase in body weight. Fig. 1.1 provides a practical way of assessing weight.

Fig. 1.1 Weight assessment chart for adults

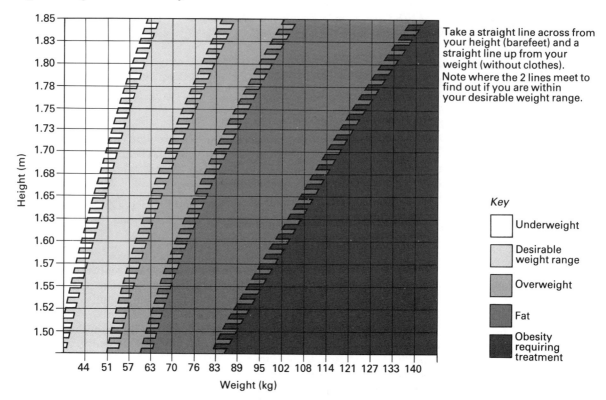

The *body mass index* (BMI) is commonly used as an index of population fatness.

$$BMI = \frac{\text{weight (kg)}}{\text{height (m}^2)}$$

The BMI values may be interpreted as follows:

BMI	Weight
Below 20	Underweight
20–25	Acceptable
25–30	Overweight
30–40	Obese
Above 40	Very obese

Diet-related risk factors
An energy intake that is chronically in excess of energy output.

Coronary heart disease

Incidence
Coronary heart disease (CHD) is a major cause of death in the UK. One person dies every 3 minutes from the disease, which is about 180 000 deaths a year. The disease causes suffering for about 2 million people. It

accounts for 2.5% of total National Health Service (NHS) expenditure and results in 35 million working days being lost per year.

Definition
The term CHD is used to describe a group of disorders which occur as a result of failure of the coronary arteries to supply enough blood to the heart muscle. This is associated with the narrowing and hardening of the arteries due to atherosclerosis, that is, the deposition of cholesterol, fatty acids and blood clots on the inside of the blood vessels (Fig. 1.2).

Signs and symptoms

- *Angina*, which is chest pain resulting from a lack of blood supply to the heart muscle.
- *Myocardial infarction*, which means a heart attack, due to an irreversible reduction in blood supply to part of the heart muscle.
- *Heart failure*, due to substantial damage to the heart muscle resulting from an inadequate blood supply. This is often associated with tiredness, breathlessness and swelling of the ankles.

Diet-related risk factors

- raised plasma cholesterol
- obesity
- diabetes mellitus

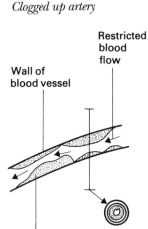

Fig. 1.2
Clogged up artery

Restricted blood flow

Wall of blood vessel

Plaque

Stroke

Incidence
Cerebrovascular disease (CVD), referred to as stroke, is a common cause of death in adults. It is the third most common cause of death in developed countries. It is a major cause of disability, particularly among elderly people. It accounts for 6% of total NHS expenditure and results in 7.7 million working days being lost per year.

Definition
The term 'stroke' is used to describe damage to brain tissue due to either cerebral infarction, causing restricted blood flow to the brain (Fig. 1.2) or, to a lesser extent, to a haemorrhage in the brain.

Diet-related risk factors

- raised blood pressure
- obesity

Raised blood cholesterol

Incidence
According to *The Dietary and Nutritional Survey of British Adults*, nearly 80% of men and women aged 35–64 years have total serum cholesterol values above 5.2 mmol/l and about 10% are over 7.8 mmol/l. Optimal levels of total serum cholesterol range from 5.2 to 5.7 mmol/l.

Definition
Cholesterol is a type of fat, essential for life, which is produced primarily by the liver, although some is obtained from the diet. It is transported in the blood attached to proteins called lipoproteins. There are two main types of these proteins. These are *low-density lipoproteins* (LDL), which carry about 70% of total cholesterol, and *high-density lipoproteins* (HDL). LDL is sometimes described as 'bad' cholesterol because the higher the level of LDL, the greater the risk of plaque formation (Fig. 1.2). HDL is described

as 'good' cholesterol because it clears away excess cholesterol from the tissues, taking it to the liver for disposal.

People with a raised total plasma cholesterol and raised LDL cholesterol and those having low HDL cholesterol can be at increased risk of developing CHD. In clinical practice most cases of raised cholesterol are described as *common hypercholesterolaemia*, due to the raised LDL cholesterol.

Diet-related risk factors

- obesity
- high saturated fatty acid intakes
- low polyunsaturated fatty acid intakes. Increasing dietary n-6 polyunsaturated fatty acids will decrease total cholesterol and LDL cholesterol. Increasing the n-3 polyunsaturated fatty acids, such as *docosahexaenoic* and *eicosapentaenoic acid* in fish oils and *alpha-linolenic acid*, does not appear to influence total cholesterol levels, but they may inhibit the formation of blood clots.

High blood pressure

Incidence

In Western societies, blood pressure (BP) gradually rises with age and it has been estimated that about 15% of the population in the UK have high BP.

Definition

The medical term for high BP is *hypertension*. The pressure exerted by the blood on the artery walls is recorded first as the *systolic pressure*. This is obtained when the heart is at the maximum contraction. Then, second, the *diastolic pressure* is measured, which is when the left ventricle of the heart is in a state of relaxation. It is important to maintain BP in order to supply blood to the body's tissues. However, if the BP becomes too high, blood vessels may become damaged. The World Health Organisation defines hypertension as a systolic BP above 160 mmHg and/or a diastolic BP above 95 mmHg.

Diet-related risk factors

- obesity
- high alcohol intake
- high salt intake
- low potassium intake

Diabetes mellitus

Incidence

Diabetes mellitus, simply referred to as diabetes, is by far the most common endocrine (hormone) disorder, and the incidence of it is rising throughout the world. The true prevalence is uncertain and in the UK it has been suggested that almost 50% of cases of *non-insulin-dependent diabetes* (NIDDM) remain undetected. NIDDM occurs mainly in older, overweight people and is the most prevalent form of the disorder. *Insulin-dependent diabetes* (IDDM) occurs mainly in young people.

Definition

For the normal uptake of glucose by the tissues to take place, the hormone insulin is required. This is secreted by the β-cells of the Islets of Langerhans in the pancreas. If there is a complete lack of insulin or the body uses it ineffectively, the normal uptake of glucose cannot take place, so diabetes mellitus results.

Diet-related risk factors

- NIDDM is more common in people who are overweight.

Constipation

Incidence
Constipation is a disorder associated with Western diets. In the UK, it has been reported to impair the quality of life of about 20% of people aged over 65 years, and around 10% of the adult population.

Definition
Constipation is characterised by infrequent bowel movements – fewer than 3 per week – a transit time (the time it takes for food to pass from mouth to anus) of 5 days or more and stool weights averaging below 50 g/day.

Diet-related risk factors

- low intake of dietary fibre

Constipation-related disorders

A number of disorders are associated with constipation and the following were referred to by the COMA Panel on Dietary Reference Values (DRVs).

Diverticular disease
Diverticulosis is a common condition in Western populations. It rarely occurs before the age of 30 years, but about 30% of the population have diverticulosis by the sixth decade and 50% by the ninth decade.

Diverticulosis is a condition in which pouches, which look like blow-outs on a rubber tyre, form in the wall of the colon (Fig. 1.3). It is associated with stool weights of less than 150 g/day. The colonic muscles need to contract strongly to transmit and expel the small stools associated with a fibre-deficient diet. The increased pressure within the bowel results in the formation of these pouches.

Fig. 1.3
Diverticular disease of the colon

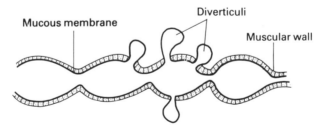

Large bowel cancer
Cancers of the *colon* and *rectum* are the second most common cancers in Western societies, affecting up to 6% of men and women by the age of 75 years.

Normal colonic cells hyper-proliferate and benign polyps, called adenomas, form. The adenomatous polyps may progress to being carcinomas. Bowel cancer is associated with stool weights of less than 150 g/day. Dietary fibre may have a protective role, due to a number of mechanisms:

- dilution of colonic contents;
- more rapid transit time, giving less time for carcinogenic action and less substrate for bacterial production of carcinogens.

Gallstones

Fig. 1.4
Gallstones

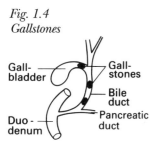

National incidence figures for gallstones are not available. However, studies have shown that the condition is twice as prevalent in women as in men, that gallstones increase in prevalence with age and that they are common in obese people.

Gallstones form in the gall-bladder (Fig. 1.4) and, should they move to the various ducts and get stuck, they will cause pain. Prolonged transit time and constipation are associated with increased levels of deoxycholic acid in bile, which is a risk factor for gallstones.

Dental caries

Incidence

In societies where the average total sugar in the diet supplies less than 10% of dietary energy, dental caries is rare. In the UK it has been estimated that pre-school children take 25–30% of food energy as sugar and older children and adults tend to take 17–25%. The COMA Panel on DRVs stated that those particularly at risk of dental caries are children, adolescents and the elderly.

Fig. 1.5
Cross section of a tooth with caries

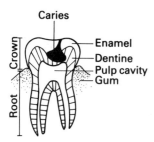

Definition

In the first instance, dental caries (Fig. 1.5) involves erosion of the tooth enamel. Once the enamel has been eroded, the amelodentinal margin is attacked and then the dentine is penetrated. Penetration of the dentine may occur slowly or may be rapid and lead to the formation of an abscess.

Bacteria – streptococci – produce lactic acid as a result of fermenting sugar and this dissolves the enamel of the tooth. In addition to this, certain streptococci have enzymes which form complex sugary compounds from glucose and fructose. These stick to the teeth and plaque then forms.

Diet-related risk factors

- non-milk extrinsic sugar
- non-fluoridated water

Health of the Nation targets

Coronary heart disease and stroke

1 To reduce death rates from both CHD and stroke in people under 65 by at least 40% by the year 2000 (from 58 per 100 000 population in 1990 to no more than 35 per 100 000 for CHD, and from 12.5 per 100 000 population in 1990 to no more than 7.5 per 100 000 for stroke).

2 To reduce the death rate from CHD in people aged 65–74 by at least 30% by the year 2000 (from 899 per 100 000 population in 1990 to no more than 629 per 100 000).

3 To reduce the death rate from stroke in people aged 65–74 by at least 40% by the year 2000 (from 265 per 100 000 population in 1990 to no more than 159 per 100 000).

Diet and nutrition

1 To reduce the average percentage of food energy derived from saturated fatty acids by at least 35% by 2005 (from 17% in 1990 to no more than 11%).

2 To reduce the average percentage of food energy derived from total fat consumed by at least 12% by 2005 (from about 40% in 1990 to no more than 35%).

Obesity

To reduce the percentages of men and women aged 16–64 who are obese by at least 25% for men and at least 33% for women by 2005 (from 8% for men and 12% for women in 1986/87 to no more than 6% and 8% respectively).

Blood pressure

To reduce mean systolic blood pressure in the adult population by at least 5 mmHg by 2005.

Alcohol

To reduce the proportion of men drinking more than 21 units of alcohol per week from 28% in 1990 to 18% by 2005, and the proportion of women drinking more than 14 units of alcohol per week from 11% in 1990 to 7% by 2005.

COMA Dietary Reference Values

The publication of the COMA report on *Dietary Reference Values for Food Energy and Nutrients for the United Kingdom* has been a major breakthrough in nutrition. In this context, one particular advantage of DRVs is the amalgamation of figures for food constituents, such as fat, carbohydrate and dietary fibre, with other nutrients. Prior to DRVs 'dietary recommendations for health' were separate from 'nutrient requirements'.

Uses of DRVs

- assessment of diets of groups of people;
- providing a guide to the adequacy, or otherwise, of individual diets;
- planning food supplies for large groups of people;
- nutrition labelling.

Terminology

The term DRV is a general one and is used to cover more specific terms.

- *Estimated average requirement* (EAR) means the estimate of the average requirement or need for *energy* or *protein* or a *vitamin* or *mineral* of a group of people. About half will usually need more than the EAR and half less.
- *Reference nutrient intake* (RNI) means the amount of *protein* or a *vitamin* or *mineral* that is enough or more than enough for about 97% of people in a group. At this level of intake, the risk of deficiency in the group is very small.
- *Lower reference nutrient intake* (LRNI) is an amount of *protein* or a *vitamin* or *mineral* that is enough for only the few people in the group who have low needs. The majority of people will need more than the LRNI. Intakes constantly lower than the LRNI will put people at high risk of deficiency.
- *Safe intake* is a term used to indicate the intake or range of intakes of a

nutrient for which there is not enough information to estimate an EAR, RNI or LRNI. It is an amount that is enough for almost everyone but not so large as to cause undesirable effects.

DRVs for energy

Many of the diseases characteristic of developed countries are associated with being overweight and obese, states resulting from a chronic excess of dietary energy intake over expenditure, and so the COMA Panel has set DRVs for energy on the basis of current estimates of energy expenditure. Recommendations for energy have always been set as the average of energy requirements for any population group and the Panel has, therefore, calculated EARs only for energy (Table 1.1).

Table 1.1
Estimated average requirement (per day) for energy

Age Months	Years	Males		Energy MJ (kcal) Females	
0–3		2.28	(545)	2.16	(515)
4–6		2.89	(690)	2.69	(645)
7–9		3.44	(825)	3.20	(765)
10–12		3.85	(920)	3.61	(865)
	1–3	5.15	(1,230)	4.86	(1,165)
	4–6	7.16	(1,715)	6.46	(1,545)
	7–10	8.24	(1,970)	7.28	(1,740)
	11–14	9.27	(2,220)	7,92	(1,845)
	15–18	11.51	(2,755)	8.83	(2,110)
	19–50	10.60	(2,550)	8.10	(1,940)
	51–59	10.60	(2,550)	8.00	(1,900)
	60–64	9.93	(2,380)	7.99	(1,900)
	65–74	9.71	(2,330)	7.96	(1,900)
	75+	8.77	(2,100)	7.61	(1,810)
Pregnancy				+0.80*	(200)
Lactation					
1 month				+1.90	(450)
2 months				+2.20	(530)
3 months				+2.40	(570)
4–6 months**				+2.00	(480)
4–6 months***				+2.40	(570)
6 + months**				+1.00	(240)
6 + months***				+2.30	(550)

*   Increment required for the last trimester only.
**   Women who practise exclusive, or almost exclusive, breastfeeding until the infant is 3–4 months old and then progressively introduce weaning foods as part of an active weaning process which last a few months.
*** Women who introduce only limited complementary feeds after 3–4 months and whose intention is that breast milk should provide the primary source of nourishment for 6 months or more.

DRVs for fat

In developed countries, there is a tendency to eat much more fat than is needed to prevent fatty acid deficiency. The COMA Panel reviewed the research on associations between fat and health and came up with proposals for population average intakes that are consistent with good health (Table 1.2). Particular reference was made to the effect of fats on blood levels of cholesterol, heart disease, certain cancers and the need for essential fatty acids. Despite suggestions that *trans*-fatty acids may increase the risk of heart disease, the evidence was not strong enough to make recommendations. However, intakes should not rise above the estimated average level.

Table 1.2
Dietary Reference Values (percentage of energy) for fat

Fat	Population average intake	
	including alcohol	excluding alcohol
Fat, total	33	35
Saturated fatty acids	10	11
Cis-monounsaturated fatty acids	12	13
Cis-polyunsaturated fatty acids including linoleic acid linolenic acid	6	6.5
Trans-fatty acids	2	2

DRVs for carbohydrate

Neither signs of deficiency nor harmful effects on health in general (or, more specifically, on dental health) have been associated with lactose in milk and milk products, or with intrinsic sugars (p. 18). On the other hand, the non-milk extrinsic sugars (p. 18) are associated with dental caries. Moreover, high intakes of non-milk extrinsic sugars (30% of energy intake) may be related to raised blood levels of cholesterol and insulin in some individuals. In the light of all this, the COMA Panel has come up with proposals for population average intakes that are consistent with good health (Table 1.3).

Table 1.3
Dietary Reference Values (percentage of energy) for sugars and starches

Carbohydrate	Population average intake	
	including alcohol	excluding alcohol
Carbohydrate, total	47	50
Non-milk extrinsic sugars	10	11
Intrinsic and milk sugars and starch	37	39

DRVs for dietary fibre

The COMA Panel considered the term 'dietary fibre' obsolete and recommended the term *non-starch polysaccharide* (NSP) in its place. The differences in terminology relate to the method of analysis.
    The COMA Panel focused attention on the following data.

1 Stool weights of less than 100 g/day are associated with NSP intakes of around 12 g/day. This is important because stool weights below 100 g/day are associated with an increased risk of bowel disease.

2 Blood levels of cholesterol may be reduced by the components of NSP that are water-soluble.
3 Specific components of NSP bind with minerals and certain groups, such as the elderly, may be vulnerable to compromised mineral status if their diets are barely adequate.

The COMA Panel based the DRVs for NSP on stool weights. An increase in the average intake of NSP from 13 to 18 g/day should increase average stool weights by about 25%. The Panel has proposed an average for the adult population of 18 g/day (range 12–24 g/day). The need to obtain NSP from a variety of *foods* – as opposed to supplements or products enriched with it – was emphasised. Although no guidance was given for subgroups of the population, it was recommended that, owing to their smaller body weight, children should eat less NSP than adults.

DRVs for protein

The DRVs for protein are derived from estimates of basic nitrogen requirements with additions for specific situations, such as pregnancy and growth. The DRVs assume that the diet includes a sufficient variety of protein-containing foods or sufficient high-quality animal protein sources to provide for *indispensable amino acid* (IAA) requirements. The figures for protein are valid if the needs for energy and other nutrients are met. Table 1.4 gives the RNIs for protein.

Very high intakes of protein may be associated with failing or poor kidney function and there is no evidence to show any benefit of protein intakes in excess of the RNI. As a result of this, the COMA Panel concluded that it was prudent for adults to avoid protein intakes of more than twice the RNI.

Table 1.4
Reference Nutrient Intakes (per day) for protein

Age Months	Years	Protein (g)
0–3		12.5
4–6		12.7
7–9		13.7
10–12		14.9
	1–3	14.5
	4–6	19.7
	7–10	28.3
Males		
	11–14	42.1
	15–18	55.2
	19–50	55.5
	50+	53.3
Females		
	11–14	41.2
	15–18	45.0
	19–50	45.0
	50+	46.5
Pregnancy		+ 6.0
Lactation		
0–4 months		+11.0
4+ months		+ 8.0

DRVs for minerals   Table 1.5 gives the RNIs for a range of minerals. If the diet consistently provides intakes in accord with these figures, mineral deficiencies are most unlikely.

Table 1.5
Reference Nutrient Intakes (per day) for minerals

Age Months	Years	Calcium (mg)	Phosphorous (mg)	Sodium (mg)	Chloride (mg)	Potassium (mg)	Iron (mg)	Zinc (mg)	Iodine (μg)
0–3		525	400	210	320	800	1.7	4.0	50
4–6		525	400	280	400	850	4.3	4.0	60
7–9		525	400	320	500	700	7.8	5.0	60
10–12		525	400	350	500	700	7.8	5.0	60
	1–3	350	270	500	800	800	6.9	5.0	70
	4–6	450	350	700	1,100	1,100	6.1	6.5	100
	7–10	550	450	1,200	1,800	2,000	8.7	7.0	110
Males									
	11–14	1000	775	1,600	2,500	3,100	11.3	9.0	130
	15–18	1000	775	1,600	2,500	3,500	11.3	9.5	140
	19–50	700	550	1,600	2,500	3,500	8.7	9.5	140
	50+	700	550	1,600	2,500	3,500	8.7	9.5	140
Females									
	11–14	800	625	1,600	2,500	3,100	14.8**	9.0	130
	15–18	800	625	1,600	2,500	3,500	14.8**	7.0	140
	19–50	700	550	1,600	2,500	3,500	14.8**	7.0	140
	50+	700	550	1,600	2,500	3,500	8.7	7.0	140
Lactation									
0–4 months		+550	+440	*	*	*	*	+6.0	*
4+ months		+550	+440	*	*	*	*	+2.5	*

*   No increment required.
** Women with high menstrual losses need more iron than the RNI, and the most practical way to achieve this is by taking supplements.

Sodium
Daily sodium intakes are 2–10 g in the UK. The COMA Panel believed that current sodium intakes were high and cautioned against trends towards increased intakes.

DRVs for vitamins   Table 1.6 gives the RNIs for a range of vitamins. Vitamin deficiencies are unlikely if the diet consistently supplies these intakes.

Table 1.6
Reference Nutrient Intakes (per day) for vitamins

Age		Vitamin A (retinol eq) (μg)	Vitamin D (μg)	Thiamin (mg)	Riboflavin (mg)	Niacin (nicotinic acid eq) (mg)	Vitamin B₁₂ (μg)	Folate (μg)	Vitamin C (mg)
Months	Years								
0–3		350	8.5	0.2	0.4	3	0.3	50	25
4–6		350	8.5	0.2	0.4	3	0.3	50	25
7–9		350	7	0.2	0.4	4	0.4	50	25
10–12		350	7	0.3	0.4	5	0.4	50	25
	1–3	400	7	0.5	0.6	8	0.5	70	30
	4–6	500	0*	0.7	0.8	11	0.8	100	30
	7–10	500	0*	0.7	1.0	12	1.0	150	30
Males									
	11–14	600	0*	0.9	1.2	15	1.2	200	35
	15–18	700	0*	1.1	1.3	18	1.5	200	40
	19–50	700	0*	1.0	1.3	17	1.5	200	40
	50+	700	10**	0.9	1.3	16	1.5	200	40
Females	11–14	600	0*	0.7	1.1	12	1.2	200	35
	15–18	600	0*	0.8	1.1	14	1.5	200	40
	19–50	600	0*	0.8	1.1	13	1.5	200	40
	50+	600	10**	0.8	1.1	12	1.5	200	40
Pregnancy		+100	10	+0.1***	+0.3	****	****	+100	+10
Lactation		+350	10	+0.2	+0.5	+2	+0.5	+60	+30

*	Certain at-risk individuals or groups may require dietary viatamin D.
**	Men and women after the age of 65 years only.
***	Increment required for the last trimester only.
****	No increment required.

DRVs discussed so far are applicable to the United Kingdom. Some countries have their own standards and figures produced by the World Health Organisation (WHO) are frequently used world wide.

WHO Dietary Reference Values

The basis of the WHO DRVs is outlined below.

Energy   The EARs for energy are the same as the UK.

Protein   The RNIs for protein are the same as the UK.

Phosphorus
Potassium   No WHO values
Chloride

Sodium   Value for population average 15–50⁺ = 3900 mg/day.

Table 1.7
WHO Dietary Reference Values for fat and carbohydrate (% total energy) and dietary fibre (g/day) for adults

Nutrient	Population nutrient goal	
	Lower	Upper
Fat (E %)		
Total	15	30
Saturated fatty acids	0	10
Cis- polyunsaturated fatty acids	3	7
Carbohydrate (E %)		
Total	55	75
non-milk extrinsic sugars	0	10
Dietary fibre (g/d)	16	24

Table 1.8
WHO Dietary Reference Values for minerals (per day)

Age Months	Years	Calcium[1] (mg)	Iron[2] (mg)	Zinc[3] (mg)	Iodine[4] (μg)
0–6		500	(4–6 months) 8.5	x	40
7–12		600	8.5	5.6	50
	1–3	400	5.0	5.5	70–120
	4–6	450	5.5	6.5	70–120
	7–10	500	9.5	7.5	70–120
Males					
	11–14	600–700	15.0	12.1	120–150
	15–18	500–600	9.0	13.1	120–150
	19–50	400–500	9.0	9.4	120–150
	50+	400–500	9.0	9.4	120–150
Females					
	11–14	600–700	16.0	10.3	120–150
	15–18	500–600	12.5	10.2	120–150
	19–50	400–500	12.5	6.5	120–150
	50+	400–500	9.5	6.5	120–150
Pregnancy		1000–1200	x	7.3–13.3	175
Lactation		1000–1200	10.5	(0–4 months) 12.7 (4+ months) 11.7	175

Key:
1 = Reference Nutrient Intake (1961)
2 = Median basal requirement on intermediate bioavailability diet
3 = Normative requirement on diet of moderate zinc availability (1992)
4 = Reference Nutrient Intake (1992)
x = No values given

Table 1.9
WHO Dietary Reference Values for vitamins (per day)

Age Months	Years	Vitamin A[1] (retinol eq) (µg)	Vitamin D[2] (µg)	Thiamin[2] (mg)	Riboflavin[3] (mg)	Niacin[2] (nicotinic acid eq)(mg)	VitaminB$_{12}$[1] (µg)	Folate[1] (µg)	VitaminC[2] (mg)
								(0–3 mths) 16	
0–6		350	10	0.3	0.5	5.4	0.1	(4–6 mths) 24	20
7–12		350	10	0.3	0.5	5.4	0.1	32	20
	1–3	400	10	0.5	0.8	9.0	0.5	50	20
	4–6	400	10	0.7	1.1	12.1	0.8	50	20
	7–10	400	2.5	0.9	1.3	14.5	1.0	102	20
Males									
	11–14	550	2.5	1.2	1.7	19.1	1.0	170	30
	15–18	600	2.5	1.2	1.8	20.3	1.0	200	30
	19–50	600	2.5	1.2	1.8	18.8	1.0	200	30
	50+	600	2.5	1.2	1.8	19.8	1.0	200	30
Females									
	11–14	500	2.5	1.0	1.5	16.4	1.0	170	30
	15–18	500	2.5	0.9	1.3	15.2	1.0	170	30
	19–50	500	2.5	0.9	1.3	14.5	1.0	170	30
	50+	500	2.5	0.9	1.3	14.5	1.0	170	30
Pregnancy		600	10	+0.1	+0.2	+2.3	1.4	370–470	50
Lactation		850		+0.2	+0.4	+3.7	1.3	270	50

Key:
1 = Safe level (1988)
2 = Reference Nutrient Intake (1970)
3 = Reference Nutrient Intake (1965)

2 The components of food

When food is eaten it is broken down into its component parts and used by the body. Fig. 2.1 shows that the body is made up of food components.

Fig. 2.1
Composition of the human body

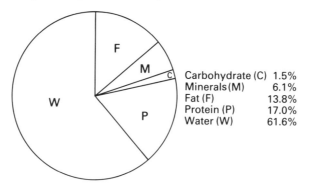

Carbohydrate (C)	1.5%
Minerals (M)	6.1%
Fat (F)	13.8%
Protein (P)	17.0%
Water (W)	61.6%

Proteins

Fig. 2.2
Monomers and polymers

About 17% of the human body is made up of proteins (Fig. 2.1). Every cell in the body contains proteins, and there are more than 10^{13} such cells. Proteins are made up of carbon, hydrogen, oxygen and nitrogen and some contain sulphur. These elements are arranged in units called amino acids which form the building blocks of proteins. The amino acids are joined together in chains by peptide links and it is the chains of these units which form the protein. Amino acids are considered as monomers and the proteins as polymers (Fig. 2.2). Cross-links may link the chains of the amino acids (polypeptide chains). Protein molecules vary in shape and on this basis can be classified into two main groups: fibrous and globular proteins (Fig. 2.3).

Fig. 2.3
Fibrous and globular proteins

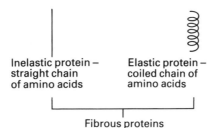

Amino acids

Twenty different amino acids are commonly found in biological materials, and these are important in human nutrition. They can be classified into 2 main groups: indispensible and dispensible amino acids (Table 2.1). Indispensible amino acids have to be supplied in the diet, while dispensible amino acids can be made in the body.

Table 2.1
Classification of amino acids

Indispensible amino acids	Dispensible amino acids
Isoleucine	Alanine
Leucine	Arginine
Lysine	Aspartic acid
Methionine	Cysteine
Phenylalanine	Glutamic acid
Threonine	Glycine
Tryptophan	Proline
Valine	Serine
Histidine Indispensible for children	Tyrosine

Biological value of proteins

Some foods are said to be of high biological value (HBV) – for example, eggs, meat, fish, milk and cheese. Plant foods, on the other hand, such as beans and bread, are said to be of low biological value (LBV). However, when mixed together – for example, beans on toast, hummus and pitta bread, dhal and chapati – the biological value is increased. The low lysine content of the wheat in the various forms of bread is complemented by the higher lysine content of the beans. Individually, bread and beans are of low biological value, but eaten together they provide the body with high biological value protein. The biological value is defined as the percentage of absorbed protein that is converted to body protein.

Properties of proteins

Proteins may be coagulated by the following:

1 *Heat*   This is particularly important in food preparation and accounts for some of the changes between raw and cooked foods.
2 *Acid*   For example, lactic acid is formed when milk is sour and may bring about the coagulation of milk protein.
3 *Enzymes*   Rennin, available as rennet, is used to coagulate milk in the preparation of curd cheese.
4 *Salt*   In cheese making, sodium chloride increases the firmness of the curd.
5 *Mechanical action*   Partial coagulation of protein occurs when egg white is whisked.

Functions of proteins

1 The growth of body cells – for example, growth of the fetus or spurts of growth during adolescence.
2 The maintenance and repair of body cells as a result of natural wear and tear or injury.
3 A source of energy: if other sources of energy are lacking, protein is used first to meet energy needs; 1 g of protein yields 4 kcals.

Deficiency and excess of protein

Kwashiorkor, which results in symptoms such as growth failure, water retention, thinning of hair, diarrhoea, anorexia and apathy, is associated with an inadequate intake of protein and energy.

Protein not required for maintenance and growth is used as energy and can therefore contribute towards a surplus of energy.

Dietary Reference Values for protein

The RNIs for protein are shown in Table 1.4 and the basis for DRVs is explained on p. 7. The values allow for increased requirements as follows:

- *pregnancy* to account for the growth of the fetus;
- *lactation* to allow for adequate production of breast milk;
- *infants* and *children*, to facilitate growth;
- *elderly*, to take account of the small amount of lean body mass per kg body weight.

Sources of protein

In the UK, approximately two thirds of the protein intake is of animal origin. Meat and meat products and milk and cheese provide 29 and 13% of protein intake respectively. Bread contributes about 15% of protein intake.

Foods with a high protein content include meat, poultry, fish, cheese, eggs, dried pulses and most nuts.

Carbohydrates

Approximately 1–2% of the human body is made up of carbohydrate (Fig 2.1). This is stored as glycogen in the liver and muscles for immediate use as a source of energy. Carbohydrates are made up of carbon, hydrogen and oxygen. Carbohydrates are considered under 2 main headings: sugars and polysaccharides. Sugar molecules are much smaller than those of polysaccharides (Fig. 2.4).

Sugars

The beginnings of words such as 'glyco' and 'sacchar' and endings such as 'ose' mean 'sugar'. Sugars may be classified in a number of ways. The *biochemical* grouping of sugars into monosaccharides and disaccharides, for example, is well established.

Monosaccharides
The chemical formula for monosaccharides is $C_6H_{12}O_6$.

Monosaccharides are simple sugars (Fig. 2.4) and examples are glucose, fructose and galactose.

1 *Glucose* is found in fruit and vegetables in varying amounts.
2 *Fructose* is found with glucose in different fruits and is present in honey.
3 *Galactose* is found with glucose as lactose, the sugar present in milk.

Disaccharides
The chemical formula for disaccharides is $C_{12}H_{22}O_{11}$.

Disaccharides are made up of 2 monosaccharides (Fig. 2.4). The simple sugars are joined together by means of a glycoside link. Sucrose, lactose and maltose are disaccharides.

1 *Sucrose* is found in different fruits and vegetables. It is made up of 1 molecule of *glucose* and 1 molecule of *fructose*.
2 *Lactose* is found in milk. The 2-constituent monosaccharides are *glucose* and *galactose*.
3 *Maltose* is formed from starch during the germination of sprouting barley. The 2-constituent monosaccharides are *glucose* molecules.

Fig. 2.4
Carbohydrate molecules

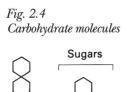

Fig. 2.4
Carbohydrate molecules

A further classification of sugars according to their *physical location* in food was put forward by the COMA Panel in its report *Dietary Sugars and Human Disease*, published in 1989. A distinction was made between sugars naturally integrated into the cellular structure of food (intrinsic) and those which were free in the food or added to it (extrinsic). The difference in physical location influences their availability for bacterial metabolism in the mouth and the readiness with which they are absorbed after ingestion.

1 *Intrinsic sugars* are those sugars contained within the cell walls of the food. The most important sources are fruit and vegetables, containing mainly fructose, glucose and sucrose.
2 *Extrinsic sugars* are sugars not contained within the cell walls. Examples include the sugars found in honey, table sugar and lactose in milk and milk products.
3 *Non-milk extrinsic sugars* are the extrinsic sugars, the exception being lactose in milk and milk products.

Properties of sugars

1 Sugars dissolve in water.
2 Sugars are known for their sweet taste
3 Disaccharides can be hydrolysed – that is, broken down by being combined with water to form the constituent monosaccharides. When sucrose is hydrolysed, the resulting mixture is of glucose and fructose and is called invert sugar. To bring about this inversion the enzyme invertase may be added or the sucrose may be heated with an acid.
4 When heated, sugars will caramelise. This happens most readily when no liquid is present.
5 With the exception of sucrose, all common sugars are reducing agents and are known as reducing sugars.

Starches

The main food reserve found in plants is the polysaccharide starch, which is made up of molecules of glucose. Under the microscope it can be seen that the starch is in the form of small granules which vary in shape and size according to the plant (Fig. 2.5).

Fig. 2.6
Amylose and amylopectin

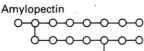

Fig. 2.5
Starch grains from different plants

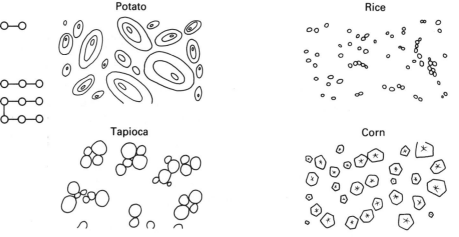

Starch is made up of 2 polysaccharides: amylose and amylopectin (Fig. 2.6).

Properties of starch

1 Starch does not dissolve in cold water.
2 Unlike sugars, starch does not have a sweet taste.
3 Starch can be hydrolysed by enzymes or acids. The molecules can be broken down, first to dextrins and eventually to monosaccharides.
4 When subjected to dry heat, dextrins form brown-coloured compounds called pyrodextrins. When starch and water are heated, water penetrates the starch granules. The granules become bigger and the liquid becomes thicker. At higher temperatures the mixture becomes more viscous becomes more viscous because the starch gelatinises.

Functions of sugars and starches

1 A *source of energy* In the cells, glucose is oxidised and energy is released: 1 g of carbohydrate provides 3.75 kcal. If energy requirements have been met, any remaining carbohydrate is changed to fat and stored in the adipose tissues.
2 A '*protein-sparing*' *function* If the diet is lacking in carbohydrate, more protein than usual will be used as an energy source.

Deficiency and excess of sugars and starches

If the diet is too low in carbohydrate, the protein will be used to provide energy at the expense of being available for growth and repair of tissues. Carbohydrate not required for immediate use is stored as fat and is a contributory factor in the development of obesity.

When non-milk extrinsic sugars are eaten in excess of around 200 g/day, blood levels of glucose, insulin and lipids may rise. High intakes of these sugars are also associated with dental caries.

Dietary Reference Values for sugars and starches

The DRVs for sugars and starches are shown in Table 1.3 and the basis for them explained on p. 7.

Sources of sugars and starches

Almost 30% of the carbohydrate intake in the UK consists of non-milk extrinsic sugars.

Foods providing *intrinsic sugars* are fruit and vegetables. Foods with a high content of *non-milk extrinsic sugars* include sugar, honey, jam and chocolate. *Starch* is present in useful amounts in foods such as bread, rice, pasta, oats, potatoes and yams.

Hidden sugar
Foods such as baked beans, salad dressings, relishes and cook-in sauces usually contain sugar. On labels sugar may be called dextrose, fructose, sucrose, glucose, maltose, corn syrup, glucose syrup, honey or molasses.

Dietary fibre

The COMA Panel on DRVs has defined dietary fibre as *non-starch polysaccharide* (NSP) where this refers to the *non alpha-glucans* as measured by the technique of Englyst and Cummings. The enzymatic chemical methods developed by these investigators identify NSP and show if the fibre fractions are *soluble* or *insoluble*. The COMA Panel has described NSP as a precisely measurable component of foods and the best measure of dietary fibre.

Functions of dietary fibre

1 *Insoluble fibre* fractions increase the weight of stools.
2 *Water-soluble* fractions may help to reduce blood levels of cholesterol.
3 Residues of fibre or the associated phytate bind minerals such as calcium, iron, copper and zinc.

Deficiency and excess of dietary fibre

Lack of dietary fibre, that is, less than 12 g/day, is associated with stool weights of less than 100 g/day and an increased risk of bowel disease. Excessive intakes are unlikely in the UK. In some parts of the world, such as rural Africa, high intakes may lead to a condition called large bowel volvulus. High intakes of fibre may be associated with compromised mineral status in groups of people whose diet is barely adequate.

Dietary Reference Values for dietary fibre

The recommendations of the COMA Panel for dietary fibre intakes are described on p. 10.

Sources of dietary fibre

In the UK, the highest fibre providers are cereals and vegetables which account for 45 and 39% of the intake respectively.

Wholegrain cereals are a useful source of dietary fibre. Breakfast cereals, particularly the high-fibre varieties, can add considerably to fibre intakes. As part of healthy meal planning as an alternative to meat, pulses, can also enhance intakes.

Fats

The amount of fat in the body varies widely according to whether a person is overweight or underweight. On average, an adult male has about 14% fat and an adult woman about 20% fat. Fat is stored in the adipose tissues, which are found around the vital organs and under the skin. A particular type of fat is an essential constituent of cell membranes. Fats are made up of carbon, hydrogen and oxygen.

Terms relating to fat

Fig. 2.7
Chemical composition of triglycerides

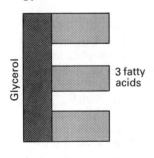

- *Triglycerides* consist of 3 *fatty acid* molecules and 1 *glycerol* molecule (Fig. 2.7). Food fats mainly consist of mixtures of triglycerides.
- *Fatty acids* are molecules consisting mainly of a carbon chain of variable length with hydrogen atoms attached. Approximately 16 fatty acids are commonly found in food.
- *Saturated fatty acids* (SFAs) contain the maximum possible number of hydrogen atoms.
- *Monounsaturated fatty acids* are molecules with 2 missing hydrogen atoms.
- *Polyunsaturated fatty acids* (PUFAs) are molecules with more than 2 hydrogen atoms missing. *Linoleic* and *linolenic* acids are the most common ones. These 2 PUFAs cannot be made in the body and need to be supplied by food. For this reason, they are known as the *essential fatty acids* (EFAs). PUFAs can be classified into *n-3* (omega-3) and *n-6* (omega-6) groups. Examples of the former are *alpha-linolenic acid, eicosapentaenoic acid* and *docosahexaenoic acid.* Examples of the latter group include *gamma-linolenic acid, linoleic acid* and *arachidonic acid.*
- *Cis* and *trans fatty acids* differ from each other in the spatial arrangement of their atoms. '*cis*' is derived from the Latin for 'on this

side' and '*trans*' comes from the Latin for 'across'. Naturally occurring unsaturated fatty acids are usually in the *cis* form.

Properties of fats

1 Fats and oils are not water-soluble.
2 Fats have plastic properties. They change their shape when pressure is applied.
3 Fats are affected by heat.

    (a) *Melting point* Most fats melt at around 30°C to 40°C. In the case of oils most are liquid at room temperature.
    (b) *Smoke point* At temperatures over 200°C most fats and oils produce a blue haze or smoke. The triglycerides are decomposed to form glycerol and free fatty acids and the glycerol is decomposed further to form a compound called acrolein.
    (c) *Flash point* If heated to high temperatures, the oil or fat may ignite.

4 Fats form soaps and glycerol when mixed with alkalis.

Functions of fats

1 Fat is a concentrated source of energy: 1 g of fat yields 9 kcals, approximately double the amount yielded from 1 g carbohydrate or protein.
2 Fat under the skin acts as an insulating layer and prevents heat loss from the body.
3 Fat around organs such as the kidneys and heart helps to protect them from physical injury.
4 Fats accommodate the absorption of the fat-soluble vitamins A, D, E and K.
5 *Linoleic acid* (n-6) and *alpha-linolenic acid* (n-3) are essential fatty acids and are important for maintaining the function and integrity of cell membranes.
6 The n-3 series of PUFAs are needed for the development and function of the brain and retina of the eye.
7 The n-3 PUFAs may be involved in preventing blood clots. Increased intakes of these PUFAs have been shown to reduce the risk of heart attacks. They also lower serum triglyceride concentrations.

Deficiency and excess of fat

Fat deficiency is not a problem in the UK. A diet that is totally fat-free would result in fat-soluble vitamin deficiencies.

    Excessive intakes of fat lead to obesity. Diets high in fat, particularly saturated fat, are of significance in the development of *cardiovascular disease*.

Dietary Reference Values for fat

The DRVs for fat are given in Table 1.2 and the basis for them is explained on p. 9.

Sources of fat

In the UK, about two thirds of the total fat in the diet is of animal origin. Fats as a group account for about 30% of the total fat intake and 25% of the intake of saturated fatty acids. Meat and meat products account for around 25% of the total fat intake and 24% of the intake of saturated fatty acids.

    The *saturated fatty acids* most abundantly present in food are *myristic acid, palmitic acid* and *stearic acid*. Myristic acid is a major constituent of butter and coconut oil. Palmitic and stearic acid are major components of hard fats, such as lard, suet, butter and cocoa butter.

Monounsaturated fatty acids are found in significant quantities in olive, rapeseed and groundnut oils.

Polyunsaturated fatty acids are generally found in specific oils. *Linoleic acid* (n-6) is present in large amounts in corn, soya bean and sunflower oils. *Alpha-linolenic acid* (n-3) is found in vegetable oils. Oily fish provide useful amounts of the n-3 group *docosahexaenoic acid* and *eicosapentaenoic acid.*

Visible and invisible fats

Visible fats are easy to identify. Examples are butter and margarine, oil and cream, and fat on meat. Fats that are not so easily identified are called invisible fats, and examples include lean meat, egg yolk, fatty fish, nuts, potato crisps and creamed cake mixtures.

Minerals

About 6% of the human body is made up of minerals (Fig. 2.1). Certain minerals are present in relatively large amounts – for example, calcium, phosphorus, iron, sodium, chlorine and potassium. Others are present in much smaller quantities, such as iodine and fluorine. Minerals found in very small amounts are called trace elements.

Calcium

The amount of calcium in the body of a healthy adult is about 1200 g. Approximately 99% is found in bones and teeth and 1% in other body tissues – for example, muscles, nerves and blood.

Functions of calcium

1 The formation and development of skeleton and teeth.
2 The normal clotting of blood.
3 The normal functioning of muscles and nerves.

Deficiency and excess of calcium

Calcium deficiency is associated with a lack of vitamin D rather than a low dietary intake of calcium. Similarly, excess calcium is associated with excess vitamin D (p. 31).

Dietary Reference Values for calcium

Table 1.5 gives the RNIs for calcium. The DRVs take into account the limited absorption of this mineral by the body and the high needs of growing *infants, children* and *adolescents* for this mineral. During *pregnancy,* the ability of the body to absorb calcium increases and therefore no increment is recommended. An increment is required while a mother is *lactating,* however, as her body needs calcium while she is producing milk for her baby.

Sources of calcium

In the UK, about two thirds of the calcium in the diet comes from animal sources. More than half of the calcium actually comes from dairy foods, with milk and cheese providing 18 and 11% of the intake respectively. Bread makes a useful contribution, providing 13% of the intake.

Useful sources of calcium include fish when the bones are eaten, such as whitebait, sardines and canned salmon, cheese, yogurt and milk, white bread, nuts, such as almonds, Brazils and hazelnuts, and pulses, such as soya beans and soya products such as tofu and tempeh.

Stability of calcium
Food preparation procedures hardly affect calcium, although foods cooked in hard water have a higher calcium content than foods cooked in soft water.

Absorption of calcium
Of the total calcium intake only about 20–50% is absorbed into the body. Absorption of calcium is poor for a number of reasons:

1 *Phytic acid* interferes with calcium absorption. However, phytic acid can be broken down by phytase.
2 *Oxalic acid*, which is particularly high in rhubarb and spinach, also interferes with the absorption of calcium.
3 *Dietary fibre* binds calcium.
4 *Fats*, particularly saturated fatty acids, form insoluble soaps with calcium.

Factors known to assist in the absorption of calcium:

1 *Vitamin D* promotes the production of the carrier protein needed for the absorption of calcium.
2 *Proteins* The amino acids formed from protein as a result of digestion combine with calcium to form soluble calcium salts, and these salts are very readily absorbed.
3 *Lactose*, the sugar present in milk, increases calcium absorption upon hydrolysis.

Phosphorus

Phosphate is present in all body cells but it is concentrated in bones and teeth. About 88% of the phosphorus in the body is found in these structures.

Functions of phosphorus

1 The formation and development of bones and teeth.
2 The release of energy in the cells. When glucose is oxidised the energy produced is stored in high-energy phosphate compounds. These compounds break down to give energy when needed.

Deficiency and excess of phosphorus
Phosphorus deficiency in humans is unknown, and this is probably owing to the widespread distribution of this nutrient in foods.

The problem of excess phosphorus is relevant to infant feeding. Cows' milk contains more phosphorus and calcium than human milk. It has been suggested that the high phosphorus content of cow's milk may reduce the absorption of calcium and lead to *hypocalcaemia*. This disorder is associated with a reduction of calcium in the circulation. When this happens, a number of symptoms may develop, including twitching of the face, hands and feet, known as tetany, and the muscles may become flaccid.

Dietary Reference Values for phosphorus
Table 1.5 shows the RNIs for phosphorus. Requirements for phosphorus are closely related to those of calcium. The maintenance of the balance between calcium and phosphorus is particularly important in infants.

Sources of phosphorus
Phosphorus, in the form of phosphate, is a major constituent of all plant and animal cells and is also present in many food additives.

Sodium

The amount of sodium in a 65–75 kg adult male is about 92 g. Sodium is present in all body fluids.

Functions of sodium
Sodium is involved in maintaining the water balance of the body and it is essential for muscle and nerve activities.

Deficiency and excess of sodium
Low intakes of sodium result in muscular cramps. A deficiency of sodium is usually associated with heat exhaustion.

Habitually high intakes of sodium are associated with high BP.

Dietary Reference Values for sodium
The RNIs for sodium are given in Table 1.5. The DRVs for adults are based on several factors, which are that current intakes are in excess of needs; a reduction in intake may reduce the prevalence of high BP; that a relationship exists between sodium intake and a rise in BP with age; and that about 10% of the population have a genetic predisposition to high BP linked with sodium at intakes above 3.2–4.7 g/day. In *infants* up to the age of 6 months, the figures relate to the sodium content of breastmilk. Thereafter in *infants* and *children* the figures have been calculated from daily losses via the skin, urine and faeces.

Sources of sodium
In the UK, 24% of the dietary sodium is provided by bread and 20% by meat and meat products.

The sodium content of foods is closely linked with food processing because salt is added to many products. Foods with a high sodium content include bacon, ham, kippers, salt cod, salted butter, vegetables canned in brine and some breakfast cereals.

Chloride

The amount of chloride in the body of an adult 70 kg man is about 84 g. Chloride is present in all body fluids.

Functions of chloride
Chloride is involved in maintaining the water balance of the body.

Deficiency of chloride
Dietary deficiency of chloride has only been reported in infants who were fed an infant formula which provided low amounts of chloride.

Dietary Reference Values for chloride
Table 1.5 gives the RNIs for chloride. The COMA Panel concluded that the intakes of chloride should equal those of sodium in molar terms.

Sources of chloride
As for sodium.

Potassium

The amount of potassium in a 70 kg adult man is approximately 110–137 g. About 95% of this is present in the fluids within the body cells. The total amount of potassium in the body is related to the amount of lean tissue.

Functions of potassium

1 Potassium has a complementary action with sodium. Together, these electrolytes enable substances to move in and out of cells. This allows nerves and muscles to function and maintains the balance between the fluid inside and outside of the cells.

2 Potassium facilitates the removal of excess sodium and this may help to prevent high BP.

Deficiency and excess of potassium
In severe cases of potassium depletion, heart failure may occur as the mineral is essential for the correct functioning of heart muscle.

High intakes of potassium are unlikely to be related to dietary sources. Toxicity is more likely to be associated with supplementation.

Dietary Reference Values for potassium
Table 1.5 gives the RNIs for potassium. For *adults* the COMA Panel concluded that it would be prudent for potassium intakes to be such that excess sodium can be excreted. In the case of *infants* and *children* the figures are based on the amounts of potassium needed for growth and estimated losses via the skin, urine and faeces.

Sources of potassium
Potassium is distributed widely in foods. Rich sources include fruit and vegetables, potatoes and fruit juices.

Iron

Fig. 2.8
Red blood cells

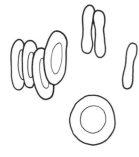

The amount of iron in the body of a healthy 70 kg adult is about 3–4 g. This is distributed roughly as follows: 2.5 g in the haemoglobin, the red pigment of the red blood cells (Fig. 2.8); 0.3 g in myoglobin, the muscle pigment and respiratory enzymes of tissues; and 1 g in the liver, spleen and bone marrow as an iron store.

Functions of iron

1 Haemoglobin carries oxygen to the body tissues. The oxygen is needed for the production of energy.
2 Myoglobin holds oxygen in readiness for muscular work.
3 The respiratory enzymes play a part in respiration at cellular level.

Deficiency and excess of iron
Iron deficiency causes haemoglobin levels to fall, which means that the amount of oxygen supplied to the tissues is not enough. This condition is called *iron deficiency anaemia*. This gives rise to a number of symptoms including tiredness, lack of energy, breathlessness on exertion and palpitations. Iron deficiency anaemia is a common condition in Britain, especially in women. Other symptoms of iron deficiency are brittle nails, which, in extreme cases, may become spoon-shaped. The tongue and corners of the mouth may become sore, and difficulty in swallowing may be experienced.

Large quantities of iron in the diet can be harmful because the iron stores may become overloaded. Iron is stored as ferritin, but if too much iron is stored the ferritin becomes conglomerated and forms a substance called haemosiderin. When this happens a condition known as *siderosis* occurs. Such a disorder is not common in the UK, but it is common among the Bantu people. These people may consume about 10 times more iron than they need (approximately 100 mg/day). This is largely derived from the iron cooking pots in which cereals such as maize are cooked and from the local beer, another rich source of iron.

Dietary Reference Values for iron
The RNIs for iron are given in Table 1.5. The DRVs allow for the low absorption of iron by the body, but assume that this is about 15% from a mixed diet. People on vegetarian diets, consuming non-haem iron, may

need more. The RNI for women of child-bearing age is higher than for other groups to allow for the blood, and hence iron, losses during menstruation, but some women may need to take iron supplements.

Sources of iron
About two thirds of the iron in the diet is obtained from plant sources, with almost half being provided by cereal foods, particularly bread. Meat and meat products contribute around 18% of intakes and vegetables about 16%.

Foods rich in iron include offal, such as liver, kidney and heart, fish, for example sardines, cockles and muscles, dried fruit, breakfast cereals fortified with iron, pulses, such as red kidney beans and soya beans, and flavourings, including curry powder and cocoa.

Absorption of iron
Only about 10% of the iron intake is absorbed into the body. Absorption of iron is poor for a number of reasons. By far the largest amount of iron in the diet is ionic or non-haem. This type of iron is readily precipitated by a number of substances present in food, as shown in Table 2.2.

The problem with phytates can, to some extent, be overcome during food preparation. For example, in the making of wholewheat bread, a long fermentation time allows phytases (enzymes present in flour) to break phytic acid down so that it can no longer bind with iron. Other factors hindering the absorption of iron include phosphorus compounds in eggs and milk and dietary fibre in plant foods.

Non-haem iron is present in food as ferric iron, which cannot be absorbed by the body. Before it can be absorbed, it has to be changed into a form of iron known as ferrous iron (Fig 2.9).

Haem iron, in contrast, is already in a soluble form when it enters the digestive tract.

Iron absorption takes place in the small intestine. Here the soluble iron enters the mucosal cells. The absorptive mechanisms differ for haem and non-haem iron. Haem iron is passed directly into the mucosal cell, but the absorption of non-haem iron is controlled by receptors bordering the mucosal cells. When a person has too little iron, as in iron deficiency anaemia, more receptors gather around the mucosal cell and more iron is absorbed.

Once inside the mucosal cell the iron binds with a protein and enters the blood stream. Depending upon the iron status of the individual, iron may stay behind in the mucosal cell. This iron combines with a different protein and is stored as ferritin. The amount of iron in the mucosal cell is an important factor in regulating iron absorption, but the precise mechanism is not fully understood.

Table 2.2
Dietary factors involved in the precipitation of iron

Precipitating agent	Food sources	Insoluble complex formed
Oxalate	Soinach	Iron oxalate
Phosphate	Rhubarb, egg yolk	Iron phosphate
Phytate	Wholegrain cereals, pulses	Iron phytate
Tannin	Tea, pulses, condiments, spices	Iron tannate

Fig. 2.9
Factors involved in the conversion of ferric iron to ferrous iron

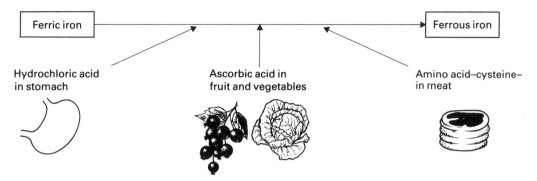

Stability of iron
Food preparation procedures hardly affect iron, but the use of iron utensils can increase the iron content of food. Meat that has been frozen may lose some iron in the thaw drip.

Zinc

The amount of zinc in the body of an adult is about 2 g. It is present in all tissues of the body, including 60% in skeletal muscle, 30% in bone and 5% in the skin.

Functions of zinc

1 It is an essential component of certain enzymes.
2 It has a structural role in a number of non-enzyme proteins.

Deficiency and excess of zinc
Zinc deficiency is associated with growth retardation. It also results in defects in those tissues of the body where there is rapid cell division, such as the skin, intestinal mucosa and the immune system.

Excess zinc has rarely been reported, but zinc toxicity has occurred when water has been stored in galvanised containers.

Dietary Reference Values for zinc
Table 1.5 gives the RNIs for zinc. The DRVs are based on the limited absorption of zinc by the body and the high needs of growing *infants, children* and *adolescents* for this mineral. During *pregnancy* an increment is allowed for the developing fetus, and also during *lactation* as extra is needed while the mother is producing milk for her baby.

Sources of zinc
Zinc is found in a wide range of foods. The best dietary sources are red meats. Fish, particularly certain crustaceans and molluscs, have a high zinc content. Cheese provides useful amounts. Pulses and unrefined cereals also contain useful quantities of this mineral.

Absorption of zinc
Approximately one third of the zinc in the diet is absorbed. This is reduced if large quantities of wholegrain cereals, rich in both dietary fibre and phytic acid, are eaten. In practical terms, the low bioavailability of zinc in wholegrain cereals is offset by the amount of zinc present in these foods.

Iodine

The amount of iodine in the body of a healthy adult is about 20–50 mg. Iodine is concentrated in the thyroid gland, the average amount present being about 8 mg.

Functions of iodine

1 Iodine is needed for the production of 2 hormones, called triiodothyronine (T_3) and thyroxine (T_4). These hormones are necessary for the maintenance of metabolic rate, cellular metabolism and the integrity of the connective tissue.
2 In the fetus, iodine is needed for the development of the nervous system during the first trimester of pregnancy.

Deficiency and excess of iodine

Goitre (Fig 2.10) may be caused by a low iodine intake. Goitre is easily recognised because a swelling of the neck is visible. This is caused by the enlargement of the thyroid gland. Lack of iodine leads to a shortage of the hormones triiodothyronine and thyroxine. This causes a fall in the basal metabolism. Lack of thyroid secretions has other effects because mucinious material tends to accumulate in various organs and under the skin. The person's features usually coarsen, giving a characteristic appearance called *myxoedema.*

High intakes of iodine can lead to toxic modular goitre and hyperthyroidism. An example of this occurred in Japanese fishermen whose intakes were 10–20 mg/day.

Fig. 2.10
A person suffering from goitre

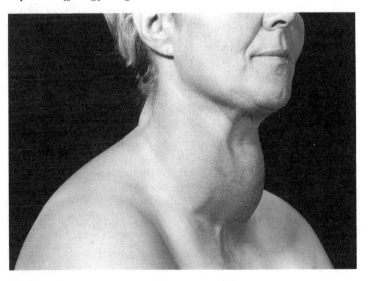

Dietary Reference Values for iodine

Table 1.5 gives the RNIs for iodine. The DRVs for adults have been derived from studies of habitual intakes and the incidence of iodine-deficiency goitre. In infants, the figures are based on studies of the iodine content of breast milk.

Sources of iodine

The amount of iodine in plant foods depends on how much of it is present in the soil in which they have been grown.

In the UK, milk makes a major contribution to iodine intakes. Cow's milk is a good source because of the iodine in supplemented foods, lactation promoters containing iodine and the use of iodophors as sterilising agents in milk production. Sea fish are also rich in iodine, as are edible seaweeds.

Vitamins

Vitamins are complex organic compounds made up of carbon, hydrogen and oxygen. These compounds are needed by the body in small quantities. Vitamins may be classified into 2 main groups: fat-soluble and water-soluble. As the name suggests, fat-soluble vitamins dissolve in fats and include vitamins A, D, E and K. Water-soluble vitamins dissolve in water and include vitamins of the B group and vitamin C.

Vitamin A (or, more correctly, retinol)

Retinol is stored in the liver. In Britain, post-mortem examinations after accidents have shown this store to be about 400 mg in the whole liver, and this will last many months or even years. The level of retinol in the blood only falls when the body's reserves of the vitamin are severely depleted.

The vitamin A content of the diet is considered in terms of retinol equivalents. It is important to draw a distinction between retinol which is found in foods of animal origin and the pro-vitamin, or precursor beta-carotene, found principally in foods of plant origin. The pro-vitamin is not as potent as retinol because it is not as well absorbed as retinol, and the conversion of beta-carotene to retinol is about 50%. The pro-vitamin is about one sixth as potent as the vitamin itself:

1 µg retinol equivalent is equal to 1 µg retinol and 6 µg beta-carotene

Functions of retinol

1 The formation of rhodopsin (visual purple), the pigment found in the retina of the eye (Fig 2.11). This pigment aids people to see in dim light.
2 To maintain the surface tissues of the body, such as the skin and mucous membranes lining the digestive and respiratory tracts. The mechanism is not entirely clear, but it seems probable that the vitamin is concerned in the formation of glycoproteins which are constituents of mucus.
3 For growth and metabolism.

Fig. 2.11
Retina of the eye

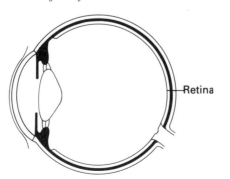

Retina

Deficiency and excess of retinol

1 In the absence of retinol the pigment rhodopsin is not formed. This results in impaired vision in dim light – night blindness.

2 If retinol is lacking, the moist membranes of the body show degenerative changes and resistance to infection is reduced. Hence retinol is also known as the 'anti-infective vitamin'. In severe cases the tear glands of the eye become blocked, and the membrane covering the eye becomes inflamed. This disorder is called *xerophthalmia* (Fig 2.12), and it can lead to permanent blindness. In the UK retinol deficiency is uncommon, but it is a major cause of blindness in some countries, such as India.

Fig. 2.12
Young child with scars on each eye as a result of severe retinol deficiency

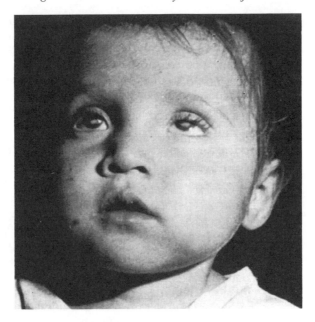

3 Retinol deficiency in children causes a reduction in growth rate. Excessive intakes of retinol are associated with the use of fish oils and supplements such as vitamin drops. Vulnerable groups are children who may be given high doses of such items by misguided mothers or adults. High intakes of retinol during pregnancy are associated with the incidence of birth defects.

In children retinol poisoning causes anorexia, irritability, dry, itching skin, swellings over the long bones and coarse sparse hair. In adults retinol poisoning causes changes to the skin, stiffness of the muscles, headaches and an enlarged liver.

People who eat large amounts of food rich in the carotenoids may develop an orange-yellow tint to the skin. This condition is known as *hypercarotenaemia*. This disorder soon clears up when the intake of carotenoids is reduced, and it does not lead to vitamin A poisoning.

Dietary Reference Values for vitamin A
The RNIs for vitamin A are given in Table 1.6 and these allow for the contribution from carotene. In *adults*, the DRVs are based on calculations

of intakes needed to maintain a store of 20 µg/g of liver. During *pregnancy* and *lactation*, an increment is recommended to allow for the needs of the growing fetus and the production of milk respectively. In *infants*, the values are based on those of breast milk. DRVs in *children* allow for growth as well as the maintenance of body stores.

Sources of vitamin A
In the UK, about three quarters of the vitamin A in the diet is in the form of retinol and one quarter of it is carotene. Meat and meat products provide approximately 40% of the intake. Fats and vegetables both provide 20%.

Rich sources of retinol are liver, kidney, fish oils, dairy products and eggs. Beta-carotene is present in large amounts in carrots and dark green and yellow vegetables. By law vitamin A must be added to margarine and it may also be added to fat-reduced spreads.

Stability of retinol
Retinol is not soluble in water and is therefore not lost by leaching. Retinol and beta-carotene are stable in most methods of cooking, frying being the exception due to the high temperatures needed. Retinol found in fatty foods may be lost during storage as a result of oxidation. Practical measures to reduce such losses include storage in a refrigerator, packaging foods or storage in dark containers.

Vitamin D (cholecalciferol)

Vitamin D is stored in the fatty tissues of the body and the liver. There are 2 main forms of the vitamin:

1 *Cholecalciferol* (Vitamin D_3) is found in foods and is produced under the skin by the action of sunlight (ultra-violet light) on 7-dehydrocholesterol which is therefore the precursor of the vitamin.
2 *Ergocalciferol* (Vitamin D_2) is produced by the action of ultra-violet light on ergosterol which comes from yeast.

Fig. 2.13
Bone

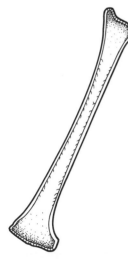

Functions of vitamin D

1 The absorption of calcium in the small intestine.
2 The uptake of calcium and phosphorus by bones and teeth and normal formation and developments of skeletal structures (Fig. 2.13).

Deficiency and excess of vitamin D
In children lack of vitamin D causes a disorder called *rickets* (Fig. 2.14). This is characterised by the failure of new bone and cartilage to calcify adequately and, as a result of this, bone deformities occur. One of the most obvious clinical symptoms of rickets in infants and young children is bow legs. In older children, the tendency is for knock-knees to develop. In females, the pelvic girdle may be so badly deformed that difficulties in childbirth may occur in adult life.

In adults lack of vitamin D causes *osteomalacia*. This is characterised by severe pain in the lower back, and tenderness may occur in other parts of the body, such as the ribs and legs.

Deficiency of vitamin D is more common in females than in males. Individuals at risk include:

1 *Asian adolescent girls* living in large northern towns who usually have little skin exposed to sunlight;
2 *women after repeated pregnancies*, due to the demands for vitamin D by the growing fetus and infant who is breast-fed;

Fig. 2.14
A child suffering from rickets

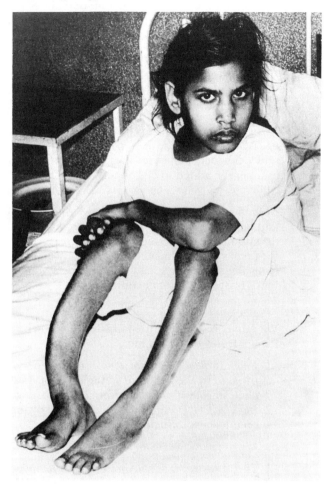

3 *infants born to mothers deficient in vitamin D.* This type of rickets is called
   'congenital rickets';
4 *the elderly,* particularly the housebound, who may be at risk owing to
   little exposure to sunshine. Intakes of the vitamin may be low, and
   losses may occur due to the consumption of laxatives, such as liquid
   paraffin, which act as solvents for the vitamin and prevent it from being
   absorbed.

As vitamin D is fat-soluble, excess of this nutrient is stored in the body and
is not excreted in the urine. High intakes of vitamin D cause calcium to be
deposited in the soft tissues of the body, causing *hypercalcaemia.* The toxic
symptoms resulting from this include loss of appetite, nausea, vomiting,
thirst and alternating constipation and diarrhoea. Children lose weight,
develop headaches and become irritable and depressed. Infants are more
prone to this disorder than adults and can be given an excessive amount in
the form of vitamin drops.

Dietary Reference Values for vitamin D
The RNIs for vitamin D are given in Table 1.6. The DRVs are based on the

need to maintain adequate blood levels of a metabolite of vitamin D throughout the year. In *adults*, it is assumed that the sun will provide enough vitamin D. However, for people confined indoors a dietary source of this nutrient is required. Asian women and children who cover their skin may also need a dietary source of vitamin D. During *pregnancy* and *lactation*, supplementary vitamin D is recommended to achieve 10 μg/day. In *infants* and *children*, needs for calcium, and consequently of vitamin D, are high because their bones are growing rapidly and so a dietary source of vitamin D is recommended.

Sources of vitamin D
The most important source of vitamin D is sunlight. By law vitamin D is added to margarine and it is also added to most low-fat spreads. Fatty fish provide the vitamin in useful amounts and so do eggs. Many breakfast cereals are fortified with vitamin D and therefore make a useful contribution to intakes of this nutrient.

Stability of vitamin D
Vitamin D is stable to heat and therefore not destroyed by cooking. This vitamin is insoluble in water and is not lost through leaching.

Vitamin E (tocopherols)

There is more than one form of vitamin E. A small group of compounds have vitamin E activity: the most active form is called 'tocopherol'. Vitamin E is found in all cell membranes in the body.

Functions of vitamin E
The main function of vitamin E in the body is that of an antioxidant. There is some evidence that increased tissue levels of vitamin E may protect against cardiovascular disease and cancer.

Deficiency and excess of vitamin E
In view of the widespread distribution of vitamin E in foods, deficiency is unlikely. However, deficiency may occur in infants born prematurely. Such infants do not have a sufficient store of the vitamin, and in these circumstances the vitamin should be given prophylactically. Deficiency is also associated with cystic fibrosis, where fat absorption is impaired.

Even in high doses there is no conclusive evidence that vitamin E is poisonous.

Dietary Reference Values for vitamin E
Requirements for vitamin E are related to the amount of PUFAs in the diet. *Safe intakes* for men and women have been set at more than 4 and 3 mg/day respectively. Needs for *infants* are based on the vitamin E content of breast milk and infant formulae should not provide less than 0.3 mg/100 ml.

Sources of vitamin E
Vitamin E is found in useful amounts in vegetable oils, nuts and seeds, cereal products and egg yolk.

Stability of vitamin E
The tocopherols are stable to heat above 100°C and, being fat-soluble, are not leached into water.

Vitamin K (naphthoquinone)

There is a small store of vitamin K in the liver. There is more than one form of vitamin K and all of them belong to a family of compounds called 'naphthoquinones'. Vitamin K is found in foods, and other forms of the vitamin are produced in the intestines by bacteria.

Function of vitamin K
For blood to clot normally 10 factors, known as blood-clotting factors, are needed. Four of these factors depend on vitamin K for their formation. Thus, vitamin K is necessary for the normal clotting of blood.

Deficiency and excess of vitamin K
If vitamin K deficiency is mild, the blood takes longer to clot. This is referred to as a 'prolonged clotting time'. If the deficiency of the vitamin is severe, the blood fails to clot altogether, which, if not treated, could result in loss of life.

Deficiency of vitamin K is not widespread in adults because of its wide distribution in foods. It is also made by bacteria in the intestines. However, vitamin K deficiency may develop in new-born babies because breast and cows' milk contain little vitamin K and, as well as this, the digestive tracts of the new-born are sterile.

Excess of vitamin K does not appear to be a problem.

Dietary Reference Values for vitamin K
The COMA Panel concluded that too little information exists to establish accurate DRVs for this vitamin. In the case of *adults*, the Panel deemed that 1 µg/kg body weight/day was safe. Infants need to be given prophylactic vitamin K at birth and thereafter 2 µg/kg body weight/day.

Sources of vitamin K
The predominant dietary form of vitamin K is *phylloquinone* and green leafy vegetables are the richest source of this vitamin. Other vegetables, fruit, dairy products, vegetable oils, cereals and meat can also provide significant amounts.

Thiamin (vitamin B₁)

The quantity of thiamin found in the body of a healthy adult is approximately 20–30 mg. This vitamin is concentrated in the heart, brain, liver, kidneys and skeletal muscles.

Function of thiamin
Thiamin is required for the release of energy from carbohydrates, alcohol and fats.

Deficiency and excess of thiamin
In the absence of thiamin, carbohydrate metabolism is affected. Glucose is only partially oxidised, and a substance called 'pyruvic acid' builds up in the body. A build-up of pyruvic acid causes a number of symptoms including muscular weakness, which may prevent the individual from walking far and cause breathlessness as a result of exercise, palpitations of the heart and nerve degeneration, which may lead to abnormal sensations from the skin, sensory loss and mood changes. These symptoms are typical of the deficiency disease *beriberi* which is common in parts of Asia where polished rice is a staple food but is uncommon in the UK.

Chronic intakes in excess of 3 g thiamin/day are toxic to adults, causing a variety of symptoms, such as headaches, insomnia and irritability.

Dietary Reference Values for thiamin
The RNIs for thiamin, based on the EARs for energy, are given in Table 1.6. As thiamin is needed for the release of energy, requirements relate to

total energy intakes. During *pregnancy* and *lactation*, the increased energy intakes result in proportional increases in daily thiamin intakes.

Sources of thiamin
More than two thirds of the thiamin in the UK diet comes from plant foods. Bread contributes almost one quarter of the thiamin in the diet.

Thiamin is widely distributed in foods. Useful sources include milk, offal, pork, eggs, fruit and vegetables and wholegrain and fortified breakfast cereals.

Stability of thiamin
Thiamin is readily soluble in water. To prevent its loss, avoid steeping and, if water is used as the cooking medium, use the minimum quantity and save the cooking liquid for sauces, gravies or soups. Thiamin is decomposed at high temperatures, especially in an alkaline environment, and therefore the addition of bicarbonate of soda to cooking liquids is not recommended. The use of baking powder can bring about considerable losses of this vitamin.

Riboflavin (vitamin B_2)

Function of riboflavin
Riboflavin is needed for the release of energy from proteins, fats and carbohydrate.

Deficiency of riboflavin
Riboflavin deficiency is not common but it may occur as part of a multiple deficiency of B vitamins. The tongue becomes swollen and red, the corners of the mouth become cracked and, in severe cases, blood vessels invade the cornea of the eye.

Dietary Reference Values for riboflavin
The DRVs for riboflavin are given in Table 1.6. The values are based on typical UK diets, intakes associated with high excretion of the vitamin and measures of tissue saturation. Increments are needed to meet the demands of *pregnancy* and *lactation*.

Sources of riboflavin
About 40% of the riboflavin in the UK diet comes from milk and milk products.

Riboflavin is widely distributed in foods, particularly those of animal origin.

Stability of riboflavin
Riboflavin is less soluble in water and more heat stable than thiamin. It is, however, sensitive to light. This is an important point to note because milk, which is an important source of riboflavin, tends to lose its riboflavin content if left in bright sunlight.

Niacin (vitamin B_3)

Niacin, in the form of *nicotinic acid* and *nicotinamide*, is present in certain foods. One of the indispensable amino acids, *tryptophan*, can be converted into niacin in the body:

$$\text{niacin} = \frac{\text{tryptophan}}{60}$$

Function of niacin

Niacin forms part of the co-enzymes involved in the oxidative release of energy.

Deficiency and excess of niacin

In severe cases of deficiency *pellagra* develops. This disorder is also known as 'the disease of the 3 Ds' because 3 of the major clinical symptoms begin with the letter 'D': diarrhoea, dermatitis and dementia.

Very high doses (3–6 g/day) of niacin may cause damage to the liver.

Dietary Reference Values for niacin

Table 1.6 gives the RNIs for niacin, which are based on the DRVs for energy. Requirements for this nutrient are estimated from measurements of urinary excretion of the vitamin's metabolites and the amount of one of the coenzymes in the body. Additional niacin is needed to meet the demands of *lactation* to maintain adequate levels in breast milk.

Sources of niacin

The main sources of niacin in the UK diet are meat and meat products, potatoes, bread and fortified breakfast cereals.

Other foods with useful amounts of niacin include fish, pulses and nuts.

Stability of niacin

Niacin is water-soluble and easily lost by leaching. For this reason, cooking liquids and meat juices should not be discarded. Niacin is more resistant to heat than thiamin or riboflavin.

Vitamin B_{12} (cyanocobalamin)

Fig. 2.15
A nerve cell (neuron)

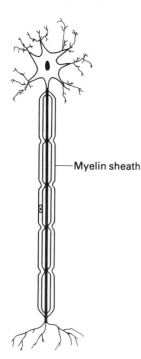

Myelin sheath

Approximately 2–5 mg of vitamin B_{12} is found in the body of a healthy adult, and more than half of this is stored in the liver.

Functions of vitamin B_{12}

Vitamin B_{12} is important in different enzyme systems in the body and is needed for growth and the formation of red blood cells. The vitamin also plays a part in the maintenance of myelin in the nervous system (Fig 2.15).

Deficiency of vitamin B_{12}

The first signs of vitamin B_{12} deficiency are tiredness and shortness of breath. This is caused by a type of anaemia in which the red blood cells are larger than normal. These large cells usually have a normal concentration of haemoglobin but the replication of these blood cells is slowed down and there are fewer red blood cells in the circulation, with the result that haemoglobin levels fall.

Lack of vitamin B_{12} affects the nervous system. Symptoms include a loss of smell and taste, difficulty in walking and in micturating. Degenerative and irreversible changes of the spinal cord occur.

Dietary Reference Values for vitamin B_{12}

Table 1.6 gives the RNIs for vitamin B_{12}. In *adults*, the DRVs have been based on the intakes of groups consuming little of the vitamin, but who do not have deficiency, and the amount of the vitamin needed to cure the deficiency and patient response to parenteral vitamin B_{12}. The RNI will create a liver store of the vitamin and prevent anaemia. An increment is needed during *lactation*. DRVs for *infants* are based on the amount of the nutrient required to cure megaloblastic anaemia in infants fed on breast milk low in vitamin B_{12}. DRVs for *children* have been interpolated between these values and those of adults.

Sources of vitamin B$_{12}$
The main sources of vitamin B$_{12}$ in the UK diet are meat and meat products and milk.

Almost all animal products contain vitamin B$_{12}$. Liver is the richest source of this nutrient. Useful quantities of vitamin B$_{12}$ are present in meat, fish, eggs, milk and cheese. Fortified breakfast cereals are useful providers of this vitamin. Vegans need to eat foods fortified with vitamin B$_{12}$ or to take supplements.

Stability of vitamin B$_{12}$
Vitamin B$_{12}$ is usually stable but some is lost by boiling in an alkaline medium.

Folate

Folic acid (pteroyl glutamic acid) is the parent molecule to a large number of compounds collectively known as folates.

Function of folate
Folates work with vitamin B$_{12}$ in rapidly dividing cells.

Deficiency of folate
Folate deficiency leads to a type of megaloblastic anaemia. Lack of folate before and during pregnancy is associated with neural tube defects such as *anencephaly* or *spina bifida*, in which the brain or spinal cord or their protective coverings fail to develop properly.

Dietary Reference Values for folate
Table 1.6 gives the RNIs for folate. DRVs for adults are based on the amounts of dietary folate needed to maintain adequate stores in the liver and concentrations in the red blood cells and serum and the amount required to prevent or cure the associated megaloblastic anaemia. Increments are needed during *pregnancy* and *lactation*. In *infants*, the DRVs relate to breast milk concentrations. In *children*, levels have been interpolated between those of infants and adults.

Sources of folate
The main sources of folate in the UK diet are potatoes, fortified breakfast cereals, bread and fresh vegetables.

Rich sources of folate include offal, yeast extract, green leafy vegetables and foods fortified with this nutrient, such as certain breakfast cereals.

Stability of folate
Folates are soluble in water and losses occur in water used for cooking vegetables. Folates are sensitive to heat and can be lost during cooking and canning.

Vitamin C (ascorbic acid)

Vitamin C is found in all body tissues in small quantities. It is concentrated in the white blood cells and in the adrenal glands. It is also concentrated, to a lesser extent, in the liver and kidneys.

Functions of vitamin C

1 The formation of all body tissues, particularly connective tissue (Fig. 2.16).
2 The absorption of iron from the intestine.

Deficiency and excess of vitamin C
In the absence of vitamin C, the formation of the connective tissue

Fig. 2.16
Connective tissue

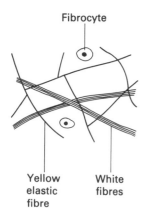

Fibrocyte

Yellow
elastic
fibre

White
fibres

collagen is impaired, the walls of the capillaries weaken and this results in haemorrhaging. The gums become swollen and red and they bleed easily (Fig. 2.17). There is a tendency for the slightest bump to cause bruising, with haemorrhages occurring around the hair follicles. Haemorrhages often occur in the feet and ankles under the skin. Wounds, including cuts, burns and fractures, do not heal. These are all symptoms of *scurvy*. Scurvy is not common in Britain, although 'widowers' scurvy' may occur in elderly men. Mild symptoms of vitamin C deficiency include mental symptoms, such as depression, hysteria and tiredness.

Excessive intakes of ascorbic acid are usually associated with the use of pharmacological preparations and result in diarrhoea and nausea. Renal stones (oxalate stones) may form in the kidneys from oxalic acid which is formed from ascorbic acid.

Fig. 2.17
Mouth of a person suffering from scurvy

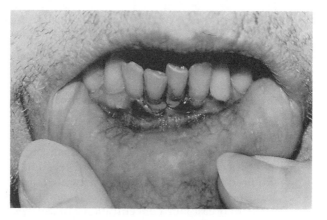

Dietary Reference Values for vitamin C
Table 1.6 gives the RNIs for vitamin C. The DRVs are based on the amount of the vitamin required to prevent signs and symptoms of scurvy, biochemical indices of vitamin C status and vitamin C turnover studies. Increments are recommended during *pregnancy* and *lactation*.

Sources of vitamin C
The main sources of dietary vitamin C are fruit and fruit juices, potatoes and other vegetables.

Citrus fruits and blackcurrants are rich sources of vitamin C and so are guavas.

Stability of vitamin C

1 Ascorbic acid is highly soluble in water and readily leaches out into water.
2 Ascorbic acid is readily oxidised and this process is more rapid at high temperatures, in exposure to light, in the presence of metals such as copper, iron and zinc, and in the presence of alkalis and of an enzyme called 'ascorbic acid oxidase'.

It is important to take account of these 2 issues when preparing foods containing ascorbic acid, otherwise most, if not all, of the vitamin may be lost. Table 8.4 summarises the precautions from 'purchase to presentation' with reference to the oxidation and water-solubility of this nutrient.

Water

Water is made up of hydrogen and oxygen (H_2O). About 60% of the human body is water (Fig. 2.1). In an adult this amounts to about 40 litres of water.

Functions of water

Water is:

1 a suitable medium in which substances such as enzymes and nutrients can be dispersed;
2 a suitable medium for the chemical reactions needed to maintain life;
3 a means of transport in the body – for example, materials are carried to cells and waste products are carried away in blood plasma.

Deficiency of water

After a matter of days without water, life ceases. Water is not stored in humans and there is a continual loss of water as a result of 'normal' bodily functions. Lack of water leads to *dehydration*. This is easily recognised: the features look sunken, with the eyes receding into their orbits; the skin becomes dry and loose and loses its elasticity; the tongue becomes dry and the person usually becomes thirsty. Sodium depletion is associated with dehydration.

Requirements for water

The adult body needs about 2–3 litres of water per day. The need for water is increased in certain circumstances:

1 *Illness*, particularly where an increase in temperature causes sweating.
2 *Vomiting* means the loss of additional water and this needs to be replaced.
3 *Diarrhoea* means the loss of additional water and this needs to be replaced.
4 *Breast-feeding* for milk production.

Sources of water

Water comes from 3 main sources: drinking water, water present in food, for example, meat, and water produced as a result of metabolic processes.

Digestion and absorption of nutrients

Any one single food may provide a number of different nutrients in varying amounts. When food is consumed it is physically broken down by the grinding action of the teeth and movement through the gut. As food travels through the digestive tract the complex nutrient molecules are broken down into smaller ones. Some nutrients are already small molecules and can be absorbed as such. For the body to absorb nutrients it is necessary that the nutrient molecules are small and soluble.

The digestive tract

The digestive tract is a hollow tube of about 9 metres in length (Fig 2.18). The innermost lining of the tube is formed by the mucous membrane, next is the submucous layer, then the muscle layer, and finally there is an outer covering. The digestive tract is supplied with nerves and blood. Various secretions are needed for the digestive process. These are produced by glands found in the lining of the gut, and various organs which have ducts leading into the digestive tract.

Fig. 2.18
The digestive tract

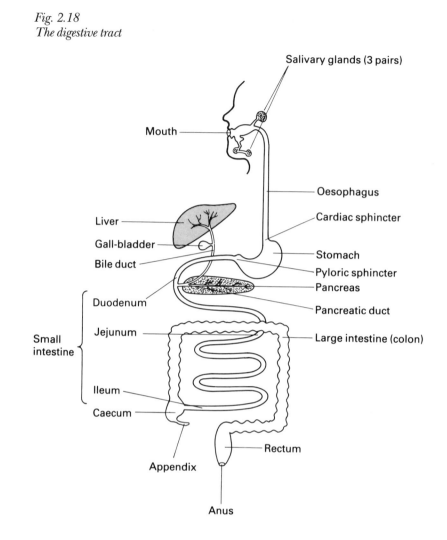

Salivary glands (3 pairs)

Mouth

Oesophagus

Cardiac sphincter

Liver

Gall-bladder

Bile duct

Stomach

Pyloric sphincter

Pancreas

Pancreatic duct

Duodenum

Jejunum

Large intestine (colon)

Small intestine

Ileum

Caecum

Rectum

Appendix

Anus

Enzymes

Enzymes are important in digestion. They are proteins which act as catalysts and, at very low concentrations, they increase the rate of chemical reactions, but at the end of the process the enzyme itself remains unchanged. In the gut the enzymes are called hydrolases. This means that these enzymes catalyse hydrolytic reactions (involving water). Enzymes are highly specific in their action. Enzyme activity is affected by temperature and pH. In order to function effectively, some enzymes require the help of other substances called 'co-enzymes' and 'activators'.

Digestion

A summary of digestion is given in Table 2.3. Food enters the digestive tract by way of the mouth, where it is chewed and mixed with saliva. The very sight and smell of food stimulates the salivary glands to produce a steady flow of saliva. The saliva enters the mouth by way of ducts leading from the salivary glands. When the food has been chewed and mixed with the digestive secretion in the mouth, it forms a bolus, or soft mass of food. This is pushed into the pharynx by the upward movement of the tongue. When the bolus reaches the pharynx, rhythmic contractions of the muscular walls of the oesophagus occur. This movement is called 'peristalsis' and it propels the bolus through the oesophagus into the stomach via the sphincter muscles.

In the stomach the food is moved about (churning movement) by the movement of the muscular walls, and mixed with gastric juice. The sight, smell, taste and physical presence of food in the stomach stimulates the secretion of gastric juice. This digestive juice is produced by gastric glands within the mucous membrane of the stomach walls. The secretion enters the stomach by way of tiny ducts. The muscular action of the stomach walls causes the food and gastric juices to be thoroughly mixed. At various intervals the pyloric sphincter muscles contract and jets of chyme are forced into the duodenum. Food stays in the stomach for about 4 to 5 hours; the time depends upon the food. A carbohydrate meal stays in the stomach for about 2 to 3 hours; protein stays longer; fatty foods have the longest stay. Absorption of certain nutrients takes place in the stomach – for example, water, glucose and alcohol.

When chyme enters the small intestine it is mixed with more digestive juices. The first juices include pancreatic juice and bile, and later the chyme is mixed with intestinal juice. Pancreatic juice is produced by cells in the pancreas and enters the duodenum by way of the pancreatic duct. Bile is produced in the liver and stored in the gall-bladder. After a meal the gall-bladder contracts and bile passes, by way of the cystic duct and bile duct, into the duodenum. Intestinal juice is produced by glands in the wall of the small intestine.

Table 2.3
Summary of digestion

Digestive juice	pH	Main components	Action
Saliva	6.7	Mucin	Aids mastication and swallowing
		Amylase	Starch → maltose
Gastric juice	1–3	Pepsin	Protein → polypeptides
		Rennin	Coagulates milk
		Hydrochloric acid	Activates pepsin
Pancreatic juice	6–7	Trypsin	Splits polypeptides and proteins
		Amylase	Starch → maltose
		Lipase	Fats → fatty acids and glycerol
Bile		Bile salts	Emulsify fats
Intestinal juice	6.5–7.5	Peptidases	Polypeptides → amino acids
		Maltase	Maltose → glucose
		Sucrase	Sucrose → glucose and fructose
		Lactase	Lactose → glucose and galactose

Absorption

Nutrients are absorbed primarily in the small intestine. The small intestine provides a vast surface area for the absorption of nutrients. Circular folds of the mucous membrane lining and hair-like projections, called 'villi', ensure this large surface area (Fig 2.19).

Fig. 2.19
Villi

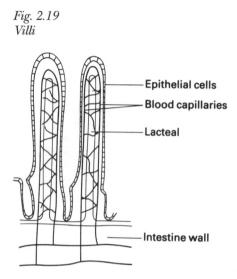

Epithelial cells

Blood capillaries

Lacteal

Intestine wall

The amino acids, monosaccharides, vitamins, minerals and water pass into the blood capillaries. The glycerol and fatty acids pass into the lacteals. This causes the lymph to have a milky appearance. In this state the lymph is called 'chyle'. The fluid contents of the small intestine pass on to the large intestine. The large intestine has a number of different functions: water is absorbed so that the liquid contents become semi-solid faeces; absorption of mineral salts continues by way of the blood capillaries; the vitamin folic acid is produced by the microbial flora, and this is absorbed in significant quantities. Mass movements in the colon causes faeces to be passed onwards to the rectum. More water is absorbed in the rectum, depending on how long the faecal material is left there.

Defecation

Faeces are usually about 60–70% water. The remaining 40–30% is made up of undigested fibrous material, micro-organisms, dead cells from the lining of the digestive tract, fatty acids and mucus. Faeces are eliminated by the process of defecation whereby faecal material leaves the gut by way of the anus.

Metabolism

Metabolism is the total of the chemical reactions by which nutrients are used to produce energy and material for growth and maintenance of body cells. Two types of metabolic reactions are involved: *catabolism* (breaking down of large molecules to small ones; and *anabolism* (building up of small molecules to large ones). Catabolic and anabolic reactions take place inside the body cells simultaneously and in stages which are catalysed by various enzymes. The production of energy is an important metabolic process. As a result of catabolic processes, carbohydrates, fatty acids, glycerol and deaminated amino acids (the nitrogen part of the molecule removed) release energy and waste products – water and carbon dioxide inside the body cells. The breakdown of these food components takes place in a series of steps involving certain catalysing enzymes. At first these 3 nutrients pass through different stages, then they follow a common catabolic pathway. The name of the common pathway is Krebs cycle, also known as the 'citric acid cycle' (Fig 2.20).

Units of energy

The units of energy referred to in nutrition are the kilojoule (kJ) and the kilocalorie (kcal).

4.19 kJ = 1 kcal

Proteins, carbohydrates, fats and alcohol all provide energy. Thus, 1 g of protein yields 4 kcal; 1 g of carbohydrate yields 3.75 kcal; 1 g of fat yields 9 kcal; and 1 g of alcohol yields 7 kcal.

Functions of energy

The body needs energy for basal metabolism and physical activity. Basal metabolism refers to the basic metabolic processes needed to keep the body alive – for example, the beating of the heart, breathing, maintenance of body temperature. The term 'basal metabolic rate' (BMR) is used to describe the rate at which energy is used to maintain basal metabolism. The basal metabolic rate is affected by a number of different factors, such as the size of the body, age and the activity of the thyroid gland.

Physical activity requires energy over and above that needed for basal metabolism. To assess how much energy is needed for different physical activities, the uptake of oxygen is measured while the activity is being undertaken.

Excess and lack of energy

If the input of energy is in excess of body needs, it is stored and leads to *obesity*. If the input of energy is less than the output, weight loss will result. In extreme cases, such as those resulting from famine and disasters, people may die from *starvation*. Starvation may arise as a result of deliberately not eating. This is a feature of a disorder called *anorexia nervosa*, which is defined as a psychiatric disease. Anorexia nervosa is more common in females than in males. It tends to occur in adolescence and early adult life.

Dietary Reference Values for energy

Table 1.1 gives the EARs for energy. In *adults*, energy needs are determined using BMRs and physical activity levels (PAL):

EAR = BMR × PAL

During *pregnancy*, there is a reduction in physical activity and metabolic rate and, therefore, a small increment in energy intake is recommended during the last trimester only. Requirements during *lactation* relate to specific circumstances (see footnotes to Table 1.1). In the case of *children* and *adolescents*, the EARs are based on lifestyle and activity levels.

Fig. 2.20
Krebs cycle

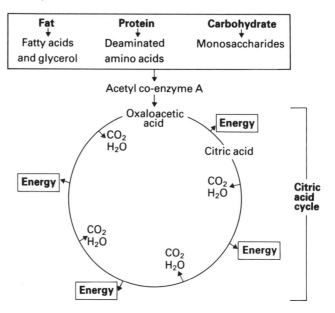

Sources of energy

In the UK diet, the main sources of energy are bread, flour and other cereals, meat, fats, dairy foods and sugar. These foods are rich in energy and are also eaten in substantial quantities.

3 Food Choice

Below is a list of factors affecting people's choice of food.

1 healthy eating
2 when the meal is to be eaten
3 occasion of the meal
4 where the meal is to be eaten
5 money available
6 time for food preparation
7 facilities for food preparation
8 level of skill
9 colour, texture and flavour of food
10 likes and dislikes
11 individual requirements
12 philosophy
13 religion
14 state of health

Healthy eating

The Balance of Good Health
The National Food Guide: The Balance of Good Health, has evolved from the government's eight guidelines for a healthy diet:

- enjoy your food;
- eat a variety of different foods;
- eat the right amount to be a healthy weight;
- eat plenty of foods rich in starch and fibre;
- don't eat too much fat;
- don't eat sugary foods too often;
- look after the vitamins and minerals in your food;
- if you drink alcohol, keep within sensible limits.

The Balance of Good Health applies to most people, but it does not apply to children under 2 years of age. Between the ages of 2 and 5 years, children make a gradual transition to family foods and the *Guide* can begin to apply. People under medical supervision or with specific dietary requirements will need to check with their doctor if they can use the *Guide*.

The basis of the *Guide* is straightforward. Foods provide nutrients to help the body to work properly and, as no single food contains them all in the amounts needed, a mixture of foods has to be eaten. *The Balance of Good Health* shows the types and proportions of foods needed to make up a well-balanced and healthy diet (Fig. 3.1).

Five groups of foods are identified in the *Guide* with the emphasis on the provision of main nutrients.

1 *Bread, other cereals and potatoes* supply starch, fibre, calcium, iron and B-vitamins.
2 *Fruit and vegetables* supply vitamin C, carotenes, folates, fibre and some sugars and starches.
3 *Meat, fish and alternatives* supply iron, protein, B-vitamins – especially B_{12}, zinc and magnesium.
4 *Milk and dairy foods* supply calcium, protein, vitamin B_{12} and vitamins A and D.
5 *Fatty and sugary foods* supply some vitamins and essential fatty acids, but also a lot of fat, sugar and salt.

It is considered advisable to select a variety of foods from the first four groups every day. If different foods within the groups are eaten, this will add to the range of nutrients consumed. The foods in the fifth group are not essential for a healthy diet, although they add extra choice and palatability.

Fig. 3.1
The balance of good health

Fruit and vegetables
Choose a wide variety

Bread, other cereals and potatoes
Eat all types and choose high-fibre kinds whenever you can

Meat, fish and alternatives
Choose lower-fat alternatives whenever you can

Milk and dairy foods
Choose lower-fat alternatives whenever you can

Fatty and sugary foods
Try not to eat these too often and, when you do, have small amounts

Recipe modification The Health of the Nation/*COMA-style*

Increasing dietary fibre (NSP) content

1 Use brown, wholemeal or ½ wholemeal and ½ white flour as a substitute for white flour, but remember to add the bran left behind in the sieve.
2 Use brown or wholemeal bread in place of white bread.
3 Choose wholemeal pasta rather than white or flavoured varieties, but allow for the additional time it takes to cook.
4 Choose brown rice in place of white rice and allow for the additional time it takes to cook.
5 Use high-fibre breakfast cereals in recipes to act as fillers – for example, in burgers and toppings.
6 Leave the skins on fruit and vegetables and keep them intact, as opposed to passing mixtures through a sieve and discarding the fibrous material.

7 Replace some animal sources of protein with pulses – for example using puréed lentils in place of some of the mince in beefburgers.

Decreasing the fat (total and saturated fatty acids) content
1 Choose lean meat, trim any visible fat and remove any fat in cooking liquids. Buy quality mince or prepare it yourself from lean meat. Choose fat-reduced sausages in place of traditional sausages.
2 Choose turkey or chicken rather than more fatty birds. Opt for the white meat as opposed to the dark meat, and remove all the skin and underlying fat to reduce fat further.
3 Go for fat-reduced varieties of cheese in preference to traditionally prepared cheeses, and try cheeses with a naturally low fat content, such as cottage cheese and fromage frais, or use smaller amounts of strong-flavoured cheeses, such as Parmesan.
4 Use semi-skimmed or skimmed milk instead of whole milk.
5 Use low-fat spreads as a substitute for butter or margarine in recipes where possible. Grill rather than fry. Dry fry in a non-stick pan if frying is a must. Coat particulate foods thoroughly with egg and breadcrumbs before frying. Drain all fried foods thoroughly on absorbent paper.
6 As a substitute for cream, use low-fat yogurt or fromage frais.

Decreasing the non-milk extrinsic sugar content
1 Use food products with no added sugar in them, such as fruit canned in its own juice and unsweetened orange juice.
2 Use fruit speads, low-sugar jams or fruit purées as a substitute for jam.
3 Use puréed bananas, finely grated carrot or chopped dried dates in place of some of the sugar in recipes for cakes.
4 Prepare fruit salad using the juice that escapes from the fruit during preparation or unsweetened fruit juice in place of sugar syrup.
5 Decorate cakes with suitable dried or fresh fruit as opposed to icings.

Decreasing the sodium content
1 Use food products with no added salt in them, such as pulses that have not been canned in brine.
2 Choose unsalted butter in preference to salted varieties.
3 Cook vegetables, rice and pasta without the addition of salt.
4 Choose alternative flavourings when preparing savoury foods, such as parsley, basil, garlic, celery.
5 If food products have added salt, simply wash it off.

When the meal is to be eaten

It is realistic to think in terms of 3 meals a day in association with rising in the morning, midday and evening. Breakfast – literally, 'to break one's fast' – is considered to be the most important meal of the day, and nutritionists are adamant that it should be a proper meal.
    Examples of breakfast include:

unsweetened orange juice   orange and grapefruit segments
porridge with milk   boiled egg with wholewheat toast

Examples of midday meals or lunches include:

Welsh rarebit with tomato salad   hummus with pitta bread
fruit and Allbran loaf   fresh fruit

Examples of evening meals include:

watercress soup
jacket potato with chicken and
    yogurt filling and ratatouille
brown bread ice-cream

carrot and orange soup
kofta curry with pilau rice and
    tomato bhurtha
fruity kebabs

Occasion of the meal

Everyday meals generally differ from those served on special occasions. Whatever the occasion, however, such meals should still take account of the guidelines for selecting foods in the meal planning scheme. Special occasions, such as when entertaining or family treats, may involve additional expense and extra time for meal preparation.

Where the meal is to be eaten

Meals eaten away from home may include packed meals, school dinners, takeaway meals and meals in restaurants.

Packed meals
Planning meals to be eaten away from home is part of everyday life for many people. Foods for packed meals should be convenient for packing, unspoilt by carriage to the eating destination and manageable to eat. Examples of packed meals include:

Cornish pasty with sticks of carrot
    and celery
wholewheat roll with salad filling
orange and apricot drink

1 slice quiche Lorraine with
    coleslaw
apple scone
flask of tea

Money available

1 Make more use of pulses as a replacement for some, or all, of the animal sources of protein.

Table 3.1
The advantages and disadvantages of different retail outlets

Outlet	Competitive prices	Wide range of products	Fresh quality food	Customer can select own goods
Super- or hyper-market	✓	✓	✓	✓
Small grocer shop	Limited	Limited	Turnover may be slow	In some only
Specialist shop	Limited	Within the product offered	Turnover may be slow	
Open market	✓	✓	✓	Frequently display goods not on sale

2 Choose foods that are in season; this is particularly relevant to fruit and vegetables.
3 Shop wisely.
   (a) Be aware of the advantages and disadvantages of different outlets (Table 3.1) and shop around for competitive prices.
   (b) Prepare a shopping list and keep to it.
   (c) Know how to recognise a 'quality' product and check labels for date marks.
4 Exciting dishes can be made from leftovers (Table 3.2).
   (a) Ensure that the leftovers are used up as soon as possible and are either eaten next day or frozen for no more than 2 to 3 months.
   (b) Chop, mince or purée leftover foods. If other foods are to be used with them, they too should be cooked. If the food is in large pieces it takes longer to cook, and longer cooking tends to toughen proteins. Large pieces of food may not reach the desired temperature all the way through so that the food could contain harmful micro-organisms.
   (c) Food should be mixed together when cool.
   (d) Good seasoning is very important because re-heated foods can be insipid.
   (e) Leftover foods may be dry. Coatings of egg and breadcrumbs can be of value in the prevention of drying out, and the use of sauces is recommended.
   (f) Losses of vitamin C in re-heated foods are probably quite high. To overcome this, include salads or fresh fruit as part of the meal.
   (g) Re-heated foods, particularly those of animal origin, tend to be less digestible than fresh foods. This is due to the toughening effect of heat on the protein. It is not advisable to give such foods to infants below 1 year old or to people who are ill or recovering from illness.

Hygienic conditions	No queuing problems	Personal service	Car parking	Home deliveries
✓	Can be very bad at peak times		✓	
✓		✓	Usually in residential areas	✓
✓		✓		✓
Not always good, e.g., side of road, dust, flies	✓			

Table 3.2
Uses of leftover foods

Food	Uses
Cooked meat	Shepherd's pie, risotto, samosas
Cooked fish	Fish cakes, fish pie, fish curry
Boiled eggs	Scotch eggs, egg curry, egg mayonnaise
Cooked beans or lentils	Spreads, burgers, roasts
Boiled potatoes	Bubble and squeak, koftas, corned beef hash

Time for food preparation

Bulk cooking for the freezer can make a valuable contribution where time saving is concerned. Convenience foods can be used to advantage and may justify the additional expense. Various pieces of equipment will save time in food preparation.

Facilities for food preparation

Some pieces of equipment will make food preparation easier and may also have a bearing on meal planning. However, preparation facilities may be very limited. The classic example is the bedsitter, where careful management is essential to cope with limited space, few pieces of equipment and possibly only one hotplate.

Level of skill

The type of meal prepared will be influenced by the level of skill of the cook. Convenience foods may be particularly helpful if skills are lacking.

Colour, texture and flavour of food

Vegetables, especially raw in salads, and sprinklings of fresh herbs can add colour to meals as well as texture and flavour. Cooking methods such as stir-frying are recommended to retain the colour and texture of foods.

Likes and dislikes

The saying 'one man's meat is another man's poison' sums up people's likes and dislikes with regard to food. When planning meals account should be taken of these likes and dislikes.

Individual requirements

Pregnancy
During pregnancy, nutritional needs increase as the fetus grows and develops (Fig. 3.2) and there is a laying down of new tissues in the mother's body. It is essential that the mother's diet provides adequate energy and nutrients to meet these needs. A good mixed diet should achieve this. The DRVs allow for additional increments of the energy, protein and vitamins required during pregnancy and are given in Tables 1.1, 1.4 and 1.6 respectively.

Some nutrients merit special attention. For example, before and during pregnancy, *folate,* is needed in additional amounts to decrease the risk of

Fig. 3.2
Developing fetus

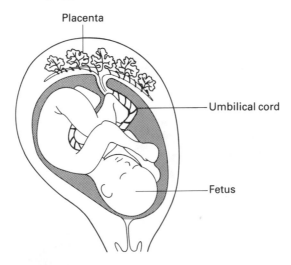

Placenta

Umbilical cord

Fetus

neural tube defects in babies. Women planning their pregnancies are advised to take a supplement of 0.4 mg folate/day and to eat foods rich in folate (p. 00). Supplements of *iron* may be recommended too, as well as drops of *vitamins A, C* and *D. Vitamin A* needs to be viewed with caution, however. Taking vitamin A supplements and eating foods rich in retinol, such as liver and liver products, during pregnancy is not advisable as these may cause birth defects. The eating of other specific foods also needs consideration – for example, ripened soft cheeses and pâté as they are frequently contaminated with *Listeria monocytogenes. Listeriosis* may cause only mild, flu-like symptoms in the mother, but there may be an associated fetal infection, resulting in the possibility of abortion, stillbirth or premature labour. *Alcoholic drinks* can also damage the unborn child.

Lactation
When the new-born infant is fed on breast milk (Fig. 3.3) the mother is said to be lactating. During this time, all the infant's needs for energy and nutrients must be supplied by the mother. It is essential, therefore, that the mother's diet provides adequate energy and nutrients to allow her to produce milk for the baby. DRVs for energy, protein, minerals and vitamins during lactation are given in Tables 1.1, 1.4, 1.5 and 1.6 respectively.

Infants and young children
Infants rely on a single food source, milk, to satisfy their nutritional needs and breast-feeding is recommended for a number of reasons.

1   Human milk is the natural food for human infants. Its content of energy, nutrients and water meets the needs of the infant. Infant formulae are similar to human milk in this respect if reconstituted properly. However, if they are not made up according to manufacturers' instructions, problems can occur; for example, if the milk is too concentrated this can lead to dehydration, causing the infant to suffer from anorexia, irritability and convulsions. If the milk is too diluted tetany can occur, causing the infant to suffer twitches and spasms.

Fig. 3.3
Breastfeeding a baby

2 Human milk contains anti-infective factors which limit the growth of harmful (pathogenic) bacteria and viruses. Some of these factors are highly concentrated in colostrum, the milk produced during the first few days of lactation. For this reason breast-feeding, if only for a few days, is better than not breast-feeding at all. Artificial feeds do not contain these anti-infective factors.

3 Breast milk is usually sterile as it is delivered straight to the baby. Artificial feeds are more likely to become contaminated. Bottles and teats need to be sterilised. Gastro-enteritis due to bacterial infection is more common in the bottle-fed infant than in the breast-fed infant.

4 Breast-feeding is convenient because the infant's food is literally 'on tap'. Infant formulae take time to make up as well as taking up storage space in the refrigerator if made up in advance.

5 Breast-feeding incurs no additional cost while bottle feeding is costly. The infant formulae have to be purchased and also the bottles and sterilisation equipment. Fuel costs of preparation also have to be taken into account.

6 Breast-feeding is believed to be advantageous for a warm, mother/child relationship because of their close contact. However, there is no evidence that bottle-fed babies have a less warm relationship. Mothers who bottle-feed are advised to hold the baby close to the breast and ensure eye contact to encourage a warm relationship.

7 The breast-feeding mother loses weight during lactation due to the energy demands of milk production. In this way the store of fat laid

Fig. 3.4
Equipment for puréeing baby foods

Hand blender

Hand grinder

down in pregnancy is used up. Mothers who bottle-feed and do not reduce energy intake tend to get fatter with each successive pregnancy.

8 Breast cancer is less common among breast-feeding communities.

Weaning

When breast-feeding or bottle-feeding starts to be replaced by a mixed diet the term 'weaning' is used. Weaning too soon may harm the infant. The infant's body needs to be mature enough to cope with the digestion of the additional foods and the excretion of the end products. The COMA report *Weaning and the Weaning Diet* advises that solid foods should not be given to infants before the age of 4 months, but that a mixed diet should be offered by the age of 6 months. During the first 4 to 5 months, infants double their birth weight and milk alone will not continue to meet their energy and nutrient requirements completely after this time. The DRVs for infants are given in Tables 1.1, 1.4, 1.5 and 1.6. Particular attention needs to be given to additional dietary sources of *energy, protein, vitamins A and D, iron and zinc.*

During weaning, the infant may be gradually introduced to a variety of foods, such as infant cereals, puréed fruit and vegetables (Fig. 3.4), egg yolk and finely chopped meat. A few pointers should be noted.

- Eggs must be cooked until solid to avoid salmonella infection. Eggs can be given after 6 months.
- Nuts, whole or chopped, should be avoided until the child is 5 years old as they may cause choking.
- Pâté and ripened soft cheeses should be avoided until the child is over 12 months old because of the risk of *Listeria monocytogenes.*
- Mildly spiced food may be tolerated, but sugar and salt should not be added to foods.
- Commercial baby foods are convenient, nutritious and prepared according to EC compositional standards.
- Infants under 12 months need 500–600 ml of breast milk or formula/day (after this time 350 ml of milk/day is recommended to meet minimal calcium requirements).
- The Department of Health recommends supplementing the diet with vitamin drops of A, C and D during the transition from milk to a mixed diet.

Pre-school children

During this transitional phase from an infant to an adult-type diet, it is important that the diet is high in nutrient-dense foods as major functional development is taking place. A nutrient-dense diet is one consisting of foods that are rich in essential nutrients in comparison with the energy they provide. The DRVs for this group are given in Tables 1.1, 1.4, 1.5 and 1.6.

Beyond the stage of infancy, it is necessary to balance the need for a diet that will benefit future health with one that will ensure proper growth and development. Pointers for this transitional phase are as follows.

- Ensure a regular pattern of meals, allowing for more frequent eating as necessary.
- Allow for a varied range of foods to be enjoyed.
- Base between-meal snacks on nutritious foods, such as celery, carrots, bread, cheese and yogurt, as opposed to fatty, sugary and salty foods.
- The development of preferences for sugary and salty foods should be discouraged as these could have implications in terms of dental caries and high blood pressure in adult life.

● Note that an adult diet is too bulky and low in energy-dense foods for children under 2 years of age. Beyond this age, lower-fat foods and those providing more starch and fibre should be introduced gradually. The Department of Health recommends the implementation of adult guidelines by the age of 5 years.

School children

This group has high energy and nutrient needs in relation to their body size compared with those of adults. This is shown by the DRVs in Tables 1.1, 1.4, 1.5 and 1.6. This is a reflection of the needs of this group for growth, which is fast, and energy, as children are very active. Caution needs to be exercised on several fronts. Salty, sugary and fatty foods should not be encouraged, as for pre-school children, and the diet should not be too bulky.

Adolescents

The adolescent or teenage phase takes place between the ages of 10–19 years. In the UK, this group represents about 14% of the population. It is a period of considerable change, centred on puberty. This process is characterised by a spurt in physical growth, in both height and weight, changes in body composition, and sexual development. The DRVs for this group are given in Tables 1.1 – 1.6.

It is important that a wide variety of foods is eaten to meet nutritional needs. *Energy* needs are high to cover the growth and physical activity taking place. *Protein* is also important for rapid growth spurts. *Calcium* needs are higher too, because of bone development – about 45% of the adult skeleton is laid down during these years. *Iron* requirements are also relatively high as there is an increase in lean body mass, blood volume and haemoglobin, and girls will need to make up for iron lost in menstruation.

Some examples of nutritional problems associated with this age group include eating disorders, such as anorexia nervosa and bulimia, faddy diets – caused by changing to vegetarianism without sufficient advice, for example – and the consumption of alcoholic drinks. Teenage pregnancies can also lead to compromised nutritional status.

Adults

The nutritional needs of adults differ from those of infants and young children, school children and adolescents because growth has ceased. At this stage in the lifecycle, food is needed to maintain and repair the tissues, for normal bodily functions, and for specific energy requirements. The DRVs for this group with the exception of dietary fibre (p. 9.) are given in Tables 1.1 – 1.6. In addition to this, alcohol intake needs careful consideration and it is advisable to keep within the Health Education Authority's sensible drinking guidelines of fewer than 14 units of alcohol a week for women and fewer than 21 for men.

Elderly people

The term *elderly* relates to people of pensionable age, which is 60 years for women and 65 years for men. Individuals aged over 75 years are classified as *very elderly*. In the UK, approximately 18% of the population is of pensionable age. Ageing involves changes which lead to a decline in physiological and psychological function. *Loss of lean body mass* is associated with the age-related fall in BMR and may also influence energy expenditure levels. *Loss of bone mass* begins in the third decade and then progresses into features such as loss of height, and roundness of the shoulders and back. *Alterations in glucose metabolism* resulting from age-related changes to the pancreas may occur and this is associated with diabetes in elderly people. The physiological changes that occur during ageing are reflected in the DRVs for this group (Tables 1.1–1.6).

In nutritional terms, the elderly are considered to be a vulnerable group for a variety of reasons:

1 Lack of interest in food can occur for different reasons. Social isolation associated with the death of a partner may lead to apathy and neglect where food is concerned and mental disturbances can also lead to this. The recovery of appetite following an infectious illness takes longer in an elderly person than it does in a younger person.

2 Lack of food may be associated with poverty. Some old people have to make a choice between keeping warm and eating.

3 Problems may result through poor food choice due to ignorance. This is particularly relevant to men who have been widowed. It may be the first time that such a person has had to cook for himself. Widower's scurvy is associated with people who live on diets of tea, biscuits and bread and butter and jam. Soft, refined carbohydrate foods may be chosen because of chewing difficulties due to ill-fitting dentures.

4 Difficulties in purchasing and preparing food may result from physical disabilities. Arthritis is particularly relevant here, as is poor eyesight.

5 Illness may have an effect on nutritional status. There may be some degree of malabsorption of nutrients; utilisation may be impaired due to the intake of drugs and there may be increased requirements of certain nutrients – for example, protein needs are higher in bedridden people.

Pointers to encourage a healthy diet for this group are as follows.

- A well-stocked cupboard is important for the housebound, particularly when outside help, such as a home help or neighbour, fails to turn up to prepare a meal. Convenience foods can be a great help in these circumstances.
- Deliveries by the milkman of heavy or bulky food items, such as potatoes or bread, help the housebound.
- Some retailers sell small quantities of food, and this is practical for elderly people who live on their own.
- Gadgets (Fig. 3.5) can be an advantage for people who are arthritic or who have other physical disabilities.
- A number of books are available, as well as free literature, to help in meal planning.
- Luncheon clubs, Meals on Wheels and home helps can be very useful. Lack of interest in food associated with social isolation may be lessened by these services.

Philosophy

Vegetarianism

By strict definition, vegetarians do not eat meat in any shape or form. However, in real terms, a vegetarian diet encompasses a wide range of dietary practices.

- *Pesco-vegetarians* exclude meat and poultry, but fish, milk, milk products and eggs are eaten.
- *Lacto-ovo-vegetarians* exclude meat, poultry and fish, but milk, milk products and eggs are eaten.
- *Lacto-vegetarians* exclude meat, poultry, fish and eggs, but milk and milk products are eaten.

Fig. 3.5
Kitchen gadgets for people with physical disabilities

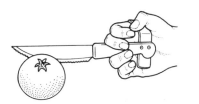

Easy grip knife

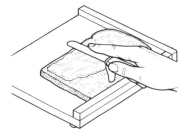

Spreading board

Onion stick

Easy grip potato peeler

Pastry blender

Pressure-release spiral action whisk

- *Vegans* exclude all foods of animal origin.
- *Fruitarians* exclude all foods of animal origin and some plant foods, namely pulses and cereals.

Some people call themselves *demi* or *semi* vegetarians because they have excluded red meat from their diet, but still eat poultry.

Vegetarianism is becoming increasingly popular, particularly among young people. It may be adopted for a number of reasons:

1 *Ethics* – because, for religious or philosophical reasons, it is considered wrong to kill or harm animals.
2 *Health* – a vegetarian diet has a number of advantages for health.
3 *Ecology* – vegetarianism is in keeping with the economic use of world food resources.
4 *Aesthetic* – the mere sight, smell or taste of meat is repulsive to some people.
5 *Economy* – a vegetarian diet may be adopted because of the high price of meat.
6 *Family* – children may be born of vegetarian parents and an adult may change to a vegetarian diet as a result of marriage.

Examples of meals for lacto-vegetarians include:

Breakfast	*Midday*	*Evening*
orange juice	tofu burger in	peanut dip with raw
muesli with milk	wholewheat bun	carrot and celery
	with salad	cheesy potato pizza
	apricot bites	and minty green
		salad
		fresh fruit salad

Examples of meals for vegans include:

Breakfast	*Midday*	*Evening*
orange and grapefruit	vegan cheese and	gazpacho
segments	tomato in	bean and okra stew
wholewheat toast with	wholewheat bun	with brown rice
peanut butter	with green salad	vegan ice-cream
	slice of date cake	

Planning a diet for a vegetarian involves taking account of the particular food restrictions in accord with the definitions of vegetarians on p. 55. Anyone serious about becoming vegetarian or vegan is advised to contact the Vegetarian or Vegan Societies for specific dietary advice. The use of *The National Food Guide: The Balance of Good Health* may be used as an overall model, but with modifications being made according to the degree of vegetarianism. In this respect, *vegans* – sometimes known as *total vegetarians* – merit particular attention.

To ensure adequate intakes of essential nutrients, the following pointers should be helpful:

- *Protein* is found in useful amounts, and of high biological value, in eggs and cheese. When combined with cereals pulses and pulse products, such as TVP, tofu and tempeh, and nuts, provide useful amounts of high biological value protein. Myco-protein (Quorn) is suitable for lacto-ovo-vegetarians (it contains egg albumen) as an alternative to meat.
- *Calcium* is present in milk, cheese and yogurt in significant amounts and these foods are suitable for lacto-vegetarians. Vegans will need to consider alternative sources of calcium, such as almonds, sesame seeds, pulses and pulse products such as tofu, which is a very rich source of calcium, tempeh and vegan cheese, which is made from soya flour.
- *Iron* is present in egg yolk and a range of plant foods, including peas, beans and lentils, wholemeal bread and dried fruits. Dried apricots are a particularly rich source of iron.
- *Zinc* is found in useful amounts in eggs, cheese and many plant foods, including pulses, nuts and seeds, wholemeal bread and oatmeal.
- *Iodine* is found in useful amounts in milk and eggs, but vegans will need to obtain this from edible seaweeds, some of which are very rich in this mineral.
- *Vitamin B_{12}* is distributed widely in foods of animal origin and so foods such as eggs and dairy products will provide useful amounts. Vegans need to eat foods fortified with this nutrient, such as soya drinks, margarines, yeast extract and breakfast cereals.
- *Vitamin D* is added by law to margarine so should not pose a problem.

The UK is home to many people who have migrated over the years from all parts of the world. The population is therefore made up of many different ethnic groups. These communities have a rich variety of cultures and eating patterns.

Hinduism

Hinduism was founded in the second millennium before Christ. In the UK, the Gujarati form the main Hindu community. They practise the doctrine of non-violence against any living entity.

Orthodox Hinduism

Orthodox Hindus abstain from eating meat, fish and eggs. The objection to eating eggs is that they contain a live embryo. Some orthodox Hindus, particularly males, will eat infertile eggs. Orthodox Hindus also refrain from drinking alcohol.

Milk and milk products are allowed because no killing is involved. Yogurt, known as 'dahi', cottage cheese, called 'panir' and 'chenna', concentrated caramelised milk, known as 'khoa', and butter which has been clarified, called 'ghee', are all widely used foods. Dahi is used in curries.

Chenna or panir is made by curdling milk in warm conditions using either tartaric acid or lemon juice. The milk is then strained through muslin and the curds are left wrapped up in the muslin. If the curds are left unpressed they are called 'chenna', but if they are pressed the product is known as 'panir'. Chenna is used to make a fudge. Panir is solid, and is usually cut up into cubes and used in dishes such as curries and pullaos.

'Khoa' is made by cooking milk until it thickens. Much liquid is lost by evaporation and the milk sugar caramelises. Indian sweets can be made by cooking khoa with ghee, sugar, fruit and nuts.

Combinations of pulses and cereals as a source of protein are important in the diet of the orthodox Hindu. Typical breads include chapatis, puri and paratha. Rice dishes include pullaos and birianis. Pulses are used in dhals and pulse flour dishes such as koftas are a feature. Koftas are made from cooked vegetables that have been mashed then mixed with mashed potato or mashed green banana, pulse flour, spices and chenna.

Non-orthodox Hinduism

Non-orthodox Hindus will eat some types of meat. However, the cow is regarded as sacred and the pig is considered to be unclean, so neither is eaten. Pig products, such as bacon, pork dripping and lard, are not used. Lamb and poultry are eaten. White fish is allowed and so are eggs. Alcohol may be consumed.

Lamb is used to make kofta curries which are meat balls, first fried and then either simmered in a curry sauce or served with a sauce such as tomato. Pasandas are made from sliced lamb covered with a mixture of nuts and spices and rolled up. The meat rolls are then fried.

Poultry, particularly chicken, is popular. Tandoori and tikka dishes involve marinating the chicken in a paste made from yogurt, lemon juice and spices. The chicken is then roasted in an oven.

White fish is popular and is used, for example, in a curry.

Sikhism

Sikhism was founded in the fourteenth century. The dietary pattern of Sikhs is similar to that of non-orthodox Hindus. Meat, however, has to be obtained from animals that have been killed in a particular way. The Sikh holy book, *Gura Granth Sahib*, states that animals should be killed at one stroke. This method of killing is in accord with practices in British abattoirs. Sikhs do not limit fish to the white variety: they also eat oily fish and shellfish. They are not permitted to drink alcohol.

Islam

Islam was founded in the sixth century. In the UK, it is practised mainly by Pakistanis and Bangladeshis and by some Gujarati. All Muslims follow the Koran, which lays down a number of rules concerning food. Muslims do not regard the cow as sacred, and so beef is eaten. The pig is considered to be unclean and is not killed for food, and products from pigs, such as dripping and lard, are not used. Other meats eaten include lamb and poultry. Meat must be ritually slaughtered by cutting the animal's throat. At the same time the slaughterer says, 'In the name of Allah, Allah is most great.' The blood is drained away and the meat cleaned because Muslims are not permitted to eat blood. Meat obtained from this method of slaughter is called 'halal meat'. The process is not unlike koshering, and kosher meat is sometimes acceptable to Muslims. Fish may be eaten as long as it has fins and scales, and both oily and white fish are allowed. Eggs may be eaten. Muslims, like orthodox Hindus and Sikhs, are not permitted to drink alcohol.

Judaism

The Bible is the source of all the Jewish food laws:

> These are the animals you may eat ... the ox, the sheep ... and any animals which have a parted hoof ... You may not eat the camel, the hare and the pig ... you shall regard as unclean. Of creatures that live in the water you may eat all those that have fins and scales. You may eat all clean birds ... You shall not eat anything that has died a natural death. You shall not boil a kid in its mother's milk, for you are the people holy to your God (*Deuteronomy*, 14).

1 Animal flesh that can be eaten includes beef, lamb, mutton, goat, chicken, turkey, duck and goose. Pork and birds of prey are not permitted.
2 All meat and poultry must be ritually slaughtered and are known as kosher. This means that the animal or bird has been killed by an appointed slaughterer, prepared according to specific rules, soaked and salted.
3 Meat and milk must not be prepared, cooked or eaten together. To ensure this, Jewish kitchens have separate kitchen and table services for meat and milk. When cooking meat and milk dishes simultaneously the cooking vessels should be kept far enough apart to prevent the foods from contaminating each other. Should a milk dish and meat dish be served to different people who are sitting at the same table a clear division must be made. It is customary to spread a special serviette for the milk dish. Meat can be eaten soon after milk as long as the mouth is cleaned by either rinsing it or by eating bread. However, if meat is eaten first, it is customary to wait 3 hours before taking any milk. When milk bread is made this is used to make small rolls in fancy shapes. This is done as a precaution to prevent the accidental mixing of the milk bread with meat.
4 Fish which have fins and scales are permitted. All shellfish and snails are forbidden.
5 No eggs with blood spots are allowed.
6 Margarine needs to be kosher.
7 Fruit and vegetables need careful attention. Any small fruit that is wormeaten is discarded; any large fruit that is wormeaten must have the

affected part cut away. Dried fruit, such as dates, must be cut open and carefully examined and rejected if infected. All vegetables should be thoroughly washed to remove any insects. If peas are at all wormeaten they should be discarded.

8 Cereals should be examined to ensure that no mites are present.

9 Certain rules apply to the sabbath day: 'Tomorrow is a day of sacred rest, a sabbath holy to the Lord, so bake what you want to bake now.' (*Exodus*, 16)

In practice, this means that food is not cooked on Saturdays, although it can be kept warm. The reason for this ruling is that in, the past, to kindle a fire would have been a major chore. As a result of this law a dish called 'cholent' is popular. This is made of meat, pulses, other vegetables and dumplings. The dish cooks slowly on a Friday evening and is left to simmer on a low heat until the synagogue service is over the next day.

State of health

Certain conditions require very careful dietary management. Two examples in this category are *coeliac disease* and *lactase deficiency*.

Coeliac disease

The term 'coeliac' comes from the Greek word *koiliakos*, which means 'suffering in the bowels'. In the UK, it has been estimated that the condition affects about 1 in 1850 people. The disease is characterised by an abnormal mucosa in the small intestine. In healthy people, the mucosa has finger-like projections called villi, but in coeliacs the villi are short and wide and the mucosa is totally flat. The damage to the mucosa is caused by gluten, the protein in wheat and rye. It is now believed that similar proteins in barley and oats may also be harmful to coeliacs. The damage that occurs impairs the absorption of nutrients from the small intestine, causing wasting and severe illness.

Symptoms of coeliac disease

In *infants*, the condition is associated with refusal to eat, weight loss, irritability, listlessness and a pot-belly. The stools are large, pale and offensive and sometimes loose. In *adults*, symptoms include breathlessness and fatigue, which is usually due to the anaemia that develops from poor absorption of iron and folate. Some adults develop other symptoms, such as abdominal discomfort, diarrhoea and vomiting.

Dietary management of coeliac disease

It is recommended that coeliacs follow a *gluten-free diet* for life. Such a diet excludes wheat and rye, and now barley and oats are excluded. Obvious sources of gluten include bread, cakes, pastries, pies, while less obvious sources include convenience foods. Food labels need to be examined and gluten-free products chosen. Apart from the restriction of gluten, it is important that the diet is adequate.

Lactase deficiency

Lactase deficiency is common in some ethnic groups, including African-Caribbean, Asian and South American people, and the incidence in these groups may reach 90%. In Western European Caucasians, it is less than 10%. The condition may be *congenital*, that is, it presents itself when infants are given milk feeds containing lactose. The condition may be *acquired*, in which case it presents later in life, following a decline in lactase activity. The disorder is due to a deficiency of the enzyme lactase. This is normally present in the brush border of the mucosa of the small intestine. Lactose in milk or other foods containing milk sugar cannot be hydrolysed in the absence of lactase, so it is passed into the colon where it is fermented by bacteria.

Symptoms of lactase deficiency
Symptoms include colic, abdominal pain and distension, increased flatus and diarrhoea. These symptoms occur because lactose exerts an osmotic effect in the small bowel, resulting in large amounts of fluid and sugar entering the large bowel. Once in the large bowel, the sugar is rapidly fermented, producing gas and osmotic diarrhoea.

Dietary management of lactase deficiency
It is recommended that people with lactase deficiency (hypolactasia) follow a lactose-free or lactose-restricted diet depending on the severity of the symptoms. Examples of foods to be restricted include milk, dairy ice-cream, made-up desserts containing milk and many 'convenience' sauces.

Slimming

The problems of being overweight and obese have been highlighted in Chapter 1. Dieting to lose weight is very popular and different approaches may be taken. The principle is one of reducing energy input – energy output has to be greater than the input for someone to lose weight. This means that the body should go into a state of *negative energy balance*.

Reducing diets
Diets that are based on 'normal' foods consumed in reduced amounts and providing energy intakes below energy expenditure are described as reducing diets. These diets should restrict energy intake, but ensure the consumption of all other nutrients, such as protein, minerals and vitamins, at an adequate level. Other methods used to achieve negative energy balance include:

- *calorie counting* – the energy values in food portions are totted up and may show a reduction in energy intake, but the diet may be inadequate with regard to certain nutrients;
- *calorie-counted meals*, are frequently chosen for their convenience, but it is advisable to read food labels carefully for salt and sugar content;
- *low-calorie foods*, for example, low-fat spreads, fat-reduced cheeses, semi-skimmed and skimmed milk, fat-reduced sausages and soft drinks without added sugar, can all play a useful part in programmes of weight-reduction;
- *meal-replacements* – in the form of foods such as biscuits and drinks, are popular and are generally used in conjunction with 'normal' foods;
- *appetite suppressants* may be taken before meals to depress the appetite – one particular type is in the form of a sweet and works on the principle that raised blood sugar levels will depress the appetite, while another is high in fibre and the bulk-forming properties of this reduce the feelings of hunger;
- *very low-calorie diets* may be used to replace 'normal' foods for a number of days or weeks, although the safety and efficacy of this approach are open to question.

4 Wheat and other cereals

The word 'cereal' is used to denote seed-grains of cultivated grasses.

Wheat

Wheat was one of the first plants cultivated by humans. It is believed to have been grown in the Middle East as long ago as 13000 BC. More wheat is grown than any other cereal, and about 90% of it grows in the northern hemisphere.

Classification of wheat

Wheat can be classified according to different criteria:

1 *Species* *Triticum vulgare* produces a flour that is suitable for making bread. *Triticum durum* produces a flour suitable for the production of pasta. *Triticum compactum* produces a flour that is recommended for cake making.
2 *Spring or winter wheat* Spring wheat is sown in spring and harvested the same year. It is grown in countries such as Canada where the winters are severe. Winter wheat is sown in the Autumn and is harvested the following year. It is grown in European countries. The protein content of spring wheat is around 12-14% whereas winter wheat contains less than 10% protein.
3 *Strength* This is associated with the quantity and quality of gluten-forming proteins in the grain. In general spring wheat produces a strong flour and winter wheat gives a weak flour. Strong flour dough is both more elastic and resistant to stretching than weak flour dough and is recommended for breadmaking, whereas soft flour is more suitable for biscuits.

Fig. 4.1
Cross-section of a grain of wheat

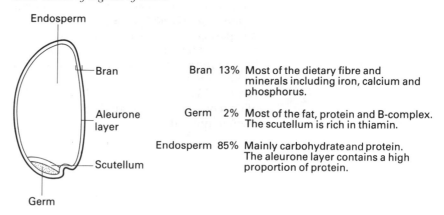

Bran 13% Most of the dietary fibre and minerals including iron, calcium and phosphorus.

Germ 2% Most of the fat, protein and B-complex. The scutellum is rich in thiamin.

Endosperm 85% Mainly carbohydrate and protein. The aleurone layer contains a high proportion of protein.

Structure and composition of wheat (Fig. 4.1)

Production of wheat flour

Fig. 4.2
Production of wheat flour

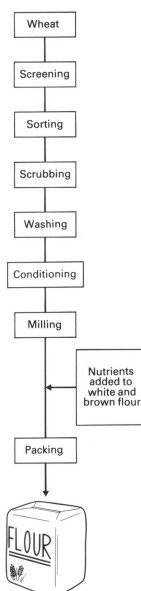

1 *The bran* forms a tough outer fibrous skin.
2 *The germ* is the seed or embryo and is situated at the base of the grain.
3 *The endosperm* is the starchy food available for the germ and forms the largest part of the grain.

1 *Screening* The harvested grain is passed through sieves to remove particles which may be larger and smaller than the wheat grain. The grain is passed along a conveyor belt where magnets remove any pieces of metal.
2 *Sorting* The grain is then sorted.
3 *Scrubbing* The grain is scoured to remove dirt and also to remove the beard and epidermis of the grain.
4 *Washing* The grain is then washed to remove fine dust, hairs and stones. The moisture is removed.
5 *Conditioning* This process ensures that all the grains have the same moisture content. The bran is toughened, and this ensures that it can readily be separated from the endosperm and germ.

Milling
This may be carried out by one of 3 methods: stone-milling, roller-milling or fragmentation.

1 *Stone-milling* Some wholewheat brown and speciality flours are milled by this method. The stones used for milling grain (Fig. 4.3) are circular and the surface of the stones is corrugated radially. Only the top stone moves, and the distance between the stones is much less towards the outer edge of the stones than it is at the centre. The grain enters the space between the stones through an opening at the centre of the upper stone and is pushed towards the outside of the stones as it becomes finer.

Fig. 4.3
A traditional grinding stone, with samples of flour displayed on it. The wheat grains are ground between two of these stones, one on top of the other.

Fig. 4.4
Roller mill

2 *Roller-milling*   Roller-milling involves two main stages:
  (a) *Breaking*   The grain is passed through grooved rollers called 'break
      rolls' which are in pairs (Fig. 4.4). These rollers rotate in opposite
      directions to each other and the top roller moves faster than
      the bottom one. At the first set of rollers the grain is sheared open
      and some of the endosperm is scraped away from the bran. The
      resulting product is then sifted through silk or fine gauze. This
      process is repeated until the grain has passed through 5 sets of
      rollers. At each stage endosperm is extracted. This process
      separates the grain into 3 main products: the particles which pass
      on to the next set of break rolls; flour which may be bagged; and
      semolina.
  (b) *Reduction*   The endosperm is reduced into a fine flour and the germ
      is extracted. The product passes through sets of rollers and is sifted,
      the coarse particles moving to the next set of rollers. The flour is
      then treated with improvers, vitamins and minerals, which are
      added according to legal requirements.
3 *Fragmentation milling*   This is a refinement of the roller-milling process.
  The white flour is processed a stage further into flour particles of
  different sizes.

Nutrients added to flour
Certain nutrients are added to flour in accordance with the 1963 Bread and
Flour Regulations (Table 4.1).
   It is interesting to note that the 1981 DHSS Report on the Nutritional
Aspects of Bread and Flour recommended that 'the addition of calcium,
iron, thiamin and nicotinic acid to flour no longer be mandatory'.

Table 4.1
Nutrients added to flour

Nutrient	mg per 100 g of flour
Thiamin	0.24
Nicotinic acid	1.60
Iron	1.65
Calcium	235–390

Types of flour

Flour can be classified according to different criteria.

Extraction rate
The extraction rate refers to the percentage of the wheat grain found in the flour. The higher the extraction rate the more bran and germ that is present in the flour.

1 *100% extraction flour* (wholewheat or wholemeal) consists of the 'whole' grain. This flour is light brown in colour.
2 *85 to 90% extraction flour* (wheatmeal or brown) is also light brown.
3 *70 to 72% extraction flour* (white flour) is white in appearance.

The higher extraction flours have more dietary fibre (Table 4.2).

Table 4.2
Dietary fibre content of flour

Flour	Dietary fibre (g)
White	3.1
Brown	6.4
Wholewheat	9.0

Fig. 4.5
Gluten formation

Gliadin

+

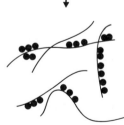

Glutenin

↓

Gluten

Protein quantity and quality
The quantity and quality of protein in flour depends upon the type of wheat used to make the flour.

1 *Weak or soft flour* is about 8% protein. It is well suited to cake-making, producing a cake with a fine crumb; and for short-crust pastry, biscuits and sauces.
2 *Medium, plain or all-purpose flour* is about 10% protein. It is suitable for most purposes in food preparation.
3 *Strong or bread flour* is much higher in protein content and can be up to 17% protein. It is recommended for breadmaking, yeasted cakes and buns, flaky and puff pastries.

Gluten is formed when 2 proteins in flour are hydrated. These proteins are gliadin and glutenin. When gliadin is hydrated it is extensible and tacky; when glutenin is hydrated it is elastic and tough. Together these proteins form a cohesive, elastic, three-dimensional network (Fig. 4.5). Gluten develops when the hydrated flour is manipulated. The degree of manipulation is critical to gluten development (Fig. 4.6). Gluten that is fully developed gives the dough a characteristic satiny surface and makes it

Fig. 4.6
Effect of kneading on gluten molecules

1 Before kneading

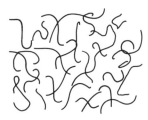

Gluten molecules folded
and tangled –
rough surface

2 After kneading

Gluten molecules aligned
and untangled –
smooth surface

Storing flour

springy, elastic and extensible. Underdeveloped gluten has a rough surface and is not springy and elastic.

Gluten gives rigidity to the structure of baked products and retains gases that expand when the dough is heated. Strong flour has a high quantity of quality protein and therefore permits a characteristic large-grained product (Fig. 4.7), whereas soft flour with its lower quantity and quality of protein produces a much finer grain.

Gluten development is sensitive to certain conditions, and ingredients used in flour mixtures need to be considered carefully. Fat coats flour and prevents water from being taken up. Sugar limits gluten development because of its attraction to water. This ingredient competes with the flour for the liquid. Ascorbic acid may be used as a flour improver but the mechanisms involved are not fully understood. Salt influences both the rate and degree of flour hydration and thus the formation and development of gluten.

Addition of leavening agent
Raising agents may be added to certain flours to produce self-raising flour. The quantity of raising agent in self-raising flour is satisfactory for a wide range of products. According to regulations, self-raising flour has to produce a minimum amount of available carbon dioxide during baking. To every 400 g of flour 4×5 ml teaspoons of baking powder are added to meet this requirement.

Methods of milling
Stone-milled ('stone-ground') has a characteristic flavour due to the heat generated during the milling process.

Wholemeal and brown flours are available as coarse, medium or fine flours. Some white flours are super-sifted. These are made from selected blends of wheat, and modifications to the grinding and sifting operations result in a granular flour.

Speciality flours
Flours may also be prepared from other cereals. Granary flour is made from malted wheat and rye.

Brown and wholemeal flours do not keep as well as white flour due to the higher fat content. Prolonged storage causes rancidity. White flour keeps for up to 6 months; brown and wholemeal flours keep for up to about 2 months. The storage life of self-raising flour is less than plain flour because of the raising agent. It keeps for about 2 to 3 months.

Fig. 4.7
Structure of bread

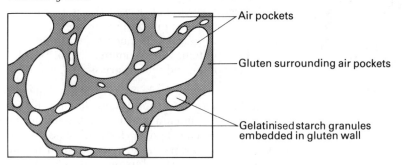

Air pockets

Gluten surrounding air pockets

Gelatinised starch granules
embedded in gluten wall

Bread by the Chorleywood process

In 1961 the Chorleywood process revolutionised the commercial production of bread. Bulk fermentation is replaced by high-speed mixing of the dough for approximately 3 minutes, and a number of modifications are made to the recipe including the addition of ascorbic acid.

Storing bread

Breads vary in their storage life. Crusty breads, such as French and Vienna, do not keep well. Chapatis are best eaten as soon as they are cooked. Other breads, such as sliced white, brown or wholemeal, keep for several days if storage conditions are adequate. To prevent mould growth, and to keep the bread moist and soft, store at room temperature in a clean, dry, well-ventilated bread bin or crock. The wrapping is best left on, but loosely fold one end of the packaging to allow some air to circulate and so keep the crust crisp. White, brown and wholemeal bread keeps for 6 months in the freezer and enriched breads for 4 months.

Nutrient content of bread

Fig. 4.8
Production of dried pasta

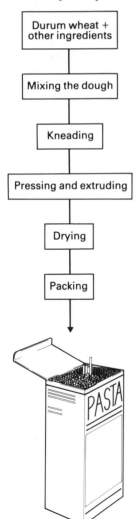

Protein constitutes about 10% of the weight of bread. *Fat* constitutes approximately 2% of the weight of bread. *Carbohydrate* is the main source of energy in bread and accounts for upwards of 40% of the weight of this food product. Most of the carbohydrate is present in the form of starch.

Dietary fibre content depends on the extraction rate of the flour used. The higher the extraction rate, the more fibre is present. Fibre profiles g/100 g of bread are as follows:

Bread	Total Englyst	Fractions Cellulose	Non-cellulosic polysaccharides Soluble	Insoluble
White	1.5	0.1	0.9	0.5
Brown	3.5	0.5	1.1	1.8
Wholemeal	5.8	1.0	1.6	3.2

The *calcium, iron* and *zinc* present mg/100 g are as follows:

Bread	Calcium	Iron	Zinc
White	110	1.6	0.6
Brown	100	2.2	1.1
Wholemeal	54	2.7	1.8

Note: The phytic acid content of bread, which for white, brown and wholemeal is 0.05, 0.35 and 0.60 g/100 g respectively, will influence the bioavailabity of the minerals present. The higher the phytic acid content and dietary fibre, the lower the bioavailability.

The *sodium* and *chloride* present mg/100 g are as shown:

Bread	Sodium	Chloride
White	520	820
Brown	540	890
Wholemeal	550	880

The salt content of bread is a subject of debate in the context of COMA's DRVs.

The *B-vitamins, thiamin, riboflavin* and *niacin* present mg/100 g are as follows:

Bread	Thiamin	Riboflavin	Niacin
White	0.21	0.06	1.7
Brown	0.27	0.09	2.5
Wholemeal	0.34	0.09	4.1

Production of pasta

Pasta is usually made from durum wheat that has been milled to produce semolina. This is then mixed with water to make a smooth but firm dough. Other ingredients such as eggs, salt, vegetable oil and vegetable colouring may be used (Fig. 4.8).

1 *Making the dough*   The ingredients are mixed together to form a dough.
2 *Kneading*   The dough is kneaded for between 10 and 20 minutes. The kneaded dough is rather like putty in consistency.
3 *Pressing and extruding*   The dough is placed in a water-lined press which is kept at a temperature high enough to keep it in a pliable form. It is then extruded under pressure into the desired shape.
4 *Drying*   The extruded dough is dried in 2 stages.

Types of pasta

Pasta comes in various colours. Wholewheat pasta contains more dietary fibre than the other varieties. There is 8.4 g of dietary fibre in 100 g of dried wholemeal pasta. The same weight of dried white pasta contains 2.9 g of dietary fibre. Wholewheat pasta has an even more 'nutty' flavour than the other varieties and takes a little longer to cook. Green pasta is flavoured with spinach. Pasta is available in a variety of shapes and sizes.

Semolina

Semolina is produced when cereals are milled – usually from wheat. The larger particles of the endosperm are sifted out during milling. When cooked, semolina has a porridge-like texture. This cereal is used in milk puddings, as a binding agent in croquettes and in sweets of Middle Eastern and Indian origin.

Couscous
This is made from semolina. Couscous is traditionally used in North African cooking.

Other cereals

Rice

The true home of rice is China and the East. Approximately 90% of the world's supply of this cereal comes from the Orient. New strains of rice which are resistant to various pests and diseases, fast-growing and also able to withstand extremes of growing conditions such as drought or flooding, have been developed. Yields of rice have also increased due to mechanisation.

Before the harvested grains of rice are milled they are cleaned and conditioned. The outer husk is then removed; in this state the rice is known as 'brown rice'. The rice may be milled further to remove the bran, leaving a white grain; this stage is called 'pearling'. The white grain may be further milled and polished with mineral substances to give it a shiny, bright surface. The different types of rice are dependent on a number of different factors.

Size and shape of the rice grain

1 *Short-grain rice* (pudding rice or round-grain rice) is plump, moist and tender with a tendency for the grains to cling together. It is suitable for making dishes such as rice pudding.
2 *Medium-grain rice* is not as plump and it is longer. It can be used as short-grain rice, and in savoury dishes such as risotto.
3 *Long-grain rice* is a narrow long-grain variety. It is suitable for savoury dishes and, if cooked properly, is light and fluffy and the grains do not stick together.

Regional varieties of rice

1 *Basmati rice* is grown in *India*. It is a narrow, long-grain variety and is often quoted as being 'the finest'. As its name suggests, this type of rice goes well with Indian food.
2 *Carolina rice* is grown in many parts of the world. It is named after the Carolina region in North America where it was first planted. Carolina rice has long grains.
3 *Patna rice* is grown in many parts of the world. It is named after Patna in North-east India. This is a long-grain variety.
4 *Arborio rice* is grown in the northern part of Italy. This is a round, plump grain and is recommended for dishes such as risotto.

Degree of processing of rice

1 *Brown rice* has had only the outer husk removed – the bran and germ still remain. Brown rice comes as short, medium and long-grain and is well known for its characteristic 'nutty' flavour, its bite and brown-green colour. It has more dietary fibre than white rice – 1.9 g per 100 g compared with 0.5 g – and it takes longer to cook.
2 *White rice* (polished) is refined rice, being made up of starchy endosperm. It comes as short, medium and long grain.
3 *Easy-cook rice* has been processed before being milled. The starch is partly gelatinised as a result of the processing. Easy-cook rice comes out fluffy, plump and the grains are separate.
4 *Pre-cooked instant rice* has been cooked after the grain has been milled and the moisture content is removed by drying. This type of rice usually takes about 10 minutes to be reconstituted.

Rice products

1 *Rice flour* may be used in foods such as shortbread to give a really short result. It can be used as a thickener for soups and puddings and in certain types of cake, such as macaroons.
2 *Rice paper* is made from the rice paper plant and not from rice. In food preparation rice paper is used to form an edible base to various biscuits and macaroons.

Oats

Oats have been cultivated for more than 5000 years. Many traditional Scottish recipes include oats in them. The world's largest producer of oats is the USA.

Oat products

1 *Rolled oats* are used to make breakfast cereals such as porridge and muesli and flapjacks.
2 *Ground oatmeal* is used in the preparation of oat cakes and digestive biscuits.

Maize

This cereal dates back as long ago as 80 000 years. The main maize-growing area in the world is the USA. China is the second main producer. Maize products include cornflour, custard powder and blancmange powder.

Barley

Barley is believed to have come from wild grasses in northern Africa and western Asia. It is grown in a temperate climate, and Britain is one of the main producers of this crop.

Barley products

1 *Pearl barley* is used in soups and stews and barley water.
2 *Malt extract and malt flour* are used in breads such as maltloaf.
3 *Beer* is made from barley.

Rye

One of the biggest advantages of rye is its hardiness. This cereal can withstand cold conditions. It is widely grown in the cold northern regions of Europe and the USSR and in the northern states of the USA.

Rye products

Rye is made into rye *flour* to make breads and crispbreads. This flour is darker in colour than wheat flour and has a lower protein content. This is why rye breads are darker than wheat breads and heavier in texture. Rye is also used to make rye whisky.

Breakfast cereals

Dr Kellogg was the originator of breakfast cereals as we know them today. He was the chief physician at a sanatorium in Michigan in the USA, and was keen to develop an easy-to-digest breakfast in place of the traditional breakfast which was rather heavy. He invented thin, malt-flavoured, toasted maize flakes.

In 1938 the Kellogg's factory in Manchester was opened. The Second World War was a great stimulus to increased breakfast cereal consumption because of the shortage of more traditional foods. Kellogg and other manufacturers have developed a wide range of products, and most of these are recognised by their brand names. Breakfast cereals are derived from cereals such as maize, wheat, rice, oats and rye. The grains used to make them may be shredded, flaked, puffed or made into granular form. Additional ingredients include sugar, honey, nuts, fruit and vitamins and minerals.

Nutrient content of breakfast cereals

Protein is found in breakfast cereals in variable quantities, ranging from 5 to 15% of the weight of the product. The biological value is enhanced by the addition of milk. *Fat* is found in small amounts, with most cereals providing less than 2% fat. The fat content is higher if nuts are present, as in the case of muesli. *Carbohydrate* is the main source of energy in breakfast cereals and this is largely made up of starch. The sugars present depend on the type of product. The starch and sugar content g/100 g of some cereals is as follows:

Breakfast cereals	Starch	Sugars Total	Individual			
			Glucose	Fructose	Sucrose	Maltose
All-Bran	27.6	15.4	0.9	0.7	12.1	1.7
Sugar Puffs	28.8	56.5	4.5	2.0	45.6	4.4
Weetabix	68.5	6.4	1.8	0.8	2.9	0.8

Note: Eating certain breakfast cereals could add considerably to the intake of non-milk extrinsic sugars.

Dietary fibre is present in variable amounts. Fibre profiles g/100 g are as follows:

Breakfast cereals	Total Englyst	Fractions Cellulose	Non-cellulosic polysaccharides	
			Soluble	Insoluble
Bran Flakes	11.3	2.1	3.0	6.2
Frosties	0.5	0.2	0.2	0.1
Shredded Wheat	9.8	1.6	2.0	6.2

Calcium, iron and *zinc* are found in breakfast cereals in variable amounts. For example, 100 g portions provide the following in mg:

Breakfast cereals	Calcium	Iron	Zinc
Cornflakes	15	6.7	0.3
Grapenuts	37	9.5	4.2
Ready Brek	65	4.8	2.7

Note: The phytic acid content of breakfast cereals will influence the bioavailability of any minerals present. The phytic acid content of All-Bran, Shredded Wheat and Ready Brek is 3.50 g, 0.94 g and 0.84 g per 100 g respectively.

Sodium and *chloride* are present in breakfast cereals in variable amounts, mg/100 g as follows:

Breakfast cereals	Sodium	Chloride
Farmhouse Bran	870	1340
Rice Krispies	1260	1980
Sugar Puffs	9	41

Note: Eating certain breakfast cereals to fill the 'fibre gap' may result in increasing salt intakes.

Vitamin D may be added to breakfast cereals and many contain 2.80 µg vitamin D/100 g. *B-vitamins thiamin, riboflavin* and *niacin* are found in breakfast cereals in useful quantities. For example, mg/100 g as follows:

Breakfast cereals	Thiamin	Riboflavin	Niacin
Bran Buds	1.00	1.50	16.0
Coco Pops	1.00	1.50	16.0
Grapenuts	1.30	1.50	17.6

Uses of breakfast cereals in food preparation

Breakfast cereals can be used in many different ways:

- *breakfast*, for example, All-Bran with milk or muesli with yogurt;
- *coatings* made from crushed breakfast cereals. Cornflakes may be used to coat foods – for example, burgers, and croquettes;
- *toppings* for savoury dishes such as vegetable au gratin;
- *stuffings* can include breakfast cereal to add variety;
- *fillers or extenders*, for example, All-Bran in meat loaf;
- *bases for cheese cakes* made from bran flakes and muesli, for example, are recommended in some recipes;
- *baked goods* such as breads, cakes and biscuits may include breakfast cereals in place of some of the flour in the recipe;
- *sweets and cakes* made from breakfast cereals are also popular and quick to prepare.

5 Flour mixtures

Bread

A quality loaf of bread has the following characteristics:

- a symmetrical shape with a well-rounded top;
- a uniform golden brown to brown crust which is both thin and smooth;
- it is well risen but not over-inflated;
- a light texture with a moist and resilient crumb;
- a nut-like flavour without a taste of yeast or a sour taste.

Ingredients and their functions in breadmaking

Basic ingredients in bread include flour, water, yeast and salt. Other ingredients are optional and may include milk, egg, fat, sugar and ascorbic acid.

1 *Flour* Bread flour or strong flour is recommended for breadmaking because the quantity and quality of the gluten formed will be sufficient to produce a loaf that has a good volume with the characteristic bread texture. The starch in the flour is a source of food for the yeast. During baking the starch gelatinises and gives rigidity to the crumb. Some of the characteristic browning of the loaf on the crust is due to the formation of dextrins from starch. Wholewheat and brown flours produce a loaf with a lower volume, a darker colour, a coarse texture and a distinctive nutty flavour because of bran and germ in the flour.

2 *Water* is necessary for the yeast cells to grow and multiply. The liquid dissolves the salt in the recipe, and sugar if used, and disperses these ingredients in the flour. The liquid helps in the even distribution of the yeast. Water hydrates the proteins in flour. The glutenin and the gliadin with water form gluten. Water hydrates the starch and during baking water is needed for gelatinisation. Steam formed from the water contributes to the expansion of the dough.

3 *Yeast* produces carbon dioxide under the anaerobic conditions which exist in the dough. The carbon dioxide formed acts as a 'leavening' agent.

4 *Salt* flavours the dough, affects the action of amylases and helps to maintain the supply of maltose for the yeast cells. It has an inhibiting effect on protein-splitting enzymes in the flour: this is desirable because these enzymes have a weakening effect on the gluten in the dough. Yeast doughs made without salt are sticky. The weakened gluten allows the gas cells to expand to excess during fermentation and baking so that the resulting loaf has an irregular shape and 'moth-eaten' appearance.

5 *Fat* has a tenderising effect on the crumb. The loaf has a better volume than when fat is not used; the crust browns more and the bread stales less readily.

6 *Sugar* is usually added to act as an 'activator' for the yeast. A high percentage of the sucrose is hydrolysed to form invert sugar; that which remains in the dough contributes to the final colour and flavour of the baked product.

7 *Eggs* give the baked product a rich flavour and darker colour.

8 *Milk* gives the baked product a browner crust than water. This is likely to be associated with the milk solids which play a part in the carbonyl-amine browning. Staling is reduced, and this is possibly associated with the casein and fat in milk.

9 *Ascorbic acid*   Vitamin C tablets may be used to make 'short-time' doughs.

Recipe balance in breadmaking
(Table 5.1)

1 *Liquid to flour*   If the proportion of liquid is too low, the dough is stiff to handle, inelastic, slow to rise and during baking expansion of the dough is limited. The resulting loaf has a close texture and poor volume and the crumb is tough because the cell walls in the dough are thicker. If too much liquid is used the dough is sticky, and when baked the texture is open and coarse.

2 *Yeast*   The amount of yeast used will depend upon the type, time available, additional ingredients and the amount of flour (p. 93). Too little yeast will delay fermentation and too much will produce a yeasty sour taste and a bread that stales quickly.

3 *Salt* should not be in excess of 2% of the weight of the flour. If too much salt is used the action of the yeast is inhibited so the bread has a poor volume, close texture and a salty taste. If too little salt is used the bread lacks flavour unless other flavourings are added and has a 'moth-eaten' appearance and a flattish top.

4 *Sugar* in amounts up to 10% of the weight of the flour is recommended as the optimum quantity. Up to this amount fermentation proceeds rapidly. If the proportion of sugar extends beyond 10% the rise is slow. It is likely that the excessive amount of sugar has an osmotic effect on the yeast cells, causing the entry of water and nutrients into the cell to be inhibited. The bread volume is reduced and the texture close.

5 *Fat* is an optional ingredient in bread, and excessive fat inhibits the action of the yeast.

Table 5.1
Basic formula for bread

500 g strong flour
300 ml water
20 g fresh yeast
10 ml salt

Preparation techniques in breadmaking

1 *Heat treatment of liquid*   The liquid should be heated to 27°C. Yeast cells are sensitive to heat (p. 93). If milk is used it should be scalded first. This may be done by heating the milk for one minute to a temperature of 92°C. If it is not scalded the dough is sticky and slack, and the bread is likely to have a coarse texture and a poor volume. Both salt and sugar dissolve more rapidly when the liquid is at these raised temperatures; also, fat melts more quickly.

2 *Dispersing the yeast*   Reconstituted dried yeast mixes readily into the flour. Compressed yeast is mixed with liquid to separate the yeast cells and the liquid acts as a convenient vehicle for distribution of the yeast.

Easy-blend dried yeast is mixed into the flour directly, and thorough mixing of the ingredients used ensures its even dispersion.

3 *Mixing* to hydrate all of the flour particles is essential. If additional ingredients, such as sugar, are included, stir the dough for a little extra time so that the flour will absorb the optimum amount of water.

4 *Kneading*   To produce a high-quality bread the gluten must be developed adequately. Kneading may be carried out by hand or using a dough hook attachment on an electric mixer or food processor. During kneading, air is incorporated and gas cell nuclei are produced in the dough. The dough becomes elastic so that it can hold gases (gas-holding capacity). Doughs that are either over- or under-kneaded leak gas.

5 *Fermentation* is necessary for the development of flavour, texture and volume. During fermentation, yeast cells produce carbon dioxide and various acids. The acids are chiefly lactic and acetic. The acidity is desirable for the fermentation process and the action of the amylases. As the dough becomes more acid it becomes less sticky. The liberated carbon dioxide changes the nature of the dough so that it becomes a foam. As fermentation continues the bubbles of gas expand, and this causes the films of gluten surrounding the gas bubbles to stretch. This enables the dough to expand during subsequent baking.

Fermentation should be continued until the dough has doubled in size. Another test is to punch the dough lightly with one finger; if the dough is ready it will barely spring back. If the dough is over-fermented the gluten strands become over-stretched so that they lose their elasticity and the dough is not able to retain efficiently gas that is produced by the yeast cells. This type of dough is much slower to rise at second rising, and it never regains the volume achieved during the first rising. The final baked product is heavy and of poor volume and also has 'off' flavours. Inadequate fermentation results in a dough that is not as manageable because the pH will not have fallen sufficiently. The flavour of the finished product will be impaired; the volume will be poor and the texture close, because insufficient carbon dioxide will have formed and the gluten strands will not be stretched enough to allow for expansion during baking.

For fermentation the dough can be placed in a mixing bowl, covered with cling film, foil or a clean damp tea towel or it can be put into a lightly oiled polythene bag. For 'short-time' doughs the mixture should be put into its tin or shaped accordingly and protected from drying out by either a loose covering of oiled cling film or polythene. A 'flying top' (where the top crust separates from the lower crust) may occur if the surface dries out. The period of time chosen for fermentation will depend upon the temperature used for this stage (Table 5.2). The

Table 5.2
Recommended fermentation times with reference to temperature

Time (hrs)	Temperature (° C)	
1	Warm place	27
1½	Room temperature	18–21
4	Cool place	10–15
12	Refrigerator	5

optimum temperature used for this type of fermentation is 27°C. If the dough becomes over-heated, the mixture rises rapidly without allowing sufficient time for it to mellow. The resulting bread has a sour taste due to the undesirable fermentation by-products. Warm dough is sticky and difficult to handle. Too much heat kills the yeast. Doughs fermented in the refrigerator need to be punched periodically because the yeast cells die when the nutrients in their immediate vicinity have been consumed. The dead yeast cells are harmful to the 'quality' of the loaf because some of the cellular contents will reduce the volume of the loaf and affect crumb structure.

6 *Knocking back* prevents the films of gluten around the gas cells from becoming over-stretched. Also, gas cells which have enlarged during fermentation are broken up to form more cells. The more gas cells, the more even the distribution of carbon dioxide and the final grain of the product is more likely to be even. Manipulation of the dough at this stage helps in the distribution of yeast cells that have formed during fermentation. Heat produced during fermentation is also distributed in the dough.

7 *Shaping* will depend upon the desired shape.

8 *Proving* (second rising) is necessary to make the knocked-back dough light, puffy and double in size. The optimum temperature for proving is 27°C. An over-proved dough collapses when put into the oven and the final crumb is uneven. The crust flattens and may balloon over the sides of the tin. If under-proved, the gas cells in the dough are inadequately inflated. This results in a loaf of poor volume and a coarse texture. In addition, the gases in the dough build up, expand and cause a 'flying top'.

9 *Finish* will vary according to the recipe.

Cooking bread

Basic bread dough is cooked at between 240°C and 250°C. For rich yeast mixtures, lower temperatures of 220°C to 230°C are required because they brown more rapidly.

During the first few minutes of baking the dough increases rapidly in volume. This is called 'oven spring'. The temperature of the dough rises, and as this happens the dough becomes more fluid. Carbon dioxide production increases and the gases in the dough to expand.

As baking progresses the yeast cells die. The flavour and aroma develop during baking. The starch in the flour takes up water and gelatinises, and the gluten coagulates. The net effect of this is a rigid structure (Fig. 4.7). Baking changes the elastic foam into a rigid foam. Bread is a solid foam. A crust forms on the surface of the dough because of loss of moisture. Browning of the crust is associated with carbonyl-amine reactions.

When bread dough is under-baked, the crust lacks colour and the texture of the bread is doughy. If over-baked, the crust is dark and the texture of the loaf dry. If the oven has not reached the desired temperature when the dough is put into it, the bread has a coarse and open texture. If the dough is put into an over-heated oven, the surface of the crust is likely to crack and have a 'flying top'.

Bread and bread doughs in food preparation

Bread can be used in many different ways:

- *bread,* for example, sandwiches, toasted sandwiches, toast with topping such as baked beans, garlic and herb breads, French bread;
- *pizza base,* with a wide variety of toppings;
- *stuffing,* for example, thyme and parsley, sage and onion;

- *bulky filler*, for example, meat loaf, burgers, Glamorgan sausages, cheese pudding, bread and butter pudding;
- *soups and sauces*, for example, bread soup, bread sauce;
- *toppings*, for example, breadcrumbs for *au gratin* dishes, slices of toast for French onion soup;
- *garnish*, for example, croutons for soups and savoury dishes such as macaroni cheese;
- *coatings*, for example, Scotch eggs, burgers, fish cakes;
- *puddings*, for example, brown bread ice-cream, queen of puddings.

Scones

A quality scone has the following characteristics:

- a symmetrical shape with a smooth surface, level top and straight sides;
- a uniform golden-brown crust that is both crisp and tender;
- a fine-grained, moist, creamy-white crumb;
- a nutty flavour with no baking powder after-taste.

Ingredients and their functions in scone-making

Basic ingredients in scones include flour, milk, leavening agent, salt and fat. Other ingredients are optional, and include sugar and eggs.

1 *Flour*   Plain or all purpose flour is recommended for scone-making. If self-raising flour is used, additional leavening agents are not required. This type of flour gives the scones a fine crumb. Browning of the crust is partly due to the formation of dextrins from starch in the flour. Flours such as wholewheat and brown may be used, but these flours will produce a scone that has a coarser texture because of the bran and germ present. The flavour will be more nutty and the colour of the crumb will be light brown and not creamy white.

2 *Milk* acts as a solvent for ingredients such as salt, leavening and sugar. Liquid is needed for the action of chemical leavening. The water in the milk hydrates both the starch and proteins so that the starch can gelatinise and the glutenin and gliadin form gluten. Steam produced from the liquid during baking acts as a leavening. The milk may be soured if the acid in it is needed in conjunction with bicarbonate of soda.

3 *Leavening agents*   Chemical leavening agents are used in scone-making. Bicarbonate of soda is used as the leaven in conjunction with various acids.

4 *Salt* is used in scones as a flavouring.

5 *Fat* is used to tenderise the scones (plastic fats are recommended). The fat functions as a shortening agent. Fat gives the crust a browner appearance and delays staling.

6 *Sugar* is used to make sweet scones. It acts as a flavouring, a tenderising agent and helps to brown the crust through a reaction between protein and reducing sugars formed. Castor sugar is preferable as granulated sugar gives a speckled appearance.

7 *Eggs* help to give a richer flavour and make the crumb cream rather than white in colour.

Recipe balance in scone-making
(Table 5.3)

1 *Liquid*   If the proportion of liquid is too low the dough is stiff, giving the scone poor volume and a close texture. The crumb tends to be coarse and not fine-grained, as the cell walls in the scone are thicker because of the poor increase in volume. If too much liquid is used, the dough is wet and the scone spreads and loses its shape during cooking.

2 *Fat*   If the quantity of fat is too low the crumb will not be as tender as is desirable. A higher proportion of fat produces a 'cake-like' scone.

3 *Salt*   If salt is omitted the scone will lack flavour unless other flavourings are used. In excess, the scone has a distinctive salty taste.

4 *Leavening*   The amount of raising agent used will depend upon the selected type. If bicarbonate of soda is used with selected acids in too high a proportion (alkali to acid), the resulting scone is likely to have a speckled appearance due to the soda being unneutralised in the mixture. The scone will be impregnated with yellow specks, and brown spots will occur on the crust. The flavour of the scone will also be impaired, tasting 'soapy'. Excess raising agent causes the scone to have a coarse open texture and the sides of the scone will be cracked. Too little raising agent results in a scone of poor volume with a close texture.

5 *Egg* must be carefully balanced against the amount of milk in the formula, otherwise the mixture will be too wet.

6 *Sugar* in excess produces a scone with a speckled appearance.

Table 5.3
Basic formula for scones

200 g plain flour
25–50 g fat
125 ml milk
12.5 ml baking powder
2.5 ml salt

Preparation techniques in scone-making

1 *Sifting the flour, raising agent and salt* ensures thorough mixing of these ingredients and a certain amount of air is incorporated. If wholewheat or brown flour is used the bran remaining in the sieve should be tipped into the bowl afterwards. Raising agent that is not mixed sufficiently causes the scones to have a speckled appearance.

2 *Mixing fat and dry ingredients*   The fat is usually cut up in the flour mixture, using a knife to break up the fat into small pieces. It is then rubbed in with the tips of the fingers or blended with a pastry blender. The fat coats the particles of flour and so acts as a tenderising agent. When this stage is completed the mixture looks like fine breadcrumbs. Sugar or other flavourings may be added at this point.

3 *Mixing the liquid and dry mixture* is usually done using a fork or a palette knife. The salt, sugar (if used) and raising agent dissolve in the liquid and this aids the even distribution of these ingredients. The liquid moistens the flour to form a dough which is at first sticky. As mixing progresses the dough stiffens, and it eventually holds together in a mass. Under-mixing may result in a scone with a rough surface or a spotted crumb and surface due to the bicarbonate of soda not being neutralised. Over-mixing promotes gluten development, making the scone tough with a coarse texture.

4 *Kneading*   The term 'kneading' is misleading because the dough only has to be stretched and folded between 10 and 20 times to develop the required degree of cohesiveness. Under-manipulation results in a scone with a rough surface. Over-manipulation develops too much gluten so that the scone has a coarse texture due to excessive gluten development.

Over-kneaded scones have a rounded top instead of a flat one. Unevenly manipulated scones tend to rise unevenly.

5 *Shaping*   Roll the dough to 20 mm in thickness. Insert the cutter as straight as possible to avoid uneven scones. Allow a 5-mm space between the scones when cutting out. For a good volume and shape leave the scones to stand for 10 to 15 minutes.

6 *Finish*   Scones can be lightly brushed with milk for a glazed appearance; dusted lightly with flour for a soft finish. Bran or other grains may be placed on top of a glaze for a textured finish. Or the scone may just be left plain for a characteristic smooth surface.

Cooking scones

Scones can be cooked in an oven or on a hot griddle. For baking, the oven should be heated to 240°C to 250°C. During baking, gases in the dough expand, the gluten coagulates and the starch gelatinises around the expanding gas bubbles. The surface dries out to form a thin crust and the colour of the crust darkens. If the oven is not hot enough the scones will be doughy and pale in appearance. If the temperature is too high the scones will be darker in colour, the crust thicker and the crumb dry.

Scone mixtures in food preparation

Scone mixtures can be used for:

- *scones*, plain, sweet or savoury;
- *pizza base*, with a wide variety of toppings;
- *cobblers*, sweet and savoury.

Shortened cakes

A quality shortened cake has the following characteristics:

- a flat or slightly rounded top;
- a uniform golden-brown, fine-grained crust;
- a soft, velvety and resilient crumb and small uniform grain;
- it is light, tender and moist rather than dry;
- it has an acceptable flavour.

Ingredients and their functions in shortened cakes

Basic ingredients in shortened cakes include flour, fat, sugar, eggs, liquid, salt and leavening. Other ingredients may include spices, fruits (especially dried) and nuts.

1 *Flour*   Soft or weak flour is recommended for cake-making. This type of flour results in a fine-grained, soft, velvety crumb and tender product. Satisfactory results can be obtained with plain flour. Self-raising flour may be used. Wholewheat or brown flour results in a darker colour, a heavier product and coarser texture due to the bran and germ. Strong or bread flour is not recommended as it produces a more open grain characteristic of bread.

2 *Fat* is needed to 'shorten' or tenderise the product (Table 5.4). It is a means of introducing air into creamed cakes and contributes to the colour and flavour as well as to the keeping qualities.

3 *Castor sugar* is recommended for cake-making. In addition to giving a sweet taste, it helps to incorporate air in creamed cake mixtures. It delays the coagulation of egg protein and the pasting of starch in the flour and this helps to give a good volume. Sugar also plays a role in keeping cakes moist.

4 *Eggs* introduce air into cakes and play a structural role in the cooked

Table 5.4
The proportion of recommended fats in shortened cakes and techniques of preparation

Method of cake making	Recommended fats	Fat to flour	Sugar to flour	Summary of preparation techniques
Rubbing in	Butter Margarine	½ or less	½ or less	Fat rubbed into flour and liquid added including egg if used
Creaming – plain medium rich	Butter Margarine	½ ¾ 1	½ ¾ 1	Fat and sugar creamed together; eggs added; half flour folded in; liquid added and remaining flour folded in
Melting	Margarine Cooking fat Lard Oil	⅓ just over	1	Fat melted with syrup, treacle and sugar; when cooled this and other liquids, including eggs, stirred into the flour
All-in-one	Soft margarine	1	1	All ingredients mixed together at the same time

product due to the coagulation of egg proteins during cooking. The fact that eggs are liquid is useful for purposes of mixing. Emulsifiers in eggs are useful in the formation of cake batters owing to their emulsifying properties.

5 *Liquid* dissolves the sugar and salt and makes possible the action of chemical leavenings. It disperses the ingredients and hydrates the flour. Steam formed from liquid during baking acts as a leavening.

6 *Leavening agent*   As in scone-making, chemical leavening agents are used.

7 *Salt* is used for flavouring.

Recipe balance in shortened cakes
(Table 5.5)

1 *Fat*   The higher the proportion of fat, the more tender and fragile the cake crumb will be and the richer the cake.

2 *Sugar*   The use of more sugar than is recommended produces a coarse-grained product and a biscuit-like crust. Cakes made by the melting method have a high proportion of sugar, and this accounts to some extent for the coarser grain and the ease with which this mixture burns.

3 *Eggs*   The richer the cake, the higher the proportion of eggs in the formula. Too many eggs results in a rubbery texture and excessive liquid in the mixture.

4 *Leavening*   Too little results in a poor volume and close texture. Too much can give the cake a coarse open texture; the surface may be cracked and the cake may collapse so that the surface is hollowed.

5 *Liquid*   Too much causes the cake to be doughy and heavy and the top may be cracked. If not enough is used the cake may be cracked on the surface, the crumb dry and tunnels are likely to develop.

6 *Salt* in excessive amounts can give the cake an unpleasant taste.

Table 5.5
Proportion of ingredients for shortened cakes

Method of cake making		Flour (g)	Fat (g)	Sugar (g)	Eggs (no.)	Liquid (ml)	Baking powder (ml)
Rubbing in		200	75–100	75–100	0–1	60–140	12.5
Creaming – plain		200	100	100	2	40–80	10.0
	medium	200	150	150	3	20–40	7.5
	rich	200	200	200	4–5	20–0	5.0
Melting		200	75	200[1]	1–2	80–100	5.0[2]
All-in-one		125[3]	125	125	2		5.0

Notes: 1 ¾ mixture of treacle and syrup   2 Bicarbonate of soda   3 Self-raising flour

Preparation techniques for shortened cakes

The ingredients should be at room temperature (15°C). Block fats need to be softened for creaming and eggs function more efficiently as emulsifiers at this temperature.

1 *Sifting* If the raising agent is not sifted with the flour and salt the cake is likely to have a speckled top. Even distribution of the raising agent is necessary to achieve a fine-grained crumb.
2 *Fat dispersion* (Table 5.4).

Cooking shortened cakes

Recommended baking temperatures cover a wide range depending upon the type of cake: 130°C to 140°C for rich fruit cakes to 190°C to 200°C for rock cakes.

During cooking the air bubbles become dispersed in the batter and carbon dioxide is liberated from the baking powder. The gas produced collects in the air bubbles and this expands. The expanding gases cause the product to rise and increase in volume. Steam also acts as a leavening.

The protein films around the gas bubbles coagulate, the starch grains gelatinise and the batter sets. As this happens the air cells rupture and leak the leavening gases but the cells do not collapse. The emulsion breaks and some of the fat appears at the interface of the cake crumb and air. As baking proceeds, moisture is evaporated from the surface of the cake and a crust forms which will be golden or darker brown. If the temperature is too low the heat penetration is slower and there is greater expansion of the batter. The batter becomes over-stretched before the proteins coagulate and the starch gelatinises. The final product has a large grain. Pre-heating the oven allows for more rapid heat penetration. Lower temperatures may also contribute to a pale crust and an uneven rise. If the temperature is too high the cake is likely to be tunnelled, the texture close and the crust may become badly cracked or peaked and darker in colour.

Test if a cake is cooked adequately:

1 An adequately cooked cake is brown in colour, well risen and begins to shrink from the sides of the tin.
2 When the ear is held over the surface of the cake there is no sound of bubbling, only a faint ticking.
3 The smell should not be musty; cooked cakes have a distinguishable smell.

4 When pushed lightly with a finger the cake should feel firm and springy in the middle as well as at the edges; if an indent remains the cake is not done; if a skewer inserted into the cake comes out sticky, not clean, the cake is not adequately cooked.

Different types of shortened cake mixtures in food preparation

- *Rubbing in*   small: raspberry buns, rock cakes, American doughnuts; large: farmhouse fruit cake, chocolate cake and Dorset apple cake.
- *Creaming*   small: queen cakes, fairy cakes, madelines; large: cherry, Madeira, Dundee, Victoria sandwich, Battenburg.
- *Melting*   gingerbread and parkin.
- *All-in-one*   Victoria sandwich, Madeira cake.

Sponge cakes

A quality sponge cake has the following characteristics:

- a flat or slightly rounded top;
- an even, delicate brown crust;
- a small uniform, resilient, golden-yellow crumb;
- it is tender, light, moist and neither sticky nor dry;
- a delicate flavour.

Ingredients and their functions in sponge cakes

Basic ingredients in sponge cakes include flour, eggs and sugar. A 'true' sponge does not include added fat in the formula.

1 *Flour* is needed for structural purposes. For a top-quality product, use a flour of fine granulation; soft or cake flour is recommended. Flours of extraction above 70 to 72% produce a heavy, darker, coarse-grained cake.
2 *Eggs* are used to incorporate air into the mixture. They are the liquid in the formula, which is necessary for the hydration of proteins in the flour, for gelatinisation of starch and as a source of steam which is a leavening agent. The coagulated egg protein contributes to the cake structure. The egg yolk contributes to the golden colour of the product.
3 *Castor sugar* is recommended. This has a tenderising effect as well as contributing to the flavour, colour and keeping qualities of the cake.
4 *Fat*   Oil is included in the recipe for a Genoese sponge.

Recipe balance in sponge cakes

Table 5.6
Basic formula for sponge cake

---

50 g soft flour

50 g sugar

2 eggs

Compared with shortened cakes, sponge cakes have a high proportion of sugar and egg to flour. Imbalance of ingredients in this mixture produces faults such as those listed on p. 80.

Preparation techniques for sponge cakes

1 *Mixing*   The egg and sugar are whisked together to form a foam. As whisking proceeds the mixture becomes thicker and lighter in colour. To test if the correct consistency has been achieved, make a figure of eight or an 'S' shape from the mixture adhering to the whisk. When this is

dropped on to the surface of the foam it should stay visible for 3 seconds if the foam is sufficiently aerated.

2 *Oil* is whisked in at this stage in the preparation of a Genoese sponge.

3 *Flour* is sifted and lightly folded into the egg foam.

If the egg and sugar mixture is under-whisked or the folding in is excessive the cake will be a poor volume, heavy and with a coarse grain as opposed to a fine one.

Cooking sponge cakes

Sponge batters must be baked as soon as they have been prepared. If they are left to stand, the large air cells rise to the top of the mixture. Baking is usually at 220°C to 230°C. During baking steam produced from the liquid in the egg acts as a leaven and the air bubbles in the batter expand. Gases diffuse in the batter as the temperature increases. The film of batter surrounding the air cells sets, and when this happens gases in the air bubbles leak out and the characteristic texture of the baked product is formed.

Higher temperatures than those given above result in the product's having a greater volume and tenderness, but the cake tends to be over-browned. The greater volume and tenderness of cakes cooked at higher temperatures are due to the batter setting more rapidly and less water being taken up by the starch in the flour.

Sponge mixtures in food preparation

Sponge mixtures can be used for:

- sponge cake; small or large, fruit flans;
- Swiss roll, plain or chocolate;
- Genoese sponge.

Pastry

Quality pastry has the following characteristics:

- a light golden brown colour;
- it cuts easily with a fork and breaks readily when bitten but without crumbling: a quality called 'tenderness';
- it is flaky with very small blisters on the surface; the flakes should be thin and the blisters plentiful for tender pastry;
- it is crisp and not soggy or doughy;
- it has an acceptable flavour.

Ingredients and their functions in pastry-making

Basic ingredients in pastry include flour, fat, water and salt. Other ingredients may be used, and these will depend upon the type of pastry: lemon juice in flaky and rough-puff pastry; a raising agent in suet-crust pastry; egg yolk and sugar in rich short-crust pastry.

1 *Flour* Short-crust pastry and suet-crust pastry are made from plain or all-purpose flour. These pastries are noted for their characteristic tenderness, and strong flour would result in a tough and chewy product. Strong flour is recommended for pastries noted for either flakiness or volume and for this reason is given in recipes for flaky and rough-puff pastries. Wholewheat and brown flours result in darker and less flaky pastries than lower-extraction flours.

2 *Fat* contributes to the tenderness, flakiness, flavour and colour.

3 *Water* is used to hydrate the flour. It is needed to form gluten which gives the dough cohesion. Water provides steam when the pastry is

Table 5.7
The proportion of recommended fats in pastry and methods of incorporating it

Pastry	Recommended fats	Proportion of fat to flour	Incorporation of fat
Short crust	$\frac{1}{2}$ lard or cooking fat and $\frac{1}{2}$ block margarine or butter	$\frac{1}{2}$	The fat is cut up in the flour and rubbed in with finger-tips or pastry blender
Short-crust pastry all-in-one	Soft margarine	$\frac{2}{3}$	The fat, liquid and $\frac{1}{3}$ of the flour are mixed with a wooden spoon; the remaining flour mixed in
Suet crust	Shredded suet	$\frac{1}{2}$	The suet is mixed with the flour and raising agent by stirring with a fork or palette knife
Flaky and rough-puff pastry	$\frac{1}{3}$ lard or cooking fat $\frac{2}{3}$ butter or margarine	$\frac{3}{4}$	*Flaky*: $\frac{1}{4}$ of the fat (lard or cooking fat) is rubbed into the flour; liquid is added, the dough formed, rolled out and fat added (Fig. 27.2) *Rough puff*: fat is cut up to sugar-lump size, stirred into flour and liquid added

being cooked, and this acts as a leavening agent producing the characteristic flakes.

4 *Salt* is used as a flavouring.

5 *Lemon juice* is recommended in flaky and rough-puff pastries.

6 *Leavening* Baking powder is included in suet pastry to give the pastry a degree of lightness. This may be in the flour itself as self-raising flour or used as an additional ingredient.

7 *Eggs* contribute to the colour and flavour of rich pastries.

8 *Sugar* is used to flavour and colour rich short-crust pastry.

Recipe balance in pastry-making
(Table 5.8)

1 *Fat to flour* Sufficient fat should be used to shorten short-crust and suet pastry and to form the characteristic flakes in flaky and puff pastries. Excess fat results in greasy pastry.

2 *Liquid* Excess liquid produces pastry that is soggy, hard and tough and difficult to handle. Too little liquid makes short-crust pastry crumbly and flaky and puff-pastry heavy.

3 *Salt* The use of less than the standard quantity will change the flavour of the pastry as will the use of excessive amounts.

4 *Egg* may be used as liquid in the recipe for short-crust pastry.

5 *Sugar* In rich short-crust pastry 25 g of sugar to 200 g of flour is used; in biscuit crust, 50 g of sugar to 100 g of flour. If less sugar than recommended is used the flavour of the pastry may not be sweet enough. If used in excess, the product may be over-sweet and may have a darkened surface.

6 *Lemon juice* in small quantities is used in the preparation of flaky and

puff pastry. If this is left out the pastry may be less flaky. If used in excess lemon-flavoured pastry is likely.

7 *Raising agent*   If chemical leavening is left out of suet pastry, the pastry will be heavy.

Table 5.8
Proportion of ingredients for different types of pastry

Pastry	Flour (g)	Fat (g)	Salt (ml)	Water (ml)	Other ingredients
Short crust	200	100	2.5	40	
All-in-one short crust	225	150	2.5	30	
Suet crust	200	100	2.5	125	12.5 ml baking powder
Flaky and rough puff	200	150	1.25	125	10 ml lemon juice

Preparation techniques in pastry-making

1 *Sifting*   The flour and salt are mixed by sifting. If a raising agent is used, as in suet-crust pastry, this is added at the same time to ensure thorough mixing.

2 *Mixing fat and flour*   The type of fat and the amount used determine the method of incorporating the fat into the flour (Table 5.7).

3 *Addition of liquid*   Cold water is recommended for mixing. Thorough mixing is essential for the hydration of the flour. Add the liquid gradually because the hydration of flour is dependent on factors such as its age and storage conditions.

4 *Rolling*   Use the minimum amount of flour for rolling. Too much can upset the recipe balance and contributes to a tough pastry. Handle the pastry as little as possible. Excessive manipulation results in tough pastry due to the development of gluten.

If there is time, pastries such as flaky and rough puff may be left to 'rest' or 'relax' in a cool place to let the fat harden and the gluten soften between the various stages of rolling.

Before being cooked pastry should be lightly pricked with a fork. This helps to prevent pockets of steam forming between the pastry and the pan. If left, these can make the pastry domed.

Cooking pastry

Pastry is cooked at between 190°C and 200°C. During cooking the fat melts; some is absorbed into the flour and some drains out of the pastry. The melting of the fat results in the formation of air spaces in the mixture. The higher the proportion of fat, the more air spaces will be formed. If the fat is in large pieces the air spaces left in its place are large. The greater the number of air spaces and the larger they are, the more flaky the product will be.

Some of the liquid in the dough turns into steam. This moves into the air spaces left by the melted fat. During cooking the steam expands and, as a result, the air spaces get bigger. The starch in the flour takes up water and gelatinises during cooking.

Further changes occur during cooking with the gluten coagulating to give a firm structure to the product, and the surface starch forming dextrins which contribute to the colour of the cooked pastry.

In recipes using pastry the weight given for the pastry refers to the quantity of flour used. For example, 100 g of short pastry means that the pastry is made from 100 g of flour.

Different types of pastry in food preparation

- *Short crust* used for Cornish pasties, quiche Lorraine, apple pie, mince tarts.
- *Suet crust* used for steak and kidney pudding, meat roly-poly, jam roly-poly.
- *Flaky and puff* used for chicken pie, Russian fish pie, vanilla slices, apple turnovers.

White sauce

A quality white sauce has the following characteristics:

- it is smooth;
- it is glossy;
- it is white;
- it has the desired degree of thickness;
- it has an acceptable flavour.

Ingredients and their functions in white sauces

Basic ingredients in savoury white sauces include fat, flour, liquid and salt. Other ingredients may be used as flavourings.

1 *Flour* is needed in a white sauce as a thickening agent. The starch in the flour pastes and gelatinises during cooking. Soft flour has more thickening power than other wheat flours owing to its higher percentage of starch, and it is recommended for white sauces. Because flours of higher extraction contain bran and germ, which are brown in colour and coarse in texture, it is not possible to make a 'smooth' and 'white' sauce with wholewheat flour.
2 *Fat* contributes to the flavour, smoothness and glossy appearance of white sauce. Fats such as butter and margarine are recommended because of their flavours. Fat plays a very important role in the production of a non-lumpy sauce.
3 *Liquid* is needed to hydrate and gelatinise the starch in the flour. Milk is generally used, but may be used in conjunction with other liquids.
4 *Salt* is used as a flavouring in savoury white sauces.

Recipe balance in white sauces
(Table 5.9)

1 *Flour and liquid*   The proportion of liquid to flour depends upon the desired viscosity of the sauce. If too much liquid is used the sauce will not be as thick as desired; if too little is used the sauce will be thicker.

Table 5.9
The proportion of ingredients in white sauces

| Sauce | To 250 ml liquid | | Consistency |
	Fat (g)	Flour (g)	
Pouring	15	15	Glazes the back of a wooden spoon and pours easily
Coating	25	25	Coats the back of a wooden spoon and only just settles to its own level in the pan
Panada	50	50	Forms a firm paste and comes away from the sides of the pan

2 *Fat*   The fat in the formula is related to the weight of the flour. If too much fat is used the sauce will be fatty; if too little is used the sauce may be lumpy and dull in appearance.

Preparation techniques and cooking white sauces

In the *roux* method the fat is melted and the flour is stirred into it, using a wooden spoon, over a low heat for about 1 to 2 minutes. The pan is removed from the heat source and half the liquid is stirred in gradually and beaten until smooth. The remaining milk is then stirred in. When the uncooked sauce is smooth and free from lumps it is returned to the heat source, brought to boiling point slowly and stirred vigorously the whole time. The flavourings are then added.

In the *beurre manié* method the fat is softened using the hands or a spoon (*beurre manié* is French for 'kneaded butter'). The flour is then worked into the fat to form a paste. The liquid in the formula is heated to just below boiling point; it is removed from the heat source and, using a whisk, small pieces of the paste are whisked into the liquid. The addition of the flour paste is therefore gradual. When the sauce is smoothly whisked, it is returned to the heat source and stirred continuously with a wooden spoon until it boils. The flavourings are then added.

In the 'all-in-one' method the ingredients are put into the saucepan over a moderate heat and whisked continuously for 2 to 3 minutes at the end of which time the sauce should be smooth and thickened.

The degree of agitation used in these sauces is critical. If stirring in the *roux* or *beurre manié* methods, or whisking in the all-in-one method is too slow the sauces are likely to be lumpy. If undercooked, the sauce is likely to be thinner than desired and to have the flavour of 'raw' starch. Gelatinisation is usually complete at about 95°C. For the desired thickness and an acceptable flavour, complete gelatinisation is essential. If over-cooked, the sauce is likely to be thicker than desired due to the loss of water by evaporation. Low to moderate temperatures are recommended because severe heat is likely to cause the sauce at the bottom of the pan to burn, and the sauce itself is likely to become lumpy.

6 Raising agents

Leavens or raising agents contribute to the lightness and porosity of food mixtures. Air, steam and carbon dioxide are all used as leavens. Air is introduced mechanically; steam is the result of a physical change, and carbon dioxide is formed by the action of chemical and biological leavens. Air, steam and carbon dioxide are considered in their own right in this chapter, but it is important to note that in any one mixture all three may function. For example, in a creamed cake mixture air is introduced by sifting the flour, creaming the fat and sugar together and beating in the egg; carbon dioxide is released from the baking powder when it is mixed with the liquid in the recipe and during cooking; and steam is formed from liquids in the recipe during cooking.

Air

Sifting

Flour can be aerated by passing it through a sieve or by sifting it repeatedly through the fingers – for example, when rubbing fat into flour. The introduction of air into scone, pastry, cake or batter mixtures is therefore partly through this method.

Creaming

In the creaming method of cake-making air is incorporated into the fat and sugar as they are creamed together. It is the introduction of air into the mixture that makes it look pale or creamy and gives it a light sheen.

Beating

Beating eggs into creamed fat and sugar results in more air being incorporated, as both the yolk (to a slight degree) and the white of egg (to a much greater degree) have the power of holding bubbles of air to form a foam. As egg proteins coagulate when heated, their power of holding air is of great value in cake-making. Nevertheless, baking powder is added to all but the richest creamed cake mixtures to produce carbon dioxide as an additional raising agent.

When a Yorkshire pudding batter is beaten a little air is enclosed in it, but as the mixture is fairly liquid and as it has only one egg in 250 ml of liquid the raw batter can hold only a small amount of air so there is no advantage in continuing to beat once the mixture is smooth. Some recipes advise leaving batters to stand before cooking to soften the starch grains. As air is lighter than the batter, any air incorporated with the flour, or during beating, tends to escape while the batter stands. Steam, rather than air, is the more important raising agent in this type of batter.

Whisking

When the white and yolk of an egg are beaten together they will enclose a certain amount of air, but the foam produced soon rises to the top of the liquid and some of the enclosed air escapes. If egg yolk alone is whisked, little air can be enclosed; but egg white alone is easily whisked to a stiff foam which is more stable than that of the whole egg. The addition of about half its weight of sugar to an egg yolk or a whole egg before whisking produces a more stable foam than the egg alone, so that in making sponge cakes, castor sugar and eggs are whisked together and flour is lightly folded into the foam. Air is the only raising agent needed for this type of cake though the steam produced during baking increases the lightness. To fix the air in the mixture it should be baked immediately the flour has been folded in; the oven heat should be moderate so as to set the mixture but not to expand the air too rapidly.

Steam

Steam is produced when the water in any moist mixture reaches boiling point. The characteristic texture of any mixture raised mainly by steam is very open and rather uneven, having pockets of air left after the steam has escaped. Yorkshire pudding, flaky or rough-puff pastry and choux pastry are all good examples of the raising power of steam; all are rather moist mixtures when raw, all are baked at temperatures of 200°C or over and all should have open textures.

Carbon dioxide by chemical means

Chemical raising agents became popular about 100 years ago. Until then yeast was used. The choice of raising agents in this group includes: bicarbonate of soda, bicarbonate of soda with acid, baking powder or self-raising flour.

Bicarbonate of soda

Bicarbonate of soda may be used as a leaven in cakes such as gingerbread and parkin. Both of these cakes have a strong flavour and dark colour due to the inclusion of treacle, syrup, brown sugar and ginger in their formulation. Strongly flavoured and dark-coloured cakes are the only ones suitable for the use of bicarbonate of soda on its own. When moistened and subjected to heat bicarbonate of soda releases carbon dioxide which acts as a leaven, and washing soda is also formed (Fig 6.1). This is alkaline and imparts a 'soapy' or 'bitter' taste and a yellowish colour to the flour. The yellow colour is probably due to the effect of alkali on the flavonoid pigments. One of the group of B vitamins, thiamin, is more likely to be lost, because in an alkaline medium this vitamin is more readily decomposed.

Fig. 6.1
Bicarbonate of soda as a raising agent

$$2\,NaHCO_3 \xrightarrow[\text{Heat}]{\text{Moisture}} CO_2 + H_2O + Na_2CO_3$$

Sodium hydrogen carbonate	Carbon dioxide	Water	Sodium carbonate (washing soda)

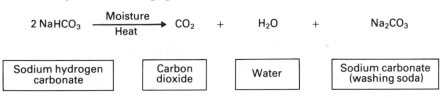

Fig. 6.2
Bicarbonate of soda with acid as a raising agent

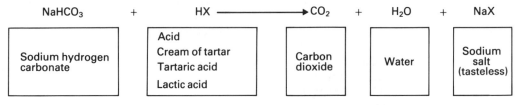

Bicarbonate of soda with acid

In order to counteract the problems associated with the use of bicarbonate of soda on its own, acids may be used (Fig. 6.2) – for example, cream of tartar and tartaric acid. When cream of tartar is used the chemical reaction is slower than when tartaric acid is used. If tartaric acid is used the reaction is so quick that much of the carbon dioxide may be lost during the preparation stages. Lactic acid, found in sour milk and buttermilk, may be used with bicarbonate of soda. Recipes for quickly prepared baking powders are shown in Table 6.1.

Table 6.1
Baking powder formulae

Slow action *(% ingredients)*	*Medium action* *(% ingredients)*
25 bicarbonate of soda	25 bicarbonate of soda
50 cream of tartar	12.5 tartaric acid
25 filler	25 cream of tartar
	37.5 filler
2 parts acid to 1 part alkali	*1½ parts acid to 1 part alkali*

Baking powder

Commercially produced baking powder is a mixture of bicarbonate of soda, acids and starchy filler. The acids are usually acid calcium phosphate (ACP). The starchy filler absorbs any moisture arising from poor storage conditions, and keeps the active ingredients – the acids and alkali – separated. Recommended proportions of baking powder in basic recipes are given in Table 6.2.

Self-raising flour

The use of self-raising flour is particularly popular because it avoids measuring raising agents and the problems of uneven blending are overcome. The available carbon dioxide yield of this flour during baking is laid down by regulations. In practical terms, to every 400 g of flour 4 ×5 ml teaspoons of baking powder are added.

Carbon dioxide by biological means

Yeasts of various kinds have been used as a leaven since their discovery by the ancient Greeks. Baker's yeast is prepared from selected varieties which are grown in liquid. The mass of yeast is separated from the liquid and then it is either compressed or dried.

Table 6.2
Recommended proportions of baking powder in basic recipes

Basic recipe	Number of level 5 ml teaspoons baking powder to 500 g of flour
Scones	5–6
Suet pastry	5–6
Plain cakes, rubbing-in method, 2 eggs	5–6
Cakes, ½ fat to flour, rubbing-in or creaming method, 4 eggs	5
Cakes ¾ fat to flour, 6 eggs	4
Cakes equal fat to flour, 8 eggs	3
Cakes equal fat to flour heavily fruited, 8–10 eggs	0
Whisked sponges	0

Fresh yeast

Compressed or fresh yeast is a creamy-beige colour with a firm but crumbly texture; it looks like putty. It is advisable to use really fresh yeast; buy it from reliable suppliers, such as bakers, and store it properly. Fresh yeast may be stored in a refrigerator for up to 2 to 3 weeks. In these conditions it is advisable to wrap the yeast in cling film or in a polythene bag or to store it in a screw-top jar. For longer storage it may be frozen. Fresh yeast keeps well for about 6 weeks in a freezer. When using frozen yeast it should be allowed to thaw for about half an hour, or it can be blended while still frozen with the warm liquid included in the recipe.

Fresh yeast is sometimes rubbed into flour or added as batter, but it is more usual to blend it with liquid in the recipe formulation before adding it to flour. Some yeast recipes state that fresh yeast should be creamed with the sugar! If this is done the leavening power is reduced (Fig. 6.3).

Fig. 6.3
Fresh yeast creamed with sugar

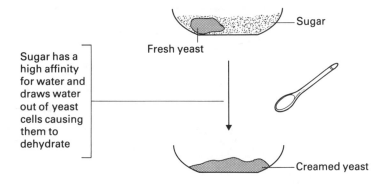

Sugar

Fresh yeast

Sugar has a high affinity for water and draws water out of yeast cells causing them to dehydrate

Creamed yeast

Dried yeast

In its dried form yeast has a longer storage life than fresh yeast; it may be kept for about 6 months. Dried yeast is available in 2 main forms: traditional dried yeast which comes in granules, or easy-mix dried yeast in the form of a fine powder.

1 *Traditional dried yeast* comes in convenient sachets or in tins. If used infrequently it is advisable to purchase the sachet type. Yeast tends to stale readily in the presence of air. Stale yeast is easily detected because it fails to froth when it is reconstituted. To reconstitute dried yeast it is usually sprinkled into warm water containing a little sugar. After about 15 minutes the mixture becomes frothy. At this stage the yeast is ready to be mixed with the flour.

2 *Easy-mix dried yeast* comes in small sachets that are vacuum-sealed. Once opened, this type of yeast deteriorates rapidly, and it is advisable to use it within 2 days of opening the sachet. Some of the easy-mix dried yeasts contain flour improvers which do away with the need for two risings. As the name suggests, easy-mix yeast is very convenient to use; it is simply stirred into the dry ingredients.

Quantities of dried yeast to fresh yeast

It is important to recognise which type of yeast a recipe specifies, and it may be necessary to work out the equivalent weight for the type of yeast that is available: 15 g dried yeast = 1 sachet easy-mix yeast = 25 g fresh yeast.

Function of yeast as a leaven

Yeast is a single-celled micro-organism. The yeasts used for bread or yeast doughs are selected strains: *Saccharomyces cerevisia* is used as a leaven in bread doughs because under the anaerobic conditions found in the dough, the cells metabolise fermentable sugars giving carbon dioxide as a waste product; alcohol is also produced, but this evaporates.

The whole action of producing carbon dioxide from yeast and flour is complicated, but, briefly stated, it is as follows. The flour contains 2% sugar and an enzyme, diastase, which changes some of the starch of the flour to a sugar, maltose. The yeast also contains three enzymes: maltase, which changes maltose to glucose; sucrase, also called invertase, which changes sucrose to invert sugar, a mixture of glucose and fructose; and thirdly zymase, which splits up both glucose and invert sugar into carbon dioxide and alcohol (Fig. 6.4).

Fig. 6.4
Enzyme action of yeast

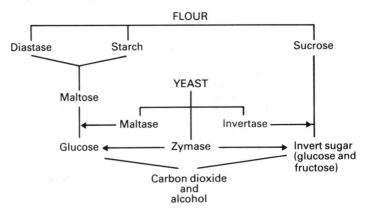

Food, moisture and warmth

Yeast gets its supply of food from the flour, and the liquid in the dough provides the water it needs. The optimum range of temperatures for yeast in bread dough is between 25°C and 27.7°C. If the temperatures are too high the yeast cells will die; if the temperatures are too low the action of yeast is retarded.

Effect on yeast of additional ingredients

As well as bread, many kinds of buns, cakes and pastry are made with yeast, and these require such ingredients as sugar, fat and eggs which all have some effect on the action of yeast.

1 Sugar, in small quantities, hastens the production of carbon dioxide, but in proportions of over 50 g to 500 g of flour it increasingly retards the action.
2 Fat in proportions of over 30 g to 500 g flour retards the action of yeast.
3 Eggs, although they contain fat which would slow up the production of carbon dioxide, have such a marked ability to hold air in a mixture that their inclusion helps to make a lighter yeast mixture.
4 Excess salt can retard the action of yeast.

To overcome the adverse effect of adding sugar, fat and milk, which contains fat, to a yeast mixture, one of the following variations on the standard method for making bread may be used.

1 Extra yeast may be used: 25 g or, for very rich mixtures, 50 g of yeast to each 500 g of flour.
2 Additional time may be allowed for rising: 2 hours or even overnight rising may be allowed.
3 The mixture may be prepared in 2 parts: a dough of flour, liquid, a little sugar and a high proportion of yeast is made and allowed to rise; then to the risen dough, extra ingredients such as sugar, fat, dried fruit and eggs are added, and further rising or proving allowed.

Biological leavens versus chemical leavens

The use of yeast as a leaven is very much in vogue at the present time. The advantages are:

1 Thiamin is not lost as it is when chemical raising agents are used.
2 Phytases present in the flour break down phytic acid when yeast doughs are made.
3 The quantity of sodium in the dough is less than when chemical raising agents are used.

7 Potatoes

Potatoes were an important staple for the Incas. They were brought to Britain by Sir Walter Raleigh in the sixteenth century. In 1690 Stevens recorded that 'The meaner people content themselves with little bread but instead thereof eat potatoes'. The Irish became so dependent on potatoes that when the crops were destroyed in 1845 and 1846 the results were devastating. There have been great developments in potato cultivation, and the world's potato crop now exceeds that of wheat in terms of volume and money.

Varieties of potatoes

It is important to know about the different varieties of potatoes, as this has implications for food preparation. Maris Piper are recommended for boiling, baking and chipping. Desirée are suitable for mashing and for potato salad, and King Edwards are ideal for baking.

Sweet potatoes are available in some areas. The red sweet potato is used for baking, mashing, cakes, soufflés and stuffings. White sweet potatoes are recommended for boiling and frying. Yams are popular in West African and Caribbean cooking, and can be cooked as potatoes but with the skin removed.

Structure and composition of potatoes

The potato consists of 3 main parts: the periderm, the vascular storage parenchyma and the pith (Fig. 7.1).

1 *The periderm*, or skin, is rich in dietary fibre and contains more protein and minerals than the fleshy part of the potato.
2 *The vascular storage parenchyma* is divided into 2 main parts by the vascular ring. The area just under the skin, known as the cortex, is thick and fibrous and contains more protein and minerals than the parenchyma lying on the other side of the vascular ring. The innermost parenchyma is rich in carbohydrate and forms the main flesh of the potato.
3 *The pith* is sometimes described as the 'water core' of the potato.

Fig. 7.1
Longitudinal cross section of a potato

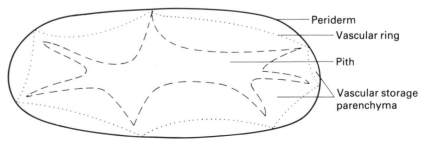

The effect of cooking on the texture of potatoes

Cooked potatoes may be floury, mealy, granular or dry and waxy, sticky or pasty. These textural qualities depend upon the behaviour of the cells within the potato during cooking. If the cells separate, the potato is usually floury; if the cells adhere to one another, the potato is usually waxy (Fig. 7.2).

Fig. 7.2
Cells in cooked floury and waxy potatoes

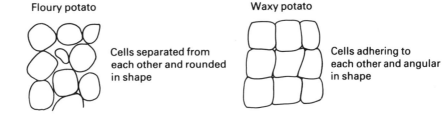

Floury potato

Cells separated from each other and rounded in shape

Waxy potato

Cells adhering to each other and angular in shape

Fig. 7.3
Gelatinisation of potato during cooking

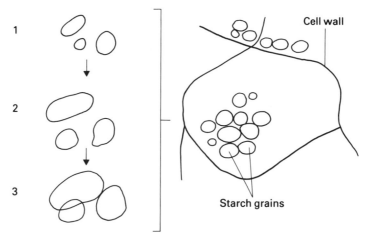

Cell wall

Starch grains

Floury potatoes have a glistening appearance, are granular and create a dry feeling on the tongue. In contrast, waxy potatoes have a translucent appearance, are pasty and feel moist.

During cooking the starch molecules in the potato take up water and swell (Fig. 7.3). Potatoes should be cooked long enough for the complete gelatinisation of starch, otherwise they will have an 'uncooked' taste and texture.

Nutrient content of potatoes, sweet potatoes and yams

Contrary to popular belief, potatoes, sweet potatoes and yams are low in energy density. This is partly due to their high water content, which is more than two thirds the weight of the product, and also to their low fat content.

Protein is found in small amounts, approximating to 1–2% of the weight of the raw flesh. *Fat* is present in tiny amounts, with these foods containing less than 0.5%. *Carbohydrate* is the main source of energy and this is mostly present in the form of starch. Carbohydrate profiles g/100 g are as follows:

Food	Carbohydrate Total	Starch	Intrinsic sugars
Potatoes	17.2	16.6	0.6
Sweet potatoes	21.3	15.6	5.7
Yams	28.2	27.5	0.7

Dietary fibre is present in potatoes, sweet potatoes and yams. Fibre profiles g/100 g of raw flesh are as follows:

Foods	Total Englyst	Fractions Cellulose	Non-cellulosic polysaccharides Soluble	Insoluble
Potatoes	1.2	0.4	0.7	0.1
Sweet potatoes	2.4	1.0	1.1	0.3
Yams	1.3	0.5	0.5	0.3

To obtain more dietary fibre from potatoes, it is necessary to eat the skins. For example, a baked potato eaten *without* the skin provides 1.4 g/100 g, but one *with* the skin provides 2.7 g/100 g, thus almost doubling the amount of fibre.

Iron is present in small amounts, with potatoes containing 0.4 and sweet potatoes and yams 0.7 mg/100 g raw flesh respectively. However, because these foods may be eaten in large quantities, they can make a significant contribution to iron intakes.

Carotene is present in white- *and* orange-fleshed sweet potatoes and yellow-fleshed yams. The orange-fleshed sweet potatoes contain 1820 to 16 000 µg/100 g of raw flesh, whereas the white-fleshed varieties provide 69 µg/100 g. Yellow-fleshed yams provide 400 to 1440 µg/100 g raw flesh. *Vitamin E* is present in sweet potatoes in significant amounts (5.56 mg/100 g). *Vitamin C* is present in potatoes in significant quantities. New and old potatoes contain 16 and 11 mg/100 g of raw flesh respectively. Sweet potatoes contain 23 mg/100 g of raw flesh, but yams contain only 4 mg/100 g. The presence of vitamin C in potatoes, sweet potatoes and yams will aid in the absorption of the non-haem iron that they contain.

Consumer choice of potatoes

1 *Quality* is an important consideration. When buying potatoes choose those which are an even size, free from soil, disease and damage – and avoid any that are green. The green colour is due to solanine. This substance is an alkaloid which, if consumed in large amounts, causes solanine poisoning.
2 *Method of cooking* will have some bearing on choice.
3 *Methods of purchase*:
   (a) Potatoes can be bought in 25-kg bags. Buying potatoes in bulk is advantageous because they cost less and the heavy brown paper sacks are convenient for storage.
   (b) They are available pre-packed in various quantities and are often washed.
   (c) They can be served from scales to shopping bag, for example, in the market or in a greengrocers.

(d) Consumers may select, weigh and pack potatoes of their own choice, for example, in a supermarket.

(e) Specially wrapped and washed large potatoes for baking are available in some retail outlets.

Storing potatoes

Store potatoes in a cool, dry, airy, dark place. Air circulation is necessary; potatoes will sweat and rot if kept in sealed polythene bags. If stored in direct sunlight they will sprout and turn green.

Preparation of potatoes

1 *New potatoes* require little preparation. A clean plastic scourer or a vegetable brush can be used to remove the skins, or the potatoes can be scraped using a sharp knife. However, the skins are tasty and nutritious, and it is enough just to wash new potatoes prior to cooking.

2 *Old potatoes* usually require more preparation. Scrub and wash thoroughly, removing eyes or blemishes and, if peeling is necessary, peel thinly. If potatoes are peeled thickly, the concentrated layer of nutrients under the skin as well as dietary fibre are lost. As potatoes are prone to browning and losses of vitamin C, preparation should be carried out just before cooking.

Potatoes in food preparation

Potatoes can be used in many different ways:

- *accompanying vegetable*, for example, mashed, boiled and baked potatoes;
- *baked potatoes* with fillings and toppings;
- *toppings to dishes*, for example, in hotpot and shepherd's pie;
- *extenders*, for example, in rissoles and fish cakes;
- *soups*, for example, in leek and potato soup;
- *sauces*, for example, in salad dressings and raita;
- *potato cakes, scones, bread doughs, pastry*;
- *soufflés, cheese cakes, puddings;*
- *sweets*; for example, chocolate fudge and coconut ice;
- *garnish*, for example, as piped potato.

Potato products

About 20% of the potato crop is processed. On a weight-for-weight basis convenience forms of potato are more expensive than raw potatoes due to the preparation and packaging costs. However, the convenience of these products is a great advantage.

1 *Canned potatoes* are available in different forms, such as diced potato salad, grated in rösti and as whole new potatoes.

2 *Dried potatoes* are available as powder or granules which fluff up as soon as they are reconstituted. Some types have added vitamin C to make good losses of this vitamin due to processing.

3 *Frozen potato products* include chips, potato waffles, potato croquettes and oven crunchies.

4 *Crisps* and ready to eat potato products such as chips and baked potatoes are popular.

8 Fruit and vegetables

Much of the appeal of fruit and vegetables in the diet is due to their colour, texture and flavour as well as nutritional value.

Classification of vegetables

Vegetables can be classified according to the part of the plant they represent (Fig. 8.1).

Fig. 8.1
Classification of vegetables according to plant structure

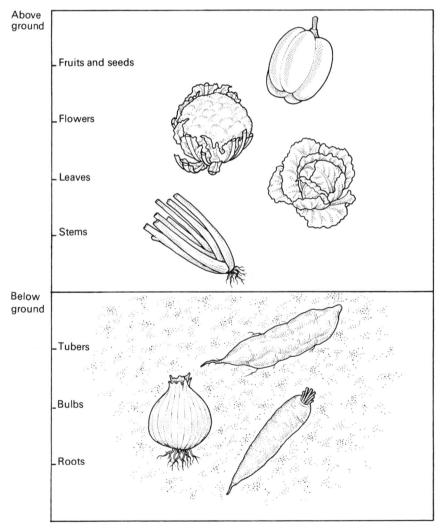

Table 8.1
Fresh vegetables with reference to classification and consumer choice

Vegetable	Description	Availability	Consumer choice
Roots			
Beetroot	Globe shaped with whiskery roots; very dark red; sweet taste	All year; new in early summer	The whiskery roots should not be broken; some stalk should remain on top
Carrots	Long and pointed or short and fat, depending on variety; orange; sweet taste	All year	Avoid woody or limp carrots
Kohlrabi	Swollen stem with a turnip-like flavour; two main types, green and purple	July–April	Buy when about the size of an orange; large roots can be tough
Parsnips	Carrot shaped; creamy white; sweet taste	September–April; best late October	Choose even-sized crisp-looking parsnips; avoid spongy or brown-marked specimens
Radish	Small, red, white or red and white; pungent flavour; usually eaten raw	All year but scarce in winter	Should be crisp and un-blemished; avoid if spongy
Salsify	Long, carrot-shaped; soft white flesh	End October–March	Choose smooth, tapered firm roots; avoid if flabby; leaves should be green-grey
Swede	Globe shaped with a swollen ridged neck; purple, yellow and white skin, yellow flesh	All year; limited supply in June and July	Avoid if blemished by spongy patches, holes or marks made by spade
Turnips	Globe shaped or cylindrical; yellow or white skin with a green or purple area near the top; whitish flesh	Autumn–spring; early variety May–August	Reject if spongy or blemished by holes, spots or brown patches
Bulbs			
Leeks	Like an elongated onion; white stem with green leaves at the top; onion-like taste	All year; best in autumn and winter	Stems should be straight and unblemished; reject any with a strong smell or hard yellow stalk or leaves
Onions	Fleshy bulbs which vary in shape and colour; usually white flesh with gold, brown, red or white skins; strong taste	All year	Look for firmness; skins should be papery; avoid slimy skins
Shallots	Like onion but much smaller	July–October	

Vegetable	Description	Availability	Consumer choice
Bulbs (continued)			
Spring onions	Young onions; look like small leeks; more delicate flavour	March–May	
Tubers			
Jerusalem artichokes	Knobbly shape; crisp flesh; white to pale yellow or pink; sweet taste	October–March	Look for the smoothest-shaped specimens; the very knobbly ones are wasteful
Potatoes	Many varieties available (see p. 94)	All year; new in spring and summer	Reject if green or indented with deep eyes
Sweet potatoes	Grooved, irregular shape with purplish skins and white to yellow flesh; mealy texture; chestnut-like taste	All year; in limited supply	Avoid if damaged; should be firm and bright in colour
Yams	Woody, brown skins; yellow flesh; mild flavour	All year; in limited supply	Avoid if damaged
Shoots			
Bamboo shoots	Crisp white pointed shoots emerging from the ground under a bamboo plant	All year	Retain crispness despite canning; canned often used in preference to fresh for convenience
Stems			
Asparagus	White, green to purple stalks	All year; best in May and June for home-grown supplies	Should be uniform size with well-formed heads; tastes bitter if stale; avoid if dry or wilted
Celery	White to pale green stalks, growing from central root and forming compact 'head'; light green leaves	All year; limited supply November–December	Stems should be firm and plump at base, not bruised; leaves should not be droopy
Fennel	Looks like bulbous celery; feathery leaves	All year; best in early summer	Reject if limp or bruised
Leaves			
Brussels sprouts	Like miniature cabbages; distinctive flavour	September–March	Each sprout should be firm and compact; avoid if strong smelling or if outer leaves are yellow
Cabbage			Avoid if leaves are limp or strong smelling; colour should be bright
Spring cabbage	Bright green crisp leaves	April–May	
Summer/autumn cabbage	Similar to spring cabbage but larger more solid head	June–October	

Vegetable	Description	Availability	Consumer choice
Leaves (continued)			
Winter cabbage	Like summer cabbage	June–October	
Savoy cabbage	Firm green head with crinkled leaves	August–May	
White cabbage	Firm compact head; light green colour	October–February	
Red cabbage	Firm, compact and purplish red	August–January	
Chicory	Greenish white to yellow or red, leaves packed firmly together, slightly bitter flavour	Autumn–spring	Choose firm, crisp heads with close packed leaves; reject if discoloured, damaged or curling at edges
Chinese leaves	Like pale green lettuce, but the large, white crinkled leaves are more solidly packed together	All year; in limited supply	Leaf edges should not be wilted or fawn-streaked
Curly kale	Dark green to purple curly-edged leaves with crimped edges; strong flavour	Winter and early spring	Avoid if the leaves are limp or turning yellow
Endive	Like a wide open lettuce with a whitish centre and vivid green outside; chewy and bitter	Late autumn and winter; in limited supply	Avoid if leaves discoloured or limp
Lettuce		All year	Choose cabbage, cos and Webb lettuces with fresh, bright leaves; avoid if hearts have yellow or brown patches or if underside is covered with slime
Cabbage lettuce	Loose, coarse leaves		
Cos lettuce	Long, coarse, crisp leaves		
Webb lettuce	Crisp, crimped leaves		
Iceberg lettuce	Crisp head; tight and solid		Should feel solid; outer leaves should not be limp or brown marked
Mustard and cress	Crisp, small leaf	All year	Avoid if droopy; buy when stalks are about 9 cm long
Spinach	Round-seeded or summer spinach and prickly-seeded or winter spinach both have tender dark green leaves	All year; best March–April	Should be bright green and crunch and squeak when handled; avoid if limp; use on day of purchase
Spring greens	May be cabbages without heads, also obtained from turnip tops	Early spring	Leaves should not be limp or yellow; use on day of purchase
Watercress	Small-leaved vegetable	All year in limited supply	Avoid if limp or yellow in colour and flowering

Vegetable	Description	Availability	Consumer choice
Flowers			
Broccoli	Flower heads similar in shape to small cauliflowers; purple or green	All year; home-grown March–May	Should have small fresh-looking heads with brittle stalks that snap easily
Cauliflower	Rounded head consisting of tightly packed, creamy white flower buds, the 'curd' surrounded by leaves	All year round	Look for firm leaves and head with creamy white flower buds; avoid if odour is strong or head coloured brown or grey
Fruits and seeds			
Artichoke (Globe)	Thistle-like plant. The flower head consists of scales with pointed tips and fleshy bases; these surround the choke; beneath the choke is the 'fond' – a greenish-grey disc considered to be a delicacy	All year but best in summer	Choose specimens with stiff leaves and slight bloom
Aubergine (Egg plant)	Purple skin, egg shaped; flesh is yellow-green, and mealy in texture	All year; in limited supply	Look for skins that are bright and shiny; avoid if wrinkled or bruised
Broad beans	Belongs to pea family; several different varieties	Summer (May–August)	If they are to be eaten whole, choose young beans with pods 5–7 cm long; larger beans need to be shelled.
Courgettes	Baby marrows harvested when 15 cm long	All year; home-grown June–October	If very small (5 cm long) can be cooked whole; if large, slice into rings; best used on day of purchase
Cucumber	Two main varieties: long, thin and smooth; and thick, rough skinned	All year; best in late summer	Choose cucumbers that are straight with a clear bloom on the skin
French beans	Many varieties; pods and seeds vary in colour, shape and size	All year in limited supply; home-grown June–mid-November	Buy when young and crisp
Marrow	Many shapes and varieties; colours may be green, whitish or irregularly striped green and white; delicate flavour	Home-grown June–November	Avoid large marrows because they tend to lack flavour and have coarse flesh and tough skin; the skin should have a dull bloom
Lady's fingers (okra)	Five-sided green pod up to 25 cm long; soft and tapering exuding a mucilaginous juice which acts as a thickener in soups and stews	All year; in limited supply	Buy when young otherwise tough and stringy; avoid brownish-coloured ones; pick smallest and brightest ones

Vegetable	Description	Availability	Consumer choice
Fruits and seeds (continued)			
Peas		Home-grown June–September	Look for small, green plump pods; avoid if pods are wet
Mangetout (sugar peas)	The earliest tender pods eaten whole when young		
Petit pois	Small seeded peas with a fine flavour		
Garden peas	There are several varieties		
Marrowfat	Large and wrinkled peas		
Peppers	Red and yellow peppers are sweeter and more mellow in flavour than green ones	All year; in limited supply	Choose specimens with smooth, glossy skins; avoid any with wrinkles or brown patches
Plantain	Looks like a big banana; fibrous texture and not as sweet as banana	All year; in limited supply	For use as a vegetable choose green unripe specimens
Pumpkin	Usually round and can grow very large; colours vary from greenish-white, green and yellow to orange	Summer and autumn	Pumpkins should be bought whole because once cut the flavour diminishes and mould appears very quickly
Runner beans	Bright green succulent pods with red seeds	Home-grown late summer (mid-July to end-October)	Avoid if tough and stringy, misshapen or pitted with brown or black; if fresh a runner bean will snap between the fingers
Sweetcorn	Yellow kernels; sweet taste	Home-grown July–October	Best eaten the day it is picked; cobs should be plump and enclosed by bright green stiff leaves; tassels at the top should be black and withered
Tomatoes	Vary in size, shape and colour; can be very small or large; the colours can be bright red or yellow	Imported all year round; home-grown April–November	Should be firm with unwrinkled skin; the colour should be bright
Fungi			
Mushrooms		All year	Avoid if brownish looking or slimy
Cup mushroom	Medium-sized		
Button mushroom	Small-sized; most immature of the cultivated mushrooms		
Flat open mushroom	Largest and most strongly flavoured form of cultivated mushroom		

Classification of fruit

1 *Berry fruits* have a fragile cell structure.
2 *Citrus fruits* have a tough leathery peel which surrounds a succulent, juicy mass of segments. Some have seeds and others do not.
3 *Fleshy fruits* may be seedless or have seeds throughout the flesh or in a central core.
4 *Stone fruits* have a single seed which is surrounded by a fleshy portion.

Table 8.2
Fresh fruit with reference to classification and consumer choice

Fruit	Description	Availability	Consumer choice
Berry			
Blackberries	Most common wild fruit in the UK; cultivated varieties also available; purple to black berries; juicy and sweet	Home-grown August–September	Use as soon as possible as this fruit spoils quickly; avoid if wet and mushy
Blackcurrants	Purple, almost black berries; smooth, tough skin; flesh juicy and acidic	Home-grown July and August	Avoid if there are a lot of leaves or if the berries are red or unripe
Cranberries	Pink to dark red small berries; hard, sharp, slightly bitter flavour	December–February; in limited supply	Should be firm and not split or squashy; not usually much choice
Gooseberries	Pink, yellow or green fruit; smooth or hairy skins; sweet or sour	Home-grown June–August	Avoid if split or blemished
Grapes	Many varieties available, e.g., Alicante with purple/black juicy berries, Almeira with pale green to golden skins, Muscat with white or golden berries	All year	Buy in bunches; avoid if split, squashed or shrivelled or showing mould near stems; choose plump grapes firmly attached to stems
Loganberries	Crimson red berries; juicy flesh surrounding firm core; similar to raspberries	Early July to late August	Choose bright, plump berries; reject if squashy or if mould is visible; or if shrivelled
Raspberries	Summer raspberries mid to bright red, large and sweet; autumn raspberries deeper red and smaller, more juicy	Home-grown July and August	Avoid if squashy or any signs of mould
Redcurrants	Bright red berries; small, glossy and juicy	July and August	Avoid if berries are squashy
Strawberries	Many varieties; red, seed-studded surface with soft, pink flesh	All year; home-grown June–September	Best eaten on day of purchase; avoid if mould visible or if berries squashy

Fruit	Description	Availability	Consumer choice
Citrus			
Clementines	Cross between an orange and a tangerine; stiff orange-like skin; the juicy, slightly acidic flesh is divided into segments; almost seedless	December–February	Fruit should be firm and heavy for its size
Grapefruit	Pale yellow skin, varies in thickness; the juicy flesh is in segments with few seeds; sharp, slightly bitter taste	All year	Avoid if skin feels spongy as this is a sign that the peel is thick and fruit juice and flesh are not plentiful; pink grapefruit are much sweeter than yellow ones
Kumquats	Look like small oranges; not true citrus; acid flavour	All year; in limited supply	Fruit should be firm and heavy for its size
Lemons	Oval-shaped, yellow fruit; skin can be thin, thick, knobbly; very sharp taste	All year; in limited supply	Choose plump lemons with smooth skins as these tend to have less peel and are more juicy than large, knobbly skinned ones
Limes	Oval shaped yellow-green fruit; similar to lemons but smaller with thinner skins; yellow flesh; very sharp taste	All year; in limited supply	Fruit should be firm and heavy for its size
Oranges Jaffa	Large, juicy, seedless with thick skins	All year	Choose oranges with fine textured skin; avoid if puffy or spongy; fruit should be firm and heavy for its size
Navel oranges	Recognised by the raised embryo growth at one end the skin is thin and smooth; juicy flesh with few pips		
Bitter oranges (Seville)	Produced commercially in Spain; good for making marmalade; thin, deep orange skins; dark yellow flesh; acidic and pippy	January and February	
Tangerines	Small bright orange fruit with loose skin; juicy segments with many pips	October–March	Fruit should be firm and heavy for its size
Ugli fruit	A cross between a tangerine and a grapefruit; same size as a grapefruit with greenish-yellow, thick, knobbly skin; flesh is juicy and sweeter than grapefruit with few pips	October–November	Fruit should be firm and heavy for its size

Fruit	Description	Availability	Consumer choice
Fleshy			
Apples		All year	Avoid if bruised or badly wrinkled
Cox's Orange Pippin	Russet coloured with orange red or crimson flush; dry skin but firm, juicy flesh with aromatic taste		
Granny Smith	Bright green skin; crunchy, hard flesh with a sharp, distinctive taste		
Bramley cooking apple	Large, green and can be flushed with red; sharp tasting, juicy flesh	October–March	
Bananas	Distinctive shape; ripe and ready for eating when yellow; the flesh is soft and sweet; green bananas are best cooked	All year	Avoid if badly bruised or squashy
Figs	Green, brown or purplish, pear shape, thin skin, sweet flesh with many seeds	July–October	Choose firm, unblemished fruit
Kiwi fruit (Chinese gooseberries)	Egg-shaped with brownish-green and hairy skin; the green flesh is soft, juicy, sweet and slightly sour	July–February	Choose firm, unblemished fruit
Melon			A ripe melon will yield to pressure applied to the stalk; a good melon should seem to be heavy for its size; gives off distinctive odour if the melon is ripe
Cantaloupe	Slightly flattened shape; rough or woody; green to yellow skins; orange-yellow flesh; succulent and juicy		
Honeydew	Most widely available; shape resembles a rugby ball; the green, yellow or white skin is slightly corrugated; juicy, sweet, pale green to pink flesh		
Ogen	Yellow to orange skin marked with faint green stripes; pale yellow in colour sometimes with a touch of green	All year; main supplies June–December	
Water melons	Largest type; round or oval; skin is glossy, deep green or green, varigated with dark grey; red to yellow flesh; very juicy; black seeds present in flesh	June–September	

Fruit	Description	Availability	Consumer choice
Fleshy (continued)			
Papaya (Pawpaw)	Fruits similar in shape and size to elongated melon; smooth skin ranging from green to yellow or orange in colour; sweet, juicy, orange-pink pulp with brown-black seeds in centre	All year; in limited supply	Choose unbruised fruit
Passion fruit (Purple granadilla)	Similar in shape and size to a large plum; tough skin, purple and deeply wrinkled when ripe; yellow pulp, sweet and juicy with small black seeds	All year; in limited supply	Dark, large, dimpled fruits are best
Pears	Elongated shape; gritty texture; dessert and cooking	All year; home-grown September–April	A ripe pear gives slightly round the stem; avoid if squashy; buy pears before they are fully ripened
Pineapples	Large oval fruit with a hard knobby skin ranging from deep yellow to orange brown; the flesh is yellow, creamy yellow, firm, sweet and juicy	All year	Choose pineapples with stiff leaves; avoid if bruised; a good pineapple has a fragrant odour and is heavy in relation to its size
Pomegranates	About the same size as an orange; the pink or bright red skin is thin but tough; crimson flesh, juicy and full of seeds held together by yellowish membranes	Autumn	Choose firm, plump fruits
Stone			
Apricots	Oval shaped with yellow skin and flesh; slightly sweet tasting	June–August and December–February	Choose ripe, firm fruit; strong colour means that the fruit is sweet; avoid if skins squashy or bruised
Avocado pear	Oval fruit with a very large stone; flesh is pale green, soft and oily; the skin can be dark green and smooth or dark greyish-green and very wrinkled; bland taste	All year	Apply gentle pressure near stalk; a ripe avocado yields a little; unripe fruit will ripen in a warm room; choose unblemished fruit
Cherries Sweet or dessert cherries	White, pink or black; small and round in shape with juicy and sweet flesh	May–August	Look for firm, dry cherries; avoid any with blemishes or if bruised

Fruit	Description	Availability	Consumer choice
Stone (continued)			
Morello cherries	Acidic and used for cooking		
Dates	Fresh dates are shiny and plump with smooth brown skin; fleshy part is juicy and sweet	September–March	Avoid if skin is damaged or flesh bruised; choose plump, firm fruits
Lychees	About the same size as a plum with a central stone; the pink to brown skin is scaly; the flesh is white and pulpy but firm, juicy and slippery	December–February	Avoid if skin is dry and shrivelled
Mango	Many varieties; can be round, kidney or pear-shaped or long and narrow; sizes vary from 125 g to 2 kg; large stone; tough skin can be green to yellow, orange and red and may be flushed with pink; juicy flesh has a delicate flavour	All year; in limited supply	Avoid if mushy looking or blemished
Nectarine	Smooth skinned peach but with a richer flavour and brighter colour	January–March; June–September	Choose unblemished fruit
Peach	Round with a velvety skin; colour varies from greenish-white to golden-yellow with crimson flushing; sweet, juicy flesh	December–March; May–September	Quality peaches are bright in colour, plump and firm; avoid bruised specimens
Plums	Dessert plums such as Victoria are sweeter than cooking plums which are acidic; a dessert plum has yellow skin flushed with scarlet and juicy flesh and may have a very dark purple skin	January–March; June–October; home-grown August–October	Avoid if bruised or if skins are damaged; look for bloom on the skin

Structure of fruit and vegetables

Fruit and vegetables are made up of different kinds of cells. Much of the edible part consists of parenchyma cells (Fig. 8.2).

Cell wall

The cell wall forms the outer layer of the cell. Young cells in young fruit and vegetables have only a primary cell wall. Older cells in more mature plant foods also have a secondary cell wall.

Fig. 8.2
A parenchyma cell

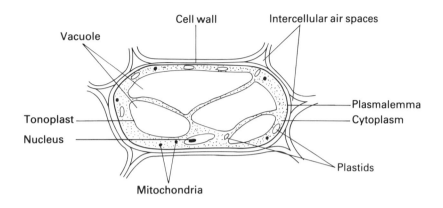

Cellulose is the major constituent of the cell wall. Other constituents include hemicelluloses and pectic substances (pectic acid, pectins and protopectin). Some fruits are particularly high in pectin content, and these include crab apples and quinces. Pectins are useful in the preparation of jams and jellies. Older fruit and vegetables may be 'woody' because lignin may be deposited in the secondary cell wall after growth of the plant has ceased.

Cytoplasm
A membrane called the plasmalemma encloses the cytoplasm in the cell. Just inside is the jelly-like cytoplasm which moves about within the cell. In the cytoplasm are the plastids. These contain fat droplets and fat-soluble pigments. In some plants, such as the potato, starch is stored in the plastids. The mitochondria and nucleus of the cell are also present in the cytoplasm.

Vacuole
The major part (about 90%) of the parenchyma cells is made up of at least one sac-like space called a vacuole. This contains cell sap. A membrane called the tonoplast separates the vacuole from the cytoplasm. Cell sap is watery, and this is partly responsible for the succulent texture of fruits and vegetables. The cell sap contains many substances – for example, sugars, salts, organic acids and water-soluble plant pigments.

Intercellular air spaces
Small air spaces are found between the cells. These are largely responsible for the opaqueness of raw plant foods. Certain plant foods – apples, for example – are so full of air spaces that they float in water.

The effect of cooking on the texture of fruit and vegetables

During cooking the cell membranes of fruit and vegetables are denatured and water and solubles in the cell sap are lost. This is one reason why cooked fruit and vegetables are less crisp than raw ones.

As a result of cooking, fruit and vegetables become translucent. This is because the intercellular gas is replaced by water. This can be seen easily by comparing the appearance of raw cauliflower with that of cooked cauliflower.

During cooking the insoluble pectic substances become soluble. As a result of this, adhesion between the cells is reduced, and this is why cooked plant tissues are more easily broken by the teeth. If undercooked, the fruit or vegetable will not be tender because the cells adhere too much. If overcooked, the cells will adhere very little, resulting in a mushy product. 'Woody' fruit and vegetables containing lignin in large amounts will never soften completely because lignin is resistant to cooking.

The pH has an effect on texture. The hemicelluloses are susceptible to breakdown by alkali. The addition of bicarbonate of soda tends to make the plant food mushy. Acid has a toughening effect on it. It is suggested that acids slow down the breakdown of the structural components – so, if lemon juice is added to whiten a vegetable (such as cauliflower), the cooking time should be extended.

Sugar in high concentrations retards the tenderising effect of cooking because it makes pectin less soluble and it also dehydrates the celluloses and hemicelluloses. In the preparation of soft berries, heavy sugar syrup is sometimes used. The fruit tends to stay whole if this is done.

The colour of fruit and vegetables

The colours of fruit and vegetables are due to the pigments present in the cells (Table 8.3). Green fruits and vegetables are rich in the chlorophylls; these are fat soluble and are found in the plastids of the cell. Orange, yellow and red fruit and vegetables are rich in a group of pigments called the carotenoids (carotene, xanthophyll and lycopene). These too, are fat soluble and are found in the plastids. Red, purple and blue plants are high in anthocyanins: pigments which belong to a larger group known as the flavonoids. The anthocyanins are water soluble and are located in the cell sap. White plant foods are rich in anthoxanthins, which like the anthocyanins belong to the flavonoid group, and are located in the cell sap and are soluble in water.

Browning

Fruits such as apples, pears, bananas, peaches and avocado pears are prone to discolouration, becoming brown or grey in colour. For browning to take place, contact between the following has to be made: phenolic compounds in the plant cells; oxygen in the intercellular air spaces or the air; phenoloxidase enzymes in the plant cells. Contact is made when the fruit is bruised or damaged or cut. To prevent browning:

Table 8.3
Plant pigments with reference to the colour of fruit and vegetables

Pigment	Predominant colour	Vegetable	Fruit
Chlorophylls	Green	Cabbage	Avocado
Carotenoids	Yellow, orange and red orange	Carrots	Oranges
Flavonoids			
Anthocyanins	Red, purple, blue	Red cabbage	Blackberries
Anthoxanthins	Colourless	Onions	Pears

1 do not prepare fruits until absolutely necessary;
2 add acids such as lemon or orange juice to the cut surface; this will depress enzyme action (for example, lemon juice on avocado pear);
3 put the fruit in a concentrated sugar solution which has the same effect as acids (for example, in fresh fruit salad);
4 store at cold temperatures to slow down the enzyme activity;
5 blanch the fruit or vegetables because the heat denatures the enzymes.

Vegetables such as potatoes develop surface discolouration when peeled or cut. The first colour change is to pink, then brown and ultimately a dark grey forms. These colour changes are due to the formation of melanin from tyrosine in the potato. An enzyme called phenolase catalyses the reaction. To prevent these colour changes:

1 do not peel or cut potatoes until absolutely necessary;
2 blanch potatoes as in the preparation of chips to denature the catalytic enzyme.

Flavour of fruit and vegetables

The characteristic flavours of fruits and vegetables are due to a mixture of compounds, and these include the following:

1 *Acids*   All fruit and vegetables are acidic.
2 *Sugars*   The sweeter flavour of freshly harvested vegetables such as peas is partly due to the sugars present.
3 *Glutamic acid*   The amino acid, glutamic acid, may play a part in the superior flavour of young fresh vegetables. The typical flavour of mushrooms and their enhancement of other flavours has been attributed to this amino acid.
4 *Sulphur compounds*   Vegetables such as cabbage, broccoli, brussels sprouts and cauliflower (which belong to the cabbage family), and onions and leeks (which belong to the onion family), owe their typical flavour to sulphur compounds. In their fresh, raw and intact states vegetables do not have much odour. When cut, onions produce a pungent odour. This is because the cells are ruptured and enzymes in the cell react with the sulphur compounds. Onions become mild in flavour after cooking because these compounds are soluble in water and are volatile. The odour of chopped raw cabbage is due to the mixing of another enzyme with the sulphur compounds. This odour becomes intense if the cabbage is over-cooked. The sulphur compounds break down and hydrogen sulphide is formed.

Solubility		Sensitivity			
Water	Fat	Acid	Alkali	Heat	Metals (iron)
	✓	Olive green	Bright green	Olive green	
	✓				
✓		Red	Blue green		Blue
✓		Bright white	Yellow		Brown

Nutrient content of vegetables

Vegetables have a high water content and, consequently, they have a low energy density.

Protein is present in vegetables in small amounts – many types contain less than 1%. Pulses contain more. Peas, for example, are about 6% protein. *Fat* is only present in small quantities, most vegetables containing less than 1% fat.

Carbohydrate is found in variable quantities as intrinsic sugars, with or without starch.

Dietary fibre is found in variable amounts. Fibre profiles g/100 g of edible weight of raw vegetables are as follows:

Vegetable	Total Englyst	Cellulose	Fractions Non-cellulosic polysaccharides Soluble	Insoluble
Carrots	2.4	0.8	1.4	0.2
Okra	4.0	1.2	2.4	0.4
Peas, frozen	5.1	3.0	1.6	0.7

Calcium is present in variable amounts. Vegetables providing significant quantities are spinach and watercress and both of these contain 170 mg/100 g. Broccoli, cabbage and swede contain more than 50 mg/100 g. *Iron* is present in vegetables in variable amounts. Frozen peas contain 1.5 mg/100 g. Spinach and broccoli provide 2.1 and 1.7 mg/100 g respectively.

Note. The bioavailability of these minerals will be reduced by the presence of dietary fibre and phytic acid in vegetables and oxalates in spinach.

Carotene is found in most vegetables in nutritionally significant amounts. Carrots are top of the league table in this respect. The average figure is 8115 µg/100 g with a range of 4300 to 11 000 µg. Spinach, watercress and tomatoes contain 3535, 2520 and 640 µg/100 g respectively. *Vitamin E* is present in most vegetables in variable amounts. Rich sources are spinach, watercress and broccoli which contain 1.71, 1.46 and 1.30 µg/100 g respectively. *B vitamins thiamin, riboflavin* and *niacin* are present in vegetables in small quantities. *Folate* is found in vegetables in variable amounts. Useful amounts are present in spinach, Brussels sprouts and broccoli, which contain 150, 135 and 90 µg/100 g respectively. *Vitamin C* is found in vegetables in variable amounts. High in the league table for this nutrient are green peppers, Brussels sprouts and broccoli, which contain 120,115 and 87 mg/100 g respectively. The presence of vitamin C aids the absorption of the non-haem iron found in vegetables.

Nutrient content of fruit

The succulence of fruit is due to its high water content. This also accounts for the low energy density characteristic of fruit.

Protein is found in small amounts in fruit – most varieties providing less than 1%. *Fat* is present in only very small amounts, with a few exceptions, such as avocados and olives which contain 19.5 and 11.0 g/100 g edible weight respectively. *Carbohydrate* is present in variable amounts. Prunes, for example, provide 38.4 g/100 g and strawberries 6.0 g/100 g. The carbohydrate is mostly present in the form of intrinsic sugars, although starch is present in some fruits, such as bananas.

Dietary fibre is present in variable amounts. Fibre profiles g/100 g of edible weight of fruit are as follows:

Fruit	Total Englyst	Fractions Cellulose	Non-cellulosic polysaccharides Soluble	Insoluble
Apples	2.0	0.7	0.9	0.4
Mangoes	2.6	0.5	1.6	0.5
Prunes	6.5	1.1	4.4	0.9

Calcium is present in small quantities. Fruit which contain reasonable amounts are blackcurrants, oranges and figs, which contain 60, 47 and 38 mg/100 g edible weight respectively. *Iron* is present in variable amounts. Prunes, for example, contain 2.9 mg/100 g and apricots 0.5 mg/100 g.

Note. The bioavailability of minerals will be reduced by dietary fibre and phytic acid in fruit.

Carotene is found in some fruit in significant quantities. Mangoes, apricots and prunes provide 1800, 405 and 155 µg/100 g edible weight respectively.

Vitamin E is present in some fruit in significant amounts. Avocados, for example, contain 3.20 µg/100 g and mangoes 1.05 µg/100 g. *Vitamin C* levels are particularly high in blackcurrants and lemons. Strawberries, oranges and grapefruit contain 77, 54 and 36 mg/100 g edible weight respectively. The presence of vitamin C aids the absorption of the non-haem iron found in fruit.

Uses of fruit and vegetables

Table 8.4
Guidelines on the use of fresh fruit and vegetables

Guidelines	Reasons
Selection	
1 Choose young fruit and vegetables	To ensure maximum vitamin C content. To ensure maximum flavour and a 'non-woody', coarse texture.
2 Purchase only if really fresh	If bruised or damaged losses of vitamin C, due to the release of the enzyme ascorbic acid oxidase, are increased. Deterioration of flavour, colour and texture is less likely in fresh fruit and vegetables
Storage	
1 Use as soon as possible after purchase	Same reasons as 2 above
2 If storage is necessary, store in a cool, dark place	To reduce losses of vitamin C. Oxidation of vitamin C is increased by light and heat.
Preparation	
1 Prepare just before required	To reduce losses of vitamin C. Once cut, ascorbic acid oxidase is released.

Guidelines	Reasons
2 Remove dirt, wildlife, withered or unwanted parts	
3 Avoid soaking in cold water	To reduce losses of vitamin C. This vitamin is water soluble
4 Use a sharp knife and do not cut, chop or shred more than necessary	To reduce the losses of vitamin C. Cutting the plant cells causes the enzyme ascorbic acid oxidase to be released. A blunt knife causes more cells to be disrupted.
5 Tear the leaves of green vegetables, e.g., lettuce, rather than cutting them with a knife	To reduce losses of vitamin C. Tearing prevents disruption of cells and prevents the release of ascorbic acid oxidase
6 Avoid the use of an iron knife	To reduce losses of vitamin C. The rate of oxidation is increased by iron
	To preserve the colour of plant foods which contain the anthocyanins and anthoxanthins. The former turn blue green or slate blue and the latter green brown when in contact with iron
7 Use acids such as lemon juice	To prevent losses of vitamin C by oxidation
	To prevent susceptible foods, e.g., apples, bananas and avocado pears from browning
8 Blanch	To prevent susceptible foods, e.g., potatoes, from darkening

Cooking

Guidelines	Reasons
1 Avoid cooking in a copper pan	To prevent losses of vitamin C. Copper speeds up the rate of oxidation
2 Use the minimum amount of water	To prevent losses of vitamin C. This vitamin is water soluble, and the greater the quantity of water the more vitamin C is lost
	To prevent losses of thiamin, riboflavin and nicotinic acid. These vitamins are water soluble
3 Place the food to be cooked in boiling water	To reduce losses of vitamin C. The high temperature denatures the enzyme ascorbic acid oxidase
4 In the case of green vegetables leave the lid off the pan for the first minute or 2	To preserve the bright green colour. Boiling with the lid off causes removal of volatile acids which, if allowed to stay, would cause the colour to change to bronze to olive green
5 Cook quickly for the minimum time	To reduce losses of vitamin C. The amount of oxidation is increased by prolonged cooking
	To prevent the breakdown of cell structure. Over-cooking causes the food to disintegrate.
	To prevent green vegetables from turning bronze to olive green
	To prevent 'off' flavours due to the breakdown of sulphur compounds
6 Never add bicarbonate of soda to the cooking liquid	To prevent losses of vitamin C. The rate of oxidation is increased by alkalis
	To prevent losses of thiamin by decomposition
	To prevent breakdown of structure. Hemicelluloses are sensitive to alkalis

Guidelines	Reasons
	To prevent discolouration. Foods in the anthocyanin and anthoxanthin groups turn from red to blue and from white to creamy yellow in the presence of alkalis
7 Add acids such as lemon juice or vinegar to foods in the anthocyanin and anthoxanthin groups	To ensure that the red stays red and the white stays white
8 Avoid acids in the preparation of green vegetables	Acids cause the bright green to turn brown to olive green
9 Add sugar (if necessary) towards the end of cooking	Sugar has a toughening effect on cell structure

Serving

1 Serve at once and do not keep warm for longer than necessary	To prevent losses of vitamin C due to oxidation
	To prevent the development of 'off' flavours due to the breakdown of sulphur compounds.
2 Serve the cooking liquid if possible as a soup or sauce	To use the vitamin C lost in the cooking liquid
3 Avoid further mashing or puréeing	To prevent losses of vitamin C. Additional processing increases the rate of oxidation

Storing fruit and vegetables

Fresh fruit and vegetables are perishable.

1 *Roots, bulbs and tubers* soon shrivel once they are out of the ground and, if exposed to sunlight, they will sprout. For long-term storage they can be kept in dry soil or sand in an outhouse. For short-term storage, they may be stored in a vegetable rack, preferably away from bright light. To prevent their drying out, a covering of polythene may be used, but it is important to allow the free circulation of some air, or the vegetables will rot.
2 *Stems, leaves, flowers, fruit and seeds* must be used as soon as possible. They should be dry, and stored by wrapping loosely in newspaper, in polythene, or in a covered pan or bowl to prevent them from withering through loss of moisture to the air around them. A vegetable drawer in a refrigerator is useful. It is advisable not to store this type of produce for more than 2 to 3 days in a refrigerator.
3 *Fresh fruit* should be used as soon as possible. Berries are especially prone to spoilage and are better suited to refrigeration temperatures. Other fruits should also be kept cool and should be stored in a cool, ventilated place.

Cooking fruit and vegetables

In their raw state most fruits and vegetables are appetising, retaining maximum texture, colour, flavour and content of vitamins such as ascorbic acid and those of the B-complex. Fruits are generally stewed or baked and vegetables are boiled, steamed, baked, grilled or stir-fried. The pressure cooker and the microwave oven are also useful for cooking fruit and vegetables.

Preserved fruit and vegetables

Frozen fruit and vegetables
Frozen fruit and vegetables are more tender than their fresh counterparts because blanching and freezing have a softening effect. The vitamin C content is equal to that found in really fresh fruit and vegetables because freezing is carried out when the foods are in prime condition.

Canned fruit and vegetables
Canned fruit and vegetables are much softer than their fresh counterparts as a result of the high temperatures used in the canning process. Much of the vitamin C content is lost. Canned fruit may include sugar syrup. To reduce sugar intake choose fruit canned in its own juice. Canned vegetables may include brine. To reduce salt intake avoid those canned in brine.

Dried fruit and vegetables
Dried fruit and vegetables are not juicy like their fresh counterparts because of the removal of water in the drying process. The vitamin C content falls dramatically although other nutrients become more concentrated. This is illustrated in Table 8.5. Dried fruit is popular as a sweetening agent in muesli and fruit bars as an alternative to sugar.

Table 8.5
Nutritional differences between dried and fresh fruit per 100 g

Fruit	Water (g)	Energy kcal	kJ	Vitamin C (mg)	Iron (mg)	Calcium (mg)	Dietary fibre (g)
Apricots							
Fresh	87.2	31	134	6	0.5	15	1.7
Dried	14.7	188	802	Trace	4.1	92	7.7
Figs							
Fresh	84.6	43	185	2	0.3	38	1.5
Dried	16.8	227	967	1	4.2	250	7.5

9 Pulses, nuts and myco-protein

Pulses

Pulses (Table 9.1) are the seeds of plants belonging to the Leguminosae family. They are also known as legumes. Peas, beans and lentils all belong to this family. Beans were one of the earliest foods to be cultivated and have been eaten since the sixth or seventh millennium BC.

Pulses are available fresh, frozen, canned or dried. The dried forms have been used as a staple food in different parts of the world for thousands of years.

Table 9.1
Some features of a selection of pulses

Pulse	Description
Aduki beans (adzuki beans)	Tiny, cylindrical shape; reddish brown with a thread-like white line on one side; smooth texture with a nutty and slightly sweetish taste
Black beans (frijol negro)	Medium size, kidney shape; black with white thread-like eye on one side; mealy texture with a sweetish taste
Black-eyed beans (cow peas)	Small, kidney shape; white with a distinctive black spot or 'eye'; smooth texture with an earthy flavour
Butter beans	Large, flat, kidney shape; cream-coloured; mealy texture; with a bland taste
Cannellini beans (pasiola beans)	Medium size, elongated kidney shape; ivory-coloured; mealy texture with a slightly nutty flavour
Chick peas (Bengal gram; garbanzos)	Medium size, shaped like hazel nuts; pale gold to beige in colour; mealy texture with a nutty flavour
Flageolets (green haricot beans)	Small, elongated kidney shape; pale green and ivory colour; smooth texture with a delicate subtle flavour
Haricot beans (Boston beans; navy beans)	Small, oval shape, off-white colour; smooth texture with a bland flavour
Lentils whole	Small, disc shape; various colours such as green or brown; the former have a subtle flavour, the latter an earthy flavour
split	Tiny, half split circles; yellow to orange colour; mealy texture with a bland taste
Mung beans (green gram)	Tiny, cylindrical shape; olive-green colour with a white thread-like line on one side; smooth texture with a bland taste
Peas Marrowfat	Small, irregular drum shape; pale green and cream colour; mealy texture with a distinctive 'pea' taste
Yellow split peas	Small, split circle shape; yellow to orange colour; mealy texture with a pea flavour
Red kidney beans (chilli beans)	Medium size, kidney shape; mahogany red with white thread-like line on one side; mealy texture with a sweetish taste
Soya beans	Small, round, black or yellow, smooth texture with a bland flavour

Nutrient content of dried pulses

Protein accounts for approximately 20% of the weight of dried pulses and it is of low biological value. Soya beans are an exception to this rule as they have a protein content of 36% and it is of high biological value. The limiting amino acids in pulses are methionine and cystine, but lysine is present in significant amounts. Cereals are rich in the two limiting amino acids but lack lysine. Therefore, if pulses and cereals are eaten together, they provide high biological value protein. *Fat* is present in pulses in small amounts, with the exception of soya beans which contain 18.6 g/100 g. *Carbohydrate* accounts for approximately 50% of the weight of dried pulses.

Dietary fibre is present in useful amounts. Fibre profiles g/100 g of dried pulses are as follows:

Pulse	Total Englyst	Fractions Cellulose	Non-cellulosic polysaccharides Soluble	Insoluble
Chick peas	10.7	2.5	3.3	4.9
Lentils	8.9	2.9	2.0	4.0
Red kidney beans	15.7	3.8	6.9	5.0

Calcium is found in pulses in variable amounts. Particularly useful sources are soya beans, haricot beans and chickpeas, which contain 240, 180 and 160 mg/100 g respectively. *Iron* is present in pulses in variable amounts. Useful sources are green and brown whole lentils, soya beans and red kidney beans, which contain 11.1, 9.7 and 6.4 mg/100 g respectively. *Zinc* is found in pulses in variable amounts. Useful sources are aduki beans, soya beans and green and brown whole lentils, which contain 5.0, 4.3 and 3.9 mg/100 g respectively.

Note. The presence of phytic acid in pulses, the tannins in the skins and their high dietary fibre content reduce the bioavailability of the minerals present.

Vitamin E is found in dried pulses in variable amounts. Soya beans, chickpeas and butter beans contain 2.90, 2.88 and 1.13 mg/100 g respectively.

B-vitamins thiamin, riboflavin and *niacin* are present in pulses in nutritionally significant amounts. Blackeye beans, pigeon peas and pinto beans contain 0.87, 0.86 and 0.68 mg/100 g thiamin respectively.

Dried pulses

Consumer choice of dried pulses
Buy pulses from places with a good turnover of stock. As pulses age their skins harden, becoming tough and leathery.

Storing dried pulses
The maximum storage life should not exceed 6 months. Store in airtight containers, but if these happen to be made of glass or other translucent materials, keep them away from direct sunlight.

Preparation and cooking of dried pulses
It is important to 'pick them over' for stones and grit and even bits of sacking if purchased loose. They should then be rinsed in cold running water in a colander.

Lentils, whole or split, and split peas do not need soaking, but all other pulses require soaking. Use plenty of water: 500 ml to 200 g of beans. Bicarbonate of soda can be added to soften pulses: 1.25 g bicarbonate of soda dissolved in 20 ml of boiling water to 500 ml water. However, this will result in the loss of thiamin which is sensitive to alkaline conditions. The old but very widely used instructions were to soak overnight, and 8 to 12 hours are generally considered enough. The faster method is to bring the pulses to the boil in plenty of water and boil for 4 minutes. Then remove the pan from the heat source and leave, with the lid on, for 1 hour. However, the longer method of soaking is probably better, so that the phytases can render the calcium and iron more available (p. 21 and 24). After soaking, the water should be drained away and the pulses rinsed again.

Put the pulses into a large pan, cover them with cold water and bring to boiling point. When they are boiling the heat can be lowered to simmering point, with the exception of red kidney beans which must be kept at boiling point for 10 minutes at least. If this is not done severe *food poisoning* with vomiting and diarrhoea can result. This is because red kidney beans contain substances called *haemagglutinins*. Cooking at boiling point for 10 minutes destroys these harmful substances. If scum appears, remove by skimming. A few drops of oil in the cooking liquid will help to prevent the pulses from boiling over. Cooking times range from between 30 and 50 minutes. If a pressure cooker is used, the pulses cook in a third of the time.

Products based on pulses

Fig. 9.1
The production of baked beans

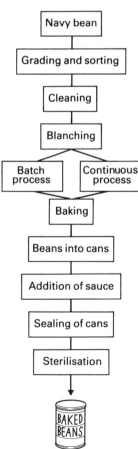

Baked beans

Baked beans are based on a recipe traditionally used by housewives in New England for their Saturday bean festivals. On the Friday evening before the festival, earthenware pots were used to soak the beans in. Early the next day the soaked beans were flavoured with salt pork, mustard and molasses. The pots were taken to local bakers who cooked the beans all day long in their ovens. In the evening the cooked beans were collected and used for the festival. The canned product was exported to Britain at the turn of the century, and during the 1920s baked beans became increasingly popular. Until 1940 the recipe included pork when, because of wartime shortages of meat, this ingredient was left out. The 'vegetarian' beans were very popular, and after the war the recipe was left as it was. The recipe for baked beans may vary to include curried beans, beans with pork sausages, beans with beefburgers and beans with mini Frankfurter sausages. Baked beans of all varieties are currently estimated to be sold in large quantities: about 900 million cans a year are sold in Britain.

Baked beans are made from a type of haricot bean, the navy bean. Approximately 90% of beans used in Britain to make baked beans come from the Great Lakes area of the United States and Canada.

Production of baked beans (Fig. 9.1)

1 The dry beans are firstly graded, sorted and cleaned.
2 The beans are blanched.
3 The beans are baked and then conveyed into the cans.
4 The sauce, which has been made from pulped tomatoes and selected spices and seasonings, is added.
5 The cans are sealed hermetically and are then sterilised.

Baked beans are a versatile food and may be eaten hot or cold. Beans on toast is a popular way of serving them; and they may also be incorporated in dishes in interesting ways.

Baked beans are about 5% protein but they also contain hidden sugar. Sucrose is added to the tomato sauce. However, newer varieties with less sugar and salt are available.

Textured vegetable protein and spun protein
Products analogous to meat can be made from soya beans. Such products are called 'meat analogues'.

Production of textured and spun protein (Fig. 9.2)

1 The soya beans for the production of textured vegetable protein (TVP) and spun protein are cleaned, cracked, hulled and flaked.
2 Most of the oil is removed by solvent extraction.
3 A defatted soya flour is then made. The 'defatted soya flour' is made into meat substitutes by one of two processes – spinning and extruding.
   (a) *Spinning* The protein is formed into a viscous solution by dissolving it in alkali. The liquid is then forced through a spinneret which has tiny holes. The liquid is extruded as thin fibres which coagulate as they pass into an acid solution. The fine hairlike fibres are then bound together with additional ingredients which include fat, albumen, flavourings and colours.
   (b) *Extrusion* The defatted soya flour is mixed with water and ingredients such as salt, flavourings and colour. The mixture is then extruded and heat applied under pressure to form a 'spongy' mass.

   Textured vegetable protein and spun protein are versatile foods, which, on a dry weight basis, are about 50% protein. Approximately 5000 to 7000 tonnes of soya protein is used in foods such as sausages, burgers and tinned soups in Britain. It is widely used in school meals and it is popular among vegetarians.

Tempeh (pronounced 'temppay')
Tempeh (sometimes referred to as the first meat analogue) is a soya-bean product made by fermentation. Tempeh has been eaten for centuries in South-east Asia. In Indonesia half the crop of soya beans is made into tempeh. In the traditional setting it is made by putting soya beans into large baskets made of bamboo. These are put into a stream where the villagers tramp on the beans with their bare feet. The soya beans split and the hulls float away downstream. The beans are then boiled, cooled and mixed with a piece of tempeh from a previously made batch. This acts as the starter for the fermentation. The beans are wrapped up in banana leaves and left to ferment in the sun. One to two days later the banana leaves are removed and the contents, which are firm, whitish-looking cakes, are sold in the village market.

   Tempeh can be made at home, and, in this respect, is comparable to homemade yogurt. Tempeh is available in health food shops.

Production of tempeh (Fig. 9.3)

1 The soya beans are split and hulled.
2 This is followed by boiling the beans in plenty of water for about 45 minutes.
3 The beans are thoroughly drained and cooled.
4 Vinegar is added and mixed with the beans.
5 The starter *Rhizopus oligosporus* is added and mixed with the beans.
6 The beans are firmly packed in containers; each layer of beans should not be more than 12 mm deep. The tempeh containers are covered with a perforated covering – for example, foil with holes punched in it. The cover should be about 6 mm above the beans and should not touch their surface.
7 The tempeh is left to incubate at temperatures of between 29°C and

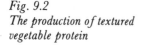

Fig. 9.2
The production of textured vegetable protein

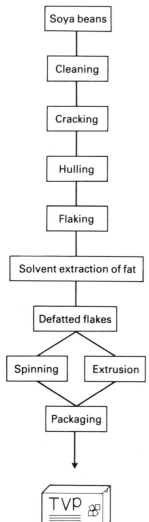

Fig. 9.3
The production of tempeh

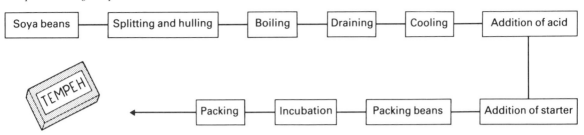

Soya beans → Splitting and hulling → Boiling → Draining → Cooling → Addition of acid

Packing ← Incubation ← Packing beans ← Addition of starter ← Addition of acid

Fig. 9.5
The production of tofu

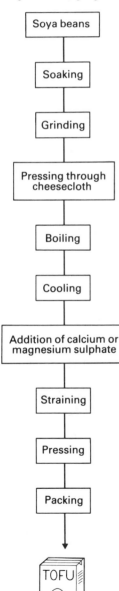

Soya beans

Soaking

Grinding

Pressing through cheesecloth

Boiling

Cooling

Addition of calcium or magnesium sulphate

Straining

Pressing

Packing

TOFU

35°C for 26 to 30 hours. The tempeh is ready when
(a) a white, fluffy layer completely conceals the beans and the beans underneath the layer are held together as a solid cake (Fig. 9.4);
(b) it does not fall apart when sliced;
(c) the smell is quite distinctive, rather like the smell of mushrooms.

Fig. 9.4
Tempeh slices in relation to the incubation time

Adequately incubated tempeh   Inadequately incubated tempeh

Tempeh will keep for 2 to 3 days in a refrigerator. It may be sliced, blanched and then frozen for longer storage.

Tempeh has great versatility in food preparation. It can be cut into rings the size of beefburgers, deep fried and served in buns as tempeh burgers. It can be cut into strips and used on pizzas and in savoury flans.

Tempeh is about 21% protein, 6% fat and 4% dietary fibre. It is particularly useful for vegans because it contains nutritionally significant amounts of vitamin B_{12}.

Soya drink
Soya drink is produced by soaking soya beans in water. The beans are then ground and filtered. The filtrate is heat treated by pasteurisation or boiling. This type of drink can be made at home and on a commercial scale. It is creamy coloured and is widely used by vegans as a drink and in food preparation. Soya drink is approximately 3% protein and 2% fat.

Tofu
Tofu was discovered more than 2000 years ago in China. It is an important soya-bean food in East Asia.

Production of tofu (Fig. 9.5).

1 Tofu is made by soaking soya beans in water at 25°C for 5 to 6 hours.
2 The beans are ground and pressed through cheesecloth.
3 The resulting milk is boiled and cooled to 50°C.
4 Calcium or magnesium sulphate is added to precipitate the protein.
5 The precipitate is then strained, using cheesecloth, and it is pressed to remove excess moisture.

Tofu can be made on a commercial scale and at home. It is a bland-tasting food which looks like a smooth-textured light cheese. Tofu is sometimes wrongly and misleadingly called soya-bean cheese. It is not entitled to this name because it is not fermented, aged or ripened. It is widely used in Oriental cooking and is popular among vegetarians. It is about 8% protein, 4% fat and a useful source of calcium.

Nuts

Nuts (Table 9.2) are defined as any seed or fruit which consists of an edible, hard, oily kernel enclosed within a hard shell. Nuts are available in different forms, including whole, shelled, chopped, ground and, in the case of almonds, blanched or unblanched, and also flaked.

Table 9.2
Some features of a selection of nuts

Nut	Description
Almonds	Small, oval and flat shape; pale brown pitted shells
Brazil nuts	Hard, dark brown, three-edged shell; firm nut and slightly oily with a flavour that resembles coconut
Chestnuts	Shiny brown, enclosed in a fleshy outer covering which breaks open when the nut is ripe
Coconuts	Hard, dark brown outer shell covered with coarse fibres; 3 indentations at the top which have to be punctured to release the milk
Hazel nuts (cob nuts)	Small, grey-brown, partly covered with leafy husks
Peanuts (strictly a legume)	Dried fibrous pod which contains the seeds or 'nuts'
Pistachio nuts	Mildly flavoured green kernels; they make attractive decorations for foods
Walnuts	Like miniature brains to look at; surrounded by brownish skin encased in hard brown shell; distinctive flavour

Nutrient content of nuts

Protein is present in nuts in significant amounts. For example, peanuts, almonds and cashew nuts provide 25.6, 21.1 and 17.7 g/100 g respectively. The biological value of the protein in nuts is low, and in order to enhance this it is necessary to eat them with cereals. *Fat* accounts for two thirds of the total weight in Brazil nuts and hazelnuts and around half the weight in almonds, cashew nuts and peanuts. The fat is mostly in the form of unsaturated fatty acids. *Carbohydrate* is present in nuts in variable amounts. Cashew nuts, peanuts and almonds contain 18.1, 12.5 and 6.9 g/100 g respectively.

Dietary fibre is present in useful amounts. Fibre profiles g/100 g of kernels are as follows:

Nut	Total Englyst	Fractions Cellulose	Non-cellulosic polysaccharides Soluble	Insoluble
Almonds	7.4	1.9	1.1	4.4
Hazelnuts	6.5	2.2	2.5	1.8
Peanuts	6.2	2.0	1.9	2.3

Calcium is found in nuts in variable quantities. Particularly rich sources are almonds, Brazil nuts and hazelnuts, which contain 240, 170 and 140 mg/100 g respectively. *Iron* is present in nuts in variable amounts. Cashew nuts, hazelnuts and almonds contain 6.2, 3.2 and 3.0 mg/100 g respectively. *Zinc* is found in nuts in variable amounts. Cashew nuts, Brazil nuts and peanuts contain 5.9, 4.2 and 3.5 mg/100 g respectively.

Note. The presence of phytic acid in nuts and the presence of dietary fibre reduces the bioavailability of the minerals present.

Vitamin E is present in nuts in variable amounts. Some nuts are a particularly rich source and these are hazelnuts, almonds and pine nuts, which contain 24.98, 23.96 and 13.65 mg/100 g respectively. *B-vitamins thiamin, riboflavin* and *niacin* are present in variable amounts. Almonds are a useful source of riboflavin and niacin, providing 0.75 and 3.1 mg/100 g respectively. Peanuts are a useful source of thiamin and niacin, providing 1.14 and 13.80 mg/100 g respectively.

Myco-protein

Quorn

Quorn is derived from myco-protein which comes from a tiny plant called *Fusarium graminearum.* The plant occurs naturally and has been around for thousands of years. Since its discovery in the early 1960s, research and development have been intensive, with the result that Quorn was officially approved by the Ministry of Agriculture Fisheries and Food (MAFF) in 1984. Up until 1990, Quorn was available as an ingredient in ready meals, but since then it has also been launched as an ingredient for cooking in its own right.

Production of Quorn (Fig. 9.6)

1 *Fusarium graminearum* is grown in a fermenter. Nutrients are added and the temperature and pH are regulated.
2 The myco-protein and excess liquid are then heat treated by the process of pasteurisation to stop further growth.
3 The myco-protein is harvested by pumping the liquid (broth) from the fermenter to a series of centrifuges. At this stage, the mixture is chilled. The myco-protein is separated from the liquid, resulting in a creamy-coloured dough that looks like raw pastry.
4 The raw myco-protein is transformed into Quorn by mixing it with vegetable flavourings and egg albumen and processing it further. The production method used depends on whether it will be made into pieces, mince, burgers or sausages.
5 The product is finally packed and chilled or frozen.

Quorn has a texture similar to that of lean meat and is marketed as a tasty alternative to meat. It is approximately 12% protein and 3% fat. It provides around 5% dietary fibre and is a useful source of vitamin B_{12} and zinc.

Fig. 9.6
Production of Quorn

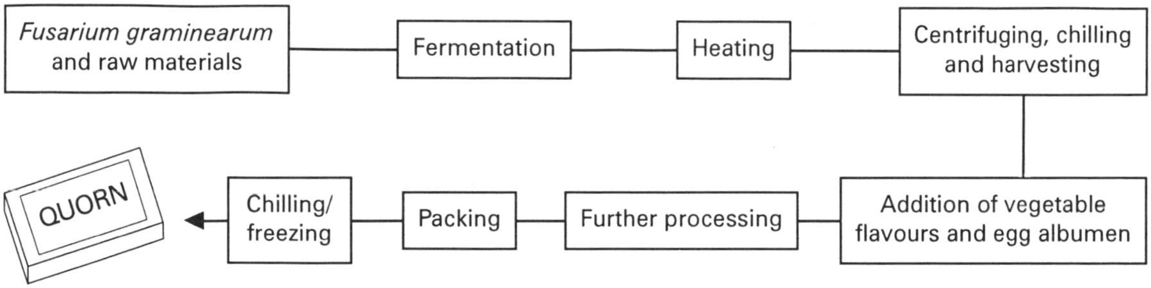

10 Meat

Meat eaten in Britain comes mainly from cattle, sheep and pigs. It includes carcass meat which is often jointed, such as leg of lamb, topside of beef and loin of pork. The 'fall-offs' from the carcass are known as offal (such as liver, kidney and tongue) and meat that has been processed into various products (for example, sausages, hamburgers and boneless joints) described as 'meat products'.

Meat production

There have been major developments in meat production during the last 100 years. Large farms produce meat on an industrial scale. Great demands are made on the farmer to produce 'good-quality' meat. Breeding is an important part of meat production and it enables the farmer to produce the types of meat in demand; that is, high-quality meat with a low fat content and at a reasonable price.

There has been much debate about the possible link between bovine spongiform encephalopathy (BSE) and Creutzfeld Jakob disease (CJD) and the whole scenario is very complicated. The Institute of Food Science and Technology in the UK has stated to its members that no definitive scientific opinion can be reached at the present time and that more research needs to be done. The slaughter of animals (Fig. 10.1) is controlled by law.

In the UK the various animals are cut up to produce the cuts shown in Fig. 10.2 (pp. 126–7) and these are suitable for different methods of cooking.

Fig. 10.1
The main stages of slaughtering

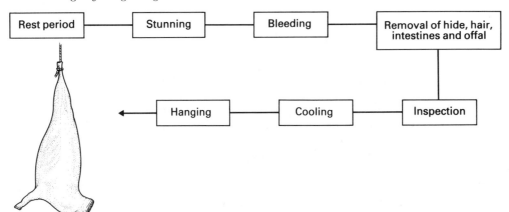

Structure of meat

Lean meat is the muscle of the animal. Muscles are made up of fibres which are so small that they cannot be seen by the naked eye. When examined under a microscope these fibres are seen as elongated cells which are dotted with nuclei (Fig. 10.3). The cells vary in length; they may be only a few millimetres or as long as several centimetres. They also vary in diameter.

Fig. 10.3
A muscle cell

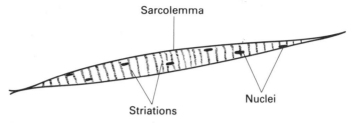

The main component of muscle cells is water. Other constituents include proteins, minerals, vitamins and the pigment myoglobin. The proteins include myosin and actin.

Groups of fibres are held together in bundles (Fig. 10.4) by a thin network of connective tissue, the *endomysium*. A sheet of connective tissue called the *perimysium* surrounds the bundle of fibres. The *epimysium* forms the outermost layer of connective tissue (Fig. 10.4).

Fig. 10.4
Cross section of muscle tissue

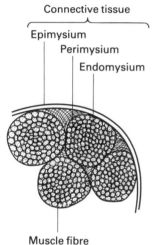

Connective tissue consists of a ground substance in which 2 proteins are embedded. These proteins are *collagen* and *elastin*. Collagen forms the main connective tissue within and around muscles and is the main component of tendons, the structures which attach muscles to bones. Collagen is pearly white in colour; it is flexible, but not as elastic as elastin, and forms gelatine when cooked. Elastin is the main component of ligaments which attach 2 bones or cartilages. Elastin is yellow in colour and, unlike collagen, does not convert to gelatine when cooked.

Fat is found in the connective tissues of muscles. This is called *invisible fat* and is described as marbling. A certain amount of marbling in meat is desirable because it helps to keep meat moist during cooking. Visible fat is easily identified by its creamy white-yellow colour. The yellowness is due to the pigment carotene. The fat tends to be yellowish in old animals and in those consuming carotene-rich foods. This type of fat is deposited under the animal's skin and is called subcutaneous fat. The organs of the animal may also be surrounded by *visible fat*.

The effect of preparation and cooking on meat

Meat is cooked to make it tender, flavoursome, appealing in colour and safe to eat.

Tenderness
Meat that is difficult to cut or hard to chew is said to be tough. It has longer and thicker muscle fibres. The meat of older animals – for example, mutton, beef and parts of an animal that are used a lot – have long, thick fibres, like the neck muscles of a sheep (scrag end). The amount of connective tissue has a bearing on tenderness. Tough meat has more connective tissue than tender meat. This too is related to the age of the animal and the activity of the muscles.

Certain procedures in food preparation can increase the tenderness of tough meat. The muscle fibres and connective tissues may be broken by *mechanical action*, as in mincing or bashing with a rolling pin or meat hammer. *Proteolytic enzymes* may be used to digest muscle fibres and connective tissue partially. Commercially prepared tenderisers may be used or enzymes obtained directly from their source, including bromelin from fresh pineapple, ficin from fresh figs and papain from the leaves of the pawpaw. When proteolytic enzymes are used it is important to perforate the surface of the meat to allow the penetration of the enzymes. Also, timing is critical; if enzyme treatment is overdone the meat will have a

Fig. 10.2
Cuts of meat and their recommended methods of cooking

Beef

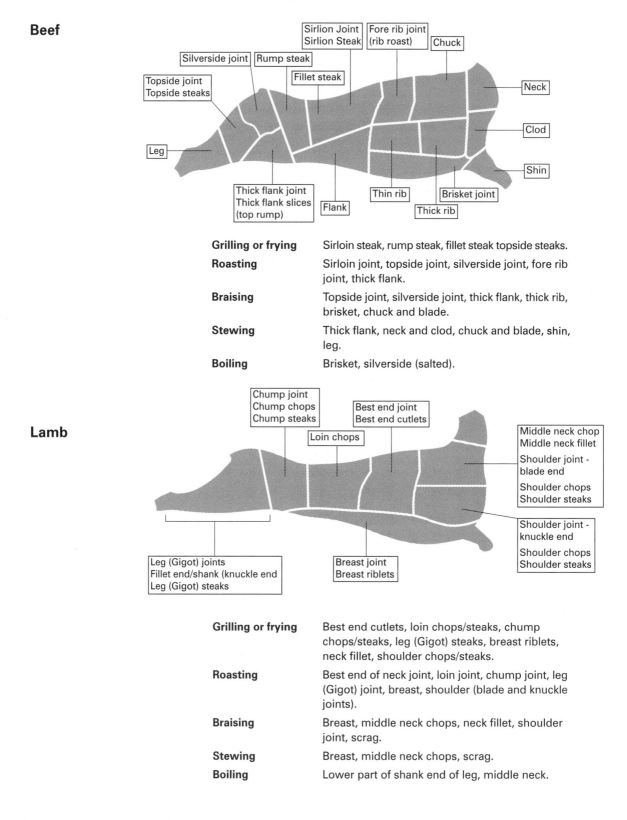

Grilling or frying	Sirloin steak, rump steak, fillet steak topside steaks.
Roasting	Sirloin joint, topside joint, silverside joint, fore rib joint, thick flank.
Braising	Topside joint, silverside joint, thick flank, thick rib, brisket, chuck and blade.
Stewing	Thick flank, neck and clod, chuck and blade, shin, leg.
Boiling	Brisket, silverside (salted).

Lamb

Grilling or frying	Best end cutlets, loin chops/steaks, chump chops/steaks, leg (Gigot) steaks, breast riblets, neck fillet, shoulder chops/steaks.
Roasting	Best end of neck joint, loin joint, chump joint, leg (Gigot) joint, breast, shoulder (blade and knuckle joints).
Braising	Breast, middle neck chops, neck fillet, shoulder joint, scrag.
Stewing	Breast, middle neck chops, scrag.
Boiling	Lower part of shank end of leg, middle neck.

Pork

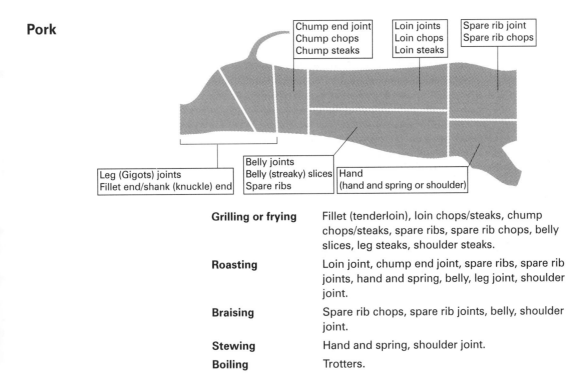

Chump end joint
Chump chops
Chump steaks

Loin joints
Loin chops
Loin steaks

Spare rib joint
Spare rib chops

Leg (Gigots) joints
Fillet end/shank (knuckle) end

Belly joints
Belly (streaky) slices
Spare ribs

Hand
(hand and spring or shoulder)

Grilling or frying	Fillet (tenderloin), loin chops/steaks, chump chops/steaks, spare ribs, spare rib chops, belly slices, leg steaks, shoulder steaks.
Roasting	Loin joint, chump end joint, spare ribs, spare rib joints, hand and spring, belly, leg joint, shoulder joint.
Braising	Spare rib chops, spare rib joints, belly, shoulder joint.
Stewing	Hand and spring, shoulder joint.
Boiling	Trotters.

Bacon

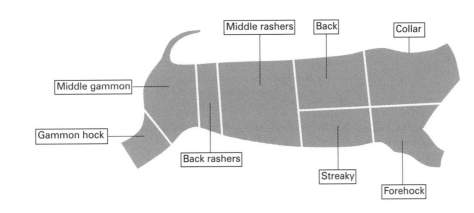

Middle rashers

Back

Collar

Middle gammon

Gammon hock

Back rashers

Streaky

Forehock

Grilling or frying	Middle gammon steaks, long back rashers, middle or through cut rashers, prime back rashers or chops, prime streaky rashers, prime collar rashers.
Roasting	Gammon hock, middle gammon, middle through cut, prime collar.
Braising	Gammon hock, middle gammon, prime collar.
Stewing	Gammon hock, middle gammon, prime forehock.
Boiling	Gammon hock, middle gammon, middle through cut, prime collar.

crumbly texture and an unpleasant flavour. Substances that increase the *hydration* or water-holding capacity of the muscle-fibre proteins may be used as tenderisers, and these include acids, alkalis and salt. However, alkalis darken meat, and salt, in the quantity needed, causes an unpleasant taste. Acids can be used successfully – lemon juice, vinegar, wine and tomatoes for example.

Cooking also affects tenderness. As a result of cooking the muscle fibre proteins coagulate and water is lost. This accounts for much of the shrinkage of cooked meat. Dry methods of cooking such as roasting and grilling cause rapid shrinkage and toughening of the tissue. Such cooking methods are suitable for tender cuts. When moist methods of cooking such as stewing and braising are used the shrinkage and toughening occur more slowly, therefore these methods are suitable for tough cuts of meat.

Initially, during cooking, the collagen in the connective tissues shrinks, and this causes the meat to 'hump'. This can be seen in the preliminary frying in the preparation of a brown stew. With further cooking the collagen is converted to gelatine. The formation of gelatine is enhanced by moist methods of cooking. This is particularly important for tough cuts of meat which have more collagen than tender cuts. Evidence of gelatine formation can be seen when the cooking liquids from tough cuts of meat have cooled. These liquids solidify because of the gel formed.

The fat melts, and this contributes to the shrinkage of cooked meat. In dry methods of cooking, such as grilling and roasting, the melted fat prevents the meat from becoming dry. In moist methods of cooking the fat floats to the top of the liquid and can be skimmed off.

Flavour

The flavour of meat is largely due to the extractives and fat. Flavour is more pronounced in less tender cuts of meat. Muscles from older animals or well-exercised parts have more extractives than the muscles of young animals or less-used parts. The flavour of extractives is not fully understood, but it is known that they include soluble inorganic salts, lactic acid and nitrogenous compounds. Fat has a distinct effect on the flavour and aroma of meat. The aroma from fat during cooking is largely responsible for the smells associated with different meats.

In dry methods of cooking the extractives and fat settle on the surface of the meat. This is why the meat on the outside of a joint is more tasty than the interior. In moist methods of cooking, the extractives and fat pass into the cooking liquid, so unless this is used in the recipe as a sauce to accompany the dish much of the flavour will be lost.

There is an association between flavour and cooking time. If less tender cuts of beef are cooked in a pressure cooker or a microwave oven, the flavour is not so well developed as in beef cooked by longer, more conventional methods.

Colour

The colour of meat is mainly due to the pigment myoglobin. This pigment accounts for about 75% of the total pigment of red meat. Some muscles contain more of this pigment than others; for example, leg of chicken is darker than breast because of its myoglobin content. The degree of pigmentation is related to muscle use. Well-used muscles and those from older animals are darker.

The colour of meat changes during cooking (Fig. 10.5). When heated, the pigment myoglobin is oxidised to form oxymyoglobin. This is associated with a change in colour from purple-red to bright red. With further heating the meat becomes greyish brown due to the formation of denatured globin hemichrome. Here the protein in the pigment is denatured and the iron in the pigment is oxidised.

Fig. 10.5
Colour changes in meat during cooking

Nutrient content of meat

Protein constitutes about 20% the weight of lean meat and it is of high biological value. *Fat* is present in meat in variable amounts depending on the cut and whether or not the meat has been trimmed of visible fat. Fat profiles g/100 g are as follows:

Meat, raw	Fat Total	Fatty acids Saturated	Monounsaturated	Polyunsaturated
Beef mince	16.2	7.1	7.1	0.5
extra lean	9.6	4.2	4.1	0.4
Breast of lamb				
lean and fat	24.7	11.9	9.4	1.2
lean only	11.5	5.2	4.2	0.5
Pork leg				
lean fat	15.2	5.1	6.4	2.5
lean only	2.2	0.7	0.9	0.4

Iron is found in meat in useful amounts and it is in the form of haem-iron. Beef, lamb and pork, raw and trimmed of fat, contain 1.8, 1.4 and 0.7 mg/100 g respectively. *Zinc* is found in meat in useful amounts in a biologically available form. Beef, lamb and pork, raw and trimmed of fat, contain 4.1, 3.3 and 2.1 mg/100 g respectively. *Potassium* and *phosphorus* are present in meat in useful amounts.

B-vitamins thiamin, riboflavin, niacin and *tryptophan* are present in meat in useful amounts. B-vitamin profiles mg/100 g of raw meat trimmed of fat are as follows:

Meat	Thiamin	Riboflavin	Niacin	Tryptophan
Beef	0.10	0.21	5.0	4.7
Lamb	0.09	0.20	5.4	3.9
Pork	0.98	0.24	6.9	4.5

Pork is a particularly rich source of thiamin.

Consumer choice of meat

1 Choose a cut of meat suitable for the method by which it is to be cooked (Fig. 10.2). Meat is a highly priced source of animal protein, and the more tender the cut the more costly it is. Cheaper cuts of meat may not always be tough but they may contain a high proportion of waste; for example, breast and shoulder of mutton.
2 Check to see if the meat is fresh. When fresh:
    (a) there is no unpleasant odour;
    (b) the colour is deep red for beef, pinkish-red for mutton, pale pink for pork and pinkish-beige for veal;
    (c) the fat is firm and not oily;
    (d) there is little, or preferably, no juice running from the meat.
3 If boning is required or any chopping of bones, it is advisable to make full use of the butcher's skills.

Storing meat

Meat is a perishable food, and to keep it fresh it is necessary to store it under suitable conditions. Meat should not be kept for more than 3 days in a refrigerator. Air should be allowed to circulate because too little air can result in decomposition by anaerobic bacteria (p. 209). Loose coverings of greaseproof paper or polythene will allow for air circulation and prevent the meat from drying out. Meat can be stored for a maximum of 2 days in an airy, cool larder protected from dust and flies by a fly-proof dish cover.

Methods of cooking meat

Grilling

Grilling (p. 240) is suitable for tender cuts of meat. This method is in line with healthy eating as much of the fat in the meat drips away during cooking. To prevent bones on cutlets from burning, they may be covered with foil. To prevent bacon and gammon steaks from curling, it is advisable to snip the fat around the edges.

Frying

Frying (p. 240) is suitable for tender cuts of meat and then usually *shallow* or *dry-frying* techniques are used. The latter method is in line with healthy eating, particularly if the meat has been trimmed of fat and is wiped on absorbent paper after cooking. *Stir-frying* – the popular Chinese method – is quick and versatile and requires tender meat cut into strips. These are quickly browned in a wok and additional ingredients, such as vegetables and sauces, are stirred into the meat.

Roasting

Roasting (p. 239), sometimes referred to as baking, is suitable for cuts of meat, as shown in Fig. 10.2. When using this method, allow 100–175 g per person for boneless joints and 225–350 g if the meat is on the bone. If the meat to be roasted is frozen, it is important to defrost it thoroughly before cooking. Table 10.1 gives details of cooking times. Before cooking it is important to note the weight of the joint in order to calculate how long it needs to be cooked. The oven needs to be pre-heated to 180 °C/gas No. 4–5 or according to manufacturers' instructions for fan ovens. Towards the end of cooking, a meat thermometer may be inserted into the centre of the joint or the thickest point for a few seconds to determine if it has reached the necessary internal temperature (Table 10.1).

When the meat is cooked, it is advisable to leave the joint to stand for about 15 minutes before carving to minimise the loss of juices. The water-holding capacity of the tissue increases as the temperature falls.

Pot roasting

Pot roasting (p. 240) is suitable for small joints of meat, particularly when no oven is available. Boned and rolled joints are thoroughly recommended for this method of cooking.

Braising

This method of cooking is described on p. 239 and cuts that are suitable for braising are given in Fig. 10.2.

Stewing

This method of cooking is described on p. 239 and cuts that are suitable for stewing are given in Fig. 10.2. The meat may be in the form of chops and steaks or cut into cubes. Vegetables and flavourings may also be added. Allow 225–350 g of vegetables per 450 g meat. The methods of preparation involve one of the following.

1 The meat, vegetables and liquid are added to a large pan or ovenproof casserole and cooked for the recommended time with the lid on (cold-water stew).
2 The meat and vegetables are first browned in fat, then the liquid is added and cooking continued with the lid on (brown stew).

Method 1 is the healthier option. The cooking time will range from $1\frac{1}{2}$ to $3\frac{1}{2}$ hours depending on the quality of the meat.

Boiling

This method of cooking is described on p. 239 and cuts that are suitable for boiling are given in Fig. 10.2. The meat is put into a large pan, covered with cold water and brought to boiling point. The heat is then reduced to simmering point and the lid put on the pan. It is important to top the water up throughout, with boiling water.

Other methods of cooking meat

Pressure cookers, microwave ovens, multi-cookers, slow-cookers and infra-red grills may also be used for cooking meat. It is advisable to follow manufacturers' instructions accordingly.

Table 10.1
Roasting meat to the desired degree of doneness at 180°C/350°F/gas No. 4–5)

Meat	Degree of doneness	Internal temperature (°C)	Cooking time (mins) per 450 g	+
Beef	Rare	60	20	20
	Medium	70	25	25
	Well done	80	30	30
Pork	Medium	75–80	30	30
	Well done	80–85	35	35
Lamb	Medium	70–75	25	25
	Well done	75–80	30	30

Preserved meat

Frozen meat

Frozen meat tends to increase in tenderness but when it is defrosted water is lost carrying with it water-soluble vitamins and minerals.

Canned meat

Canned meat tends to become tender as a result of canning but some of the

B-group vitamins are lost. The fat content is variable; for example, 3% in jellied veal and 27% in luncheon meat.

Cured meat

The flesh of the pig preserved by using curing salts is called 'bacon' or 'ham'. Beef, namely silverside and brisket; tongues; and the breasts of ducks and turkeys may also be cured.

Offal

The word 'offal' is derived from 'off-fall'. In the USA offal is called 'variety meats'; this term highlights the wide variety in this meat group (Table 10.3).

Nutrient content of offal
Protein is found in variable amounts and it is of high biological value. Heart, liver and kidney are about 20% protein, whereas tripe is about 7% protein. *Fat* is present in offal in small quantities.

Iron is present in offal in useful amounts and it is in the form of haem-iron. Liver is a particularly rich source of iron. Raw liver: calf, chicken, lamb and ox provide 11.5, 9.2, 7.5 and 7.0 mg/100 g respectively. *Zinc* is present in offal in useful quantities and it is in a biologically available form. Liver is a rich source of zinc. Raw liver: calf, lamb, ox and pig provide 14.2, 4.0, 4.0 and 7.0 mg/100 g respectively. *Potassium* and *phosphorus* are present in offal in useful amounts.

Retinol is present in liver in large quantities. Raw liver: calf, chicken, lamb, ox and pig provide 18 800, 9700, 17 300, 14 200 and 17 400 µg/100 g respectively. *Carotene* is also present in variable amounts. *Vitamin D* is found in liver in useful amounts. *B-vitamins* are present in offal in useful amounts. Liver is a particularly rich source of vitamin B_{12} and folate.

Using offal
Offal should be used on the day it is purchased and should not be kept for longer than 24 hours in a refrigerator. Recommended cooking methods are given in Table 10.2, and these are closely related to the toughness or tenderness of the particular offal type.

Meat products

Sausages
Sausages can be divided into three main types: fresh, cooked and dry.

1 *Fresh sausages*, such as those made from beef and pork, are made from raw meat, fat, carbohydrate filler, seasoning, water and casing. They have a high fat content whether grilled or fried. Both fried and grilled pork sausages, for example, contain 25% fat. Beef sausages are not quite as high in fat as pork sausages; a fried and a grilled beef sausage contain 18% and 17% fat respectively. Sausages with reduced fat containing half the fat of ordinary sausages are available.
2 *Cooked sausages*, such as liver sausage, frankfurters and polony have similar ingredients to fresh sausages. Sausages of this type are pre-cooked and, in some cases, smoked. Some cooked sausages can be eaten as they are or they may need to be heated before being served. Cooked sausages are high in fat content; frankfurters and polony contain 25% and 21% fat respectively.
3 *Dried sausages* such as salami have similar ingredients to sausages but the meat is cured and then dried. Many are also smoked. The fat content of salami is very high at 45%.

Hamburgers
Hamburgers are made up of minced beef, pork fat, onions which have been

Table 10.2
Fresh offal and cooking methods

Type	Description	Recommended cooking methods
Heart	The heart of the ox and calf are the largest, ox heart being darker; pigs' heart is smaller; sheep's heart is smaller again; ox heart is usually sold sliced; others are generally left whole	Small hearts may be kept whole and stuffed and pot roasted, braised or casseroled
Kidney	Ox and calves' kidneys are lobulated; ox kidney is reddish brown; calves' kidney is much lighter brown; other kidneys are dark brown and bean-shaped; ox and calves' kidneys are coarse in texture and have a strong flavour	Pig and lamb – grill fry Ox and calf – braise stew
Liver	Ox and calves' livers are the largest and dark red in colour; sheep's liver is similar in appearance but smaller; pigs' liver is brownish; ox and pigs' liver are coarse textured and strong flavoured; calves' and lambs' livers are fine-textured and delicate-flavoured	Calf, pig and lamb – grill fry braise Ox – braise stew casserole
Tongue	Ox and calves' tongues are the largest; ox and lambs' tongues are the most widely available	Boil and press
Tripe	The stomach linings of ox: from the first stomach 'plain', from the second stomach called 'honeycomb' and from the third called 'thickseam'; tripe is purchased bleached and partly boiled	Stew Fry
Feet	Pigs' trotters are most widely available and are used mainly to make gelatine and brawn	Boil to make stock or brawn; pigs' trotters can be stuffed and roasted

cooked and chopped, carbohydrate filler and seasonings. Hamburgers are usually grilled or fried. The fat content is very similar to that of beef sausages.

Boneless joints
To make boneless joints, a mixture of good quality lean meat, salt and water is put into a tumbling machine. As a result of the agitation, the meat holds together when it is cooked, being bound by meat proteins in much the same way as an egg solidifies and binds mixtures together.

Meat extracts
Meat extracts, such as beef-flavoured cubes, are used to make stock or to add to the flavour of stock. The cube is usually dissolved in boiling water. These extracts are by-products of the meat-processing industry.

Gelatine
Gelatine, which is the setting agent in most jellies other than preserves, is derived from the connective tissue, collagen, by boiling or stewing. It is prepared commercially from bones, skins and hoofs of young animals. Grease and other impurities are removed and the resulting gelatine solution

is concentrated and dried. It is sold as powdered gelatine or in a less concentrated form as 'packet jellies' to which synthetic colouring and flavouring are added.

Guidelines for using gelatine

1 Use the envelopes of gelatine provided by some makers or measure it: 8 level 5-ml teaspoons or 2 level tablespoons to 15 g.

2 Add gelatine to cold or warm, not boiling, water or fruit juice and stir it while heating it. Use a bright metal spoon so that undissolved granules can be seen.

3 Never boil a gelatine solution as this makes it too concentrated and gives it the taste of glue, and may reduce its setting power.

4 If gelatine is to thicken a milky mixture it must be dissolved in 140 ml of warm water to each 30 g, and this solution must be added at once, while hot, to the rest of the ingredients. If it is allowed to cool first it forms 'ropes' in the mixture which it does not set.

11 Poultry and game

Poultry

Poultry is the name given to birds that are reared for their meat or eggs or both.

1 *Chickens* can be classified according to their age.
   (a) *The poussin* is a very young bird about 5 to 6 weeks old. It is a light-weight chicken weighing about 225 g.
   (b) *The spring chicken* is a little older than the poussin, usually 8 to 10 weeks old, and larger, weighing about 905 to 1130 g.
   (c) *The roasting chicken or broiler* is a bit older than a spring chicken – about 8 to 12 weeks old and weighing about 1100 to 1800 g.
   (d) *The boiling fowl* is very much older – 12 to 18 months – and usually weighs from about 1800 to 2700 g.
2 *Turkeys* are generally slaughtered at about 6 to 10 months. The average weight is about 5.5 to 6.5 kg.
3 *Ducks* are killed when they are about 12 to 16 weeks old and weigh from about 1800 to 2700 g. The Aylesbury duck is one of the most popular breeds.
4 *Geese* are killed at about 6 to 9 months old and weigh from about 3.5 to 6.5 kg.

Poultry production

There have been tremendous developments in the poultry industry since the 1950s when poultry was considered to be a luxury food. Today it is available at prices that are competitive with meat. Methods of production have become intensive, and cross-breeding has been widely practised. The various types of poultry are reared in batches.

1 *The battery hen* (p. 146) is bred mostly for egg production. When egg-laying capacity declines the bird is slaughtered and may be used for poultry products or sold as boiling fowl.
2 *Broiler chickens* (roasting chicken) are produced by the deep litter method (p. 146).

The slaughtering process (Fig. 11.1) is controlled by law.

Fig. 11.1
The main stages of slaughtering poultry

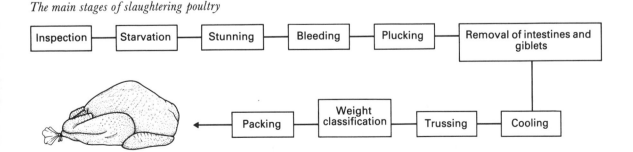

Structure of poultry

Poultry has the same basic structure as meat (p. 124). The amount of connective tissue is higher in well-exercised muscles and in older birds. The legs of poultry are not quite as soft in texture as the white meat from the breast, and a boiling fowl is not as tender as a very young chicken (poussin). Differences in colour of the flesh are related to the pigment *myoglobin*. White meat does not contain this pigment. Fat content also has a bearing on the colour of the flesh.

Nutrient content of poultry

Poultry is comparable with meat in nutrient composition. One major difference is the fat content (Table 11.1) and this depends on factors such as the type of bird, age and which parts are eaten.

Table 11.1
Fat profiles of raw poultry g/100 g:

Poultry	Fat Total	Fatty acids Saturated	Monounsaturated	Polyunsaturated
Chicken				
Dark meat	2.8	0.8	1.3	0.6
Light meat	1.1	0.3	0.5	0.2
Dark and light meat with skin	13.8	3.8	6.4	2.6
Turkey				
Dark meat	2.5	0.8	1.0	0.6
Light meat	0.8	0.3	0.3	0.2
Dark and light meat with skin	5.2	1.7	1.9	1.2
Duck				
Meat	6.5	2.0	3.2	1.0
Meat with skin	37.3	10.7	19.0	5.6

Consumer choice of poultry

1 The type of bird chosen will depend on the purpose for which it is intended.
2 Birds may be purchased in different forms:
  (a) *completely eviscerated*, that is, feathers and hair removed, drawn and trussed with the giblets wrapped inside the carcass (these birds may be fresh or frozen);
  (b) *rough plucked*, which means that most of the feathers have been removed (these birds are sold fresh);
  (c) *portioned*, for example, legs or breasts of chickens. These can be purchased fresh or frozen.
3 Check for freshness:
  (a) As with all meat the smell should not be unpleasant.
  (b) The colour of the skin should be white for chicken and turkey and creamy-white for duck and goose.
  (c) The skin should show no signs of bruising or cuts.
  (d) The flesh should be firm.
4 A high quality bird has meaty legs and a well-fleshed or plump breast.

Storing poultry

Fresh poultry should be stored with the giblets removed. The same principles apply to poultry as to meat (p. 130).

Frozen poultry is of particular concern. It should be defrosted thoroughly at refrigerator temperatures away from any thaw drip. This can be done by placing the bird on a rack over a tray or meat tin. As with fresh poultry the giblets should be removed. Frozen poultry should be cooked only when it is fully thawed. If frozen poultry is cooked before it has defrosted, salmonella food poisoning is likely because the internal temperature of the meat will not be high enough to destroy the micro-organisms.

Cooking poultry

The same principles apply to poultry as to meat. Recommended cooking methods are closely related to the age of the bird and the activity of the various parts. Poussin, spring and broiler chickens, duck, goose and turkey are all suitable for roasting. Joints such as breast or legs of chicken may be grilled or fried. Boiling fowl is best cooked by moist methods such as boiling, stewing and casseroling. All poultry may be casseroled. When cooking by moist methods it is important to remove the skin beforehand, because if left on it is not appetising.

Game

The word 'game' is used to describe any animal or bird that is shot for sporting purposes and is protected by game laws. Game can be divided into two main groups: *game birds* or feathered game and *furred game* (Table 11.2).

Structure of game

Game, with the exception of young game, tend to have tougher flesh than that of poultry, beef, sheep and pigs. Game birds and animals have to fend for themselves in the quest for survival and, as a result, the flesh of moving parts, especially the legs, tends to be tough. The amount of visible fat is less in game than poultry and meat (with the exception of birds in the duck family). This too is probably due to the active life style of these creatures.

Nutrient content of game

The nutritional value of game is similar to that of meat (p. 129). The major difference is the lower fat content. Many traditional game recipes include the use of streaky bacon, for example, or the practice of larding to prevent the meat from being dry. The lower fat content is highly desirable in the light of recent dietary recommendations.

Consumer choice of game

1 Game should only be sold by wholesalers or shops with a licence to sell it.
2 Check how long the bird or animal has been hung (Table 11.2). It might be necessary for hanging to continue after purchase.
3 Check that the game is fresh:
  (a) For feathered game, avoid if the smell is too high and follow the same guidelines as for poultry (p. 136).
  (b) For furred game the flesh should not smell too high. The flesh should feel firm and be free from bruising. For larger animals, such as deer, the same principles that apply to carcass meat should be followed (p. 130).
4 For quality in game birds and small animals look for 'meaty' legs and a plump breast. For large animals such as the deer, remember that the choicest parts are the leg and saddle. Buy game when it is young if tender meat is required for roasting. Ideally, purchase early in the season (Table 11.2). If older game is purchased it will require moist methods of cooking.

Cooking game

The same principles that apply to meat also apply to game. Suggested methods of cooking are given in Table 11.2.

Table 11.2
Game with reference to season, hanging and cooking

Game	Season	Recommended hanging time (days)	Suggested methods of cooking
Feathered game			
Grouse (red)	12 August to 10 December	Up to 7	Young – roast Older – braise, casserole
Pheasant	1 October to 1 February	Up to 7	As for grouse
Wild duck	12 August to 1 March	1–2	As for grouse
Furred game			
Hare	September to March	2–3	Whole or saddle – roast Legs–casserole, stew
Rabbit	September to April	2–3	As for hare
Venison	August to February	Up to 21	Leg or saddle – roast Shoulder – braise, stew Chops ⎫ Loin ⎪ Saddle ⎬ braise Neck cutlets ⎭

12 Fish

Fish includes sea or salt-water fish, fresh-water fish and shellfish. Fish used to be a relatively cheap food, but today it costs about the same as meat.

Classification of fish
(Table 12.1)

1 *Sea fish* can be classified according to their way of life:
   (a) *Demersal fish* live at the bottom of the sea. They are caught in nets dragged along the sea-bed by trawlers.
   (b) *Pelagic fish* swim freely near the surface, usually in shoals. They are caught in nets hung vertically from the surface of the sea by boats known as 'drifters'.
2 *Freshwater fish* are caught mostly for sport, and, with the exception of eels, salmon and trout, are not readily available to the consumer. Eels, sea trout and salmon spend part of their lives in fresh water and part in the sea.

Fish may be further classified according to their *shape* as *flat* or *round* fish and, according to their fat content, as fatty or white fish.
3 *Shellfish* are of two main kinds:
   (a) *crustacea*, which have legs and a partially jointed shell and include crabs, crayfish, lobsters, prawns and shrimps;
   (b) *molluscs*, which have a hard outer shell and no legs. These may be bivalves, which have a shell in two hinged parts such as oysters, mussels and scallops, or they may have a shell like a snail, such as cockles and winkles. Shellfish have no backbone.

Table 12.1
Fresh fish with reference to classification and consumer choice

Fish	Description	Season	Consumer choice
Fatty or oily fish *Round*			
Herring	Salt-water pelagic fish; small – up to 37.5 cm long; silver-blue, scaly skin; fine textured flesh; delicate flavour	All year; best June–March	Whole; fillets
Mackerel	Salt-water pelagic fish; bigger than herring – up to 40 cm long; the skin on the back has a geometric dark blue–green pattern; oily flesh; pronounced flavour	All year; best winter and spring	Whole; fillets

Fish	Description	Season	Consumer choice
Fatty or oily fish *Round (continued)*			
Pilchard	Salt-water pelagic fish; small – similar to herring – up to 35 cm long; black shading to silver white on the back	All year (in canned form)	Whole
Salmon	Salt water fish which goes up rivers to spawn; up to 90 cm long; silvery-coloured skin with patches of dark grey on the back; pinkish-red flesh; close texture; characteristic flavour	At its best June–July	Whole; steaks
Sardines	Salt-water pelagic fish; young of the pilchard family; up to 15 cm long	All year (in canned form)	Whole
Trout Rainbow trout	Reared on fish farms; up to 25 cm long; green-gold skin; whitish flesh	All year	Whole
Whitebait	Salt water pelagic fish; young of the herring or sprat; up to 5 cm long; silver skin, grey-white flesh	Best February–July	Whole
White fish *Round*			
Cod	Salt water demersal fish; up to 1½ m long; grey to olive-green skin with dark patches on its back; coarse-textured, white flesh; mild flavour	All year; best October–April	Whole; fillets; steaks
Coley or saithe	Salt-water demersal fish; up to 90 cm long; similar skin to cod but black colouring on its back; coarse flesh with greyish tinge	All year	Fillets
Haddock	Salt-water demersal fish; up to 90 cm long; silver skin with darkish grey back; characteristic mark called St Peter's thumbprint on the lateral line behind the head; finer texture than cod	All year; best November–February	Whole fillets

Fish	Description	Season	Consumer choice
White fish *Round (continued)*			
Hake	Salt-water demersal fish; up to 1 m 20 cm long; dark grey skin on the back and silver on the underside; white, flaky, tender flesh	Best June–January	Cutlets; fillets
Whiting	Salt-water demersal fish; up to 45 cm long; black skin, brownish-olive green, whitish yellow on underside; fine textured, flaky flesh	All year; best November–February	Whole fillets
Flat			
Halibut	Salt-water demersal fish; up to 2 m 10 cm long; brown skin, mottled on upper side; firm flesh, white and dry	Best August–April	Steaks
Plaice	Salt-water demersal fish; up to 75 cm long; upper side grey-brown with orange spots; underside creamy white; soft white flesh	All year; best January–April	Whole; fillets
Sole Dover sole Lemon sole	Dover and lemon sole: salt-water demersal fish; up to 45 cm long; skin of Dover sole is brownish with black markings, rough on the upper side and creamy white on the under-side; skin of lemon sole is yellowish brown with dark spots on the upper side and smooth with whitish underside; Dover sole: fine textured and delicate flavour; Lemon sole: coarser, not so well-flavoured	All year; Dover sole is best from May–February; Lemon sole is best from December–March	Whole; fillets
Shell fish *Crustaceans*			
Crab	Greyish-brown shell on live crab, brownish pink and dark cream coloured when cooked; average weight 900 g to 1 kg 360 g; 2 large claws and 8 feet contain white meat; brown flesh inside shell	All year; best May–October	A fresh crab feels heavy; avoid if there is any sound of water inside

Fish	Description	Season	Consumer choice
Shell fish *Crustaceans (continued)*			
Lobster	Blue-black shell when on live lobster, bright red when cooked; weighs up to 1 kg 360 g; elongated shell and 2 large claws contain flesh	All year; best April–August	Choose a lobster that feels heavy for its size; reject if the tail does not spring back when straightened; avoid a white shell as this is a sign of age
Prawn	Soft grey shell when raw, bright pink when cooked; up to 10 cm long	All year	Usually purchased boiled with or without its shell
Molluscs			
Cockles	Small and circular, about 2.5 cm in diameter; white and fluted shell	All year; best September–April	Usually purchased cooked and shelled
Mussels	Small and oval; up to 6.25 cm long; blue-black, smooth shell	September–March	Shells should be closed and not broken
Oysters	Roundish, up to 10 cm long; greenish-grey shell, ridges outside	September–April	Avoid if the shells are open

Structure of fish

Fig. 12.1
Fish muscle

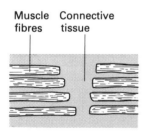

Muscle   Connective
fibres   tissue

Fish with backbones (vertebrate fish) have two types of muscle. Most of the edible part is made up of the lateral muscle. In some types of fish there is a second muscle which is superficial and fans outwards on both sides of the lateral line. The main muscle, the lateral muscle, is usually colourless, salmon being an exception. This particular fish is pink in colour due to a carotenoid pigment. The superficial muscle is dark red/brown and contains a high proportion of fat and myoglobin.

The structure of fish (Fig. 12.1) resembles that of meat. The muscles are made up of fibres and connective tissue. The proteins actin and myosin are found in the muscle fibres as in meat. However, unlike meat, the muscle fibres of fish are short, usually about 2.5 cm, and thick, compared to the thin and hair-like fibres characteristic of meat muscle. The short fibres of fish are found in parallel layers embedded at either end in connective tissue. There is much less connective tissue than in meat. The fat is found dispersed among the fibres.

The effect of cooking on fish

The main reasons for cooking fish are to bring about changes in texture, to develop flavour and to destroy micro-organisms. Tenderising is not an objective of cooking fish because the muscle fibres are not tough and there is not much connective tissue. During cooking, the collagen is converted to gelatine and the layers of muscle fibres separate and form flakes. Cooking alters the appearance, with the flesh losing its translucency. If over-cooked, the fish shrinks and becomes tough and dry. The proteins of fish coagulate at temperatures from 60°C to 70°C. During cooking the flavour develops, and as with meat, this is due to the extractives.

Nutrient content of fish

Protein accounts for about 15–20% of the weight of fish and this is of high biological value. *Fat* is present in significant amounts in fatty fish. The fish in this group are useful sources of the physiologically important long-chain n-3 (omega-3) polyunsaturated fatty acids. Fatty acid profiles g/100 g of raw whole fish, are as follows:

Fish	Eicosapentaenoic acid	Docosahexaenoic acid
Herring	0.8	1.0
Mackerel	0.7	1.1
Salmon	0.5	1.3

Calcium is found in fish in variable amounts. The highest calcium providers are those in which the bones are eaten, such as sardines, whitebait and canned salmon. *Iron* is present in fish in variable amounts. Molluscs are particularly rich in iron. *Zinc* is present in fish in useful quantities. Molluscs, and oysters in particular, are rich sources of zinc. *Sodium*, *potassium* and *phosphorus* are plentiful in fish. *Iodine* is found in sea- and saltwater fish in significant amounts.

Retinol is found in fatty fish and some molluscs in useful amounts. *Vitamin D* is found in significant amounts in fatty fish. Herrings are very high in vitamin D, providing 19.0 µg/100 g. Canned pilchards and sardines in tomato sauce provide 14.0 and 8.0 µg/100 g respectively. *Vitamin E* is found in fish in variable amounts. Levels are particularly high in fatty fish. Sardines and pilchards canned in tomato sauce and tuna canned in oil contain 3.08, 2.56 and 1.94 mg/100 g respectively. *B-vitamins* are found in fish in variable amounts. Some fish are rich in niacin. Mackerel, salmon and red snapper contain 8.6, 7.2 and 6.3 mg/per 100 g respectively.

Consumer choice of fish

1 Fish, such as salmon, Dover sole, crabs and lobsters, tend to be more highly priced than herrings and mackerel.
2 Fish may be purchased whole, in fillets, cutlets or steaks (Fig. 12.2). As with boning meat, filleting is best done by the expert, the fishmonger.

Fig. 12.2
Cuts of fish

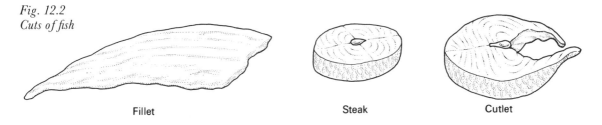

Fillet   Steak   Cutlet

3 Check for freshness:
   (a) There is no unpleasant odour around fresh fish.
   (b) The skin of really fresh fish is bright in appearance and glistening; it is moist and has a transparent outer slime and the scales are plentiful.
   (c) The gills of fresh fish are brightly coloured and the eyes are bright, moist and not sunken.

(d) The flesh of fresh fish is firm and elastic. This can be tested by pressing the surface of the fish with the finger. If fresh, the indentation quickly disappears.

Storing fish

Fresh fish is perishable. Cook on the day of purchase. Fresh fish does not keep well; during the 24 hours' maximum period of storage it may be kept in a cool place with loose greaseproof paper wrapping. In the refrigerator it can be placed in the chilling tray.

Methods of cooking fish

The aim in cooking fish is to conserve and to add to its natural flavour and to prevent the flakes from falling apart.

Frying

Despite dietary goals, this is a popular method of cooking fish. The fish is coated with egg and crumbs or batter and fried in shallow or deep fat. The coating keeps in the juice of the fish and becomes crisp and savoury during cooking. Filleted flat fish can be coated with dry flour and herring with oatmeal before frying in shallow fat.

Grilling

This is another method of cooking to conserve the flavour of fish. It is suitable for whole, flat fish, herring or mackerel and cutlets not more than 25 mm thick. The flesh of whole fish is scored with a sharp knife, the outer surfaces are painted with liquid fat and dredged lightly with flour. The grill should be moderately hot and the fish turned only once to keep it from breaking.

Baking

This is an alternative to frying, and one that is just as savoury. Extra flavours may be added in a savoury stuffing.

Moist methods of cooking

Fish should not be boiled because much flavour is lost and the flakes easily separate.

1 *Poaching*   To poach fish, cook it in very little liquid adding salt if desired, lemon juice or vinegar, onion and herbs for flavour. Simmer gently and from time to time baste the fish. The cooking may be done in a slow oven and the liquid may be used in a sauce.
2 *Steaming*   A perforated steamer is not suitable unless the fish is wrapped in aluminium foil, as juices are lost into the water below. To steam fish, put it on a lightly greased plate, cover and cook over boiling water.

Preserved fish

Smoked fish

Fish is smoked to give it a characteristic flavour.

1 *Herrings* may be smoked to produce kippers, bloaters, buckling and red herrings.
2 *Haddock* may be smoked to produce finnan haddock, smokies and smoked haddock fillets.
3 *Cod* may be smoked to produce smoked cod fillets.
4 *Salmon* may be smoked to produce smoked salmon.

Canned fish

Canned fish is popular despite the fact that the high temperatures of the canning process affect both the texture and flavour of the fish. Examples are salmon, tuna, sardines, pilchards, mackerel, herring, kippers, crab and prawns. Fish may be canned in brine, oil or sauces such as tomato. Canned fish provide useful amounts of calcium because the canning process softens the fish bones, enabling the consumer to eat them. Canned oily fish are useful sources of vitamins A and D.

Frozen fish
Most of the fish consumed in Britain has been frozen. Quick freezing of fish is usually carried out immediately after it leaves the nets. This fish is often in better condition than fresh fish that has had a long journey from the coast.

Fish products

Fish fingers
Frozen blocks of white fish fillets or minced fish are cut. The fingers are then dipped into batter, breadcrumbed and re-frozen. The energy value is increased as a result of this processing. A raw frozen cod steak contains less than 1% fat. A raw fish finger contains almost 8% fat and even more, 13% if it is later fried.

Fish cakes
Minced fish is mixed with a potato purée and seasonings. Fish cakes are then shaped, coated with batter, breadcrumbed and frozen. The energy value is not as high as fish fingers because the fat content is much lower. The fat content is, however, increased substantially from less than 1% to just over 10% if they are fried.

13 Eggs

Most of the eggs eaten in Britain are hens' eggs.

Egg production

The production of eggs has grown into a thriving industry. Free-range eggs are produced by hens which have space to move about. The diet of the free-range hen is not controlled like that of the battery or litter hen. The birds are fed on grains but they can also search for other food on the ground. Hens kept in batteries or deep litter cannot move about in the open. They are kept under cover in artificial light, at a constant temperature and are fed and watered. Battery hens are kept in cages, and deep litter hens are kept in large buildings which have floors covered with sawdust or wood shavings.

Grades and sizes of eggs

According to EC legislation, shell eggs for consumers must be Grade 'A'. This means that they have the following qualities:

- naturally clean and fresh;
- internally perfect with shells intact;
- air-space not exceeding 6 mm in depth;
- yolk that does not move away from the centre of the egg on rotation.

Commission Regulation EC No. 1511/96 of 29 July 1996 gives new weight bands and an extra large category (Table 13.1).

Table 13.1
Sizes of eggs

Description	Letters	Weight (g)
Very large	XL	73 and over
Large	L	63–73
Medium	M	53–63
Small	S	under 53

Other grades of eggs are *B/C* and these are broken out of their shells and used as liquid whole egg, yolk or white after being pasteurised. These eggs are used by food and other manufacturers. A final group of eggs is described as *Industrial* and these are designated for non-food uses, such as shampoo and soap.

Structure and composition of eggs

Eggs are made up of 3 main parts: shell, white and yolk (Fig. 13.1).

1 *Shell* About 11% of the egg is shell. This is made up primarily of *phosphate* and *calcium carbonate*. The shell is porous, and odours and

bacteria can enter through it to the egg white and yolk. The shell may be white or brown, depending on the breed of the hen, and, to some extent, the type of feed. The colour does not relate to the quality of the egg. Just inside the shell of the egg are 2 membranes. These are made up of proteins called keratin and mucin. One of the membranes is closely associated with the shell; the other with the liquid content of the egg. As an egg gets older the contents shrink and the 2 membranes separate, forming an air space at one end of the egg.

2 *Egg white*   The egg white or albumen forms about 58% of the egg. It is found in 3 layers, 2 of which are thin and watery and the remaining 1 thick and viscous. The thin white is found immediately around the yolk and as an outer layer to the thick white near the inner shell membrane. The thick white lies between the layers of thin white. The ratios of thick and thin white are related to the storage conditions of the egg (p. 149). The main components of egg white are water and protein. Most of the protein is ovalbumin, conalbumin and ovomucoid.

3 *Egg yolk*   The yolk forms about 31% of the egg. This is separated from the egg white by the vitelline membrane also known as the 'yolk sac'. The yolk is held in position by the chalaza. These rope-like structures keep the yolk in the centre of the egg. The yolk is made up of a small area of white yolk which is surrounded by yellow yolk. The germ (embryo) is positioned at the surface of the yolk and is attached to the white yolk. The higher the carotenoid intake, the more yellow the yolk. The colour of the yolk is not an indication of quality. The main components of egg yolk are water, fat and protein. Vitellin is the main protein.

Fig. 13.1
Structure of a hen's egg

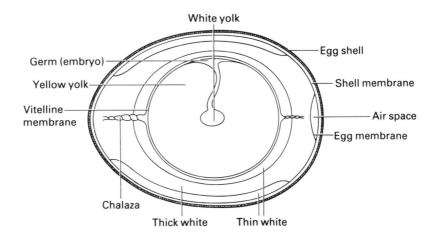

Nutrient content of eggs

Protein is present in the yolk (16.5 g/100 g) and in the white (9 g/100 g) and it is of high biological value. *Fat* is present in the yolk (30.5 g/100 g) and the profile, per 100 g, is as follows:

| Fatty acids (g) | | | Cholesterol (mg) |
Saturated	Monounsaturated	Polyunsaturated	
8.7	13.2	3.4	1120

Calcium and *phosphorus* are present in the yolk in useful amounts (130 mg and 500 mg/100 g respectively). *Iron* is concentrated in the yolk (6.1 mg/100 g), but difficulties in absorption occur due to the binding of this mineral with the protein conalbumin. *Zinc* is present in the yolk in useful amounts (3.9 mg/100 g).

Retinol is found in the yolk in significant quantities (535 µg/100 g). *Vitamin D* is found in the yolk, which is a particularly rich source of this nutrient (4.94 µg/100 g). *Vitamin E* is found in the yolk in significant amounts (3.11 mg/100 g). *B-vitamins* are present in eggs. Riboflavin is found in egg yolk and white in useful quantities and thiamin and vitamin B_{12} are concentrated in the yolk.

Fig. 13.2
Characteristics of fresh and stale eggs

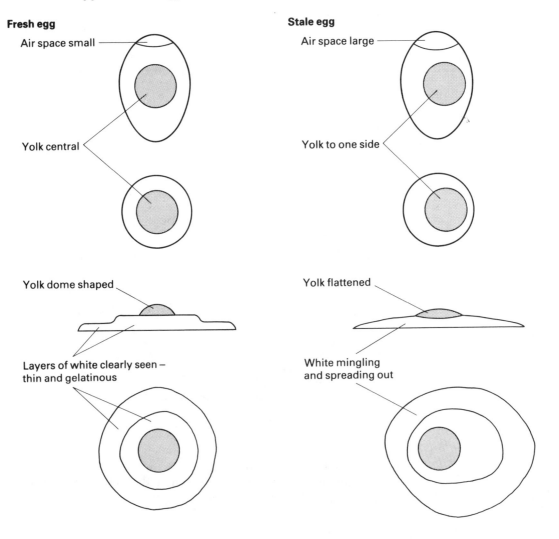

Fresh egg

Air space small

Yolk central

Yolk dome shaped

Layers of white clearly seen – thin and gelatinous

Stale egg

Air space large

Yolk to one side

Yolk flattened

White mingling and spreading out

Consumer choice of eggs

1 Hens' eggs are more widely available than other eggs.
2 Free range eggs usually cost more than mass produced eggs.
3 The consumer can choose different sizes of eggs (Table 13.1).
4 It is advisable to purchase eggs where there is a fast turnover.
5 Check that the eggs are not broken or cracked.

Storing eggs

Store eggs with their blunt end – that is, the one with the air space – facing upwards. The most desirable temperature range is between 7°C and 13°C. The egg rack in a refrigerator is a suitable storage place. Stored in these conditions the eggs can be kept for about a month. Under warmer conditions eggs deteriorate more quickly. When storing eggs keep them away from strong-smelling foods.

   Use eggs as fresh as possible because as they get older certain changes take place (Fig. 13.2) which affect their performance in food preparation.

1 Water is lost by evaporation and this is replaced by air through the shell. As a result, the air space gets bigger.
2 Water from the white of the egg passes to the yolk. This causes the yolk to get bigger, which has a weakening effect on the yolk sac or vitelline membrane and makes the yolk flatten.
3 The egg white becomes thin so that, when the egg is broken, the white spreads out. There are several theories as to why this happens, all associated with the enzyme lysozyme.
4 The egg white may turn yellow and become cloudy.
5 The yolk loses its central position because the thin white cannot keep the yolk centrally in the egg.
6 There is a loss of carbon dioxide from the egg through the shell during storage. As a result of this the pH of the egg increases – that is, it becomes more alkaline.
7 During storage bacteria may cause spoilage. These can enter the egg through the porous shell. Proteins in the egg are broken down by bacterial action and this gives rise to hydrogen sulphide.

   To test for freshness, place the egg in a bowl of water. If the egg lies on its side it is fresh; if it stands with the blunt end facing the surface of the liquid it is less fresh, and if the egg floats it is stale and should not be used.

Functions of eggs in food preparation

The functions of eggs in food preparation can be classified according to different properties of the egg. The 3 functional properties of relevance to food preparation are: coagulation, emulsification and foaming.

Coagulation

The proteins of egg coagulate during cooking (Fig.13.3). The egg-white proteins coagulate at temperatures ranging between 60°C and 65°C. This is associated with a loss of translucency; the white becomes opaque and it no longer flows. When the egg white has reached 70°C it is firm. The egg-yolk proteins coagulate at a slightly higher temperature than egg-white proteins. Coagulation begins at 65°C and the flow properties are lost at 70°C.

   In the preparation of egg dishes it is important to avoid overcooking. If overcooked, the proteins squeeze together leaving little room for the pockets of water. Whole egg dishes such as boiled, poached and fried eggs become rubbery and egg dishes with added liquid, such as scrambled egg and egg custard, separate to produce lumps of protein and a watery liquid. This is known as syneresis.

Fig. 13.3
Coagulation of egg proteins

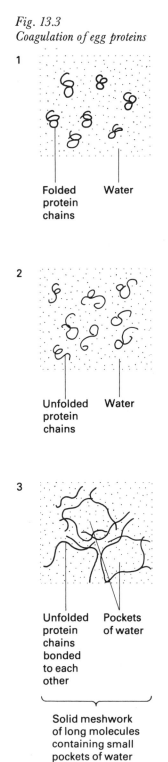

1

Folded
protein
chains   Water

2

Unfolded
protein
chains   Water

3

Unfolded   Pockets
protein   of water
chains
bonded
to each
other

Solid meshwork
of long molecules
containing small
pockets of water

- *Boiled eggs* are put in a pan of water and simmered 'until done'. If the egg is superficially cracked, the addition of salt or vinegar to the water will reduce the risk of the egg white's leaking from the shell into the water. The addition of these substances speeds up coagulation. Soft-boiled eggs have whites that are soft and jelly-like and yolks in the form of a thick liquid. They take from 3 to 5 minutes to cook. Hard-boiled eggs take longer to cook. The white becomes firmer and opaque and the yolk becomes paler and has a mealy consistency. If over-cooked, the egg develops a rubbery texture. If a hard-boiled egg is not really fresh it will have a large air space and the yolk will be to one side (Fig. 13.2). Undesirable colour changes can take place when an egg is boiled. These colour changes are associated with the prolonged application of heat and alkalinity. The egg white begins to brown due to a reaction between glucose and amine groups of proteins found in the egg white. This reaction is noticeable in Scotch eggs that have been baked in the oven and in Russian fish pie where boiled eggs are baked inside the pie. The egg yolk may develop a surface layer of greenish grey. This is due to the formation of iron sulphide from the iron in the yolk and hydrogen sulphide which comes from the proteins containing sulphur. To avoid these colour changes, use fresh eggs, boil for the shortest time possible, serve at once or cool them in cold water.
- *Poached eggs* are made by cracking the egg open and putting it into boiling water. The egg is left until the white becomes jelly-like and the yolk semi-liquid with a thick covering of white. Over-cooking results in a rubbery egg. If the egg is not fresh and there is a high proportion of thin white, the poached egg will look ragged in appearance. Salt or vinegar is usually added to the cooking water to speed up coagulation. An alternative method is to use an egg poacher: the egg is kept in shape by the special compartment it is cooked in.
- *Fried eggs* are prepared by cracking the egg and emptying the contents into a pre-heated frying-pan with just enough fat to allow basting. The fat should be about 137°C. If the temperature is lower, the egg spreads; if higher, it will become over-cooked and cause spluttering. Fresh eggs are essential; a thin watery white spreads, gives the egg a ragged appearance and the yolk is more readily broken. To reduce fat intake use a small amount of fat or a non-stick pan with a lid, and allow the egg to set in the steam.
- *Scrambled eggs* are prepared by blending the egg white and yolk together. Milk may be added with seasoning and the mixture is put into a pre-heated pan containing a little fat. The mixture is cooked slowly and stirred thoroughly throughout the cooking process. If overcooked this mixture becomes a curd-like mass surrounded by a watery liquid. Scrambled eggs cooked properly are fluffy, soft and moist.
- *Omelet* contains ingredients similar to scrambled egg. An omelet mixture is fried and, as the mixture sets, it is lifted to allow uncooked mixture to come in contact with the pan. The texture should be soft and flexible. Over-cooking creates a rubbery product.
- *Egg custards* are made from egg, milk, sugar, salt and vanilla flavouring. They may be cooked by either stirring in a pan over a source of heat or by baking. The characteristic thickening that occurs when a stirred or baked custard is cooked is due mainly to the coagulation of egg protein. About 50 g of egg (that is, a grade 5 egg) will be enough to thicken 250 ml of milk. Milk proteins provide less than 1% of the coagulable protein. Baked custards are susceptible to curdling. This happens if the heat treatment is severe. The recommended temperature for cooking is 177°C.

Place the dish containing the custard in a water bath – a *bain marie*. Use a roasting tin filled with enough hot water to protect the custard from the direct heat of the oven. If this precaution is not taken, the custard is likely to have a porous texture and release a watery liquid when cut. This is called 'syneresis' and can be compared with water being squeezed out of a wet sponge. Baked custards should be firm but tender, smooth and free of porosity. To test if a baked custard is cooked, insert a knife into the centre of the custard. The custard is cooked if the knife comes out clean. The rapid application of a high temperature to a stirred custard also results in curdling – that is, a custard that has flecks of rubbery protein and a runny liquid that cannot coat the back of a spoon. This can be avoided by cooking the egg custard in a double boiler with a cold water start. The custard thickens at 82°C. The mixture should not reach 87°C if curdling is to be avoided. A stirred custard is done when it can coat a spoon with a thick velvety coating. If curdling occurs, the custard may be improved by pouring the mixture into a cold dish and beating it. Whether the custard is baked or stirred, scalding the milk (heating to 85°C) is desirable because this shortens the cooking time and is believed to improve the flavour and texture of the finished product.

Stirred custard can be used as a sauce or cold in trifle. Baked custards are dishes in their own right. Dishes such as bread and butter pudding and cheese flan with egg and milk in their recipes also depend on the coagulation of egg protein to form a smooth, tender, non-porous gel.

The following are other functions associated with coagulation.

1 *Supplementary thickening* Eggs may be used as a supplementary thickening agent – for example, in the lemon base of a lemon meringue pie, or to thicken sauces such as hollandaise sauce.
2 *Binding* Eggs are useful binding agents in burgers, rissoles, fish cakes and potato croquettes.
3 *Coating* A surface coating of egg coagulates. This helps to prevent the food within from disintegrating and from absorbing excessive amounts of fat during frying. Foods coated with egg are usually also coated with some kind of cereal such as breadcrumbs – for example, Scotch eggs, fillets of fish and potato croquettes.
4 *Glazing* Whole egg, egg yolk or white may be used to glaze foods to give an attractive finish to the dish. For example, whole egg or egg yolk is used to glaze the pastry tops of savoury pies, and egg white is used to glaze Eccles cakes.
5 *Garnish* Slices of hard-boiled eggs can be served with kedgeree. Egg white and yolk from a boiled egg can be separated and passed through a sieve, or better still, through a food processor, and used to garnish foods such as veal escallopes or dressed crab.

Emulsification
Egg yolk contains *lecithin* which is an emulsifying agent. The emulsifying properties of egg yolk are used in the preparation of cakes and mayonnaise. If vinegar and oil are shaken up together and left to stand, the liquids separate, with the oil forming the top layer and the vinegar the bottom layer. Such liquids are immiscible. If an emulsifying agent such as egg yolk is used, the 2 liquids are held together as an emulsion. Mayonnaise is an emulsion of oil in vinegar. The oil is suspended in minute droplets in the vinegar, and this mixture is stable because of the lecithin from the egg yolk.

Emulsifying agents have one part of the molecule which attracts water (hydrophilic) and another part which does not (hydrophobic). In an emulsion of this kind the molecules of lecithin surround the oil droplets with the hydrophilic part of the molecule in the vinegar and the hydrophobic part in the oil droplets (Fig. 13.4).

Fig. 13.4
Action of lecithin as an emulsifying agent in the preparation of mayonnaise

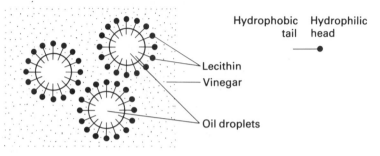

Foaming
When egg white is whisked, bubbles of air are incorporated into it forming an egg white foam (Fig. 13.5). Examples of foods which rely on this property of eggs are meringues, soufflés and soufflé omelets. When egg whites are beaten they become foamy. During the early stages of beating, the bubbles of air are large and tend to coalesce or join together. If beating is stopped the egg white drains away from the air bubbles. As beating continues the air bubbles become smaller and the liquid egg white forms a thin film around each bubble. If beating is continued the foam becomes thicker, with smaller air bubbles, and whiter, eventually forming soft rounded peaks. As beating progresses the peaks become stiff and pointed. Cooking brings about coagulation of the foam which makes it permanent. Below are some critical factors in the preparation of egg white foams.

Fig. 13.5
Formation of egg white foam

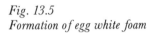

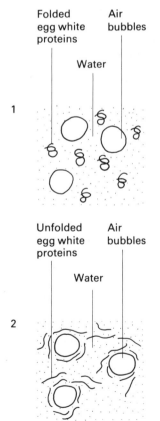

1   The bowl should be large enough to allow the egg white to increase in volume as a result of beating.
2   Beaters with either fine wire or thin blades produce smaller air bubbles, and consequently the result is a finer foam.
3   The eggs should be fresh. If the white has become alkaline, the foam is less stable and tends to leak.
4   The eggs should be stored at room temperature, 21°C. Cold egg whites do not whisk so easily because of the greater viscosity.
5   The egg white should be free of any traces of fat. This means using clean utensils and avoiding mixing yolk with the white. Fat interferes with the formation of the foam and reduces the volume.
6   If agents are added to stabilise the foam, such as salt, lemon juice or cream of tartar, these should be added after the 'foamy' stage has been achieved to avoid interfering with the formation of the foam.
7   If sugar is added before the foam is prepared it is necessary to beat for longer, but this type of foam is more stable.
8   The eggs should be beaten adequately to the desired stage. If under-beaten, an egg-white foam has large air spaces which coalesce and the foam leaks. If over-beaten, the air spaces also coalesce and leakage occurs.
9   Use the foam as soon as it is ready. If left to stand it tends to stiffen.

Whole egg can be used to produce a foam – for example, in making a sponge cake (p. 82).

14 Milk

The natural food for young mammals is milk. It has been described as a 'near perfect food'. In Britain milk is obtained mainly from dairy cows.

Milk production

Friesians are noted for their high milk yield, and Guernseys and Jerseys produce milk with a high butterfat content. About 3860 litres of milk are produced by a cow during lactation – that is, the period of time after a cow has calved. A farmer gets a licence to sell milk when the herd has been tested and certified as being free from *tuberculosis*.

Milking cows

Cows are milked twice a day, early in the morning and again in the late afternoon. Because milk is an ideal medium for the growth of micro-organisms, it is essential that strict attention to hygiene is applied.

1 *Milking house and equipment* The milking house must be light and airy, have a plentiful supply of water, be efficiently drained and have surfaces which are easy to clean. The floor must be cleaned daily.
2 *Dairy workers' cleanliness* The dairy worker should be clean, wear a washable overall and headcover, and refrain from smoking in the milking house. Any exposed part of the skin – for example, a cut or abrasion – should be covered with a waterproof dressing.
3 *Cows' cleanliness* The cows must be kept clean. Long hairs on various parts of the cow's body should be clipped, and the udders and teats should be washed and dried before milking.

Fig. 14.1
Milk being collected from a cow in the closed system

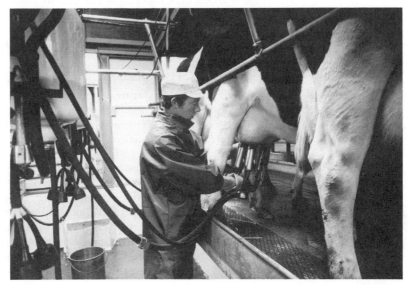

4 *Milking machines*   If the cow is in good health, the udder is washed and dried and the milk is collected into a closed bucket or pipelines to a refrigerated bulk vat (Fig. 14.1). Most farmers record the amount of milk produced by each cow. Samples are taken regularly and tested for butterfat and sometimes protein.

Transport
The milk is collected by insulated tanker. The tanker driver has to check that the milk is not dirty, that it has a sweet smell and that it is at the desired temperature. If the driver is not satisfied, arrangements are made for a separate collection. One tanker may collect milk from several farms. The milk is taken to the dairy or creamery. When the milk has been unloaded the tanker is thoroughly cleaned and sterilised.

Testing the milk

Bar-code labels are used by the different farms, and samples of milk are analysed at central testing laboratories. The milk is tested for composition, hygiene and antibiotics. The results of these tests determine whether the milk will be used and what price will be paid to the farmer.

At the dairy or creamery a milk sample from the tanker is analysed. These tests determine whether the milk is used as milk or for milk products. Tests include measuring for non-fat solids (mainly protein and lactose) and butterfat content.

Heat treatment

Most of the milk sold in the UK is heat treated. Approximately 5% of the milk is left untreated and it can only be sold under special licence. There are 3 main methods of heat treatment: pasteurisation, sterilisation and ultra-heat treatment.

Pasteurisation
About 86% of the heat-treated milk is pasteurised. The usual method is the High Temperature Short Time (HTST) method, where the milk is heated for 15 seconds to a temperature of 71°C. The Holder method is less common. This takes longer because the milk is heated for 30 minutes to a temperature of 63°C to 65°C. After the milk has been heated it is cooled rapidly to below 10°C. The milk is then bottled.

Pasteurised milk differs from untreated milk in nutritional value. Up to about 10% of the thiamin and vitamin B_{12} is lost and 25% of the vitamin C may be lost. The flavour and appearance of pasteurised milk is not spoilt by the heat treatment, and it will keep for up to 5 days if it is kept cool.

Sterilisation
This is a method of heat treatment applied to milk in sealed bottles. Using the batch process, the bottles of milk are heated to a temperature of 104°C to 113°C in autoclaves for 15 to 40 minutes. The bottles are then left to cool naturally. Using the continuous process the bottles of milk pass through hot-water tanks on a conveyor belt and then go on to a steam chamber under pressure at 107°C to 113°C, also for 15 to 40 minutes. The bottles are then passed into water cooling tanks.

Sterilised milk has lost about one-third of the thiamin and half of the vitamin B_{12}, folic acid and vitamin C. The flavour and appearance are affected by the high temperatures of sterilisation: some of the milk sugar (lactose) caramelises, and this gives sterilised milk a cooked taste and a creamy appearance. Sterilisation destroys micro-organisms more completely than pasteurisation. Sterilised milk will keep for several weeks (as long as it is not opened) without refrigeration.

Ultra-heat treatment (UHT)
The milk is heated for 1 second to a temperature of not less than 132.2°C
and is packaged under aseptic conditions. It is similar to pasteurised milk
in nutritional value and the heat is so quick that the colour and
flavour changes are not so obvious as in sterilised milk. This type of milk
has a long storage life. It can be kept unrefrigerated for about 6 months (as
long as it is not opened).

Homogenisation

The term 'homogenisation' means 'to make uniform'. When milk is
homogenised the composition of the milk is uniform. The fat becomes
dispersed evenly throughout the milk (Fig. 14.2). The process of
homogenisation causes the fat globules to break down to a uniform size
because the milk is forced through tiny holes under pressure. Homogenised
milk does not separate to form a cream layer.

Fig. 14.2
Effect of homogenisation on the size of fat globules

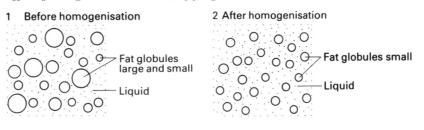

Composition of milk

Milk is an emulsion: that is, minute droplets of fats are suspended in a
watery solution which contains proteins, lactose (milk sugar), vitamins and
minerals. The main proteins in milk are caseinogen, lactalbumin and
lactoglobulin. The last 2 proteins are the whey proteins.
  Milk may be bluish white or a golden colour. The yellowness is due to
the pigment carotene.

Nutrient content of milk

Protein constitutes just over 3% of the weight of milk and it is of high
biological value. *Fat* in milk is dependent on the type of milk. Whole, semi-
skimmed and skimmed milk are 3.9, 1.6 and 0.1% fat respectively.
  Carbohydrate is present in milk in the form of lactose and this constitutes
about 5% of the weight of milk.
  Calcium is found in milk in useful amounts – approximately 120 mg/
100 g. *Potassium* and *phosphorus* are present in milk in useful quantities.
  Retinol, carotene and *vitamin D* are present. The profiles of these vitamins
µg/100 g of milk are as follows:

Milk	Retinol	Carotene	Vitamin D
Whole	52	21	0.03
Semi-skimmed	21	9	0.01
Skimmed	1	Trace	Trace

Note. The lower the fat content, the lower the amount of these fat-soluble
vitamins in the milk.
  B-vitamins are present in milk and it is considered a particularly useful
source of riboflavin.

Table 14.1
Different types of milk

Milk	Colour of bottle top	Heat treatment	Homogenised (no cream layer) (√)
Heat treated			
Ordinary	Silver	Pasteurisation	
Channel Islands and S. Devon	Gold	Pasteurisation	
Semi-skimmed	Red with silver stripe	Pasteurisation	√
Skimmed	Blue with silver check	Pasteurisation	√
Homogenised	Red	Pasteurisation	√
Sterilised	Blue	Sterilised	√
Ultra-heat treatment (UHT)	Pink	Ultra-heat treatment	√
Untreated			
Ordinary	Green	None	
Channel Islands and S. Devon	Green with gold stripe	None	

Consumer choice of milk

Milk varies according to the heat treatment, whether or not it has been homogenised and the fat content (Table 14.1).

Storing milk

Collect milk from the doorstep as quickly as possible. If no refrigerator is available it should be kept cool by leaving it in a current of cold air rather than in a non-ventilated cupboard. For storage, the floor is cooler than a raised surface. One way of keeping milk cool is to put the bottle into a basin which is half filled with cold water, and then to place a piece of muslin saturated with cold water over the top, ensuring that the muslin rests in the cold water. The water should be changed at regular intervals to keep it cool. Milk should be kept covered to protect it from being contaminated by dust and flies. In a refrigerator milk should also be covered and kept away from strong-smelling foods: it has a bland flavour and readily absorbs the flavours of such foods.

Guidelines for keeping milk fresh

1 Keep milk from different deliveries separately.

2 If a jug is used to store milk the jug should be rinsed after use, then washed, scalded in boiling water and drained.

3 Milk keeps better if it is kept in its original container. These containers are sterile when the milk is put into them.

Fat content* %	Flavour	Keeping qualities
3	Creamy; 'typical' of milk not spoilt by heat treatment	Up to 5 days if kept cool
4	As above but richer	As above
1.5 to 1.8	Similar to silver top but not as creamy	As above
Less than 0.3	Like silver top but not creamy	As above
3	Smooth and creamy	As above
3	'Cooked' taste and creamy	Several weeks without refrigeration
3	Similar to silver top but 'distinctive' taste	Up to 6 months without refrigeration
3	Very like silver top	Up to 2 days in a refrigerator
4	Similar to gold top	Up to 2 days in a refrigerator

* Legal minimum

Milk in food preparation

Milk has many uses in food preparation:

- *drinks*, in hot chocolate, milky coffee and milk shake;
- *soups*, in cream of chicken and tomato soup;
- *sauces*, in parsley sauce, bread sauce and custard;
- *batters*, in pancakes and Yorkshire pudding;
- *egg custard-type mixtures*, in quiche Lorraine and bread and butter pudding;
- *milk puddings*, in rice pudding and milk jelly;
- *baked goods*, in bread, scones and cakes;
- *glaze*, for brushing over the surface of scones to give a smooth, shiny surface.

Overcoming some problems when using milk

Milk scorching at the bottom of the pan
When milk is heated, the proteins lactalbumin and lactoglobulin and some of the calcium phosphate are precipitated. This precipitate falls to the bottom of the pan where it settles. As heating continues, the precipitate scorches because it is in contact with the heat source. This problem can be overcome if a thick-bottomed pan is used over a moderate heat, or if the milk is heated in a double boiler.

Skin on boiled milk
When milk is heated in an open pan a skin develops on the surface. This happens because water is evaporated from the surface and the protein

casein is concentrated, along with some milk fat and calcium salts. Steam produced from the water in milk forms under the skin and this causes the milk to boil over. This problem may be overcome by removing the skin as it forms, although this will result in appreciable losses of milk solids. An alternative method is to agitate the milk during cooking by 'whisking'. This causes a foam to form on the surface and prevents skin formation. Skin may form on milky drinks, such as cocoa and coffee, even after cooking has ceased. For this reason, toppings of foams such as whipped cream may be used.

Curdling of milk during cooking
Milk has a tendency to curdle when mixed with acid ingredients. A typical example is in the preparation of cream of tomato soup. The curdling tends to happen after the milk has been added to the tomato mixture. There are several ways of tackling this problem. One method is to add the tomato mixture to the milk, rather than the milk to the tomato mixture. Another tip is to ensure that both the milk and tomato mixture are hot when mixed together. It also helps if some kind of thickener is added to either the tomato mixture or milk before these foods are mixed together.

Other types of milk

Frozen milk
To prepare milk for freezing it is pasteurised and homogenised. The milk is poured into polythene bags and frozen rapidly in a bath of brine. Milk processed in this way will keep in a freezer for about a year.

Concentrated milks
1 *Condensed milk* can be made from whole, semi-skimmed or skimmed milk. It is homogenised and heated. Sugar is added at this stage. The milk is passed into an evaporator and boiled under vacuum. The milk is concentrated to approximately $2\frac{1}{2}$ times that of the original milk, and it is then drawn off, cooled and sealed under aseptic conditions into tins or barrels.

   Condensed milk has all the nutrients found in liquid milk but in concentrated form. The carbohydrate content is higher because of the added sugar. Skimmed varieties of condensed milk have lost fat and also vitamins A and D, which are fat soluble. Condensed milk is easily identified by its 'sugary' taste.

   The storage life of the unopened can is 'indefinite'. The sugar content has a preservative effect. Once the can is opened it should be treated as fresh milk.
2 *Evaporated milk* has been processed in a similar way to condensed milk. There are, however, several differences. Evaporated milk does not have added sugar; it is sterilised in the can and it is concentrated to about twice the density of the original milk.

   Evaporated milk has lost about 60% of its vitamin C and 40% of the thiamin. Other nutrients are concentrated due to the loss of moisture. Evaporated milk has a pronounced flavour and distinctive tan colour. This is due to the reaction between lactose and proteins that takes place when the milk is sterilised in the can. This type of milk does not have a cream layer because of the homogenisation process. Evaporated milk has a long storage life. It will keep indefinitely if the can is not opened. Once the can is opened, it should be treated as fresh milk.
3 *Dried or powdered milk* can be made from whole or skimmed milk. Before the drying process, the milk is pasteurised, homogenised, heat treated and, usually, pre-concentrated in a vacuum. There are 2 main methods for drying milk.

(a) *Roller drying*   The milk is spread on hot, revolving rollers. The water evaporates rapidly and a thin film of powder is left on the rollers. This is scraped automatically by a blade which is fixed to the roller. The film of milk is cooled rapidly, then ground into a powder and sifted. It is then packed into airtight containers. Dried milk prepared in this way does not have a great deal of consumer appeal because the resulting milk has a 'cooked' taste and the powder tends to clump when mixed with water.

(b) *Spray drying*   The milk is sprayed into a hot-air chamber. The water is rapidly lost from the droplets of milk by evaporation and the remains drop to the floor of the chamber in the form of a fine powder. The temperature is controlled to make sure that the protein in the milk is not coagulated. This stops the milk from having a cooked flavour. The tiny grains of milk powder are cooled quickly and packed into airtight containers. Spray drying is more expensive than roller drying, but the milk produced by spray drying is more soluble in water than roller dried milk and it does not have such a pronounced flavour.

Dried whole milk has all the nutrients that are found in liquid milk in concentrated form, with the exception of some vitamins – for example, vitamin C, thiamin and vitamin B_{12}. These nutrients are lost as a result of the heat treatment. Dried skimmed milk also loses these same nutrients; the fat content is less; also fat soluble vitamins are lost. Therefore dried skimmed milk has less retinol and vitamin D than dried whole milk. The storage life of the unopened can is approximately 6 months. Once dried milk has been reconstituted it should be treated as fresh milk.

15 Fermented dairy foods

Cheese and yogurt are fermented dairy foods. The production and characteristics of these products are due to the activities of micro-organisms. Cheese and yogurt are dependent on the lactic acid bacteria.

Cheese

The very first cheese was produced by accident about 4000 years ago. The milk collected from sheep or goats by nomads in the desert was poured into bags for storage. The bags were made from the dried stomachs of animals. After travelling in the hot desert the milk in the bags turned into a type of soft cheese.

In Britain evidence of cheesemaking dates back to the time of the Roman occupation. In some areas of Britain, cheese is still made on farms, using traditional methods.

Today there are over 400 varieties of cheese. These are made in different parts of the world from the milk of a variety of animals, such as cows, sheep, goats and buffalo, by different methods.

Classification of cheese

Cheeses may be classified according to their country of origin and the place where they were originally made. For example, Cheddar cheese is a well known British cheese from Cheddar. Cheeses may also be classified according to the methods used for making them, and these include cheeses that are soft, semi-hard, hard, with internal mould, or with external mould (Table 15.1).

Production of Cheddar cheese

In England and Wales about 60% of all the cheese produced is Cheddar (Fig. 15.1).

1 *Heat treatment of milk*   Once the milk has been accepted at the creamery it is pasteurised (p. 154). It is then cooled to a temperature of 31°C. Large volumes of the cooled milk are pumped into cheese vats.
2 *Addition of starter culture*   The starter is added to the milk, 2% by total weight. The starter culture is added to sour the milk; it works by converting the milk sugar lactose into lactic acid. The lactic acid acts as a preservative and contributes to the flavour of the cheese.
3 *Addition of rennet*   The addition of rennet is described as 'renneting'. Rennet is extracted from the dried stomach of the calf. Rennet contains *rennin*, the enzyme which causes milk to clot. Rennet is added about 30 minutes after the starter has been added. The temperature is controlled during the 'setting' period.
4 *Cutting the curd*   After about 40 to 45 minutes a firm curd is formed. The curd is cut to release the whey.
5 *Scalding*   The curd is heated for about 40 to 45 minutes, during which time it is stirred continuously by paddles.

Table 15.1
Cheese with reference to classification and consumer choice

Country of origin	Name of Cheese	Type	Characteristics		
			Colour	Texture	Flavour
Britain	Caerphilly	Semi-hard	Creamy white	Semi-smooth	Mild, slightly salty
	Cheddar	Hard	Golden or orange-red	Close	Mellow, nutty
	Cheshire	Hard	Orange-red, white or blue veined	Loose, crumbly	Mild, mellow, slightly salty
	Derby	Hard	White or honey-coloured with patches of green if sage is added	Smooth	Mild
	Double Gloucester	Hard	Straw to light red	Close, smooth	Mellow, quite pungent
	Lancashire	Semi-hard	White	Soft, crumbly	Mild
	Leicester	Hard	Rich red	Soft, crumbly	Mild, mellow
	Stilton blue veined	Internal mould	Creamy white with blue veins	Soft, close	Rich, creamy, mellow
	Wensleydale blue	Internal mould	Blue veins	Soft, close	Rich, creamy, sweet
France	Brie	External mould	Whitish	Semi-liquid	Mild
	Camembert	External mould	Whitish	Semi-liquid	Pungent
	Port Salut	Semi-hard	Creamy	Soft, rubbery	Mild
Holland	Edam	Semi-hard	Red or yellow skin – orange inside	Firm, leathery	Mild
	Gouda	Semi-hard	Red or yellow skin – paler than Edam inside	Soft	Mild
Italy	Parmesan	Hard	Skin varies, cream inside	Very hard, granular	Sharp
Switzerland	Emmental	Hard	Pale yellow	Firm with big holes	Mild, sweet

Fig. 15.1
The production of Cheddar cheese

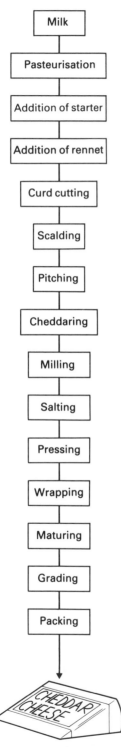

Fig. 15.2
A cheese grader

6 *Pitching*   The curd may be allowed to settle at the bottom of the vat and the whey run off; or, the curds and whey are pumped into shallow coolers and the whey is run off from there once the curd has settled.

7 *Cheddaring*   The curd is passed into the Cheddar master tower and left there for approximately 90 minutes. The curd drains and fuses. It also becomes silky in texture and more acid.

8 *Milling*   The blocks of curd are milled to form small fragments which are known as 'curd chips'.

9 *Salting*   About 2% of salt is added to the curd chips. The salt is sprayed over the curd chips through a series of fine jets. To ensure thorough mixing, stirrers operate. The addition of salt influences the flavour of the final product and helps to preserve it.

10 *Pressing*   Pressing the curd gives the cheese its characteristic texture and shape.

11 *Wrapping*   The blocks of cheese are put into polythene bags under vacuum to exclude air. The wrapped blocks are then put into boxes.

12 *Maturing*   The cheese passes into the cheese store to mature. It may stay in the store for a few weeks or several months. The cheeses become more mature the longer they stay in the store. The temperature in the cheese store is kept constant, between 5°C and 10°C.

13 *Grading*   After 8 weeks Cheddar cheese is usually graded. The cheese grader (Fig. 15.2) decides which of the cheeses will be sold as mild ones and which cheese should be stored for a longer period to be sold as medium or mature cheese.

A cheese mark (Fig. 15.3) is given to cheese that comes up to selected quality standards in England and Wales. This is useful for consumers when buying cheese.

14 *Packing*   The cheese may be cut into retail size portions or into 4.5-kg blocks. A range of packaging materials may be used. For short-term storage film wrapping is used; for longer-term storage vacuum packing is necessary.

Other cheeses

Fig. 15.3
The cheese mark for quality selected British cheeses

QUALITY
SELECTED

Cottage cheese

Traditionally the farmer's wife made cottage cheese from the milk that was left after the cream had been separated. This is also known as 'low-fat' cheese. It is recognised by its mild flavour and particulate texture. This type of cheese may be flavoured with added herbs, vegetables and fruit.

Cream cheese

By strict definition, cream cheeses are not true cheeses. They are not made from a basic curd but from cream. Cream cheese has a soft, buttery texture and a mildly acid taste.

Processed cheese

Processed cheese is not a true variety of cheese. It is a product made from cheeses, usually the hard ones, such as Cheddar.

Low-fat cheeses

A number of manufacturers have produced low-fat varieties of cheese. These are particularly useful for people wishing to lower their energy intake because these cheeses contain less than half the fat of their traditional counterparts.

Home-produced cheeses

Soft cheeses can be made on a domestic scale by the consumer. All equipment and utensils used to make cheese should be scrupulously clean.

Recipe for acid curd cheese

570 ml pasteurised milk

Juice of 1 large lemon (30 to 40 ml).

Flavourings: for example, salt, chopped vegetables or fruit

Method

1 Heat the milk to a temperature of 38°C.
2 Pour the warmed milk into a bowl and then add the lemon juice.
3 Leave the mixture to curdle. This usually takes about 15 minutes.
4 Transfer the curd formed, using a perforated spoon, into a colander lined with muslin positioned over a basin.
5 Tie the corners of the muslin together and leave the curd to drain for an hour.
6 When the whey has drained away from the curd, transfer the curd into a clean basin and add any selected flavourings.

Recipe for rennet-curd cheese

570 ml pasteurised milk

5 ml junket rennet

Method

1 Heat the milk to a temperature of 38°C.
2 Add the junket rennet.
3 Leave the mixture undisturbed for 20 minutes to allow it to set.
4 When the curd has set, using a knife, cut the curd a few times. This causes the whey to be released.
5 Transfer the curd formed by means of a perforated spoon, into a colander lined with muslin positioned over a basin.

6 Tie the corners of the muslin together and leave the curd to drain for an hour.

7 When the whey has drained away from the curd, transfer the curd into a clean basin and add any selected flavourings.

Nutrient content of cheese

Protein is present in cheese in useful amounts, but the quantity is variable depending on the type of cheese. For example, Cheddar, feta and cottage cheeses contain 25.5, 15.6 and 13.8 g/100 g respectively. The protein is of high biological value. *Fat* is found in cheese in variable amounts. Fat profiles g/100 g of cheese are as follows:

Cheese	Fat Total	Fatty acids Saturated	Monounsaturated	Polyunsaturated
Cheddar	34.4	21.7	9.4	1.4
Reduced fat	15.0	9.4	4.4	0.4
Cottage cheese	3.9	2.4	1.1	0.1
Fromage frais	7.1	4.4	2.1	0.2

Carbohydrate is present in cheese in small amounts and this is in the form of sugars, particularly lactose.

Calcium is found in cheese in useful amounts – many cheeses providing well over 500 mg/100 g. Cheddar, Leicester and Mozzarella contain 720, 660 and 590 mg/100 g respectively. Some cheeses are a useful source of *zinc*. For example, Emmental, Wensleydale and processed cheese provide 4.4, 3.4 and 3.2 mg/100 g of zinc respectively. *Potassium* and *phosphorus* are present in cheese in useful amounts. *Sodium* and *chloride* are highest in the hard and semi-hard cheeses and in those with moulds.

Retinol, carotene and *vitamin D* are found in cheese in useful amounts. The cheeses with the highest fat content are richer in these nutrients than those with less fat. Fat-soluble vitamin profiles µg/100 g of cheese are as follows:

Cheese	Retinol	Carotene	Vitamin D
Hard cheese, average	335	225	0.26
Processed cheese	270	95	0.21

B-vitamins thiamin, riboflavin and *niacin* are present in cheese and cheese is considered to be a useful source of riboflavin in particular.

Consumer choice of cheese

1 The fat content of cheese is an important consideration:
   (a) Choose cheeses which have a lower fat content – for example, Edam instead of Cheddar, or cottage cheese instead of cream cheese.
   (b) Choose the low-fat range of cheeses which have less than half the fat of ordinary cheeses.
   (c) Use a strong-flavoured cheese, such as mature Cheddar or Parmesan, but use it in smaller amounts.
2 The cheese mark (Fig. 15.3) is a useful guide when buying cheese.
3 If strong flavours are preferred it is advisable to buy mature varieties. For a more delicate flavour a mild cheese is more suitable.

4 Cottage cheese may easily be flavoured at home. This could be more economical than buying flavoured varieties.

5 Processed cheese is useful for sauces, burger toppings and sandwiches.

6 Cream cheese is useful for making cheese cakes.

Storing cheese

To retain the flavour and moisture content it is necessary to wrap cheese. It should be stored in a cool place, 10°C to 15.5°C, or in a refrigerator. Hard cheeses keep well and semi-hard cheeses quite well, but the softer varieties are best eaten within 2 to 3 days of purchase. If cheese has been stored in a refrigerator let it stand at room temperature for about half an hour before it is served to allow the full flavour to be appreciated.

Cheese in food preparation

Uses of cheese in food preparation include:

- *sauces*, for cauliflower cheese and macaroni cheese;
- *fillings*, in toasted sandwiches, omelets and baked potatoes;
- *toppings*, for vegetable *au gratin*, French onion soup, pizza and Welsh rarebit;
- *dips and spreads* – for example, in cottage cheese with pineapple, and cream cheese with chives;
- *biscuits*, in cheese straws or twists;
- *soufflés*;
- *flans*, in quiche Lorraine;
- *fondues*;
- *cheese cakes*.

Overcoming some problems when using cheese

Lumpy cheese sauce

If cheese is added to a hot liquid in large pieces, it does not blend well and results in a lumpy sauce. The same thing happens if smaller pieces of cheese are added when the liquid is cold. In both cases the cheese does not blend well because it is not heated sufficiently to melt the fat. This problem can be overcome by grating or slicing the cheese before it is added to the liquid and by ensuring that the liquid is hot.

Watery, stringy and matted cheese sauce

If the liquid to which cheese is added becomes overheated the cheese shrinks and water is forced out (curdles). This results in a watery, stringy and matted sauce. To overcome the problem, over-ripened or mature cheeses, which are less sensitive to high temperatures, may be used. Another way to overcome this problem is to use processed cheese. This blends to give a smooth sauce because of the emulsifiers in the cheese. However, sauces made with processed cheese lack flavour. To be sure of a good cheesy flavour and smooth sauce a compromise is to use a mixture of mature cheese and processed cheese.

A stringy, matted sauce also occurs if the cheese is added to an acidic sauce. At a pH below 5.6 the cheese tends to become stringy and matted. It is therefore advisable to blend the cheese well before adding acid ingredients such as French mustard or tomato purée.

Tough, rubbery and fatty cheese on toast

If cheese is overheated – for example, if it is under a hot grill for too long – the fat melts and oozes out, and the protein shrinks to form a tough curd. Water loss also contributes to this shrinkage. Keep the cooking time to a minimum in order to prevent this from happening. The same principles apply when cooking cheese-topped baked potatoes and pizzas with cheese toppings.

Yogurt

In 1975 the Food Standards Committee defined yogurt as 'an acidified coagulated product obtained from milk by fermentation with lactic acid producing bacteria'. Yogurt is thought to have originated in the Balkans and Eastern Mediterranean countries. In its traditional setting yogurt was made from the whole milk of cows, ewes or goats. The milk was boiled in open pans and became concentrated as a result of evaporation. The concentrated milk was cooled and yogurt from a previously prepared batch was added. The bacteria from the added yogurt multiplied quickly and produced enough lactic acid to coagulate the milk.

Yogurt has gained a reputation among health-food fanatics as being associated with the prolongation of life. This belief owes its origin to the work of a Russian bacteriologist, Metchnikoff. After studying the bacteria used to make yogurt he wrote a book called *The Prolongation of Life* in which he related the good health and long lives of Balkan peasants to the effects of certain bacteria found in the yogurt.

Yogurt has been sold in Britain for more than 60 years, but it was not until the early 1960s that sales of this product increased dramatically. This increased popularity of the product was associated with the introduction of fruit yogurt. The new image was of a palatable dessert and not just a sour-milk product. Sales of yogurt have continued to rise ever since: in 1980 about 100 000 tonnes were sold in the UK.

Fig. 15.4
The production of yogurt

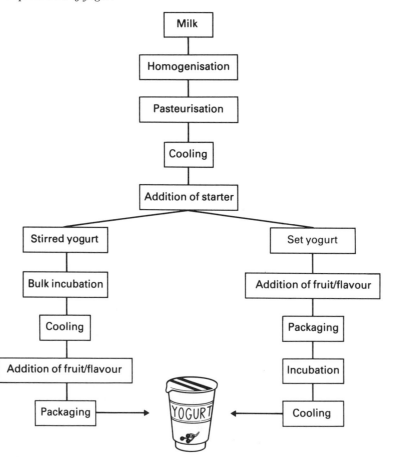

Yogurt production

Most of the yogurt for sale in Britain is classified as 'stirred' but some is 'set' (Fig. 15.4).

1 *The milk for yogurt*   In some countries yogurt is made from ewes' and goats' milk. These types of milk give a distinctive taste to the final product and the consistency varies. When yogurt is made from ewes' milk it is particularly firm and smooth. This is because ewes' milk is rich in protein and fat. In Britain commercial yogurt is made from homogenised cows' milk.

2 *Pasteurisation*   Milk destined for yogurt production is usually pasteurised for 15 to 30 minutes at temperatures ranging from 85°C to 95°C. The heat treatment of pasteurisation has a stabilising effect on the proteins in milk. The heat treatment also creates an almost sterile environment.

3 *Cooling*   The milk is then cooled to temperatures between 40°C and 43°C. The temperatures given here are ideal for the optimum growth of the fermenting bacteria.

4 *Addition of the starter*   This is described as 'inoculation'. The quantity of starter added is usually between 0.5% and 2%. This is usually a mixed culture of *Lactobacillus bulgaricus* and *Streptococcus thermophilus*. The streptococci grow and ferment the lactose in the milk to give lactic acid, and diacetyl is produced. Diacetyl gives yogurt its creamy buttery flavour. Lactic acid production goes on until the pH is 5.5 and the oxygen level in the mixture is reduced. These conditions are ideal for the growth of *Lactobacillus bulgaricus*, the organism responsible for the production of acetaldehyde which contributes to the characteristic flavour of yogurt.

5 *Incubation*   The inoculated milk is incubated for 4 to 6 hours at 37°C to 44°C, or 12 hours at 32°C. The period of incubation is critical to the acidity of the final product. The desired level of acidity is between 0.8% and 1.8% lactic acid. During incubation the yogurt thickens because of the coagulation of the proteins.

6 *Cooling*   The yogurt is cooled to 4.5°C. This helps to reduce the further production of lactic acid. The yogurt is kept at this temperature throughout storage and distribution. At this lower temperature the bacteria are retarded in their activities but are still alive. Unless the yogurt has been heat treated after fermentation it will contain live bacteria.

Additives

1 *Colouring* may be added, and this must comply with the list of acceptable food dyes given in the Colouring Matter in Food Regulations.

2 *Stabilisers and thickeners* may be added to help maintain viscosity during processing; to prevent the yogurt from separating during transport and storage; and to assist the suspension of added ingredients such as fruit and nuts in flavoured yogurt.

3 *Emulsifiers* may be used but their use in yogurt is not widespread.

4 *Preservatives* may be present in fruit yogurt. Permitted preservatives according to the preservatives in Food Regulations include sulphur dioxide or benzoic acid or ethyl 4 hydroxybenzoate or propyl 4 hydroxybenzoate or sorbic acid.

5 *Retinol and vitamin D* may be added to yogurt.

Additional ingredients
Yogurt may be flavoured. About 90% of the yogurt on sale in Britain contains fruit. The fruits used to flavour yogurt, in order of popularity, are strawberry, black cherry, raspberry, peach and pear. Yogurt may also be sweetened, and sucrose is generally used for this purpose.

Home-produced yogurt

A yogurt maker can be used but there is no need to use special equipment. All equipment and utensils used to make yogurt should be scrupulously clean.

Recipe for yogurt

570 ml pasteurised, sterilised, UHT or evaporated milk

50 g dried skimmed milk powder (optional)

1 level tablespoon plain yogurt

Method

1 If pasteurised milk is used this should be boiled and allowed to cool to the desired temperature. If sterilised or UHT or evaporated milk is used there is no need to boil it.
2 The milk should be heated to a temperature of 43°C.
3 Add the dried skimmed milk powder (if used) and the yogurt and blend the mixture together.
4 Warm a vacuum flask by filling it with boiling water. Empty the flask and then pour in the yogurt mixture. Put the lid on the flask and leave for 7 hours.
5 Pour the yogurt into a basin and stand the basin in cold water and then gently stir the yogurt.
6 Cover the basin and put it into the refrigerator for about 4 hours where the yogurt will thicken further.
7 Finally, flavourings may be added if desired.

Yogurt made in this way will keep for about 4 to 5 days in a refrigerator.

Nutrient content of yogurt

Protein constitutes approximately 5% of the weight of yogurt and, like milk, it is of high biological value. *Fat* is present in variable amounts depending on the variety. Fat profiles for cows' milk yogurts g/100 g are as follows:

Yogurt	Fat Total	Fatty acids Saturated	Monounsaturated	Polyunsaturated
Whole milk, plain	3.0	1.7	0.9	0.2
Low-fat, plain	0.8	0.5	0.2	Trace
Greek	9.1	5.2	2.7	0.5

Carbohydrate is found in variable amounts depending on the variety. It is usually present in the form of sugars, particularly lactose and galactose.

Calcium is present in useful amounts. For example, whole milk, low-fat and low-calorie yogurts provide 200, 190 and 150 mg/100 g respectively. *Potassium* and *phosphorus* are present in yogurt in useful amounts.

Retinol and *carotene* are present in yogurt in small amounts. *B-vitamins thiamin, riboflavin* and *niacin* are found in yogurt and it is considered to be a useful source of riboflavin.

Consumer choice of yogurt

1 When buying yogurt make sure that it has been stored in a chilled cabinet. Do not buy it if the cap is blown or domed in the centre.
2 Plain yogurt is very versatile. Low-fat yogurts are ideal in the context of the 'healthful' diet.
3 If the yogurt is not required for immediate use, choose yogurt that has been heat treated after fermentation.
4 Large pots or multipacks of yogurt are more economical. About 10% of the yogurt sold in the UK is in large pots, either 450 g or 500 g.
5 Flavourings can be added to natural yogurt. This may be more economical and also cut down on the sugar intake. Sweet yogurts that are prepared commercially usually contain added sugar.

Storing yogurt

Non-heat treated yogurt can be stored for about 10 days. If yogurt is kept longer than the recommended storage time the bacteria multiply enough to increase the acid level and the flavour of the yogurt is impaired. Eventually the curds and whey separate so that the yogurt no longer has a smooth creamy texture. If yogurt has been heat treated after fermentation it will keep longer.

Yogurt in food preparation

Uses in food preparation include:

- *drinks*, with fruit in them;
- *desserts*, with fruit or nuts added and in cheesecakes;
- *salad dressings, dips* and accompaniments to curries;
- *a substitute for cream or cream fillings*;
- *toppings*, for moussaka and on baked potatoes;
- *garnish*, for soups.

16 Fats, oils and cream

Fats in the diet are obtained from animal and vegetable sources:

1 *Milk fat* is used to make butter and ghee (clarified butter) and cream.
2 *Animal fat*, found around various organs of the body and in and around muscles, is used to make lard, suet, dripping, cooking fats and margarine.
3 *Fish oils* from fish such as herrings, anchovies, pilchards and sardines may be used to produce margarine and cooking fats.
4 *Nuts, seeds, pulses and cereals* can be used to produce oil. The name of the oil usually indicates its origin – for example, ground nut oil, corn oil, soya bean oil. Oils are used in the manufacture of margarines, low-fat spreads and cooking fats.

Fats and oils

Butter

Butter has been made for centuries, and reference to it is found in the Old Testament in Proverbs: 'Surely the churning of milk bringeth forth butter.' The seventeenth and eighteenth centuries have been described as 'the golden age of butter in English cookery'. The consumption of butter rose considerably at about this time: 'swimming in butter' seems to have been the desirable way of serving certain foods.

Production of butter
Butter is an example of a 'water-in-oil' emulsion. It is made from cream which comes from cows' milk (Fig. 16.1).

1 *Pasteurisation*   The cream is heat treated. This is done by heating it for 2 to 4 seconds at 95°C.
2 *Holding*   The cream destined to be fresh or sweet cream butter is cooled to about 4.5°C. This temperature is maintained for several hours to allow the fat globules to harden uniformly. This cooling process helps to prevent fat from being lost in the buttermilk. Cream destined to be ripened or lactic butter requires the addition of a 'starter', and the temperature is held at 15.5°C to 18.5°C for 3 to 4 hours. The cream is then cooled to 7°C.
3 *Churning*   This is carried out at a temperature of about 4°C. During churning the cream revolves so that the fat globules coalesce to form grains of butter.
4 *Separating and washing*   The buttermilk is drained off, and chilled water used to replace it washes the grains of butter. The washing process is important, because if any buttermilk is left behind it reduces

Fig. 16.1
The production of butter

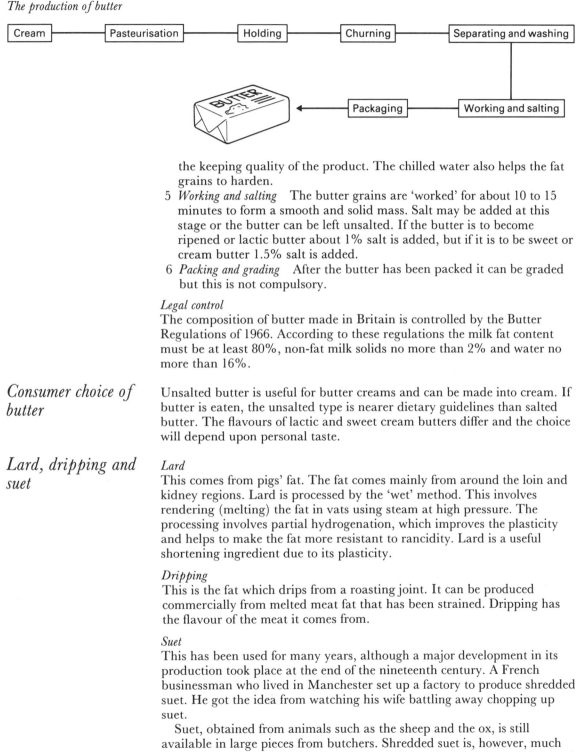

the keeping quality of the product. The chilled water also helps the fat grains to harden.

5 *Working and salting*   The butter grains are 'worked' for about 10 to 15 minutes to form a smooth and solid mass. Salt may be added at this stage or the butter can be left unsalted. If the butter is to become ripened or lactic butter about 1% salt is added, but if it is to be sweet or cream butter 1.5% salt is added.

6 *Packing and grading*   After the butter has been packed it can be graded but this is not compulsory.

Legal control
The composition of butter made in Britain is controlled by the Butter Regulations of 1966. According to these regulations the milk fat content must be at least 80%, non-fat milk solids no more than 2% and water no more than 16%.

Consumer choice of butter

Unsalted butter is useful for butter creams and can be made into cream. If butter is eaten, the unsalted type is nearer dietary guidelines than salted butter. The flavours of lactic and sweet cream butters differ and the choice will depend upon personal taste.

Lard, dripping and suet

Lard
This comes from pigs' fat. The fat comes mainly from around the loin and kidney regions. Lard is processed by the 'wet' method. This involves rendering (melting) the fat in vats using steam at high pressure. The processing involves partial hydrogenation, which improves the plasticity and helps to make the fat more resistant to rancidity. Lard is a useful shortening ingredient due to its plasticity.

Dripping
This is the fat which drips from a roasting joint. It can be produced commercially from melted meat fat that has been strained. Dripping has the flavour of the meat it comes from.

Suet
This has been used for many years, although a major development in its production took place at the end of the nineteenth century. A French businessman who lived in Manchester set up a factory to produce shredded suet. He got the idea from watching his wife battling away chopping up suet.

Suet, obtained from animals such as the sheep and the ox, is still available in large pieces from butchers. Shredded suet is, however, much more convenient to use. Suet may be used in sweet and savoury dishes such as puddings, dumplings, stuffings and pastry.

Fig. 16.2
Refining oil

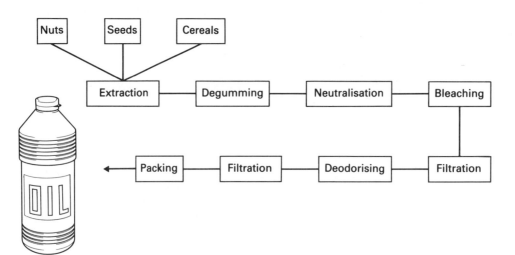

Oils

Production of oil (Fig. 16.2)

1 *Extraction*   The oil is extracted from its source by crushing, flaking and then heating the material. The oil is dissolved in a solvent which has a low boiling point and the solvent is then removed by evaporation. The residue left after the oil has been extracted is a protein-rich cake.
2 *De-gumming*   The oil is mixed with a salt solution. The impurities in the oil are precipitated in the solution and this is strained off.
3 *Neutralisation*   The oil is washed with alkali to remove free fatty acids.
4 *Bleaching*   The oil is kept under vacuum, and fuller's earth is added to absorb the colour pigments.
5 *Filtration*   This process removes the fuller's earth.
6 *Deodorising*   A steam distillation process removes the volatile impurities.
7 *Filtration and packing*   After the oil has been deodorised it is filtered once more and then packed.

Consumer choice of oil

1 Some oils have flavours that are particularly well suited to salad dressings; olive oil is highly esteemed for this purpose.
2 The temperature at which the oil breaks down is an important consideration in the selection of oils for frying.
3 Some oils are richer in polyunsaturates than others; sunflower oil is a well-known example.
4 Some oils are more expensive than others; for example, olive oil is more expensive than corn oil.

Margarine

Margarine has been described as the first 'tailor-made food' because it was developed to meet food needs. In France Napoleon III played an important part in the story. He was anxious to maintain food supplies for French factory workers and for the army. He therefore invited scientists to produce research ideas that would lead to the development of an alternative to butter which could be produced easily and economically and also have good keeping qualities. The best idea came from a food research chemist called Mège Mouriès. Using beef suet, he developed a fat that was a butter

Fig. 16.3
Production of margarine

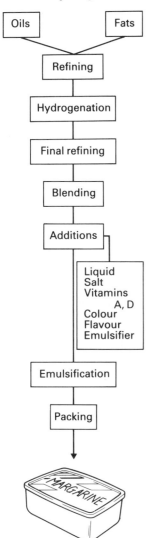

replacement and at the same time much cheaper to produce.

The margarine industry has expanded considerably and today is a thriving industry. In the UK, about 383 000 tonnes of margarine are made every year.

Production of margarine

Margarine is an example of a 'water-in-oil' emulsion. It is made from oils (Fig. 16.3).

1 *Refining*   Oils derived from vegetables, animals and fish may be made into margarine after they have been refined (p. 172).
2 *Hydrogenation*   The oils are selectively hardened by the process of hydrogenation. Hydrogen is added and the oil is made more stable and has a higher melting point as a result of the process.
3 *Refining*   The oil is refined again; this process is called 'final refining'.
4 *Blending*   The selection of fats and oils in the blend depends on factors such as cost, desired melting point, spreadability, plasticity and target groups (for example, vegetarians). The selected fats are heated and, when the melting point is achieved, they are passed through pipes into a compounding tank.
5 *Liquid and salt*   The type of liquid added depends on the margarine being made. Religious or dietary laws may require water to be used. Usually, ripened or cultured skimmed milk or whey is used. Salt may be added to make up 2% of the final product.
6 *Other ingredients*
   (a) *Vitamins A and D* must be added by law.
   (b) *Colouring* may be added in order to give a satisfactory colour.
   (c) *Butyric acid* may be added to improve the flavour.
   (d) *Emulsifiers* are needed to prevent the fat and liquid in the margarine from separating.
7 *Emulsification*   The liquid mixture and fat blend is then mixed together in a machine called a 'votator'. The resulting water-in-fat emulsion is mixed again to form a homogeneous product.
8 *Packing*   The margarine is packaged according to its texture; hard margarine in blocks, and soft margarine in tubs.

Legal control

As in the case of butter the composition of margarine is controlled by law. The Margarine Regulations of 1967 state that margarine must be at least 80% fat with not more than 10% by weight as butter fat. The water content must not be in excess of 16% and specified amounts of vitamins A and D must be added.

Consumer choice of margarine

Currently there are more than 100 brands of margarine to choose from.

1 *Block margarine* can be used for cooking or spreading. It is recommended for making pastry.
2 *Soft margarine* first appeared in 1964. It is useful because it spreads straight from the refrigerator. This helped to make it a popular alternative to butter. Soft margarine is particularly useful in the preparation of cakes and pastry made by the 'all-in-one' methods. Included in this category are the polyunsaturated margarines, popular in the context of the 'healthful' diet. More than two-thirds of the margarine bought in Britain is soft margarine.

3 *Low-fat spreads* are not the same as margarine because they do not comply with the margarine regulations. They do not contain the legal amounts of fat or water. The fat content is too low and the water content too high. In principle, most low-fat spreads are made in a similar way to margarine. Details of processing are kept secret by the manufacturers. Low-fat spreads are useful for programmes of weight reduction and in the context of the 'healthful' diet. In food preparation they cannot be used as a substitute for margarine or butter because of the high liquid content, but various manufacturers have produced recipes which have been specially adapted.

4 *Kosher margarine* has been prepared especially for practising Jews. Tomor margarine is prepared from vegetable oils. It does not contain any fat of animal origin and is processed under strict supervision in a special way. Vegetable margarines are suitable for vegetarians, vegans and Hindus.

Cooking fats

Cooking fats were originally described as 'shortenings'. They were first used in the USA as a substitute for lard. They are virtually pure fat products and are based on blends of vegetable and fish oils and animal fats. Some are vegetable fat only. The method of processing is similar to that of margarine. The selected oils are partially hydrogenated. The fats and oils are blended and cooled to produce the required consistency and the texture is usually improved by the incorporation of air. Emulsifying agents may be added. Such cooking fats are called 'high ratio fats'. Cooking fat from sunflower oil which is high in polyunsaturates is available. 'Shortenings' or 'cooking fats' are useful in pastry making, and those designated 'high ratio' are suitable for cakes based on batters with a high moisture content.

Nutrient content of fats and oils

Fat is undoubtedly the macronutrient found in greatest amounts in these products. Fat profiles g/100 g of fats and oils are as follows:

Fats and oils	Fat Total	Saturated	Fatty acids Monounsaturated	Polyunsaturated
Butter	81.7	54.0	19.8	2.6
Dairy-fat spreads	73.4	28.1	29.9	11.3
Low-fat spreads	40.5	11.2	17.6	9.9
Lard	99.0	40.8	43.8	9.6
Suet	86.7	48.0	32.1	2.1
Corn oil	99.9	12.7	24.7	57.8
Sunflower oil	99.9	11.9	20.2	63.0

Sodium and *chloride* are present in significant amounts in salted butter, margarine, dairy-fat spreads and low-fat spreads.

Retinol, carotene, vitamin D and *vitamin E* are present in useful amounts in butter, margarine, dairy-fat spreads and low-fat spreads. Some oils are very rich in vitamin E, such as sunflower, corn and peanut oils, which contain 49.22, 17.24 and 15.16 mg/100 g respectively. Fat-soluble vitamin profiles per 100 g of these fats are as follows:

Fat	Retinol (μg)	Carotene (μg)	Vitamin D (μg)	Vitamin E (mg)
Butter	815	430	0.76	2.00
Margarine	780	750	7.94	8.00
Dairy-fat spread	800	845	5.80	5.06
Low-fat spread	920	985	8.00	6.33

Storing fats

During storage fats may become rancid. If this happens they develop 'off' flavours and odours. In a cool store free from dampness oils can be kept for up to 3 months, shredded suet for 1 month and other fats for up to 1 week. In a refrigerator most fats can be kept for up to 1 month. Fresh suet and low-fat spreads will keep well for 2 weeks. Keep fats away from strong-smelling foods because they absorb flavours.

Functions of fats in food preparation

Fig. 16.4
Aeration test

1   Mixture has sufficient air incorporated

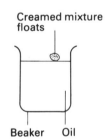

Creamed mixture floats

Beaker   Oil

2   Additional air needed

Beaker   Oil

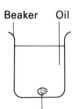

Creamed mixture sinks

Aeration

Creamed cakes, such as a Victoria sandwich, depend on the incorporation of air into the fat. A fat that has been 'creamed', using an electric whisk or a wooden spoon, contains tiny bubbles of air. This is called a foam. The air bubbles act as 'gas cell nuclei', and during cooking carbon dioxide and steam diffuse into these nuclei. The result is a well-risen product with a light texture.

A number of factors are relevant to the aeration process:

1   The plasticity of fat is critical in the formation of a foam.
2   The presence of emulsifying agents in the fat promotes a fine dispersion of air in the mixture.
3   Castor sugar in the fat helps in the aeration process.
4   The amount of air incorporated is very important, and equipment such as an electric whisk is recommended for this process. Creaming with a wooden spoon is hard work.

To test if a creamed mixture has been aerated sufficiently, just drop a speck of mixture from a fine skewer on to the surface of a beaker of oil. If the creamed mixture floats, it has been creamed enough (Fig. 16.4).

Shortening agent

Fats give foods such as biscuits, shortbread and pastries – notably short-crust pastry – their characteristic 'short' (crumbly) texture. They function as shortening agents by coating particles of flour. This is known as 'waterproofing the flour' (Fig. 16.5). When the flour particles are coated in this way, contact between water in the recipe and the proteins in the flour is inhibited. When this happens the product is likely to be 'short' and not chewy or tough, because gluten formation, which is responsible for these conditions, depends upon water reaching the proteins in the flour. Even when gluten does form, the fat keeps the gluten in short lengths and long elastic strands do not develop.

A number of factors need to be considered when fats are used as shortening agents. Fats that are almost pure fats are the most effective shortening agents. Fats such as butter and margarine are not as efficient as shortenings because of their water content. Lard and pure vegetable fats are useful shortening agents. Plastic fats are good shortenings because they coat the flour readily. Liquid fats (oils) coat the flour particles so thoroughly that gluten development is minimal and the product is very crumbly

Fig. 16.5
Fat as a shortening agent

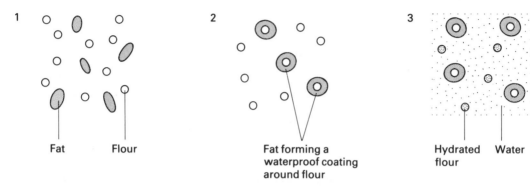

1   Fat   Flour

2   Fat forming a
     waterproof coating
     around flour

3   Hydrated   Water
     flour

Fig. 16.6
Fat in 'all-in-one'
short-crust pastry

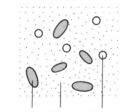

1

Fat Water Flour

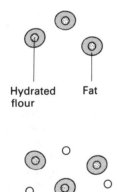

2

Hydrated   Fat
flour

3

Hydrated Flour Fat
flour

indeed. The proportion of fat is a critical factor; enough fat to inhibit gluten development is necessary. On the other hand, too much fat can cause an unmanageably crumbly and greasy product. Methods of mixing are also relevant. The fat should be thoroughly mixed with the flour before the water is added. Alternatively, as is the case in 'all-in-one' short-crust pastry, the water in the recipe is taken up by one-third of the flour and the hydrated flour is then coated with the fat so that the further development of gluten is inhibited (Fig. 16.6).

Flakiness
The fat in the pastry mixture separates the layers of gluten and starch. During cooking the fat melts and the layers are kept separate by steam from the liquid in the recipe. Flakiness shows itself as 'blistering' on the surface and as distinctive flakes in the pastry. It is particularly noticeable in pastries which have a high fat content, such as flaky and puff pastry.

Flakiness of short-crust pastry occurs when plastic fats are used. The use of oil tends to result in a non-flaky pastry. When making flaky pastry, it is recommended that hard fats be incorporated in the various foldings. This type of fat should not be allowed to melt and soak into the dough. During cooking much of the fat comes out of the pastry, and flakes, separated by air spaces, are clearly definable.

Other functions of fats

1 The retention of moisture in baked foods, such as cakes and bread, during storage is partly due to the presence of fat. Cakes with a low-fat content dry out quickly.
2 Fats used in the preparation of flour-based sauces play an important role in preventing the flour particles from clumping (Fig. 16.7).
3 Fats contribute to the flavour of foods: olive oil in salad dressing; sesame-seed oil in tahini; ghee in curries; and butter in shortbread.
4 The colour of some foods depends on fat in the recipe. For example, pastry made with a white fat lacks the rich, golden colour that margarine or butter provide. Palm oil gives a yellow to orange colour to food.
5 Fats are sometimes used as glazes to give a shiny finish to foods; for example, glazed peas, carrots and potatoes. Sauces made with little or no fat tend to have a dull appearance.
6 Fats may be used as basting agents to prevent foods from drying out

Fig. 16.7
Function of fat in the preparation of white sauce

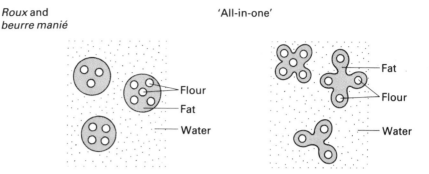

Roux and
beurre manié   'All-in-one'

during cooking – for example, the basting of a roast joint. Foods to be grilled, such as very lean meat, are usually glazed with a thin film of fat for this same reason.

7 Fat is used as a cooking medium. Fats that have a high smoke point are recommended for frying. If the smoke point is low, the fat breaks down imparting 'off' flavours to the fried food. Fats for frying should be free from water, salt or non-fat solids and should either be tasteless or have an acceptable flavour.

8 A thin layer of fat to grease cooking vessels prevents foods from sticking; for example, dripping in a Yorkshire pudding tin. In the interest of the 'healthful' diet, non-stick pans are preferable to greasing.

Cream

Cream has been eaten for many years. Samuel Pepys made an entry in his diary in 1664 in which he described the pleasure he got from eating cream. Trends in consumption of cream vary: peaks in sales of this product occur at Christmas, Easter and during the soft fruit season.

Production of cream

According to the 1970 Cream Regulations, cream is 'that part of milk rich in fat which has been separated by skimming or otherwise and which is intended for human consumption'. Cream is similar to milk in that it is a 'fat-in-water' emulsion. The fat content of different creams is given in Table 16.1.

1 *Separation of cream*   The oldest and simplest method of separating cream is by gravity. This method relies on the fact that, if fresh milk is left to stand the fat globules cluster together, and because they are lighter than the other components of milk they rise to the surface where they form a cream layer. This method of separating cream is tedious because the fat globules tend to rise to the top of the milk very slowly. Cream produced commercially is separated by means of centrifugal force.

2 *Heat treatment*   Most cream is heat treated, only a small proportion of cream is left untreated. Untreated cream is available from farms which hold a special licence. If the cream has been heat treated the method is shown on the label. Cream may be pasteurised, sterilised or ultra-heat treated (p. 154). The cream may be homogenised (p. 155).

Table 16.1
Types of cream

Cream	Fat* content (%)	Heat treatment	Other points	Uses
Single cream	18	Pasteurised	May be UHT	Pouring cream; single cream will not whip
Whipping cream	35	Pasteurised	May be frozen or UHT and lightly homogenised	When whipped, can be used as a piping cream and as a filling for cakes and pastry; can also be pouring cream
Double cream	48	Pasteurised	May be frozen or UHT; may be partly homogenised	Pouring cream; whips to $1\frac{1}{2}$ times its original volume; when whipped can be used as a piping cream and as a filling; floats on coffee and soups
Clotted cream	55	Scalded		Thick and spreadable, with a granular texture; rich creamy colour
Soured cream	18	Pasteurised		Piquant refreshing taste; used in sweet and savoury dishes
Half cream 'coffee cream' 'top of the milk'	12	Pasteurised	May be UHT	Pouring cream for coffee and low-fat substitute for single cream
Whipped cream	35	Pasteurised	Has additions, e.g., sugar and emulsifiers; usually frozen	Suitable for sweet dishes requiring whipped cream
Aerosol cream	35	UHT	May contain additions, such as sugar; collapses within $\frac{1}{2}$ hour of being released from can	Topping for flans, fruit and trifle but must be served at once
'Spooning' or or extra thick textured cream	30	Pasteurised	Can be made from whipping cream	'Spoonable', will not whip
Extra thick double cream	48	Pasteurised		Thick cream, 'spoonable', will not whip.
Sterilised cream	23	Sterilised	May contain certain additives	'Spoonable'; will not whip; caramelised taste due to sterilisation process
Sterilised half cream	12	Sterilised	May contain certain additives	Thin cream for pouring

* Legal minimum

Cream making at home

It is possible to make cream on a small scale using unsalted butter and milk.

Recipe for cream

150 g unsalted butter

115 ml milk

Method

1 Pour the milk into a saucepan, add the butter and put the pan over a gentle heat until the fat has melted.
2 Leave the mixture to cool.

3 Pour the milk and butter mixture into a blender. Liquidise at top speed for 30 seconds.
4 Pour the mixture into a jug and leave to cool in a refrigerator.

Nutrient content of cream

Protein is found in cream in small amounts, constituting about 2–3% of the product. *Fat* is the main source of energy in cream. Fat profiles g/100 g are as follows:

Cream	Fat Total	Fatty acids Saturated	Monounsaturated	Polyunsaturated
Double	48.0	30.0	13.9	1.4
Whipping	39.3	24.6	11.4	1.1
Single	19.1	11.9	5.5	0.5
Half	13.3	8.3	3.9	0.4

Carbohydrate forms about 3–4% the weight of cream and this is present as lactose.

Calcium is present in cream and the amount varies with the fat content. The lower the fat content, the higher the amount of calcium. For example, double cream and half cream contain 50 and 99 mg of calcium per 100 g respectively.

Retinol, carotene and *vitamin D* – the higher the fat content, the higher the levels of fat-soluble vitamins.

Consumer choice of cream

1 The choice of cream will depend on its use (Table 16.1).
2 Buy cream from the chill cabinet only.
3 Half cream helps to lower the intake of fat.

Storing cream

Pasteurised cream keeps for about 10 days in a refrigerator. Sterilised cream is usually tinned and keeps up to 2 years. UHT cream keeps for between 2 and 4 months. Frozen cream keeps up to a year in a freezer.

Cream in food preparation

Uses of cream in food preparation include:

- *drinks*, in coffee, milk shakes and hot chocolate;
- *sauces and soups*;
- *fillings*, for cakes and pastries;
- *puddings*, in trifles and *soufflés*;
- *dips and toppings*, soured cream on baked potatoes and clotted cream with scones.

Preparation of whipped cream

Cream is whipped to incorporate air bubbles. When cream is whipped it is transformed from a liquid into a foam (Fig. 16.8). The air bubbles that are introduced into the cream are stabilised by a thin layer of denatured milk protein. The protein layer becomes surrounded by fat globules and liquid fat helps the fat globules to clump. Whipped cream loses its sheen, has a matt finish and stands in soft peaks. A number of factors are critical in the preparation of whipped cream:

1 There must be sufficient fat to enclose the air bubbles. If the fat content is too high the globules of fat form butter granules before the air can be introduced. The optimum level of fat for whipped cream is 38–42%.

Fig. 16.8
Whipped cream

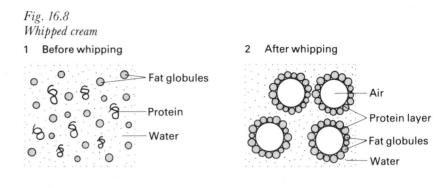

2 Cream that has been homogenised does not whip as well as non-homogenised cream. The formation of a foam is impaired because the fat globules in homogenised cream are reduced in size and stabilised by a protein membrane.

3 The temperature of the cream is important. It should be cooled to below 8°C, and all the equipment used is best kept cool as well. The lower temperatures have an effect on whipping quality. The colder the cream the more solid the fat content.

4 Whipping time is critical. Underbeating does not introduce sufficient air, and overbeating causes the foam to collapse and the cream separates to form yellow granules of butter and buttermilk.

5 The quantity of cream whipped at any one time is an important consideration, because if the mixing container is too full the cream will take longer to form a foam.

17 Sugars and sweeteners

Sugar

Honey was used long before sugar was known, and it was the main sweetener up until the time that sugar became available. Sugar was cultivated in India 2500 years ago. Some writers described it as 'Indian salt'. Sugar did not arrive in Britain until about the thirteenth century.

Production of sugar

Most of the sugar produced comes from sugar cane (Fig. 17.1), accounting for approximately 60% of the world's sugar production. The remaining 40% comes from sugar beet (Fig. 17.1).

Sugar cane contains about 18% sugar and sugar beet contains about 15%. Early stages of production involve different methods of extraction according to the source, but both give rise to raw brown sugar with a film of molasses.

Fig. 17.1
Sugar cane and sugar beet

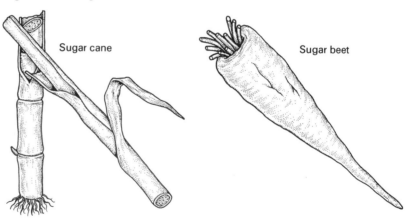

Sugar cane   Sugar beet

Sugar refining
(Fig. 17.2)

1 The raw brown sugar is mixed with a raw syrup to soften the molasses adhering to the sugar crystals. Centrifugal machines are used to spin off the molasses. This is described as 'affination'.
2 The sugar is dissolved in water, a process called 'melting'.
3 Milk of lime is added to the sugar solution and carbon dioxide is bubbled through the liquid. This stage is called 'carbonation'.
4 At this stage the liquid is cloudy and it is filtered.
5 After the filtration process the liquid is brown. In order to remove the colour and dissolved impurities, it is filtered through animal charcoal creating a colourless liquid. This is called the 'char' process.
6 The sugar liquor is concentrated and crystallised in a vacuum pan.
7 When the crystals are the required size they are separated from any liquor that is left in a centrifugal machine.
8 The sugar crystals are then dried.

Fig. 17.2
Refining sugar

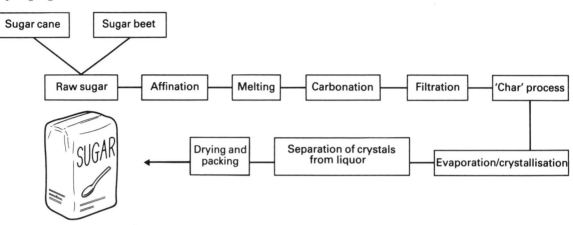

Consumer choice of sugar

Table 17.1
Sugar in food preparation

Type	Description	Consumer choice	Uses
Black treacle	Processed from filtered molasses and partially inverted; thick dark brown, heavy syrup with a strong flavour	Gives strong colour and flavour to foods; because it is partially inverted helps keep baked goods moist	Gingerbread, parkin, Christmas pudding, baked beans, curry sauces
Castor sugar	Processed from granulated sugar by milling and sifting; fine white crystals	Small crystals useful in creamed cake mixtures because they allow more air cells to be incorporated; stabilises egg white and whole egg foams	Victoria sandwich, fairy cakes, meringues, Swiss roll, Genoese sponge
Coffee crystals	Processed as granulated sugar and colour added; large brown crystals	Large crystals dissolve slowly in coffee so that the bitter taste of coffee comes through	Coffee
Cube sugar	Processed from moist granulated sugar, then moulded into cubes and dried	Convenient way of adding sugar to drinks; quick dissolving to sweeten drinks quickly	Hot drinks such as cocoa, coffee, tea
Demerara	Comes from raw sugar or sugar syrup remaining after white sugar has been extracted; sugar crystals are coarse and pale amber; delicate syrup flavour	Large crystals for crunchy toppings or cakes and crumbles	Coffee, apple crumble

Type	Description	Consumer choice	Uses
Golden syrup	Partially inverted; selected refinery syrups	Distinctive flavour; because it is partially inverted helps keep baked goods moist	Treacle pudding, gingerbread
Honey	A form of invert sugar; can be cloudy and thick or clear and like syrup	Prized for its flavour; because it is inverted helps keep cakes moist	Honey cake; as a spread; in drinks
Icing sugar	Processed from granulated sugar by milling it to a fine white powder	Useful for making icings because the fine powder dissolves easily	Icing, e.g., royal, fondant; decorating cakes as a powder
Maple syrup	Processed from sap that comes from the maple tree; light brown syrup, distinctive taste	Popular American syrup	Served with pancakes
Molasses	Processed from molasses; heavy brownish-black as syrup; also available in crystal form; distinctive, strong taste	Used in bread and cakes, giving strong colour and characteristic flavour	Vegans use this type of sugar – they cannot use refined sugar because it is clarified with animal charcoal
Muscovado sugar	Similar to molasses sugar but not as dark		
Nibs	Produced alongside cube sugar as by-product; coarse white nibs	Useful as a decoration for cakes	Bath buns
Preserving sugar	Processed as granulated sugar	Useful for preserves; large crystals dissolve slowly and do not settle as a dense layer so the mixture need not be stirred so frequently	Jam, marmalade
Rainbow sugar crystals	Processed as granulated sugar: food colour added to give pastel shades	Colours are the attraction	Toppings for biscuit and cake decoration
Soft brown sugar	Processed from sugar syrup remaining after white sugar has been extracted; dark brown or light brown and moist; the darker version has a more distinctive flavour	Dark type is good in mincemeat; the light one is good sprinkled on porridge and grapefruit	Both sugars are used in baked goods, e.g., Dundee cake

Storing sugar

The storage life depends on the type of sugar. Sugar in powder, granular or cubed form will keep for about 3 months if unopened. Syrups and honey keep for up to 1 year. Once opened, sugar tends to absorb moisture because of its hygroscopic properties and syrups tend to evaporate, so that some of the sugar crystallises.

Functions of sugar in food preparation

1 *Flavourings*   Sugar is used as a flavouring in drinks, puddings and cakes.

2 *Tenderiser*   There are several reasons why sugar has a tenderising effect in baked products. The uptake of water by flour is decreased when sugar is present, and as a result gluten formation and development is hampered resulting in a tender cake. As well as this, sugar increases the coagulation temperature of eggs and delays pasting of the starch in the flour. This gives more time for the gas cells to expand before the cake batter sets, thus giving a light result.

3 *Aeration of creamed cakes*   This is dependent on the addition of sugar. Sugar added to plastic fats during creaming accommodates the incorporation of air into the mixture. As the crystals of sugar are mixed with the fat, air, incorporated by the process of mixing, adheres to the sugar crystals. This air is introduced as small bubbles into the fat. Fine sugar crystals such as those provided by castor sugar are ideal for this purpose, because the finer and consequently more numerous the sugar crystals the higher the number of air cells incorporated. Powders such as icing sugar and liquids such as honey do not function in this way.

4 *Aids moisture retention*   Sugar helps because of its hygroscopicity (water-attracting properties). Fructose is particularly hygroscopic. Honey contains a high proportion of fructose, and black treacle and golden syrup contain fructose because of the inversion process. Cakes made with honey, black treacle or golden syrup keep well because the fructose functions as a humectant (that is, it absorbs moisture from the atmosphere).

5 *Colour*   Sugar affects colour in baked products – for example, in yeast breads and cakes sugar contributes to the carbonyl-amine-browning of the crust. Brown sugar in mixtures contributes to the colour.

6 *Activator*   The term 'activator' is used because in mixtures leavened with yeast sugar is useful as a means of activating the yeast. Fermentation tends to be slow if sucrose is not included. Fermentation is generally more rapid when sugar is approximately 10% of the weight of the flour. If more than 10% is used, the fermentation is retarded by the osmotic effect of the sugar on the yeast cells.

7 *Stabiliser*   The stabilising effect of sugar on egg-white foam is useful in food preparation. Once sugar has been mixed into such a foam, as in the preparation of meringues, it can be spread without rupturing the air cells.

8 *Reduces the risk of curdling*   The addition of sugar to both stirred and baked custards is useful because it raises the coagulation temperature and thus reduces the risk of curdling. Also, baked custards with sugar in the recipe are more translucent and tend to have a finer skin on the surface than when sugar is not used.

9 *Decreases the thickness of starch-based sauces and puddings*   This is because sugar raises the temperature at which the sauce thickens, and is particularly noticeable when the product has cooled.

10 *Preservative*   Foods such as jellies and jams have a long storage life because the high sugar content prevents microbial growth. Sugar in high concentrations also helps to maintain the shape of fruit in preserved fruit.

11 *Coating*   Sugar syrups are useful in the preparation of fruit salad because the syrup protects the surface of the cut fruit from contact with atmospheric oxygen, reducing the risk of browning.

12 *Icings and sweets*   Sugar is the main ingredient of icings for cakes.

Sweeteners

Some sweetening agents have a sweetness that is similar to the sweetness of sucrose, and others have a sweetness that is many times greater. In 1982 the Food Additives and Contaminants Committee referred to the first type as 'bulk sweeteners' and the latter as 'intense sweeteners'.

Need for sweeteners

1 Diabetics need to control the consumption of foods sweetened with carbohydrates that are readily absorbed, such as sucrose. Bulk sweeteners used in place of an equivalent amount of sucrose produce a lower insulin demand. This means that diabetics can eat foods sweetened in this way, such as jams and confectionery, freely. Some of the bulk sweeteners are not as sweet as sucrose, and so the use of intense sweeteners is useful.

2 'Sugar-free' foods have been promoted particularly in the interests of dental health. Dental caries is initiated by acids produced from the carbohydrates by bacteria in the mouth, and it is suggested that the use of a sweet substance that does not ferment might reduce the risk of tooth decay.

3 'Slimming' foods may include the use of intense sweeteners without contributing significantly to the energy value of the diet.

4 Foods with a high concentration of carbohydrate may be improved by the use of sweeteners. For example, soft-scoop ice-cream made with sucrose tends to become both gritty and grainy and is very sweet. The use of bulk sweeteners helps to overcome this.

Sorbitol

This bulk sweetener is found naturally in fruits such as apples, berries, pears and plums. It is approximately half as sweet as sucrose. Sorbitol is useful because it is stable at high temperatures, which enables it to be used to make confectionery, sweets and jams. This is particularly satisfying to those people suffering from diabetis mellitus. Sorbitol is claimed to be less cariogenic than sucrose.

Saccharin

This intense sweetener was discovered in 1879. It was obtained from coal tar and was found to be 300 times sweeter than sucrose. It became popular among diabetics before the turn of the century. During the First World War the shortage of sugar was a great stimulus to the use of saccharin. It was also used to overcome the taste of medicines, and was found to be better than sugar for this purpose because sugar tended to crystallise and clog up the screw tops of bottles. Saccharin is popular with the 'diet conscious'. However, it does have an after-taste. It is used in the production of soft drinks and in diabetic foods.

Aspartame

This is a mixture of 2 amino acids, aspartic acid and phenylalanine, and has a sweetness that is about 200 times greater than sucrose. It is used to sweeten soft drinks and can be purchased under various trade names. It has one major advantage over saccharin in that it does not leave an after-taste. It is, however, unsuitable for children suffering from a genetic deficiency called 'phenylketonuria', found in 1 child in every 15 000. Individuals with this disorder cannot metabolise the amino acid phenylalanine.

Forms of sweetener

Sweeteners are available in 3 main forms: pellets or tablets, liquids and powders. The pellets or tablets are useful for sweetening drinks, particularly if the pellets are contained in 'one-by-one' pocket dispensers. The liquids are available in bottles that allow for 'one-drop-at-a-time' dispensing. The powders are useful for sprinkling on food.

To find out the sweeteners on which proprietory brands are based, examine the labels carefully. Some sweeteners may be blends; for example, a powder made up of sorbitol and saccharin is available and advertised as being particularly suitable for diabetics.

Some sweeteners are actually combined with sugar and are sold as 'low calorie' sugars in granular and cube form. An example of this is granulated sugar and saccharin.

Consumer choice of sweeteners

1 Bulk sweeteners such as sorbitol are useful for diabetics.
2 Intense sweeteners such as saccharin are useful for people who are trying to reduce their energy intake. The sweetener and sugar blends serve a similar purpose.
3 Avoid aspartame sweeteners if there is a phenylketonuric in the family.

Use of sweeteners

1 If liquid sweeteners are used, add them one drop at a time so that the product will not be over-sweetened.
2 Some sweeteners are not heat stable, and this will have implications for cooking. Many of the manufacturers' recipes incorporate sweeteners towards the end of cooking for this reason.
3 Some sweeteners leave an after-taste, so find one that suits your palate.

Alternatives to sugar and sweeteners

One way of satisfying a 'sweet tooth' is to turn to alternatives to both sugar and sweeteners. It is unrealistic to expect people to change their eating habits overnight and deny the desire for sweetness. In his book *The Saccharin Disease*, Captain Cleave pointed out that the desire for sweetness is one of the strongest where food is concerned.

In the context of the 'heathful' diet, many of the adaptations that were adopted in the Second World War when sugar was rationed are prudent today. Wartime recipe books are full of interesting recipes which make use of various dried fruits and vegetables, such as carrots, parsnips and beetroot, to sweeten cakes and puddings.

One major advantage of using foods other than sugar and sweeteners as a means of sweetening is that other nutrients, apart from energy, are provided in significant amounts. For example, if dried fruits are used, the quantity of fibre in the recipe is increased; if carrots are used, the carotene is increased. However, it is important to note that the products made with less or no sugar will be different. If, for example, dates are used to sweeten a creamed cake mixture in place of sugar, the volume of the cake is less, due to reduced aeration. The texture will be closer, the colour darker and the flavour of the dates comes through.

Use of alternatives in food preparation

1 *Dried fruit*, such as dates, figs, prunes and apricots, are useful sugar substitutes in cakes, puddings, muesli and some types of sweets. To get a really sweet taste it helps if the fruit is broken by chopping or blending it with some of the liquid in the recipe. The use of fruits in cakes helps to keep the product moist. Dried fruits, especially dates, blended with water are useful as syrups for fruit salads and, as purées, are tasty fillings for cakes.
2 *Fresh fruit*, such as bananas, are particularly suitable in cakes for the reasons given above. Puréed bananas make a sweet spread for sandwich and cake fillings and can be used to sweeten dishes such as apple pie.

Puréed bananas sweeten several types of vegan ice-cream.

3 *Fresh fruit juices* that seep out of fruit are ideal for fruit salad, and can be topped up with the juice of a freshly squeezed orange or cartons of unsweetened fruit juices, such as apple, orange or pineapple.

4 *Vegetables* such as carrots and parsnips, particularly young ones, are useful sweetening agents. When these foods are used in cakes it is important to cut them up adequately; grating finely on a grater or in a food processor is recommended. Purées of these foods may be used in sweet recipes – for example, in fudge. If used in this way they are best blended in with the fudge mixture so they work on the dilution principle. Sweet potatoes are useful in purée form as a sweetener in cakes and scones.

18 Flavourings

Much of the enjoyment of eating depends on the flavourings added during preparation and also when the food is about to be eaten.

Herbs

The word 'herb' comes from the Latin *herba*, which means grass or herbage. Herbs are green plants which include roots, stems, leaves, flowers and seeds. They owe their distinctive aromas and flavours to volatile oils. Herbs have been used since the earliest times for medicines, perfumes and in food preparation. General points about herbs used in food preparation are given in Table 18.1.

Table 18.1
Herbs used in food preparation

Herb	Description	Uses
Angelica	Has a hollowed grooved stem which is reddish at the base; jagged edged leaves and yellowish or greenish flowers	Fruits and leaves can be added to sauces and salads; available in candied form and used as a decorative garnish in sweet dishes such as trifle
Basil	2 kinds of plant: bush basil is a short-stemmed plant, and sweet basil is tall and with long pointed leaves; the flowers are whitish to pale red; scent is clove-like and flavour of the leaves spicy and aromatic	Goes well with tomatoes; gives subtle flavour to soups, sauces, fish and other savoury dishes and stuffings
Bay leaves	Leathery leaves which grow on a small tree; the flower is yellowish in colour; leaves have a strong scent and a bitter taste which is less noticeable when the herb is dried	In bouquets garnis; can be used in sweet and savoury dishes, e.g., milk puddings and meat stews (it is important to remove bay leaves before eating)
Borage	Tall plant with hairy leaves and blue flowers; both leaves and flowers are used giving a slightly salty cucumber flavour	The leaves give a delicate flavour to salads and fruit drinks; the flowers are an attractive decoration in fruit salad
Capers	A shrub with long slender stalks; the leaves are oval and the flowers white or pale pink; the closed flower buds are pickled in vinegar, salt or wine; sweet-sharp flavour	In sauces such as tartare sauce; sandwich spreads; garnish for cold appetisers
Chervil	Soft-leaved delicate looking plant bearing tiny white flowers which resemble parsley; the leaves have a delicate flavour – sweet and aniseed-like	In sauces such as parsley; in salads and in bouquets garnis; garnish for vegetables, soups and casseroles

Herb	Description	Uses
Chives	Thick clumps of hollow, tubular leaves with mauve shaggy flowers; the leaves have an onion-like flavour with a sharp but sweetish taste	Flavouring salads and dressings; garnish for soups, omelets and potatoes
Coriander leaves	The stem is branched and the leaves vary according to the part of the plant; the flowers are pink and mauve; the leaves have a delicate flavour	Popular in curries (parsley can be used as a substitute)
Dill	Feathery leaves and yellow flowers; the leaves have a sharp aromatic flavour	Goes well with cucumber, in salads and fish sauces
Fennel	Fern-like feathery appearance; leaves have a pronounced aniseed flavour	Used as garnish and in sauces to serve with fish
Garlic	A bulb composed of bulblets called cloves which are tooth-like in appearance; sharp and pronounced flavour	Soups, stews, curries, patés and pizzas, garlic bread, salad dressings; very little garlic is needed to yield a strong flavour, and recipes are based on the use of cloves, not bulbs
Horseradish	Long, thick fleshy root, leafy stem and white flowers; the root is used raw or dried and has a 'hot' flavour similar to mustard	Grated root may be mixed with cream or white sauce and eaten with roast beef or smoked and fresh-water fish; adds flavour to salad dressings
Marjoram	Leaves are small and ovate and flowers pink and white; leaves have strong, distinctive, spicy taste	In bouquets garnis and mixed herbs; in soups, salads, pizzas
Mint	14 varieties, e.g., spearmint, apple mint, peppermint; spearmint has wide pointed leaves and a purple flower; the flavour of the leaves is very strong and the aroma penetrating during cooking	Mint sauce to serve with lamb; to flavour vegetables during cooking; in marinades for kebabs; in fruit cups and salad dressings
Oregano	Branched erect reddish stem with ovate leaves and purple flowers; stalks and leaves are used; spicy scent and slightly bitter taste	In soups, stews, pizzas and salad dressings
Parsley	Curly leaves and stems yield a greenish/yellow flower; the stem has more flavour than the leaves; a distinctive sweetish flavour	Sprigs are a popular garnish and flavouring for sauces such as parsley sauce served with ham or fish
Rosemary	Shrub with slender leathery leaves, dark green on one side and off-white on the other; flowers are purple/blue; flavour of the leaves is pungent, aromatic and sweet	Traditionally used with roast lamb; gives flavour to soups, stews and salads
Sage	Shrub-like plant; both stem and leaves are felted and wrinkled slightly and grey-green in colour; the flowers are blue-purple or pinkish; flavour of the leaves strong and slightly bitter	In sage and onion stuffing and served with pork, goose and duck; use sparingly as the flavour is strong
Savory	2 kinds, summer and winter; low-growing plant with a woody, shrub-like stem; leaves are long and slender and flowers white or pink-purple; flavour of leaves is pungent and peppery	Goes well with all kinds of beans; in soups, salads, stuffings, and in mixed herbs

Herb	Description	Uses
Tarragon	Tall plant with long leaves bearing pinkish-yellow flowers; leaves have aromatic flavour	In sauces such as tartare; in marinades and wine vinegar; goes well with fish and chicken. French tarragon has a much better flavour than Russian
Thyme	2 kinds of thyme, wild thyme and garden thyme; both have small shiny leaves and pinkish flowers; flavour strong, pungent, aromatic and clove-like	In mixed herbs and as a flavouring in stuffing, e.g., thyme and parsley, in soups and salads; strong flavour, so use sparingly

Fresh herbs

Herbs can be grown in pots or in herb gardens. They are sold in supermarkets, greengrocers' shops and at market stalls. Herbs may be stored for 1 week by tying them loosely but securely in polythene bags and placing them in the lowest part of the refrigerator (vegetable drawer). Garlic is an exception to this rule, and may be kept in a vegetable rack or in a dry, airy place for several months. For long-term storage herbs may be frozen, dried or made into butters or vinegars. Fresh herbs must be chopped to release the volatile oils if both aroma and flavour are to be appreciated.

Dried herbs

Most herbs can be purchased in dried form. Dried herbs should be bought regularly because flavour will be lost with prolonged storage. One herb particularly well suited to drying is the bay leaf, which is dried by hanging the branches in a dry, airy place for a few weeks. Store dried herbs in screw-top bottles away from light.

Dried herbs are useful flavourings but they are not suitable for garnishing. As a result of the drying process the herbs lose moisture and shrink, and the flavour becomes concentrated. If using dried herbs it is important to use only one-third of the amount specified for fresh herbs.

Frozen herbs

Most herbs can be frozen, but they must be really fresh. Before freezing, rinse them lightly in cold water and drain thoroughly. The herbs can be packed into polythene bags and frozen. They can then be chopped when they are needed. Another method is to chop the herbs before they are frozen. They can also be chopped and put into ice-cube trays with a little water. When the 'herb ice cubes' have frozen the cubes can be tipped into a polythene bag and used as required. Frozen herbs are useful flavourings but as they are wet they are not suitable for garnishing.

Herb butters

Well-known and popular herb butters include garlic butter (used in garlic bread) and parsley butter (served as a garnish for steaks). The crushed garlic or chopped green herb is simply mixed with butter. In the interest of the 'healthful' diet, herb butters can be made using low-fat spreads.

Herb vinegars

Herb-flavoured vinegars are useful for making salad dressings – for example, tarragon vinegar. Herb vinegars can be made simply by quarter-filling a vinegar bottle with the herb leaves, which have been freshly picked, washed and dried of excess moisture, and filling the bottle with hot vinegar. The bottle is then corked and kept for approximately 1 month. The vinegar is then decanted and may be used at once or stored.

Herb mixtures

The most obvious example of a herb mixture is dried mixed herbs. A mixture of dried herbs can also be purchased as bouquets garnis, usually in little bags, some of which look very like tea bags. There are many variations in the particular herb mixture. Bouquets garnis can also be purchased fresh or made by the consumer from fresh herbs. To make one, take a small piece of muslin and some string, put the herb mixture on the muslin (for example, 1 bay leaf, 1 sprig of thyme and 1 sprig of parsley). Draw the edges of the muslin together and secure them with the string, making a small bag with the herbs inside. When using a bouquet garni remember to remove it before the food is served.

Spices

Spices are dried aromatic parts of plants which include roots, bark, leaves, flowers and seeds. They owe their distinctive aromas and pungent flavours to volatile oils. Spices have been used since the earliest times and have been imported to Britain for hundreds of years. Spices were a valuable commodity in medieval times when they were used as currency. General points about spices used in food preparation are given in Table 18.2.

Spices can be purchased whole or powdered. It is essential that they are purchased from a retailer with a fast turnover because flavour is lost during storage. Powdered spices lack the aroma and pungency of whole spices, because when they are ground the volatile oils evaporate. All spices should be stored in airtight containers.

Powdered spices are convenient despite flavour losses. A pestle and mortar is needed to grind whole spice. For curry powders or garam masala, a curry stone is recommended. Whole nutmeg is easily grated and can be used to flavour a wide variety of dishes.

Table 18.2
Spices used in food preparation

Spice	Description	Uses
Allspice	Also known as 'pimento' and 'Jamaica pepper', it is the dried berry of a West Indian shrub called allspice; the ripened berries are smooth, round and reddish brown; the spicy, pungent taste is due to pimento oil; the aroma resembles that of nutmeg, cinnamon and cloves	Whole or ground to flavour sauces, soups, pickles, chutneys, milk puddings and meat dishes such as potted beef; not to be confused with mixed spice
Caraway seeds	The seeds come from a feathery plant which grows in Europe and are pale to dark brown with a distinctive aroma and pungent, liquorice-like taste	In soups, salads, seed cake and popular in some Jewish foods
Cardamom	Dried, tiny black seeds of plant grown in India, Sri Lanka, Sumatra and China; the seeds have a strong camphor-like smell and pungent taste; the whitish-green pod can be eaten crushed	In curry recipes, pilau rice and sweet dishes; if whole cardamoms are used do not eat the pod surrounding the seeds – it is parchment-like

Spice	Description	Uses
Chilli	Red chillies can be imported fresh or dried whole; crushed dried chillies are pungent and should be used sparingly; powdered chilli is not so pungent	In pickling if dried; if fresh useful in Mexican dishes, e.g., chilli con carne
Cinnamon	Bark of a species of laurel native to tropical Asia; the light tan, paper-thin bark is rolled as a stick or powdered, pungent sweet spice	To flavour puddings, cakes and biscuits; useful in punch; used in Indian meat and rice dishes; enhances the flavour of shepherd's pie and moussaka; if sticks are used remove them before eating
Cloves	Dried, unopened flower buds of a species of myrtle cultivated mainly on islands off the East African coast; distinctive pungent aroma; available whole or powdered	Goes well in apple dishes and adds to the flavour of bread sauce and baked gammon; used in Indian meat and rice dishes; if used whole remove before eating
Coriander seeds	Tiny round beige seeds of the coriander plant grown in southern Europe, India and South America. The seeds have a spicy sweetish taste with a hint of orange; available whole or powdered	In curries along with the leaves of the plant; in pickling spice and as a seasoning for meat dishes
Cumin seeds	Cultivated in India, Eastern and Southern Europe and North Africa; the seeds have a pungent aroma and a sharp taste; available whole or powdered	In chilli and curry powder, in curries, pickles and Mexican dishes
Dill seeds	Widely cultivated in America, Asia and Northern Europe; the seeds are rich in aromatic oils; flavour is mild, aromatic, slightly sweet and caraway-like	In pickling, especially for cucumber
Fenugreek	Native to Asia but cultivated in many parts of the world; highly aromatic flavour leaving a bitter after-taste	In curry powder, chutneys, pickles and sauces
Ginger	Cultivated in India, China, Japan, Jamaica and West Africa; the root is available fresh or dried in powdered form; the root and stem can be preserved in syrup or crystallised; hot, sweet flavour	In curries, sauces, cakes, biscuits and pickling
Mace	Dried, fibrous network which grows round the nutmeg; golden colour and flavour like nutmeg but stronger and more pungent; available in blades or ground	In pickling, in sauces and soups and savoury meat dishes; use sparingly due to strong flavour; if not available nutmeg may be used instead
Poppy seeds	Tiny greyish-black seeds of the poppy; originated in the Near East and popular in Central Europe; spicy and sweetish	Topping for breads; filling for cakes, e.g., Jewish cakes; added to curry mixtures
Saffron	Dried stigmas of a variety of crocus; cultivation spread from western Asia to India, China and then west to the Mediterranean; gives food a deep yellow colour; aromatic flavour with slightly bitter taste; available whole or ground	To colour and flavour rice dishes such as Spanish paella; Italian risotto; in Indian festive dishes; it is the most expensive spice of all – turmeric can be used in its place

Spice	Description	Uses
Sesame seeds	About 20 species, the most common being *Sesamum indicum*; cultivated widely in many parts of the world; the seeds have a rich, sweet, slightly burnt flavour	Toppings for breads; in salads and oriental sweets such as halva; in tahini
Turmeric	Dried root of a plant similar to ginger; cultivated in China, India, Java and other places; has a distinct spicy taste and aroma sometimes described as earthy; gives a yellow colour to foods	An ingredient in curry powder, savoury rice dishes and piccalilli; try not to spill it as it stains work surfaces, hands and clothes yellow
Vanilla	Dried pods of a tropical orchid which grows in Mexico; available as a pod or essence; the former can be used several times over if wiped and dried after use; add the latter in small quantities in drops; sweet-flavoured	In custards, ices and many sweet dishes; pod can be infused in milk or stored with sugar to make vanilla sugar

Spice mixtures

1 *Mixed spice* is a blend of sweet spices including cloves, allspice and cinnamon. This mixture is very useful in puddings, cakes and biscuits.
2 *Curry powder* is a blend of many spices and is golden brown in colour. Spices used in a curry powder may include cayenne, coriander, turmeric, cumin, ginger, mace, cloves, cardamom, fenugreek and pepper. There are many recipes for curry powder. If curry powder is mixed with clarified butter or vinegar it comes out as curry paste. Curry powder or paste can add flavour to foods other than curries.
3 *Garam masala* is an aromatic spice mixture of (for example) large black cardamoms, cinnamon, black cumin, cloves, black peppercorns and nutmeg. Garam masala is not a standardised mixture: it is usually added to curries towards the end of cooking.

Condiments

The word 'condiment' comes from the Latin *condimentum*. Condiments are generally salty, spicy, piquant or stimulating. The four basic ones are salt, pepper, mustard and vinegar.

Salt

Salt has been a valuable commodity since the second millennium BC. The word 'salt' comes from the Latin *salarium*, which means 'salt-money', and even today a good worker is described as being 'worth his salt'. Salt or sodium chloride, as it is known chemically, is made up of sodium and chlorine. It is found in many different parts of the world and comes from 3 main sources: underground, underground lakes and the sea.

Consumer choice of salt

1 *Rock salt* has crystals which are large and coarse.
2 *Sea salt* is in the form of small flakes. One well-known example is Maldon salt.
3 *Table salt* comes as small crystals and is obtained by evaporating a salt solution that has been purified. Because the process of evaporation is carried out in vacuum pans, the name 'vacuum salt' is used to describe this type of salt. Magnesium carbonate is added to prevent it from caking.

4 *Iodised salt* is a table salt that has sodium or potassium iodide added.
5 *Celery salt* is table salt that has been mixed with a blend of crushed celery seeds. It is convenient to use when only a small amount of celery is needed in a recipe or when celery is expensive.
6 *Garlic salt* is table salt that has crushed dried garlic mixed with it. This type of salt can be used as a replacement for fresh garlic.
7 *Salt substitutes* such as low sodium, high potassium salts are widely available and may be used as a substitute for salt.

Storing salt
Salt should be stored in a dry atmosphere. If it becomes damp it cakes.

Salt in food preparation
As well as being a condiment for use at table, salt is added to foods such as vegetables, pastry, cakes, soups, sauces and many other dishes to give additional flavour.

Pepper

Pepper was the most popular spice with the Romans in the first century AD. White and black pepper come from the plant *Piper nigrum*, and the various red peppers, such as cayenne, paprika and chilli, are all from the capsicum family. Although the various types have their own characteristics they all have one common quality: they are all pungent.

Consumer choice of pepper

1 *Black pepper* comes from the immature berries of the pepper plant that have been dried in the sun. The berry is made up of an outer husk which is black and an inner kernel which is white. The inner kernel is hot and the outer husk is aromatic. Black pepper has a much stronger taste than white pepper. It is available as ground or whole pepper.
2 *White pepper* is made from the mature berries, and the outer husk is removed. The inner white kernels are dried and used to make white pepper. White pepper is more expensive than black pepper and is much milder. It is available as ground or whole pepper and is useful for white sauces.
3 *Green peppercorns* are the fresh green berries which have been canned. The flavour of the peppercorns is pungent but not hot. These peppercorns have a soft texture and go well with meat and fish dishes.
4 *Cayenne pepper* is a fiery red pepper. It is useful in cheese dishes such as cheese straws and scones, and it is also good with fish. Cayenne is made from the dried ripe berries of the plant.
5 *Paprika* is also a red pepper but it is not as hot as cayenne pepper. It comes from the seeds of sweet peppers that are grown in Hungary and is traditionally used in Hungarian goulash.

Storing pepper
In order to retain flavour and colour buy pepper regularly and keep it in a container with a tight fitting lid.

Pepper in food preparation
Pepper is useful as a flavouring and, in the case of red pepper, a colouring in many foods. To obtain the best flavour of black and white pepper, use a pepper mill and grind the peppercorns as they are needed.

Mustard

Mustard has been used for thousands of years, but it was the Romans who introduced this condiment to Britain. The various species of mustard plant are all related to the cabbage family.

Making mustard

The characteristic pungency of mustard comes from an essential oil which is formed when the ground seeds are mixed with water. This reaction depends upon the enzyme *myrosin*. For the full flavour to be developed, the mustard powder and water mixture should be left for 10 to 15 minutes. It is essential that boiling water, salt or vinegar are not mixed with the mustard powder. These additions will destroy the enzyme, so that the mustard will not be hot and it is likely to have a bitter taste. Ingredients such as vinegar and salt may be added once the pungency has had sufficient time to develop. Make up fresh mustard as needed because it tends to lose its pungency during storage. If it must be kept, keep it covered because it forms an unappetising crust on the surface if it is left exposed to the atmosphere.

Consumer choice of mustard

1 *English mustard* is made from brown and white mustard seeds. The mixture of seeds is ground and made into a powder called 'mustard flour'. This is mixed with other ingredients, including wheat flour, turmeric, sugar and salt. English mustard is available in powder form or ready made.
2 *French mustard* (Bordeaux mustard) has a mild flavour but is dark in colour. The whole mustard seed and its seed coat go into this mustard. Other ingredients in Bordeaux mustard include vinegar, sugar, tarragon and other herbs and spices. It is available as made-up mustard.
3 *Dijon mustard* is paler in colour than Bordeaux mustard because the seed is removed, and it is more pungent. There are many varieties of Dijon mustard – for example, a mustard with mustard seeds, spices and the juice from grapes that have not fully ripened. Like Bordeaux mustard, Dijon mustard is sold made up.
4 *German mustard* is very similar to Bordeaux mustard.
5 *American mustard* looks like English mustard but it has a sweet taste and is much milder. American mustard is made mainly from ground white mustard and turmeric.

Storing mustard

Dry mustard should be stored in containers which have tight-fitting lids. If it is purchased ready made, keep the lid on during storage, otherwise it will dry out.

Mustard in food preparation

Mustard adds 'kick' to sauces and goes well in cheese dishes such as Welsh rarebit. French mustards make appetising marinades for barbecued meats. Mustard is often added to salad dressings because it helps to stabilise the emulsion as well as adding to the final flavour of the dressing.

Vinegar

The word 'vinegar' comes from the French *vin aigre* which means 'wine that has soured'. It is believed to be one of the oldest condiments. It is formed by an oxidation process whereby alcohol is oxidised to form acetic acid, thus creating the characteristic aromatic taste.

Consumer choice of vinegar

1 *Malt vinegar* is a traditional English vinegar made from beer. It is dark brown and is strongly flavoured. This type of vinegar is useful in the preparation of pickles and chutneys.
2 *Wine vinegar* is associated with France and is a by-product of the wine

industry. It is particularly useful in salad dressings and sauces, because it tastes milder than malt vinegar. The colour depends on whether red or white wine is used to make it.

3 *Cider vinegar* is made from cider and tastes like cider.
4 *Distilled vinegar* contains much more acetic acid than other vinegars. The high acidity makes it particularly useful for pickling. This type of vinegar is colourless and has a strong flavour.
5 *Other vinegars* are available with flavourings; for example, herbs (such as tarragon), spices and fruit.

Storing vinegar
Vinegar should be kept in sealed containers.

Vinegar in food preparation
As well as a condiment for use at table, vinegar can be used as a tenderising agent for tough cuts of meat. It gives an appetising 'sting' to sauces, it is an important ingredient in most salad dressings and a key ingredient in sauces such as mint sauce and sweet and sour sauces. It is used extensively as a preservative in pickles and chutneys.

Essential oils and essences

Volatile or essential oils and essences are extracted from plants.

1 *Almond oil* is obtained from bitter almonds.
2 *Lemon oil* comes from lemons.
3 *Orange oil* comes from oranges.
4 *Peppermint oil* is obtained from the peppermint plant.

Artificial essences are not as expensive as natural ones. The range of such essences is very wide: rum, brandy, apple, vanilla, and anchovy are just some examples.

Essences and essential oils are best stored in dark bottles away from the light. These flavourings oxidise rapidly, and for maximum flavour should not be kept in storage for long periods.

Sauces

Soya sauce

Shoyu or soya sauce has been used since ancient times in Chinese and Japanese cooking. It is well known for its characteristic taste which is meaty, salty and slightly sweet. The colour is dark brown. This sauce has been popular for more than 300 years in Britain. Soya sauce is made from fermented soya beans. It is used for flavouring sauces, soups and stews, and is good as a marinade. It goes well in stir-fry dishes.

Tabasco sauce

A chilli sauce called Tabasco sauce is well known for its hot or fiery taste and red colour. It originated in the Tabasco region of Mexico and is made from chillis crushed into a pulp. This pulp is packed into barrels and salt is added. The mixture is left to mature in the barrel over a period of 3 years. After this time it is mixed with distilled vinegar, and, finally, the skin and seeds of the chillis are removed before the sauce is bottled.

Tomato ketchup	This red, sweet-tasting sauce is made from tomato paste, sugar, vinegar, salt and spices. It is used mainly as a condiment but also in food preparation as a flavouring (for example, in dips and in meat loaves).
Worcestershire sauce	This sauce dates back to Victorian times, and the exact recipe is a closely guarded secret. The sauce is dark brown and the flavour is aromatic, pungent and both sweet and sour. It is used to flavour soups, stews and sauces and is also used as a condiment.

Extracts

Bovril	This meat extract is a thick, dark brown paste with a salty taste. It was made for the first time in 1874 in Quebec and was known as 'Johnston's Fluid Beef'. Bovril is a concentrated flavouring which can be used as a spread or to flavour foods such as gravies, stews and casseroles.
Yeast extract	This thick, dark brown paste also has a characteristic salty taste. Yeast extract has been produced since the turn of the century and is made from yeast cells. The yeast cells are broken down by various methods such as hydrolysis and autolysis. The liquid that comes away from the cells is evaporated and flavourings may be added. Yeast extracts may be used as spreads and as flavourings in food preparation. They are frequently used in vegan cooking. Yeast extracts are useful sources of some of the B vitamins.

Flavour enhancers

Monosodium glutamate	The seaweed *Laminaria japonica* was traditionally added to foods by the Japanese. This ingredient has the ability to make foods really tasty. In 1908 a chemist, Dr Kikunae Ikedo, discovered that the seaweed contained monosodium L-glutamate. Only very small amounts were needed to intensify the flavour of foods such as meat and fish. Monosodium glutamate is described as a 'flavour enhancer' or 'flavour potentiator' because it brings out the flavour of food. The product comes from proteins in plants – for example, maize and sugar beet – by a type of hydrolysis. It looks like salt because it is white and crystalline. It can be used in food preparation to enhance flavours and is particularly important in Chinese cooking. It is widely used in manufactured foods. Excessive intakes have been associated with a disorder called the 'Chinese restaurant syndrome'. The symptoms are headache, palpitations and pains in the chest and neck.

Other flavourings

1 *Vegetables*   A stick of celery is often included in soup recipes. Tomatoes, particularly canned or puréed, are often included in meat dishes, such as burgers and shepherd's pie. The use of only a few mushrooms makes

all the difference to soups and stews. Green peppers, in very small quantities, can add to the taste of salads and savoury rice dishes.

2 *Fruit*   Lemons complement the flavour of sweet and savoury foods. The juice and zest may be used together for maximum flavour of the fruit.

3 *Meat*   Bacon is often used in very small amounts as a flavouring, for example, in tomato soup and quiche Lorraine.

4 *Cheese*   Even small amounts of cheese can make all the difference to sauces, toppings or vegetarian burgers made from cereals and pulses. Strong-flavoured cheeses are recommended for this, such as mature or farmhouse Cheddar or parmesan.

5 *Fats and oils*   Butter, margarine and olive oil may be added to flavour foods. Both butter and margarine play a part in the buttery taste of short-crust pastry, and olive oil adds flavour to salad dressings.

6 *Sugar and sweeteners* are used to sweeten foods.

7 *Beverages*   Cocoa, coffee, tea, fruit juices and alcoholic drinks can be used to flavour foods.

19 Beverages

Flavoured drinks are a popular way of meeting the body's needs for water. Some are stimulants, and certain drinks contribute to the energy value of the diet. Other nutrients may also be provided: tea, for example, contains useful amounts of fluoride, and fruit juices contain useful amounts of vitamin C.

Tea

About 5000 years ago the Emperor Shen Nung is said to have tasted some boiled water contaminated with leaves from a wild tea bush. The Emperor discovered that the water had a 'wonderful flavour and fragrance'. Today approximately one-third of the world's production of tea is consumed in Britain, where the average daily consumption of tea is about $4\frac{1}{2}$ cups, which is more than 1600 cups a year. It is not surprising that tea has become known as 'the Englishman's drink'.

Production of tea

Fig. 19.1
The terminal bud and 2 young leaves from a tea plant

Growing tea

Tea comes from a plant belonging to the camellia family. Tea plants are evergreen and grow well in tropical and sub-tropical regions where they like an acid, well-drained soil. Tea bushes are pruned regularly and kept to an average height of 90 to 120 cm. Every 7 to 14 days the tea is plucked. This is done by hand, and a skilled tea picker can collect about 30–35 kilos in one day. Only the young leaves of the plant are used to produce tea; these leaves are called the 'flush'. The finest teas are produced from the terminal bud and the 2 small leaves from each tea shoot (Fig. 19.1). Regular pruning ensures that there is an abundance of young shoots.

Much of the tea imported into Britain is grown in India, Kenya, Sri Lanka and Bangladesh.

Processing of tea (Fig. 19.2)

1 *Withering* The green tea leaves are taken to the tea factory on the tea plantation. The weighed leaves are spread thinly on 'withering' racks, where they may be left for up to 24 hours. About 50% of the moisture is lost by evaporation during withering.
2 *Rolling* The withered leaves are put into rolling machines where the cells of the leaves are disrupted and the natural juices released. At this stage sifting separates the fine leaves and terminal bud from the larger leaves. Thereafter the fine and coarse teas are processed separately.
3 *Fermentation* The leaves are spread on racks and left in a damp atmosphere for about 3 hours. The word 'fermentation' is not strictly correct; 'oxidation' would be a more accurate description. During this stage the tannin in tea is oxidised; the enzymes released in the rolling process play an important role in this. At this stage tea develops its characteristic colour, aroma and flavour. The leaves come out a bright copper-red colour.

Fig. 19.2
Processing tea

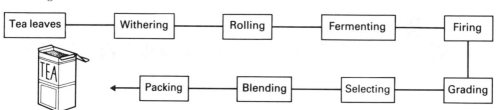

4 *Firing*   The leaves are 'fired' in a current of hot air. Firing takes about 20 to 30 minutes, and the leaves are then dry, crisp and dark brown or black in colour.

5 *Grading*   The tea is sifted and graded into leaf tea, broken and small leaf tea, fannings and dust. It is packed and despatched to the various purchasing countries.

6 *Selection*   When the tea arrives in Britain it is stored in warehouses, and samples are distributed to tea buyers by selling brokers. This gives the buyers time to taste the different teas before they are auctioned. The tea is cleaned and assessed for quality and cost.

7 *Blending*   Most teas are in the form of blends. As many as 30 different teas may be used to make up a blend. To obtain a standard product the tea blenders make up and taste samples, using tea from different estates. When the mix is right (that is, when it compares favourably with the original standard), it is blended on a factory scale.

8 *Packing*   The tea may be packed loose, or it may be made into tea bags before being packed.

Other types of tea

1 *Green tea*   After the leaves have been picked they are crushed and dried. The drying is carried out at a high temperature to inactivate the oxidising enzymes. The fermentation is left out altogether so the tannins in the leaf are not oxidised. Green teas have more tannin than black teas. Examples of green teas are Hyson and Gunpowder. Only just over 1% of the tea purchased in Britain is of this type. Green tea produces a pale greenish-yellow liquor.

2 *Scented tea*   Flavourings such as mint leaves, rose petals, orange zest and cloves may be added to tea at the firing stage. These additions are usually sifted out. These teas are available as loose tea and as tea bags.

3 *Instant tea* is made from an infusion of tea that has been either freeze dried or spray dried. The dried product is then packed in airtight containers.

Constituents in tea

A good cup of tea has the following qualities:

- subtle aroma;
- clear and bright appearance;
- deep amber liquor;
- 'briskness'.

To understand these qualities it is important to know about the constituents of tea.

Essential oils
Much of the appeal of a cup of tea lies in its characteristic aroma. This is due to the presence of essential oils or volatile compounds. Black tea is known to have more than 300 such compounds.

Caffeine
Tea has a stimulating effect, and caffeine is responsible for this.

Tannins
Tea leaves are rich in tannins. These play an important part in the colour and flavour of tea. Tannins are phenolic compounds:

1 *Thearubigins* constitute from 7% to 20% of the dry weight of black tea and give depth of colour to the tea.
2 *Theoflavins* account for about 2% of the dry weight of black tea and give a characteristic sparkle to the tea.

Nutrient content of tea

Tea contributes fluoride to the diet. In Britain where tea is such a popular drink it has been suggested that the adult intake from tea may be as high as 1 mg of fluoride daily.

Consumer choice of tea

1 The choice of tea will depend on personal taste. Some people prefer 'green teas' and others are partial to the scented varieties.
2 Loose tea, tea bags or instant tea are available. Tea bags are very popular and are quick and convenient to use.
3 Tea should be purchased from retailers with a fast turnover; stale tea is lacking in flavour.

Storing tea

Tea becomes stale and loses its flavour during storage, particularly in a damp atmosphere. During storage, volatile compounds are lost and the flavour of the less volatile tannins tends to predominate. Storage temperatures should be below 30°C and the tea should be kept in closed containers. The recommended storage time for loose tea is 1 month, for all other tea from 2 to 4 months.

Tea making

Tea is made by steeping the leaves in hot water, but other factors are important:

1 *Quality of the tea*   If the tea has been stored in the wrong conditions, or kept for too long much of the flavour will be lost.
2 *Type of water*   If hard water is used this tends to produce a 'scum' and a distinctive flavour. It is likely that the calcium and magnesium salts in the hard water bring about these effects by precipitating soluble compounds in the tea. Alkaline water tends to result in a darker liquor. This is believed to be due to ionisation of the thearubigins.
3 *Boiling water*   To avoid a flattish taste bring the water to a rolling boil.
4 *Temperature of the water during steeping*   If the steeping temperature is too low, extraction from the leaves will be poor. If the tea is kept so hot that it boils when steeping, the tea itself will be very astringent. For the best extraction warm the teapot with boiling water, have a tight fitting lid and position the teapot away from any source of direct heat once the tea is in it.
5 *Steeping, infusing or brewing*   This is best done for 3 to 6 minutes. If the infusion time is less, the tea will be weak and lacking in colour. If the tea is infused for too long, much of the flavour will be lost because of the loss of volatile compounds and the tea will become more astringent due to the flavour of the tannins.
6 *Addition of lemon juice*   When tea is served with a slice of lemon it has a lighter colour. This is believed to be due to acid depressing the ionisation of the thearubigins.

Coffee

Coffee first became popular in the Middle East. Originally the berries were eaten whole or they were crushed and fat was added to them. Eventually the berries were fermented to produce a 'stimulating' drink. It was the Turks who brought coffee to Europe in the seventeenth century.

Production of coffee

Fig. 19.3
Coffee berries and coffee beans

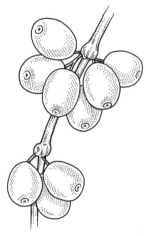

Growing coffee

Coffee comes from an evergreen plant that grows well in tropical and sub-tropical regions. The white, fragrant blossom of the coffee bush yields dark green berries. When the berries ripen they are deep red in colour and are called 'cherries'. The fully ripened berries are picked by hand; a skilled picker can collect about 90 kg in 1 day. The seeds found inside the cherries are the coffee beans (Fig. 19.3). The beans are oval, with one side rounded and the other flat. They are surrounded by an inner husk, a layer of pulp and finally the red skin.

Most coffee is grown in Brazil, Colombia, Mexico, El Salvador, Kenya, Indonesia, the Ivory Coast and Guatemala.

Processing of coffee (Fig. 19.4)

1 *Curing*   The cherries are taken to a processing plant where they are cured by one of 2 methods:
   (a) *The 'wet' method*   The cherries pass through a machine which removes the fleshy part of the fruit. The 2 seeds enclosed by the inner husk are put into vats for 24 to 40 hours to ferment. The process of fermentation is important for the development of the coffee aroma and for removing any pulp that remains attached to the husk. The beans are then washed and dried by spreading them out in the sun. The dried beans are then put into a hulling machine where the husk is removed. At this stage the beans are olive green.
   (b) *The 'dry' method*   This method is not as costly as the wet method of curing. The cherries are left to dry in the sun and then they are put into a hulling machine where the pulp and husk are removed together.
2 *Grading*   The coffee beans are graded according to size and quality.
3 *Selection*   The beans are either distributed to brokers or they may be purchased direct from the country of origin.
4 *Blending*   This is done by experts in order to produce a standard product. It also gives consumers a range of different blends to choose from.
5 *Roasting*   This is carried out in rotating drums where the temperature is at least 200°C. During roasting the cell walls in the beans are ruptured so that most of the aromatic oils are driven to the surface. Roasting brings about various chemical changes which are important for the

Fig. 19.4
Processing coffee

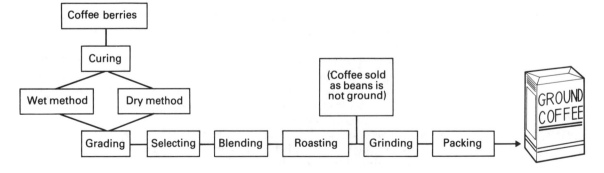

aroma, taste and colour of the final product. The beans may be light-roasted for a mild flavour or dark-roasted for a slightly bitter flavour. During roasting the coffee beans become porous. When the ground coffee is finally mixed with water the porosity allows for greater contact between the 2 ingredients.

6 *Grinding*   This determines the aroma, flavour and colour of the coffee. However, once ground, coffee stales rapidly.

7 *Packing*   The roasted beans or ground coffee are stored in vacuum packs or airtight containers. Ground coffee is sometimes made into coffee bags.

Other types of coffee

1 *Coffee and chicory* mixtures are not quite as expensive as pure coffee, and the resulting drink is strong.

2 *Instant coffee* was introduced to Britain in 1939. It is made from freshly brewed coffee. The liquid coffee is dispersed into a fine mist in a stream of warm air and the water evaporates, leaving coffee powder. Alternatively, the coffee may be freeze-dried.

3 *De-caffeinated coffee* is becoming more popular. Coffee labelled 'de-caffeinated' must not contain more than 0.1% caffeine, by law.

4 *Coffee concentrates* are particularly useful in the preparation of coffee flavoured foods such as coffee cake.

Constituents in coffee

A good cup of coffee has the following qualities:

- high aroma;
- deep amber to rich brown liquor, depending on the type of roast;
- silky feel on the tongue;
- mellow as opposed to bitter;
- slightly astringent and not 'flat'.

To understand these qualities it is important to know about the constituents of coffee.

Volatile compounds
The aroma of coffee is a complex matter. Over 100 compounds have been identified as playing a part in this.

Caffeine
Caffeine has a stimulating effect. The amount of caffeine found in the prepared beverage depends on how the coffee is made. Coffee made in a percolator contains less caffeine than coffee made by the filter or 'drip' method.

Carbon dioxide
During roasting carbon dioxide fills the spaces in the beans, and it is this gas which gives coffee some of its characteristic 'zip'. The carbon dioxide in the beans makes ground coffee float when it comes in contact with water.

Organic acids
Chlorogenic acid, which constitutes approximately two-thirds of the acid in a cup of coffee, has a marked effect on the final taste. Other organic acids contributing to flavour are caffeic, citric, malic and tartaric acids.

Colour compounds
The colour of the final drink is related to the degree of roasting. A light roast produces a light cinnamon colour, and a heavy roast a dark brown. As well as this, some of the carbohydrates in the bean are caramelised during roasting so that they too contribute to the colour.

Nutrient content of coffee

One of the B vitamins, nicotinic acid, is provided by coffee in useful amounts. The quantity provided depends upon the degree of roasting. Coffees with a dark roast have more nicotinic acid than those with a light roast.

Consumer choice of coffee

1 Many blends are available, each with its own distinct flavour.
2 It is usual for dark roasted coffee to be used as an 'after-dinner' beverage; this type of coffee has a slightly bitter 'Continental' flavour, and it is also used for espresso coffee. A more general-purpose coffee with a mild taste is made from lightly roasted beans.
3 Some consumers prefer coffee that is mixed with ingredients such as chicory. This is particularly popular in France.
4 De-caffeinated coffee is preferred by some individuals who believe it is better for them than ordinary coffee. Coffee taken in large quantities can produce anxiety symptoms, cardiac arrhythmias, insomnia and gastro-intestinal discomfort. These symptoms are not associated with de-caffeinated coffee.
5 The consumer can choose from coffee beans, ground coffee, instant coffee or coffee bags. Coffee beans ground at home have an appealing aroma and yield an excellent cup of coffee if they are fresh. If ground coffee is purchased loose it has a limited storage life (Table 20.2). Vacuum-packed ground coffee keeps fresher longer. Instant coffee is a convenient and economical way of making coffee. Coffee bags have the advantage of convenience with the flavour and aroma of ground coffee.
6 Coffee should be purchased from retailers with a fast turnover.

Storing coffee

Roasted coffee beans, particularly after grinding, become stale quickly. During storage carbon dioxide is lost, resulting in a 'flat' cup of coffee. Volatile compounds are also lost, and they may become less soluble in water. This means that the aroma will be missing. Coffee becomes stale more quickly in a damp atmosphere. It should be stored at a low temperature and in a container preventing direct contact with the air. Recommended storage times for the various types of coffee are shown in Table 20.2.

Coffee making with ground coffee

1 *Quality of the coffee*   Use fresh coffee kept for no longer than the recommended storage times.
2 *Degree of grinding*   This will depend on the method used to make the coffee; for example, the coffee should be very finely ground if a coffee-filter is used. If the coffee is insufficiently ground the beverage will be weak and lacking in aroma.
3 *Quantity of coffee*   It is suggested that for every cup of coffee of average strength, 1 dessertspoon of ground coffee is used.
4 *Type of water*   This affects the quality of the drink; soft water is ideal.
5 *Boiling the water*   Once boiling point has been reached, the water used to make coffee should not be allowed to continue to boil. Coffee made with water that has continued to boil tastes 'flat'.
6 *Temperature of the water*   This should not be higher than 95°C. If the water is at a higher temperature than this, the drink has a bitter taste because more soluble constituents are extracted.
7 *Brewing time*   2 minutes is recommended, because this allows time for the extraction of the desirable flavours but is not long enough to extract the components which would impart a bitter flavour.

Cocoa

The Aztecs had been drinking chocolate for hundreds of years before the Spanish explorer Don Hernando Cortés conquered Mexico in 1519. Cocoa beans were taken back to Spain by Cortés but the drink was not introduced to England until the 1650s. In 1824 a young Quaker, John Cadbury, opened a grocery shop in Birmingham where he sold 'cocoa nibs'. In the cellar of his shop he experimented by roasting and grinding cocoa beans, and in 1831 he opened a warehouse and began manufacturing cocoa.

Production of cocoa

Fig. 19.5
Cocoa pod and cocoa beans

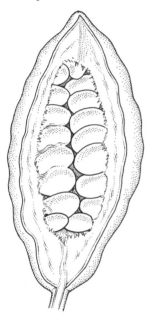

Growing cocoa

Cocoa comes from the cocoa tree, which is native to the rain forests of the Amazon but is now cultivated in other parts of South America and West Africa. Cocoa trees require a deep, rich soil, and the ideal climate is about 20 degrees north and south of the Equator. The cocoa pods grow from the branches and trunk of the tree. Each pod weighs about 450 g and is 225 mm long. When the pods have ripened they are a rich golden colour. Each pod has between 20 and 40 seeds in it, and it is these seeds that are called 'cocoa beans' (Fig. 19.5). They are like almonds in shape and size, and are covered with a sweet pulp. The ripened pods are removed from the trunk and branches of the cocoa tree. They are then taken to a collection point.

Approximately 60% of the world's cocoa is produced in West Africa. Other cocoa-producing areas include Brazil, Mexico, Ecuador, the Dominican Republic, Trinidad and Sri Lanka.

Processing of cocoa (Fig. 19.6)

1 *Fermentation*   The beans and pulp are removed from the pods and are either heaped in boxes or put between leaves of plantains or large bananas and left to ferment for 5 to 6 days. The contents of the heaps are turned from time to time to ensure that the beans are mixed evenly. The pulp that surrounds the beans drains away and the temperature within the heap rises to 50°C. This stage allows the beans to develop the 'chocolate' flavour.
2 *Drying*   The beans are dried by spreading them out in the sun.
3 *Sorting and cleaning*   Beans that are mouldy or damaged by insects are rejected, and the remainder are shipped in sacks to Britain where they are taken to a cocoa-processing plant. At this stage they are sorted and cleaned.
4 *Roasting*   The beans are put into rotating ovens to roast. During this stage the shells of the beans are loosened and the flavour and aroma of cocoa is acquired.
5 *Kibbling and winnowing*   The beans are 'kibbled'; that is, they are broken down into small pieces. Next, the shells, which are brittle, are removed, using an artificial wind in a winnowing machine. The broken, roasted cocoa beans without their shells are called 'nibs'.

Fig. 19.6
Processing cocoa

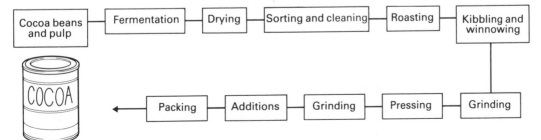

6 *Grinding*   The cocoa nibs are ground between steel rollers to produce a thick chocolate-coloured liquid. The liquid is called 'mass', and it solidifies when it has cooled.

7 *Pressing*   The solid mass is 55% cocoa butter, and about half of this is pressed out so that a solid block of cocoa is left. The cocoa butter is not wasted; it is used in the manufacture of chocolate.

8 *Grinding*   The solid block of cocoa is ground into a fine powder.

9 *Additions*   Ingredients added are salt, sodium carbonate and vanilla flavouring.

10 *Packing*   The cocoa in powder form is then packed into tins or cartons.

Constituents in cocoa

Cocoa contains only traces of tannins and caffeine. Consequently it does not have the same stimulatory effect as tea and coffee. This is why cocoa is particularly suitable as a bedtime drink.

Nutrient content of cocoa

Folic acid and iron are found in cocoa in useful amounts. As a beverage, cocoa is made with milk and this adds significantly to the nutritional value.

Storing cocoa

Cocoa loses its flavour during prolonged storage. The recommended storage time is 3 months in a clear, dry, well-ventilated storage area. Keep cocoa in its original container, sealed until required.

Making cocoa

To make cocoa it is usual to blend the cocoa powder with a little of the measured cold milk. The rest of the milk is boiled and then blended with the dissolved cocoa.

Other beverages

Soft drinks

Drinks such as Coca-Cola, lemonade, orange squash and lime cordial are all soft drinks. The first 2 examples are ready to drink and the last two need to be diluted. These beverages contribute water to the diet and energy because sugar is used as a sweetening agent. Coca-Cola is particularly popular. As a result of new technological developments many of these soft drinks are available without sugar, so that the energy value is lower.

Fruit juices

Juices obtained from fruit by mechanical processes are popular. The virtue of these drinks again is water, and also vitamin C is provided. Some fruit juices are sweetened, and the energy value of such drinks is higher. In the interests of the 'healthful' diet choose the unsweetened varieties.

Mineral waters

Drinks such as Perrier, Vichy and Evian waters are popular because of their refreshing qualities. The dietary virtue of such drinks is the water content. Small quantities of sodium, calcium and magnesium salts are found in mineral waters. Many of the mineral waters are aerated with carbon dioxide.

Alcoholic drinks

Drinks such as beer, cider, wine, whisky and brandy all contain alcohol, which is a drug. The drug, even in small quantities, impairs judgement. As with all beverages, alcoholic drinks contribute water to the diet. The energy value depends upon the drink in question. For example, dry white wine provides less energy than sweet white wine. As far as other nutrients are concerned, beer provides very small amounts of nicotinic acid and riboflavin, and some wines are rich in iron.

20　Food hygiene

Microbiology

Some very basic knowledge of microbiology is fundamental in the prevention of food poisoning.

Bacteria

Fig. 20.1
A bacterial cell

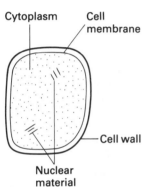

Cytoplasm

Cell membrane

Cell wall

Nuclear material

Bacteria are widely distributed in the environment. They are single-celled organisms which are so small that they are not visible to the naked eye. A bacterium consists of a mass of cytoplasm, some nuclear material and a cell wall (Fig. 20.1). Some bacteria have a slime layer surrounding the cell wall or a capsule. Certain bacteria have thread-like structures called 'flagella' which help to propel them in liquid.

The shape of the bacterial cell varies, and this is important in the classification of bacteria. There are 4 main shapes (Fig. 20.2).

Bacteria reproduce by dividing into two.

Under adverse conditions some bacteria form spores. A spore forms inside the bacterial cell and the remainder of the cell disintegrates around it. Spores are hard, resistant bodies which can survive in adverse conditions for long periods. Spores germinate as soon as conditions are favourable for growth.

Bacteria produce various substances, some of which are harmful to humans: these are called toxins:

1　*Endotoxins* are formed inside the bacterial cell. These toxins are released from the bacterial cell when the cell dies. Illness resulting from endotoxins can only take place if the living bacteria are consumed.
2　*Exotoxins* are secreted by bacteria into their surroundings, and foods containing exotoxins will cause illness even if the bacteria themselves are dead.

Fig. 20.2
Different shapes of bacteria

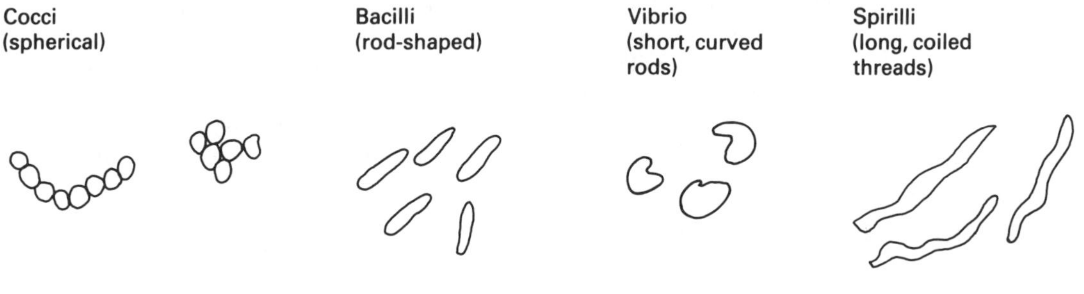

Cocci
(spherical)

Bacilli
(rod-shaped)

Vibrio
(short, curved rods)

Spirilli
(long, coiled threads)

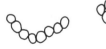

Yeasts

Yeasts are not as widely distributed as bacteria. They are found mainly on plant foods in nature.

Like bacteria, yeasts are single celled, but the cells are bigger. They come in a variety of shapes, including oval, rod-shaped and spherical.

Yeasts reproduce by a process called 'budding'. When yeast cells bud part of the cell forms a bulge: this bulge is called a 'bud'. The bud grows and eventually breaks away to form a new cell.

Table 20.1
Food poisoning

Causative micro-organism	Source	Associated foods
Bacillus cereus spore-forming aerobic bacilli	Soil, dust and water	Cereals, e.g. rice and cornflour
Campylobacter non-spore-forming aerobic bacilli	Intestines of humans and other animals, especially young pets such as kittens and puppies	Poultry, milk, shellfish and mushrooms
Clostridium botulinum spore-forming anaerobic bacilli	Soil	Home-canned foods
Clostridium perfringens spore-forming anaerobic bacilli	Intestines of humans and other animals, soil, dust, flies and bluebottles	Meat dishes prepared in advance
Listeria monocytogenes non-spore-forming aerobic cocci	Soil, manure, food waste and other decaying organic matter	Cook–chill foods, raw and processed meat, raw vegetables, soft cheeses
Salmonella non-spore-forming aerobic bacilli	Intestines of humans and other animals, including cats	Meat, poultry particularly cold and re-heated poultry, cream and eggs
Staphylococcus aureus non-spore-forming aerobic cocci	Skin, nose, hands, throat boils, scratches, burns, raw cows' and goats' milk	Cold meat, ham, tongue and meat pies

Moulds

Unlike bacteria and yeasts, moulds are usually made up of more than 1 cell and are known as multicellular organisms.

Moulds grow as a tangled mass, made up of thin thread-like strands called 'hyphae'. The mass of hyphae is called the 'mycelium'. Moulds may be septate or non-septate. The former has cross-walls which divide the hyphae into cells. The latter does not have cross-walls, so the hyphae are just continuous tubes (Fig. 20.3).

Moulds usually reproduce by a process called 'sporulation'. In septate moulds spores break off either singly or in chains. In non-septate moulds

Fig. 20.3
Moulds

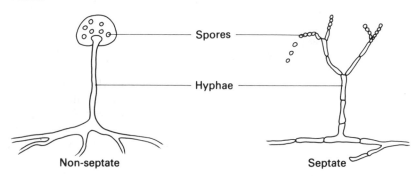

Non-septate   Septate

Incubation period	Symptoms	Duration (days)
1–5 hours	Abdominal pain, vomiting and sometimes diarrhoea	¼–1
3–5 days	Headache, nausea, malaise, fever, severe abdominal pain and diarrhoea	1–10
18–36 hours	Headache, dizziness nausea, fatigue, vomiting, dry skin, mouth and throat, constipation, paralysis of muscles and respiratory failure	Death within 1–8 days or slow recovery
8–22 hours	Nausea, abdominal pain and diarrhoea	½–1
1–90 weeks	Mild flu-like illness to meningitis and meningoencephalitis and possibly abortion in pregnant women	Variable
12–36 hours	Headache, vomiting, fever, abdominal pain and diarrhoea	1–8, but can be fatal
1–7 hours	Acute vomiting, abdominal pain, diarrhoea and sometimes collapse	¼–1

the spores are formed in a spore case. The ripened spores are released, and they germinate when they reach a suitable environment for their growth.

Factors affecting the growth of micro-organisms

1 *Food*   All micro-organisms need food to survive.
2 *Moisture*   All micro-organisms need a supply of water to maintain life.
3 *Temperature*   This is critical to the growth rate, and all micro-organisms have an optimum growth temperature as well as minimum and maximum ones.
4 *Oxygen*   This affects the growth of micro-organisms. If they are aerobic they need oxygen. If anaerobic they do not require oxygen.
5 *pH (measure of acidity or alkalinity)* Most micro-organisms grow well in neutral conditions.
6 *Time*   All micro-organisms need time to reproduce.

Food poisoning

Food poisoning may be defined as an illness caused by eating food which is either contaminated or contains naturally harmful substances. Food poisoning is classified into 3 main types: *bacterial*, *biological* and *chemical*. Of these 3 types, bacterial food poisoning (Table 20.1) is the most usual. Biological food poisoning results from eating plants containing harmful substances – for example, poisonous mushrooms and green potatoes. Chemical food poisoning may result when chemicals such as weed killers and insecticides are eaten in large doses.

Guidelines for the prevention of food poisoning

In order to prevent food poisoning it is essential to prevent contamination with bacteria, and growth of bacteria.

Personal hygiene

1 Hands should be washed thoroughly with soap and hot water before food is handled and always after going to the lavatory or using a handkerchief. When raw meat or poultry is being prepared it is essential to wash the hands immediately afterwards.
2 Hands should be free from cracks, roughness and abrasions, and nails should be short, clean and unbroken.
3 Rings should be removed and nail varnish should not be used.
4 Any cuts, sores, boils or abrasions on the hands or fingers should be covered with clean, waterproof plasters.
5 Fingers should not be licked. Care should be taken not to finger parts of the body, such as the nose, mouth or hair. If these parts are touched, the hands should be washed at once.
6 Use clean, disposable paper tissues for blowing the nose rather than handkerchiefs.
7 Wear some form of protective clothing such as an overall.
8 Hair should not come in direct contact with food. Hair can be tied back or covered during food handling.
9 Individuals suffering from any illness should not prepare food for others.
10 It is not hygienic to allow animals into a kitchen.

Kitchen hygiene

1 There should be nothing in the kitchen to attract vermin. If any food is spilt it should be cleaned up at once, and leftovers from meals disposed of hygienically.
2 All equipment and utensils should be kept scrupulously clean.
3 Work surfaces should be washed every day; the floor may need to be swept more than once a day. It should be washed when spills occur and cleaned thoroughly at least once a week.
4 Cloths, such as dishcloths and tea towels, should be washed daily; soaking in bleach and boiling are recommended. Dirty cloths are dangerous sources of infection.
5 Dispose of all scraps promptly. Many kitchens have small waste bins, such as pedal bins. It is usual to line bins of this type with plastic bags. Bins kept indoors should be emptied at least daily, cleaned with detergent and then drained. They should be disinfected regularly.
6 Larger bins should be kept outside and are best positioned away from windows leading to the kitchen or larder. Bins should have a tightly fitting lid and can be raised above the ground by about 30 cm so that the area around is easy to clean, and metal bins are less likely to become rusty. Plastic bin bags are useful because they reduce the amount of work in keeping the bin clean and help to prevent odours. Bins should be washed regularly and disinfected.

Handling food

1 All the guidelines for personal hygiene should be followed.
2 Direct handling of food should be avoided if possible – particularly cooked food.
3 Food should be covered to prevent contamination.
4 Equipment and utensils should be clean.
5 Cook food thoroughly.

6 Hot food should be eaten while it is still hot.
7 If the food is to be eaten cold it should be cooled rapidly and refrigerated within 90 minutes. Cold food should be kept below 5°C in a refrigerator.
8 Cooked food should not be stored too long; up to 3 days in a refrigerator is the maximum time. For longer storage freezing is advisable.
9 It is not advisable to reheat food. Careful planning can minimise the problem of leftovers.

Table 20.2
Approximate storage life of some foods

Food	Shelf life (months)
Beverages	
Tea – loose	1
other	2–4
Coffee – instant	3
beans, loose	2 weeks
vacuum-packed	12
ground, loose	1 week
vacuum-packed	10
Cocoa	3
Canned foods	6–12
Chutneys	24–36
Dried fruit	2–3
Dried pulses	6
Flour	
Wholewheat	2
Brown	2
White	6
Self-raising	2–3
Cornflour	6
Jams	24–36
Pickles	12
Raising agents	
Dried yeast	6
Baking powder	2–6
Bicarbonate of soda	1–2
Salt	Indefinite, if dry; if damp 1–2 weeks
Spices	1–2
Sugar	
Icing, granulated and cubes	3
Honey and syrup	12
Vinegar	1–2

Hygienic storage of food in the home

Perishable food – that is, meat, fish, milk, fruit and vegetables and cooked dishes made of these foods – should be stored for the shortest time possible. Ideally, these foods should be bought on the day they are needed. When this is not possible they must be stored in cool conditions. Perishable foods should be stored at a temperature below 10°C, and preferably a refrigerator should be used.

Larders or food cupboards are really best for the storage of non-perishable foods. However, a cold slab in a north-facing, well-ventilated food cupboard is useful if the following conditions are provided:

1 It is important to allow good ventilation.
2 The food cupboard should be safe from vermin and pets. A door that closes tightly and gauze over the windows are essential.
3 The floor, walls and shelves should be washed at least once a week and any spills dealt with immediately.
4 Lower shelves should be kept for perishable goods; higher ones that are not easily reached for longer-term storage.
5 It is not advisable to store foods on the floor. A minimum height of 450 mm is recommended so that the floor is easily cleaned.
6 Hot foods should never be put into the larder when hot as this will cause the atmosphere to become warm and moist.
7 To ensure that foods do not sit on a shelf too long, a system for using existing stock before new additions is useful.
8 Storage containers should be scrupulously clean and existing stock should not be 'topped up' with new.
9 Keep a check on the approximate storage times (Table 20.2).

Vegetable racks or cupboards are recommended for the storage of certain fruits and vegetables. These are ideally positioned a little way from food preparation and cooking areas because of any soil bacteria they may be harbouring.

21 Preservation of food

Foods are preserved to prolong their 'shelf life'. As soon as animals have been slaughtered and plant foods have been harvested deterioration begins. This involves two main processes. Firstly, cells break down due to enzymes present in the food: this process is called *autolysis*, meaning self-destruction. Secondly, the disrupted cell structures are vulnerable to the activities of *micro-organisms*. The complex organic components of food are broken down by micro-organisms causing changes in the odour, flavour, colour and texture of food. For effective food preservation it is necessary to prevent both autolysis and microbial growth.

Commercial preservation of food

Dehydration

Traditionally, foods were dried in the sun. The original processes have advanced considerably, and moisture is now removed by the application of heat in a controlled flow of air.

Methods of drying

1 *Sun drying* This method is practical in hot dry climates, but the process is slow and the foods being dried are vulnerable to contamination.
2 *Fluidised bed-drying* Warmed air is circulated around the food while it is agitated to stop it from sticking. This method is particularly suitable for vegetables.
3 *Spray drying* is used for liquid foods such as milk. The liquid is sprayed through fine nozzles into a current of hot air. The water evaporates and leaves behind a fine powder.
4 *Roller drying* is used for pasted foods such as instant breakfast cereals. The paste forms a film on the surface of a heated roller or drum. During the rotation of the roller or drum the food dries and it is finally removed by scrapers.
5 *Accelerated freeze-drying (AFD)* involves an initial freezing process which is followed by gradual heating in a vacuum cabinet. During this process ice crystals form and change to vapour without going through the liquid stage. The product is porous but differs little from its original form. The porous nature of the food makes it suitable for instant rehydration – for example, coffee, meat and vegetables.

Quality of dried food

Drying alters the cellular structure of food. Compare, for example, fresh apricots with dried apricots. Retinol, thiamin, ascorbic acid and vitamin E are lost during the drying process. Characteristic volatile odours are lost as a result of drying. Foods with a high fat content are vulnerable to rancidity and discoloration.

Canning

Fig. 21.1
Commercial canning

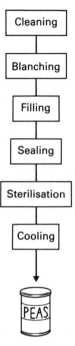

The origin of canning dates back to 1795 when the French government offered a prize for a practical method of preserving food. Eventually in 1809 François Appert preserved meat in glass bottles that were boiled in water.

Canning involves the application of heat and aims at destroying micro-organisms and their spores. The heat-treated or sterilised food must be kept in an airtight container to prevent contamination.

Canning is carried out in 6 main stages (Fig. 21.1):

1 The food is cleaned, and inedible parts such as the bones in meat and stones in fruit are removed.
2 Vegetables are usually blanched either by immersing them in boiling water or exposing them to steam. Blanching inactivates enzymes in the food, and bubbles of air are driven out of the food, reducing its bulk.
3 The cans are automatically filled. Fruits and vegetables and certain other foods are topped up with liquid such as brine or syrup. The filled cans are usually exposed to steam or hot water. This causes air to be driven out.
4 The cans are sealed with a lid in an automatic machine so that they are airtight or hermetic.
5 The cans are sterilised.
6 The cans are then cooled gradually.

Aseptic canning

This process involves the separate sterilisation of the food and can. The cans are filled in such a way that micro-organisms cannot enter.

Quality of canned food

The sterilisation process causes the loss of heat-sensitive nutrients such as ascorbic acid and thiamin. There are also changes in colour, flavour and texture.

Freezing

Fig. 21.2
The effect of large ice crystals on cell structure

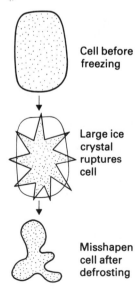

Cell before freezing

Large ice crystal ruptures cell

Misshapen cell after defrosting

The Romans are known to have kept foods packed in snow, but it was the Eskimos who stored meat for months in deep wells cut out of ice. In 1916 this practice was noted by Clarence Birdseye during a trading expedition to Labrador.

Freezing controls the growth of micro-organisms in two ways. The growth rate is reduced due to the low temperature and water is unavailable because it has been converted to ice. Also, the chemical changes in food are slowed down because of the low temperature. Before freezing foods, inedible parts are removed and it is usual to blanch fruit and vegetables to inactivate enzymes. The number of bacteria is also reduced by blanching.

Commercially, foods are frozen by the quick-freezing process. This method is desirable because ice crystals that form in the food are small; large ice crystals change the texture and appearance of food (Fig. 21.2).

Methods of freezing

1 *Plate-freezing* is the oldest of the large-scale methods of freezing. The food is packed between hollow metal plates, and refrigerant is passed through the plates.
2 *Blast-freezing* involves exposure of the food to a blast of pre-cooled air in a specially designed tunnel.
3 *Fluidised bed-freezing*, a development of blast-freezing, is suitable for foods of small particle size.
4 *Immersion-freezing* involves placing the food in the refrigerant. Brine may be used for fish.
5 *Cryogenic freezing* uses liquid nitrogen. This method allows a faster rate of

temperature loss, and the frozen food has tiny ice crystals. It is more costly than the other methods but it is recommended for foods such as strawberries.

Quality of frozen food
During blanching of fruit and vegetables ascorbic acid and thiamin are vulnerable. Nutrients in the form of thaw drip may be lost when foods are thawed – for example, thiamin from meat. Textural changes may occur; soft fruits, for instance, can become mushy because the cell structure of the fruit collapses.

Addition of chemicals

Foods may be preserved by the addition of anti-microbial substances such as:

1 *salt*, used in the curing of meat such as bacon;
2 *sugar*, used in the manufacture of jam and crystallised fruit;
3 *acids*, such as vinegar, used in pickling;
4 *permitted chemical preservatives*, such as benzoic acid in soft drinks and sulphur dioxide in dried fruit.

Low-sugar jam
Because consumers are becoming more health-conscious and are moving away from sweet foods, there is a demand for reduced-sugar jams. Changes in the quantity of sugar have implications for labelling and the word 'jam' cannot be used to describe the product. The EEC Commission is currently preparing proposals to cover low-sugar jams. In the meantime the Jams and Similar Products Regulations of 1982 allow the use of the descriptions 'jam', 'jelly' and 'marmalade' for products which have 60% or more soluble solids.

Reduced-sugar jams – that is, those with less than 60% soluble solids – do not have enough sugar to form a pectin-sugar gel, and calcium salts are added to increase the strength of the gel. However, the use of calcium is not always successful because it has a tendency to encourage syneresis, causing jams made in this way to separate. Apart from this problem, the low-sugar jams are not shelf-stable. To overcome this the product is either stored chilled or preservatives are added. However, syneresis is more likely at refrigerator temperatures, and consumers are becoming increasingly concerned about the use of additives.

Short-term preservation of food on a commercial scale

Irradiation
Although radiation destroys micro-organisms it has no effect on the enzymes in food, so degradation is not prevented. Food irradiation is permitted in some countries. For example, in 1974, potatoes in Japan were irradiated to preserve them from sprouting. In Britain the method is being considered by the Advisory Committee on Irradiated and Novel Foods.

The commercial development of irradiation is limited due to a number of factors such as the cost of equipment, stringent tests needed for safety and the development of undesirable flavours in certain foods.

Chilling
Refrigerators were developed after the First World War. Chilling is based on the principle that microbial activity is reduced in cold storage conditions.

Controlled gaseous atmospheres
The humidity and the composition of the atmosphere are controlled.

Vacuum packing
Food such as meat or cheese is packed in impermeable plastic material, and the air is sucked out under vacuum. This method prevents the growth of aerobic micro-organisms because of the absence of oxygen.

Permeable packaging
Some types of plastics are semi-permeable and allow the transfer of gases such as oxygen and carbon dioxide and water vapour. This type of material is used for foods such as tomatoes, and is useful because it delays ripening and extends shelf-life by more than a week. Other packaging materials are completely permeable. Sometimes crusty bread is packed in a plastic covering dotted with tiny holes. This type of packaging is advantageous because otherwise trapped moisture would condense and the crust would lose its characteristic crispness.

Home preservation of food

Commercial methods are not always practical in the domestic environment and some are potentially dangerous. Canning and bottling are not recommended because of practical difficulties in reaching the desired temperatures for the production of safe food.

Methods of preserving foods recommended for consumer use include freezing, drying and chemical methods.

Freezing

Most foods are well suited to freezing, but there are some exceptions:

- *Eggs*   The egg shell shatters around raw whole eggs. Boiled eggs become tough and the white turns grey. Egg yolk frozen on its own becomes gummy (this problem is overcome if either salt or sugar is added).
- *Cream*   Single cream separates when thawed after freezing.
- *Yogurt* separates when frozen.
- *Milk*   Pasteurised milk separates when frozen.
- *Cheese*   Both cream and cottage cheeses separate when frozen.
- *Egg-based sauces*, such as mayonnaise and egg custard, separate when frozen.
- *Sauces, casseroles and soups thickened with cornflour* separate when frozen.
- *Gelatine*   Dishes such as moulded jellies which rely on this thickener as a stabilising agent do not freeze well.
- *Jam* tends to lose its 'set' when frozen.
- *Soft meringues, macaroons and royal icing* thaw into a soggy mass.
- *Vegetables* lose a certain amount of crispness. Foods such as cucumber, tomato and lettuce are not suitable for salads once they have been frozen. Garlic-flavoured foods have a limited storage life due to the development of 'off-flavours'.
- *Fruit*   Both avocado pears and bananas usually become discoloured due to enzyme activity. If these foods are puréed or mashed with lemon juice and are used in a recipe the problem is overcome. Strawberries and pears become mushy because large ice crystals rupture the cellular structure of these foods.

Table 21.1
Recommended storage times for frozen foods

Food	Time (months)
Vegetables	12
Fruit	12
Meat	
Beef joints	12
mince	3
stewing	6
Lamb joints and chops	8
stewing	6
Pork joints	6
chops	4
bacon	3
Fish	
white	8
oily	4
shell	2
Cheese	
Cheddar, Cheshire, Double Gloucester, Edam	6
Camembert, Stilton	3
Eggs	
whole egg beaten, egg white, yolk with added salt or sugar	6
Butter	
salted	3
unsalted	6
Ice-cream	3
Bread	3
bread dough	4
part-baked rolls	2–4
sandwiches	1
fresh yeast	6 weeks
Scones	6
Pastry	
raw and cooked short crust and flaky	6
Sponge cake (fatless)	6
'Shortened' cakes (with fat)	3
Prepared dishes and meals	
stews and casseroles	2
fish or liver patés and meat loaves	1

Guidelines for freezing food

1 Use fresh food.
2 Preparation procedures should be hygienic.
3 Foods should be packed, sealed and labelled.
4 Do not put warm or hot foods into a freezer.
5 To retain the texture of the food, freeze as quickly as possible. The fast-freeze switch is useful for this.
6 Pack foods in small quantities; large blocks of minced meat, for example, take much longer to freeze and thaw than small portions.
7 Avoid packing foods close together when bulk freezing, to avoid slowing down the freezing process.
8 As soon as foods are frozen they should be moved to their appropriate storage shelves in the freezer.
9 To reduce running costs switch the fast-freeze control off as soon as the food has frozen.
10 When taking frozen foods out of the freezer open the door quickly, remove the item and close the door.
11 As soon as the food has been removed make a record of this in a freezer inventory.
12 A freezer thermometer is useful for testing the temperature. The temperature should be a steady −18°C in all parts of the cabinet.
13 Make sure the freezer is defrosted regularly (p. 251).
14 In case of breakdown, keep the address and phone number of a servicing organisation.
15 It may be worth having a special type of insurance.
16 A freezer alarm is worth having if the freezer is kept in an outhouse or garage.
17 Plugs for freezers with built-in buzzers are useful because they immediately warn consumers of blown fuses.
18 Freezers should be kept full in order to reduce running costs.
19 Do not store foods for longer than recommended (Table 21.1).
20 Some foods need defrosting thoroughly.
21 Foods that have been allowed to thaw should not be refrozen unless they have been thoroughly cooked.

Freezing vegetables
Enzymes present in vegetables are active, and must be inactivated in order to prevent discoloration, textural changes and any loss of flavour and aroma. The aim of blanching is to heat the vegetables enough to inactivate the enzymes and then to cool them rapidly to prevent softening.

The vegetables should be washed, unwanted parts removed and then cut up for blanching.

1 Half-fill a large pan with water.
2 Bring the water to boiling point.
3 Put either a wire basket from a chip pan or a special blanching basket into the pan of water to heat it.
4 Lift the wire basket out of the water, put the vegetables into the basket and immerse the basket with its contents in the boiling water.
5 Bring the water back to the boil, and as soon as it is boiling, time the procedure (Table 21.2).
6 When the blanching time is up lift the basket out of the pan and immerse it in iced water for the same length of time as for blanching.
7 Immediately drain the vegetables thoroughly in a colander and spread them on to absorbent paper.

Table 21.2
Recommended blanching times for vegetables

Type of vegetable	Blanching time (mins)
Aubergines	5
Broad beans	3
Broccoli	
small	3
medium	4
thick	5
Brussels sprouts	3
Carrots	5
Courgettes	
whole	3
sliced	$1\frac{1}{2}$
French beans	
whole	3
cut	2
Parsnips	2
Peas	2
Peppers (green or red)	3
Spinach	3
Swede	$2\frac{1}{2}$
Sweetcorn	5

Freezing fruit

Any leaves, twigs, foreign bodies or unsound fruit should be discarded. The fruit should be washed quickly. Soft fruits are prone to breaking so it is advisable to place them in a sieve or colander, pass this through clean cold water in a large bowl, and then drain the fruit. There are different methods of freezing fruit:

1 *Dry or plain*   The fruit is packed into rigid containers or it is frozen open. For the latter method the fruit is laid on a tray and put into the freezer. When frozen the fruit is packed. It is advisable to open-freeze for between 4 and 6 hours to prevent drying out.
2 *Dry and packed with sugar*   This involves coating the fruit with sugar to form a protective glaze around the fruit by drawing moisture from the fruit and producing a syrup coating.
3 *In sugar syrup*   Fruits may be frozen in syrups. Sugar syrup forms a barrier between the fruit and air and helps to prevent oxidation and discoloration.
4 *Purées* are particularly suitable for misshapen fruits and are useful for making soufflés, sorbets and sauces.

Freezing meat and poultry

A whole carcass or a side or a quarter of an animal may be available cut up into joints. Alternatively, a number of specific cuts may be purchased. It is much less trouble if the meat has been cut up already by the butcher who has the required skills. It is useful to buy either 'quality' mince and freeze it in handy portions for future use or to make the mince by grinding meat down after trimming away any visible fat.

All poultry should be cleaned, plucked and drawn. Birds may be frozen whole or in portions. Never stuff poultry before freezing. Herbs and seasoning tend to develop 'off' flavours during the first 3 months of storage so the storage time is reduced. Also, stuffings may have a high bacterial content, and this may not be destroyed when the thawed food is cooked.

Freezing fish
Fish should be really fresh. It should be gutted, scaled, trimmed of fins and thoroughly cleaned with clean cold water.

Freezing baked foods

1 *Bread*   Yeast doughs may be frozen uncooked: the dough is lightly kneaded and wrapped, allowing time for some expansion of the dough. For baked dough freezing should be carried out as soon as the product has cooled.
2 *Pastry*   Short-crust, flaky and puff pastries all freeze well uncooked and are ideally stored in measured quantities, separately wrapped ready for use. Foods such as apple pies or Cornish pasties may be frozen uncooked. Raw pastry may be cooked while still frozen, but if meat fillings are used, thaw the product before baking to ensure thorough cooking. A mixture of rubbed-in flour and fat for use in short-crust pastry and crumble mixtures can be stored in the freezer.
3 *Scones*   It is recommended that scones are underbaked before freezing and then thawed at 150°C in the oven for 15 minutes.
4 *Cakes*   Rubbed-in mixtures lose some of their quality when frozen, but large cakes, rich in dried fruit, and creamed and sponge mixtures freeze well.

Freezing meals

1 Avoid using fat in large amounts because it becomes rancid during storage.
2 Avoid using salt in large amounts: salt increases the rate of rancidity.
3 Onions and garlic both change flavour when frozen, so are best added to the meal after freezing.
4 Spices and herbs change flavour, so it is sensible to add these later or to use them in moderation before the food is frozen.

Thawing frozen food
Foods such as vegetables, casseroles and coated fish are cooked from frozen. To thaw foods, a refrigerator or microwave oven is recommended. Thawing at room temperature is suitable for fruit.

When thawing poultry, arrange a grid over a shallow pan such as a meat tin and put the poultry on the grid so that thaw drip collects in the meat tin. Do not let the drip come into contact with other foods or they may become contaminated with salmonella.

Drying

Drying is particularly suitable as a way of preserving herbs (p. 190). Fresh, clean and drained parsley may be dried by tying the stems in loose bundles. The bundles are then tied to a shelf which is positioned halfway between the top and bottom of an oven set at 100°C. The parsley is left to dry for about an hour. Alternatively, the parsley may be dried by placing the stems on an oven shelf and heating them for 1 minute at 200°C. The temperature is then reduced.

The colour of dried parsley is never like that of fresh or frozen parsley. To enhance the colour, blanch the herb by dipping it into boiling water before drying.

Jam

Good quality jam is clear and bright, has the full flavour of the fruit and is set without being stiff: in a few jams such as strawberry or cherry the set is less important than colour and flavour.

The keeping quality of jam depends mainly on the proportion of sugar, on the amount of boiling and on the exclusion of air and moisture in covering and storing it.

Setting jam
The setting of jam depends on the pectin in the fruit which, with the right proportion of acid and sugar, will form a gel. The pectin in ripe fruit is soluble, and can be set free from the cell walls of the fruit by crushing or by stewing for a short time. In under-ripe fruit pectin is in an insoluble form called 'pectose' which can be freed from the fruit and converted to pectin by stewing with acid. In over-ripe fruit however, it has changed to pectic acid and has lost its setting power so that over-ripe fruit is useless for jam making. Of the three ingredients needed to form a gel, sugar is the only one that can be added in a known quantity; acid and pectin are contained in varying amounts in different kinds of fruit and in fruits of different degrees of ripeness. They are diluted in fruit grown in very wet weather. Acid is needed in jam making not only to change pectose to pectin and to help the pectin to form a gel but also to improve the flavour and colour of jam and to prevent crystals of sugar forming in it during storage.

1 Fruits that contain plenty of pectin and acid are: cooking and crab apples; black and red currants; green gooseberries; damsons. These all contain so much pectin that water is added to prevent the jam being too stiff.
2 Fruits that contain an adequate amount of pectin and acid are: apricots; blackberries (picked early in a dry season); plums; raspberries and loganberries. Water is only added to the harder kinds of fruit in this group to soften them and to free the pectin; it will all be boiled away before sugar is added.
3 Fruits that contain little pectin and little acid are: blackberries (gathered late in the season); cherries; pears; most strawberries. No water is added to these fruits but acid may be added. They may be mixed with other fruit or fruit juice rich in acid and pectin, such as apples, red currants and gooseberries, or commercially prepared pectin may be added.

Adding acid
To each 1 kg fruit add 20 to 40 ml lemon juice or 2.5 to 5 ml tartaric acid; the acid is added to the fruit before cooking is begun.

Mixing fruits
A fruit with a little pectin mixed with one rich in pectin is often improved in flavour as well as in setting quality. Examples are: cherry or strawberry with red-currant juice; cherry or strawberry with gooseberry juice; blackberry and apple, and pear and apple. The amount of sugar is calculated on the total quantity of mixed fruits. If one fruit is harder, it is cooked for a little while before adding the softer fruit.

Fig. 21.3
Testing for pectin

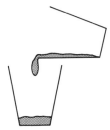

Good clot

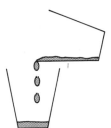

Fair clot

Poor clot

Commercially prepared pectin

Pectin can be bought in liquid or powder form or mixed with sugar. It is useful for making jam from fruits listed above as deficient in pectin but is unnecessary with fruits that will normally make a well-set jam.

Choice of fruit

Fruit for jam must be perfectly sound and picked in dry weather so that moulds and yeasts will not have begun to develop on it. It should be just ripe, or a mixture of ripe and under-ripe.

The amount of sugar to add

1 To fruits very rich in pectin add 1.25–1.5 kg sugar to each 1 kg fruit (water will have been added up to 900 ml per 1 kg for stewing).
2 To fruit with an adequate amount of pectin add 1 kg sugar to each 1 kg fruit.
3 To fruit poor in pectin add 750 g sugar to each 1 kg fruit. When the jam is boiled sufficiently for it to set and keep well it should contain 65% sugar, 5% of which will be the natural sugar in the fruit and 60% added sugar.

As the amount of sugar needed depends on the amount of pectin, a test must be made with the softened fruit before sugar is added.

To test for pectin

When the fruit has been simmered to extract pectin and is soft, put 1 teaspoonful of the juice, free of skin and pulp, into a tumbler and cool it for 2 to 3 minutes, then pour on to it 3 teaspoonfuls methylated spirit and again leave it for 1 minute. Gently free the juice from the bottom of the tumbler and pour it into a second tumbler.

One firm clot of juice shows a high proportion of pectin; several smaller but firm clots show an adequate amount of pectin; thin, soft, broken clots show very little pectin (Fig. 21.3).

If the pectin seems inadequate, either the fruit must be simmered a little longer to extract more pectin or, if it has already been simmering for over $\frac{3}{4}$ hour, more pectin must be added by using a fruit with plenty of pectin or commercial pectin extract.

Equipment for making jam

1 *A preserving pan* or a large saucepan is needed: it may be made of aluminium, stainless steel or heavy quality enamelled iron. If a solid hot-plate is used the base of the pan must be flat. A pan with a thick base distributes the heat more evenly than a thin one and therefore lessens the chance of burning the jam.
2 *A wooden spoon* is needed with a handle so long that it cannot slip right into the jam.
3 *Jam-jars* must be scrupulously clean and not chipped.
4 *Covers for jam-jars* may be of cellophane with rounds of waxed paper, and in sizes to fit the jars used.
5 *Rubber rings* are used to fix cellophane covers.
6 *A jug, jug measure or large cup* is needed for filling jars, and a saucer to hold beneath the jug to catch any drips.
7 *Equipment for testing the pectin* is methylated spirit and 2 tumblers.
8 *Equipment for testing for setting-point* is a thermometer, a saucer chilled on ice if possible, or a clean, dry wooden spoon.

General method for making jam

1 Select suitable fruit, sound, partly under-ripe and free of bruises.
2 Wash the fruit to remove dust and soil and drain it. Hard fruit may be stirred round in a bowl of cold water, soft fruit dipped quickly in and out of cold water in a colander, but very soft berries should be rolled gently about on a clean, damp cloth instead of washing.
3 Prepare fruit by removing any damaged parts, leaves, stalks, stones and cores as necessary, and by cutting large fruit in halves or apples and pears in quarters.
4 Wash the jam-jars using a detergent if they are really dirty, rinse them in very hot water and drain them; do not wipe them with a cloth. Dry and heat them by putting them open end upwards on several layers of paper on an oven tray in a very slow oven. Heating prevents the jars from cracking when the hot jam is poured in.
5 Grease the preserving pan with butter to prevent fruit sticking to the pan and also to prevent scum forming, as the butter later floats on the surface.
6 Simmer the fruit gently in the water or juice until it is very soft and until its juice is flowing freely. For very hard fruit a lid on the pan prevents too much loss of moisture and hastens the softening of the fruit. The sugar will later harden all fruit skins, so that unless they are softened at this stage they will spoil the finished jam with their toughness. Soft fruit such as raspberries or strawberries will need 10 to 20 minutes simmering; fairly hard fruit such as apricots and some plums will need 30 to 35 minutes; and very hard fruit, or fruit with tough skins such as blackcurrants, will need 45 minutes and oranges even longer – up to 3 hours.
7 Test the juice for pectin and take the necessary steps to ensure an adequate amount.
8 Warm the sugar in a slow oven while the fruit is simmering; this makes it dissolve quickly and avoids cooling the panful of jam too much.
9 Add the sugar to the fruit, warm it steadily and stir it until all is dissolved.
10 Boil the jam quickly, stirring from time to time to prevent fruit from sticking and burning on the bottom of the pan and to prevent the formation of scum. The shorter the time taken to reach setting-point the better will the colour and flavour be, as the acid in fruit, with the sugar, produce a slow darkening of the colours and a gradual change in flavours.
11 Test the jam for setting-point when it makes a faint knocking noise as it boils and when the bubbles begin to break more slowly. First remove the pan from the heat. The tests for setting are:
   (a) *The wrinkle test*: put half a teaspoon of jam on a cold saucer, cool it quickly then push it with a fingernail across the saucer; if it forms wrinkles while still tepid the jam should set.
   (b) *The flake test*: dip a clean, dry wooden spoon into the jam, twirl it horizontally above the pan to cool the spoonful of jam, then allow the jam to run off the spoon. If broad flakes form and break off short, the jam is ready; if it still trickles in an unbroken stream, it needs more boiling.
   (c) *Temperature*: while still boiling the temperature of the jam should reach 104°C–105°C when it is ready. This temperature will only be reached if the sugar has been concentrated to a 65% solution.

Fig. 21.4
Filling jars with jam

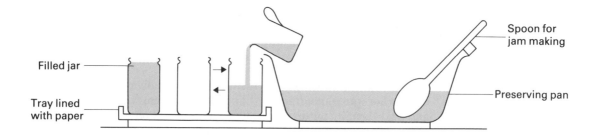

12 Fill the jars. Stir the jam steadily, off the heat, to break up the scum.
(The scum is simply air entrapped by the stickiness of the jam as
bubbles rise, and if these bubbles can be broken before they set there
will be no scum to remove.) If the scum has dried and set it must be
removed, as it spoils the appearance of the jam. Fill the jars as shown in
Fig. 21.4.
13 Cover the jars. At once slip a waxed disc on to the top of each full jar
and with the back of a teaspoon press any bubbles gently out to the
edges. Wipe the rims of all jars with a cloth wrung tightly out of very
hot water. Damp each cellophane cover on the upper side, making sure
that the underside is dry, and stretch it very tightly over the hot jar. Fix
it with a rubber band. When the cover is cold it should be concave.

Lastly, wipe the outside of all jars with a cloth wrung out of hot water
to remove any sticky patches and, when they are cool, label jars neatly
with the name of the jam and the date.

Marmalade

The word 'marmalade' comes from the Portuguese *marmelada*, a preserve
made from quinces, but it now generally means a preserve made from citrus
fruits – that is, from oranges, lemons, grapefruit or limes.

The same guidelines apply to marmalade making as to jam making, but
as the citrus fruits contain a very high proportion of pectose in the pith and
pips, they need long simmering in a large amount of water to extract the
pectin. Because citrus fruits, with the exception of lemons and limes, contain
a fair amount of acid but not enough to form a gel with their very high
proportion of pectin, they all need some lemons or some tartaric acid in
recipes for marmalade.

Bitter oranges are popular for marmalade as they give the sharp, slightly
bitter tang that is usually liked for breakfast. Bitter oranges come from
Seville or Malaga in Spain, from Italy or South Africa; Seville oranges are
usually considered the best and may be recognised by their dark orange,
deeply pitted skins and by the stalks which are often still attached to them.

It is important that the skins of citrus fruits should be soft before sugar is
added to marmalade otherwise the sugar hardens them to an inedible
toughness.

Low-sugar jams

Advantages of low-sugar jam

1 The lower amount of sugar in jam is more desirable in the context of the
'healthful' diet.
2 Low-sugar jams have a more fruity flavour, which some consumers prefer.

3 If there is a glut of garden produce the jam will cost less to make because less sugar is used.

Disadvantages of low-sugar jam

1 Low-sugar jams produced at home will not have a firm set.
2 The storage life is reduced and the product is more likely to separate.
3 If fruit has to be purchased, the product is likely to be more expensive because of the increased fruit content.

Guidelines for making low-sugar jam

1 Use fruit with good setting properties such as plums, apricots, early blackberries, raspberries and loganberries.
2 The fruit is softened as for jams in general and the sugar added. The amount of sugar used is usually $\frac{3}{4}$ that of fruit, so if 400 g of fruit is used, then 300 g of sugar is required.
3 The tests for setting applied to low-sugar jams are the flake test or the wrinkle test (p. 223). Other methods for testing are not suitable for low-sugar jams.
4 When the setting point is reached the jam should be poured into clean, hot jars and airtight covers should be put on straight away (p. 224).

Jellies

The guidelines for making and testing jam all apply to the making of jelly, but the amount of sugar must be calculated on the yield of strained juice from the fruit.

Equipment for jelly-making

This is the same as for jam, with the addition of a woollen or felt jelly-bag or a strong linen cloth for straining the juice. A jelly-bag may have a wooden hoop at the top and be made to hang from a suitable hook. A felt jelly-bag and a jelly cloth are both hung from the 4 legs of an upturned stool or chair. The bag should have four loops of tape to hang it by; the cloth should be tied on firmly with tape.

Method for making jelly

Choose and prepare the fruit as for jam, but skins, cores or stones need not be removed. Simmer the fruit in the water (or sometimes only in its own juice) until it is very soft. Mash it to a pulp with a wooden spoon. Scald the jelly-bag by dipping it in boiling water and draining it, then fix it in position with a large bowl below.

Pour the pulped fruit and juice into the jelly-bag and leave it until it stops dripping in 2 to 3 hours, or it may be left overnight.

Fruit rich in pectin may be removed from the bag after an hour, thinned again to a soft pulp with water, simmered for another $\frac{1}{2}$ hour and this pulp also strained.

The juice, or the mixture of juices, is tested for pectin and then measured.

1 For juice giving a very good pectin clot allow 1 kg sugar to each 1 litre.
2 For juice giving a good pectin clot allow 800 g sugar to each 1 litre.
3 For juice giving an adequate pectin clot allow 600 g sugar to each 1 litre.

For most jellies have the juice boiling and warm the sugar before adding it, but for a deeper colour in apple or gooseberry jelly add cold sugar to cold juice. Dissolve the sugar and boil and test the jelly for setting-point just as for jam.

All scum must be removed as it spoils the look of the clear jelly, and the hot jars must be filled quickly before a skin can form on the jelly. The jars of jelly must not be tilted before the jelly has cooled and set.

Pickles

Pickling is a 'chemical' method of preserving, in which vegetables and fruits are stored completely covered with spiced vinegar to which sugar is sometimes added.

1 The vinegar should contain 5% acetic acid in order to be sufficiently acid to prevent the development of micro-organisms. Brown malt vinegar gives a good flavour; white malt vinegar gives a poorer flavour but keeps the colour pale. Spices improve the flavour and possibly also the preservative action.
2 Vegetables are usually treated first with salt to extract some of the water and to prevent the growth of some bacteria; the salt may be used dry or as a strong solution or brine.
3 Fruit is usually cooked gently in the spiced vinegar with added sugar.
4 Vegetables and fruit for pickling must be perfectly fresh and sound, as for all preserving.
5 The only equipment needed is a supply of screw-topped jars with waxed cardboard discs to prevent the vinegar coming in contact with the metal, or wide-necked bottles with fitting corks which may be coated with melted paraffin-wax.

Recipe for brine

100 g salt to each 1 litre cold water

Recipe for spiced vinegar

to 1 litre vinegar:

1 teaspoon blade mace
1 teaspoon stick cinnamon
1 teaspoon cloves
1 teaspoon allspice berries
1 teaspoon peppercorns
2 teaspoons bruised root ginger

Method

Put the vinegar and flavourings in a double saucepan or a deep earthenware basin over a pan of water, cover it with a lid or plate. Boil the water and then keep it just hot over a low heat for 2 hours. Strain the vinegar through a nylon strainer or muslin and bottle it for future use.

The spices may be added to cold vinegar, bottled and stored for 2 months before use.

General method of pickling

1 Wash any soil off vegetables, prepare them in the usual way, removing outer leaves of cabbage and any damaged parts and cutting large vegetables into suitably sized cubes or slices.
2 Put the prepared vegetables in an earthenware bowl and cover them with brine and float a china plate on top to keep them under liquid; alternatively, pack them in layers with salt, finishing with a covering of salt. Leave them for 12–48 hours, then drain the brined vegetables or rinse and drain the dry salted ones. Drain thoroughly, or vinegar will be diluted.
3 Pack drained vegetables loosely but neatly into clean, dry, cold jars, only to within 20 mm of the top. Fill the jars with the spiced vinegar (cold for a crisp result, hot for a soft one) to 10 mm above the vegetables. Screw on the caps and label.

Store most pickles for 2 or 3 months before using them. Cabbage may be eaten 2 weeks after pickling; it gets less crisp on longer storage.

Chutney

'Chutney' is the name given to a hot, sweet pickle or condiment originating in India, where it usually contained mangoes and chillies. It is now widely varied, but always includes fruit, sweet and hot spices, vinegar and sugar and is usually of the consistency of jam although it does not gel. Very roughly the proportions are:

1 kg fresh fruit

250–500 g dried fruit

250–500 g onion

250–500 g sugar

500 ml vinegar (which may be spiced)

a variety of spices, including some hot ones

salt to taste

The sweet, savoury, hot and sour flavourings may vary widely.

The fruit may be any of which there is a glut, such as apples, blackberries, gooseberries, marrow, plums, rhubarb and tomatoes, either green or ripe.

The fruit and onions are chopped or minced and stewed in their own juice until soft, then cooked with all other ingredients until the right jam-like consistency is reached. For long storage the chutney should be more liquid than for quick use.

The pan should be aluminium or stainless steel, or an earthenware casserole may be used in an oven. Copper, brass and enamel are all acted upon by the strong acid and may spoil the flavour of the chutney; an enamel surface will be roughened, and copper and brass may produce verdigris.

Note: A pressure cooker may be used for the first stage of cooking but pressure should be reduced, the lid removed and the last stage completed with the lid off.

22 Food issues

Food additives

Many packaged foods contain additives and those commonly used include *preservatives, antioxidants, colours, flavour enhancers, sweeteners, emulsifiers* and *stabilisers*

Preservatives

These additives help to keep food safe for longer. According to its definition, a 'preservative' is a substance capable of inhibiting, retarding or arresting the growth of micro-organisms or any deterioration of food due to micro-organisms or of masking the evidence of any such deterioration.

Antioxidants

These additives stop oils, fats and fat-soluble vitamins in foods from combining with oxygen and going rancid. According to its definition, an 'antioxidant' is a substance capable of delaying, retarding or preventing the development in food of rancidity or other flavour deterioration due to oxidation.

Colours

These additives restore the colour lost from food during processing and also make food look brighter. Of the 52 permitted colourings, E150, caramel, is the most widely used.

Flavour enhancers

These additives are classified as miscellaneous and referred to as flavour modifiers. Flavour enhancers are widely used in savoury foods and have the ability to make flavours seem stronger.

Sweeteners

There are two types of sweeteners (p. 185). These are being used more and more with reduction in sugar intakes in mind. According to definition, a sweetener is any substance, other than a carbohydrate, the primary organoleptic characteristic of which is sweetness.

Emulsifiers and stabilisers

Emulsifiers help foods to mix together, such as oil and water, which would normally separate. *Stabilisers* prevent the foods from separating again once mixed. These additives are used in sweet and savoury foods.

Safety of additives

In the UK, most additives go through a long and strict safety review in order to be, and stay, approved. Those that have 'E' numbers have been accepted as being safe throughout the EC.

Food terms

Convenience foods

Convenience foods may be defined as processed foods in which a considerable amount of the preparation has been carried out by the manufacturer. Examples of convenience foods include frozen foods, breakfast cereals, cooked poultry dishes and ready meals. The growth in the convenience food industry, and of ready meals in particular, is associated with factors such as a busy lifestyle.

Fast foods

Fast foods (that is to say, fast service foods) is a general term for a limited menu of foods that lend themselves to production-line techniques. Examples of this category of foods include pizzas, hamburgers and jacket potatoes. The growth of the fast food industry is associated with a move towards a less structured, more individualistic form of eating. Eating has become less of a household ritual. There is also a social dimension to fast food outlets and this is capitalised on in advertising and promotion.

Functional foods

This group of foods has been described as the third generation of health foods to hit the European market. The first generation were foods such as fiuit juices and wholemeal bread in the mid 1970s. The second generation comprised foods with reduced amounts of fat and sugar in the mid 1980s. Functional foods, also known as *neutraceuticals* and *pharmafoods*, are big business in the Japanese market. The term *functional foods* is applied to food ingredients and manufacturers' products that are designed and promoted to provide identified health benefits. There is a wide range of functional foods in Europe, with the greatest innovation taking place in the UK and France. In contrast to Japan, where the emphasis during the early development of these foods focused on fibre-enriched drinks, European manufacturers have centred their activities on dairy foods. Examples of functional foods include bio-yogurts, fruit juices with soluble fibre added, spreads with added omega-3 fatty acids and milk with added folic acid.

Genetically modified foods

Genetic modification has evolved as scientists have learnt to identify genes, and which genes control which characteristics. Scientists are also learning how to transplant genes from one plant or animal to another. Genetic modification offers a short-cut to improving crops and livestock. There are concerns about the genetic modification of foods. For example, could it harm the environment, is it ethical and what about food safety? These issues have been addressed by government. Government has accepted that food should be labelled if it contains genes that would not be expected to be there and which might cause real concern to some people on ethical grounds.

Novel foods

'Novel foods' are defined as foods or food ingredients which have not hitherto been used for human consumption to a significant extent in the UK and/or have been produced by extensively modified or entirely new food production processes. Thorough safety evaluations, including toxicological and nutritional ones, must be carried out to ensure that there are no health risks. All of these studies are assessed by the Government's Advisory Committee on *Novel Foods and Processes*.

Organic foods

The EC and national legislation controls the use of the word *organic* in relation to crops or food. The term 'organic' is used to describe:

- food grown without most 'artificial' fertilisers or pesticides and in a way that emphasises crop rotation, making the most of natural fertilisers and ensuring that the life of the soil is maintained;
- animals kept in ways which minimise the need for medicines and other chemical treatments.

Food legislation

The primary aims of the legislation controlling food are to:

- protect the health of consumers;
- prevent food fraud.

These aims are achieved by a combination of primary legislation and secondary legislative measures. The former are the *Acts*, and the latter *Regulations* or *Orders*.

The Food Safety Act 1990

The primary legislation in the UK is the Food Safety Act 1990. The Act is applicable in England, Wales and Scotland. In Northern Ireland, the Food Safety (Northern Ireland) Order 1991 applies.

The intention of the Act is to ensure that food shall be in as wholesome a condition as possible when it is eaten. The Act, and legislation associated with it, prescribe legally enforceable standards of composition and treatment and render infringement a criminal offence. The Act prohibits the addition to food of any substance that would make it *'injurious to health'*. *It is also required that Ministers 'have regard to the desirability of restricting, so far as practicable, the use of substances of no nutritional value as foods or ingredients of foods'*. The Act empowers Food and Health Ministers to make regulations concerning foods and, once approved by Parliament, these are published as legally binding *Statutory Instruments*.

The Food Safety (General Food Hygiene) Regulations 1995

These regulations aim to ensure that the same food hygiene rules are enforced in all European Union countries. The Regulations must be adhered to by anyone who owns, manages or works in a food business.

Weights and Measures Act 1985

The Department of Trade and Industry has responsibility for weights and measures legislation. Most of the Act applies to England, Wales and Scotland. In Northern Ireland similar controls are in the Weights and Measures (Northern Ireland) Order 1981.

Of particular importance to consumers is the section dealing with *short weight*. Any person who, in selling or purporting to sell any goods by weight or other measurement or by number, delivers or causes to be delivered to the buyer:

1 a lesser quantity than that purported to be sold;
   or
2 a lesser quantity than corresponds with the price charged,
   shall be guilty of an offence.

The Food Labelling Regulations 1996

Principal provisions of the Regulations

1 Require all food which is ready for delivery to the ultimate consumer or to a catering establishment, subject to certain exceptions to be marked or labelled with: the name of the food; a list of ingredients; the appropriate durability indication; any special storage conditions or conditions of use; the name and address of the manufacturer or packer or of a seller, and, in certain cases particulars of the place of origin of the food and instructions for use.

2 Require, where the labelling of a food places special emphasis on the presence or low content of an ingredient in a food, an indication of the minimum or maximum percentage of that ingredient in the food.

3 Make special provision for labelling of food which is not prepacked and certain similar foods, fancy confectionery products, food which is packed in small packages and indelibly marked bottles, certain foods sold at catering establishments and seasonal selection packs.

4 Specify additional labelling requirements for food sold from vending machines and for alcoholic drinks, and require any compulsory indication of the strength of an alcoholic drink to be in the form '% vol.'.

5 Require specified cautionary statements to be given with raw milk and a warning to be given with products consisting of skimmed milk together with non-milk fat.

6 Specify an additional labelling requirement for food packaged in a gas so as to extend its durability and specify additional labelling requirements for food containing sweeteners, added sugar and sweeteners, aspartame or more than 10% added polyols.

7 Specify requirements as to the manner of marking or labelling of food.

8 Prohibit a claim in the labelling or advertising of a food that it has tonic or medicinal properties. Imposes conditions for the making of: claims relating to foods for particular used and similar foods; reduced or low energy value claims; protein claims; vitamin claims; mineral claims; cholesterol claims; nutrition claims; and claims which depend on another food.

9 Specify labelling requirements in the giving of nutritional information for a food, whether or not a nutrition claim is also being made.

10 Impose restrictions on the use of certain words and descriptions in the labelling or advertising of food.

11 Permit the use of the word 'wine' in composite names for drinks other than wine or table wine.

Indication of durability

The *minimum durability* of a food shall be indicated by the words '*best before*' on the packaging, followed by: the date, up to and including which, the food can reasonably be expected to retain its specific properties if properly stored; any storage conditions which need to be observed if the food is to retain its specific properties until that date.

Where a '*use by*' date is required, it shall be indicated by the words 'use by' followed by: the date up to and including which the food, if properly stored, is recommended for use; any storage conditions which need to be observed.

23 Introduction to kitchens and equipment

Kitchen planning

Fig. 23.1
Shapes of kitchens and basic arrangement of work surfaces

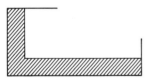

One sided

Galley

L-shaped

U-shaped

1 *Location* The kitchen is the focal point of the home. Considerations include accessibility, light, views and essential services.
2 *Types* Separate working kitchens (enclosed or isolated kitchens) are designed for meal preparation and may include facilities for other domestic tasks. Working kitchens with dining spaces and dining kitchens allow for meal preparation, other domestic tasks and activities such as eating and watching television.
3 *Size and shape* (Fig. 23.1) For a family of 4 a minimum of 8 square metres is recommended for an enclosed kitchen and 12 square metres for one which includes a dining area.
4 *Ergonomic aspects* 'Ergonomics' is defined as 'the study of work and its environment in order to achieve maximum efficiency'. Lines joining the centre points of the sink, cooker and refrigerator form the work triangle (Fig. 23.2). To prevent unnecessary walking, the sides of the work triangle should be between 3600 mm and 6600 mm. The selected heights for work surfaces and shelves should be aimed at minimising the amount of movement required (Table 23.1). Sufficient space should be allowed for kitchen users to stand or sit and to operate kitchen equipment efficiently and safely (Table 23.2). A sequence of work surface/cooker/work surface/sink/work surface is recommended (Fig. 23.2).
5 *Surfaces* (Tables 23.3, 23.4 and 23.5)
6 *Kitchen units* These may be designed to cover an area from the floor to the ceiling and from the floor to work surface or to cover parts of walls as wall units. Considerations include the amount and shape of available space, money, versatility, style of kitchen, hygiene (for example, plastic coatings on shelves are easy to keep clean) and efficient operation (for example, handles, catches or levers).
7 *Kitchen sinks* It is an advantage to have the sink near a window with a pleasing view. Main sinks should be a minimum of 500 × 350 mm and 175–200 mm in depth. For maximum efficiency a double sink is recommended.

Table 23.1
Recommended heights for work surfaces and shelves

Height (mm)	Purpose
800	Manual jobs on work surface
900	Skilled jobs on work surface
1500	Maximum height deep shelf over cupboard
1750	Maximum height narrow shelf over cupboard
1800	Maximum height narrow shelf

Fig. 23.2
Work triangle in an L-shaped kitchen

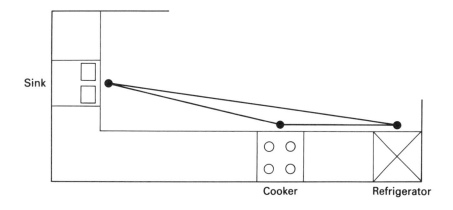

Sink

Cooker   Refrigerator

8 *Lighting*   According to the Department of the Environment in *Safety in the Home*, burning and wounding accidents are more likely if consumers work in their own light. Daylight needs to be adequately supplemented by artificial light. Work-surface lighting may be provided by strip lights fixed to the underside of wall cupboards or shelves above the work surface, or by lights positioned on the ceiling above the work surfaces. Lights on cooker hoods will illuminate cookers. Dining areas may be lit by low-hung pendent fittings or cylindrical 'down lights' mounted on or recessed into ceilings.

9 *Heating*   Kitchens generate a lot of heat, but back-up heating may be needed in cold weather. According to the National House Builders Regulation Council Standards, kitchen temperatures should be between 12°C and 15°C.

10 *Ventilation*   Kitchen waste products such as moisture, heat, grease, and fumes need to be removed otherwise condensation, excessive heat and stale air will prevail. Efficient kitchen ventilation will remove these waste products at or as near to their sources as possible without causing draughts. Open windows create draughts which carry grease-laden steam and odours to other parts of the house. For efficient ventilation extractor fans and cooker hoods are recommended.

Table 23.2
Recommended work spaces and clearances in the kitchen

Space (mm)	Purpose
800	Width of work surface next to counter
900	Width of passage for carrying large items
1000	Free space in front of appliance that opens
1100	Clearance to squat
1200	Clearance to bend from waist

Table 23.3
Kitchen floor coverings

Floor covering	Slip-resistant	Resilient	Quiet	Resistant to domestic chemicals and heat
Vinyl	Only if surface is textured	Resilient but heels and heavy objects cause indentations	✓	Not resistant to heat
Rubber	Good when dry and if surface is studded or ribbed; poor when wet	✓	✓	Not resistant to heat; oils and fats cause deterioration
Cork	✓	✓	✓	Not resistant to heat; resistant to chemicals if vinyl skinned
Linoleum	Good as long as it is not highly polished	Heavy objects dent it but thick quality linoleum is resilient		Damaged by alkalis
Carpet	✓	Resilient but heavy objects dent it	✓	Stains easily
Quarry tiles	Slippery when polished or wet	Hard and cold; noisy for the feet		Grease can stain it
Ceramic tiles	Poor when wet	Hard and cold; noisy for the feet	✓	

Table 23.4
Wall coverings for kitchens

Wall covering	Easy to clean	Impervious to smells	Grease resistant	Water resistant	Hardwearing	Not too costly
Paint – gloss vinyl	✓	✓	✓	✓	✓	✓
Washable wallpaper	✓	✓	✓	✓	✓	✓
Vinyl wall covering	✓	✓	✓	✓	✓	✓
Ceramic tiles	✓	✓	✓	Water can penetrate poor joins	Break if knocked hard	Expensive
Cork					Tends to chip	Expensive

If sealed or vinyl skinned

Waterproof	Hardwearing	Easy to clean	Not too costly
✓	✓	✓	✓
✓	✓	✓	✓
Not waterproof unless sealed or vinyl skinned	Tends to chip	Only if sealed or vinyl skinned	More expensive than vinyl
An absorbent material depending on thickness	✓	✓	✓
Water spilt seeps through to the under-lying floor	✓	✓	✓
✓	Tends to chip	✓	Expensive
✓	Tends to chip	✓	Expensive

Table 23.5
Kitchen work surfaces

Work surface	Easy to clean	Hard-wearing	Heat resistant	Scratch-proof	Water-proof	Resistant to chemicals	Quiet	Not too costly
Plastic laminates	Especially if contoured	✓	Fairly	Scratches	✓	✓	✓	✓
Hard woods	Needs constant attention and has to be sealed	Chips	Shows heat marks	Scratches	Wipe up immediately to protect seal		✓	✓
Ceramic tiles	✓	Will not withstand hard knocks	✓	✓	Moisture can seep through poor joins	✓	Noisy	Expensive
Stainless steel	✓	✓	✓	Scratches	✓	✓	Noisy	Expensive
Marble	Not if stained	✓	Could mark or crack		Slightly porous and moisture stains it	Stained by grease, oil and acids	Noisy	Very expensive

Cooking appliances

Cooking appliances may be classified into three main types: ovens, surface heating units and grills (Fig. 23.3).

Fig. 23.3
Cooking appliances

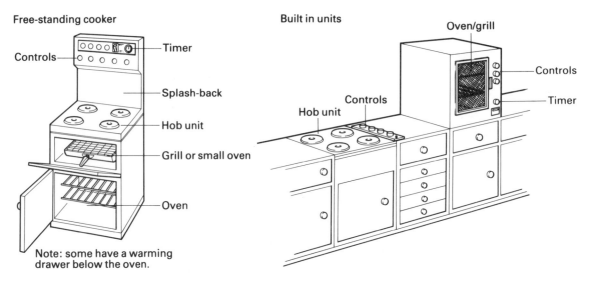

Free-standing cooker

Controls — Timer

Splash-back

Hob unit

Grill or small oven

Oven

Note: some have a warming drawer below the oven.

Built in units

Oven/grill

Controls

Timer

Hob unit

Controls

Ovens

Fig. 23.4
Principles of thermostats

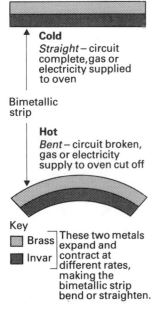

↑ **Cold**
Straight – circuit complete, gas or electricity supplied to oven

Bimetallic strip

Hot
Bent – circuit broken, gas or electricity supply to oven cut off

Key

☐ Brass | These two metals
■ Invar | expand and contract at different rates, making the bimetallic strip bend or straighten.

1 *Solid fuel ovens* are traditionally made of cast iron, and heat from the fire is conveyed to the oven and heating plates.
2 *Electric ovens* have heating elements in the base or sides of the oven compartment. A thermostat (Fig. 23.4) controls the temperature in the oven.
3 *Gas ovens* may be heated by direct and indirect methods (Fig.23.5) and are thermostatically controlled.

Autotimers

Most ovens include automatic timers. These consist of clocks which can control starting time, duration of cooking and time at which cooking finishes. Foods are cooked from a cold start, and this has implications for the choice of dishes.

1 Avoid foods such as yeast doughs, scone mixtures and flaky and puff pastries as these all need high temperatures at the start of cooking. Soufflés and meringues are likely to separate if left to stand.
2 Meat, poultry, fish, eggs and milk should have a maximum standing time in the cold oven of 2 hours in warm weather as these foods spoil.
3 Ensure that the oven is cool before putting foods to stand in it.
4 Fruit and vegetables baked in their skins are particularly suitable for autotimed cooking. Peeled vegetables may be glazed lightly with fat or, in the context of the 'healthful' diet, moistened with a little water. Frozen vegetables may be covered with foil.
5 Hotpots, stews and casseroles should be covered with tight-fitting lids to prevent drying out.
6 Cover strong-smelling foods (for example, garlic) carefully.

Fan-assisted ovens

There are two main types of fan-assisted oven. In one, the fan circulates heat round the oven shelves; in the other, heat is directed through ducts on the oven shelves. Fan-assisted ovens heat up quickly and the temperature is even. They are economical because the temperature needed for cooking is on average 10°C lower than usual and cooking time is reduced on average by 10 minutes per hour. Fan ovens tend to be noisy.

Fig. 23.5
Heat distribution in gas ovens

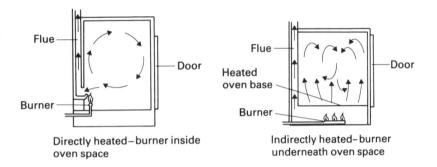

Directly heated – burner inside oven space

Indirectly heated – burner underneath oven space

Easy-clean ovens

1 *Non-stick coatings* of plastic polytetrafluoroethylene (PTFE) allow dirt to be removed by wiping the surface with a damp cloth.
2 *Continuous cleaning ovens* are lined with a type of vitreous enamel which contains a catalyst. When temperatures above 200°C are reached foods adhering to the lining are oxidised continuously and removed. An occasional wipe over is all that is required.
3 *Pyrolytic ovens* have specially insulated oven doors which keep automatically closed during cleaning. At temperatures around 500°C food particles on the lining are oxidised to a fine ash, which is removed by wiping with a damp cloth. Fumes formed during cleaning are deodorised by a filter in the roof of the oven. The pyrolytic method of cleaning adds considerably to the cost of the oven.

Surface heating units

1 *Solid fuel heating plates* are made of cast iron. The heating plates are covered with insulated lids to keep the heat in.
2 *Electric heating plates* generate heat which is transferred to the base of the pan by conduction. Solid surface plates (disc rings) consist of a cast iron plate in which the heating elements are set. In radiant rings the heating element is housed in a spiral tube. Ceramic heating plates have a smooth, flat surface made of ceramic glass which is non-porous and durable. Radiant heating elements in insulated bowls are positioned under the surface.

   A recent development is the magnetic induction hob. An induction coil connected to an electronic circuit produces a high-frequency magnetic field; this is housed underneath the ceramic surface. When a metal pan is put on the surface it heats up straight away because the magnetic field is instantly converted to heat. The heat ceases when the pan is removed.

3 *Gas heating plates* are usually open gas flames with a pan support above the burner and a well which collects spilt foods under the burner. Heat transfer is by convection from the gas flames to the overlying pan. Ceramic gas hot plates are being developed.

Grills (broilers)

Grills are used to provide a source of radiant heat which is directed on to the food in the grill pan positioned under the heat source.

1 *Electric grills*   The heating elements in the grill are tubular and designed to cover the whole of the cooking area.
2 *Gas grills*   A burner produces a flame which is directed horizontally on to a steel fret. The metal becomes hot and radiates the heat downwards. When low gas settings are used cooking is uneven, so surface combustion burners are superior. The mixture of gas and air enters the grill through metal gauze, and a piece of metal shaped into an 'H', attached to the centre of the gauze, distributes heat evenly.

Additional features
Some grills may be used as a second oven. Some include a rotisserie, which is a motor-rotated spit.

Consumer choice

Considerations for choice of cooking appliances include type of fuel available; needs; space; economics; personal preferences; and finish.

Cooking food

Food is cooked:

1 to make it *safe* to eat, i.e., by destroying micro-organisms and toxins present in food;
2 to increase the storage life for short-term storage;
3 to make food *palatable*, for example, raw meat would be difficult to chew (and just imagine trying to eat uncooked grains of rice!).

Heat transfer

Heat energy can be transferred by conduction, convection and radiation.

1 *Conduction* is a comparatively slow method of heat transfer. When molecules get hot they move rapidly, and this *kinetic* energy is transmitted from molecule to molecule as they touch. The object to be heated must be in direct contact with the heat source. Examples include a metal pan positioned on the coils of an electric hob unit and a metal spoon used for stirring a hot liquid which gradually heats up, starting at the bowl of the spoon and finally making the handle hot.
2 *Convection* is the rapid transfer of heat energy through gases and liquids. As gases or liquids are heated they become less dense and consequently rise. The cold gases or liquids then flow downwards to the heat source. In this way a flow from bottom to top and top to bottom is set up. Examples of the use of convection in cooking include boiling vegetables in water in a pan, frying chips in deep fat or oil and baking bread in an oven.
3 *Radiation* is a rapid method of heat transfer. The energy travels as electromagnetic waves. The energy is transmitted directly from its source to the object heated. The food cooked by radiant heat should be near to the heat source because the further away it is the fewer rays it receives, and consequently it is heated less. Examples of the use of radiation in cooking include grilling and the use of an electric pop-up toaster.

Methods of cooking

Methods of cooking may be broadly considered in the following categories:

Moist methods

1 *Boiling* is cooking in water at 100°C. True boiling gives rise to rapid bubbling and evaporation of water as steam (for example, cooking starchy foods such as rice or pasta, where the quick bubbling lifts the grains off the bottom of the pan and prevents sticking). Simmering is not true boiling; the temperature is lower, 90°C; and bubbles rise slowly at one side of the pan. Foods such as meat and green vegetables are suitable for simmering.

2 *Braising* is cooking meat, poultry, fish or vegetables on a bed of fried root vegetables, called a 'mirepoix', and with enough stock or water barely to cover the mirepoix. It is a combination of stewing, steaming and pot roasting; the food being braised is basted at intervals with the hot liquid; it is kept covered with greased paper or foil and a weighted lid. Meat is browned, either in hot fat before the moist cooking or under a hot grill afterwards. All the liquid from the braising pan is used with the dish; it may be reduced to a thin glaze or thickened with starch, and should be brown and savoury. The mirepoix vegetables are usually overcooked. Braising may be used to make tough cuts of meat tender.

3 *Poaching* is cooking below simmering point with water only half-covering the food, in a shallow pan, the food being basted with the hot liquid from time to time. Poaching is used for foods that require only low temperatures or gentle handling – for example, fish and eggs.

4 *Steaming* (Fig.23.6) is cooking in the steam from boiling water. The equipment must be arranged so that no water touches the food but so that steam can circulate freely around or under it. Steamers are available that fit over a pan of boiling water and allow the steam to enter through perforations in the base. Secondly, tiered steamers have an inner tube with an outlet to pass steam into the upper tiers and a cap that must be kept on the top of the tube. A third method is to put the food in a covered basin set in boiling water to reach half-way up the basin. A fourth method is to put a plate on a pan of boiling water covering the food on it with a pan lid.

   In all methods of steaming the lid must fit well so that steam does not escape and a kettle must be kept boiling, ready to replenish the water as it boils away. Steaming is suitable for cake-mixture puddings and for fish and vegetables.

5 *Stewing* is cooking in a small amount of liquid which is allowed to simmer only and which is always served with the cooked food. It is useful for tough foods such as tough cuts of meat, and for soft foods such as fruit which easily break up in cooking. Stewing may be preceded by frying for tender meat, or by 'fat-steaming' for vegetables. Stewing is most easily carried out over a long period by using a casserole in an oven set at 120°C–140°C. See also slow cooking pots (p. 244).

6 *Pressure cooking* (p. 245).

Dry methods

1 *Baking* is cooking in an oven by heat radiated from the hot metal lining of the oven and by convection currents set up in the hot air. The hot air in the oven rises and therefore the top shelf is usually the hottest; middle and lower shelves may be 3°C–5°C cooler than the top shelf. Steam given off by the food in the oven keeps it from getting too dry. Baked food has a crisp brown surface when cooked, as in pastry, cakes or baked meat.

Fig. 23.6
Steaming

Steamer over saucepan

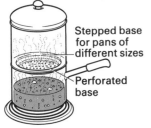

Stepped base for pans of different sizes

Perforated base

Tiered steamer

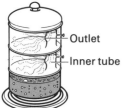

Outlet

Inner tube

Saucepan method

Trivet

Plate method

Plate

2 *Grilling* (broiling) is cooking by radiant heat from a metal fret heated by a gas flame or an open electric element. The grill is made red hot, and the food is placed on a grid standing in a grill pan. Food to be cooked by grilling should not be over 25 mm thick. Foods suitable for grilling include very tender cuts of meat such as fillet and rump steaks; chops and cutlets of lamb and pork; liver and kidney; bacon and sausages; wings and breast of chicken, some fish, mushrooms and tomatoes. Grilling may be used to brown the tops of dishes finished *au gratin*. (See also infra-red grill and electric sandwich toasters, p. 244.)

3 *Roasting*   Today the term is used to describe the cooking of meat or potatoes in an oven. A modern return to true roasting is the electrically heated rotisserie or the revolving spit fitted to some grills and in some ovens.

4 *Pot-roasting* is cooking meat in a little hot fat in a strong, covered pan on top of the cooker; it is useful where no oven is available, as in camp or in a caravan. The meat must be basted occasionally and turned over in the hot fat, and once the meat is brown it must be cooked very gently or it will be dry.

Frying (Fig. 23.7)

Frying is a quick method of cooking. In the interests of health frying should be avoided, but if it is the chosen method of cooking, dry frying is preferable. Whatever method is used, thoroughly drain the fried food on absorbent paper to remove excess fat.

Table 23.6
Recommended temperatures for deep fat frying

Food	Temperature (°C)	Browning of dry bread in seconds
Raw, starchy foods, e.g., potatoes, doughnuts	170–175	(1–1½ minutes) 60–90
Fish coated in batter	175	(1 minute) 60
Fish coated in egg and crumbs or flour	185	30
Re-heated foods	195	20

Fig. 23.7
Methods of frying

Deep frying

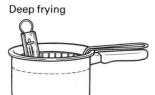

Shallow frying

Stir frying

1 *Guidelines for deep frying*
(a) To avoid any risk of fire the pan must be little more than two-thirds full so that the fat will not spill over. For the same reason a naked flame must not lick up the side of the pan.
(b) The fat should be at the required temperature while frying is in progress; this is best done by checking the thermometer readings. See Table 23.6 for recommended temperatures.
(c) Boiling water must not be near the frying-pan because drops of water splashing into the hot fat will cause the fat to spurt.
(d) All food must be coated in batter or egg and crumbs unless it is itself starchy – for example, raw potato chips or doughnuts.
(e) After use, the fat should be warmed gently until all bubbling stops; this is to ensure that no water is left in it which would hasten its decomposition. It should then be strained through a fine strainer to remove all crumbs of food as these get charred during frying and

also cause the fat to decompose.

(f) The fat should be stored in a covered light-proof container.

2 *Guidelines for shallow frying*

(a) Food should not be more than 25 mm thick.

(b) There should be enough fat in the pan to come half-way up the food.

(c) Most foods must be coated with a starchy substance that will form a crisp coating and prevent moisture escaping into the fat; exceptions are meat and some vegetables.

(d) The fat must be at the correct temperature for the food to be fried: if the fat is too cool, the food will absorb it and will be greasy; if the fat is too hot, the outside of the food will be overcooked and the inside will be undercooked.

(e) The food must be lowered gently into the hot fat to prevent splashing.

(f) One piece of food should be lowered into the fat at a time and the fat allowed to heat up again after each addition.

(g) The frying-pan should never be filled with food, but space should be allowed for turning the pieces, for checking the rate of cooking and for lifting them out.

3 *Guidelines for dry frying*   This is conveniently done using a non-stick pan; alternatively, a thin film of oil may be sprayed into an ordinary pan to prevent the food from sticking to the surface. Pancakes are traditionally dry-fried. Cooking in a wok may involve dry frying, for example, stir-fry vegetables.

Microwave ovens

Microwave ovens are not replacements for conventional ovens. According to the magazine *Which?* a microwave oven is 'an addition to, rather than an alternative to, a conventional cooker'. A microwave oven is described as the 'freezer's natural mate'.

Principles of microwave cooking

Microwave ovens cook foods by generating electromagnetic waves (Fig. 23.8). Electricity is converted to microwaves by the *magnetron*. The waves are channelled into the oven space by the waveguide. A *mode stirrer* or *turntable* ensures the even distribution of heat. The microwaves penetrate the food to about 5 cm. The waves are attracted to tiny molecules of water in the food. When the microwaves are absorbed, the molecules of water vibrate at high speed (more than 2000 million times per second). The vibrating molecules cause friction, which produces heat. The *metal lined casing* and *door seal* prevent leakage of microwaves. Steam escapes by way of the *oven vent*, and an *air filter* (cooling fan) permits cool air to pass into the oven. As microwave cooking does not brown food, *browning* devices may be included such as a browning element/integral grill or a browning dish.

Guidelines for using a microwave oven

1 Follow the manufacturer's instructions carefully.

2 Use the oven to cook, heat or defrost foods. Do not use it for storage.

3 Use microwave cookware, glass, china or paper. Metal repels the microwaves and should be avoided.

4 If required, cover foods using cling film, kitchen paper, roasting bags or oven-proof glass.

Fig. 23.8
Design features of a microwave oven

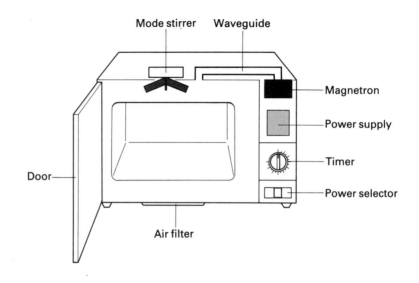

5 Set the timer according to instructions.
6 When not in use keep a vessel of water inside the oven. If an empty oven is turned on the microwave energy can damage the magnetron.
7 Check the manufacturer's instructions for maintenance. Periodically check the door seal; if damaged, microwaves may escape and be dangerous to the user. If in doubt, arrange for qualified help.

Advantages of a microwave oven

1 It saves time and energy, for example, a baked potato cooks in a fraction of the time it takes using conventional methods.
2 It can save on washing up if foods are cooked and served in the same vessel.
3 It is easy to clean.
4 There are no problems of cooking smells or condensation.
5 Flavour retention of foods is superior to conventional methods.
6 It can be used to defrost, speeding up food preparation.
7 It is mobile and can be used in rooms other than the kitchen.

Disadvantages of a microwave oven

1 It takes up work surface space.
2 It is not suitable for cooking all foods, for example, pastry and biscuits.
3 Metal pans must be avoided, therefore not all conventional cookware is suitable.
4 Timing is critical if over-cooking is to be prevented.
5 It needs to be maintained carefully, for example, door seal needs to be checked.
6 Money required for initial outlay.

Consumer choice of microwave ovens

A defrost control allows short bursts of microwave energy and rest periods and does away with manual control; variable power allows for flexibility of cooking speeds; a temperature probe is useful when cooking joints of meat; a rotating platform reduces the need to turn dishes or to stir foods; browning mechanisms save additional effort such as flashing under a hot grill or glazing.

Small electrical cooking appliances

There are many small electrical cooking appliances (cooking aids) to choose from. A summary guide is given in Table 23.7.

Table 23.7
Advantages and disadvantages of small electrical cooking appliances

Type and design	Operation	Advantages	Disadvantages
			Money needed for initial outlay and repairs
Water-heating appliances Kettles Body of kettle — Socket — Heating element	Heating element inside kettle heats water. Automatic kettles turn off when water boils, based on principle of bi-metallic strip	• Energy saving • Leaves heating units on hob free for cooking • Can be used in rooms other than kitchen	• Takes up work surface space
Coffee percolators Perforated basket Stem Heating element — Socket Heating chamber Warming element	Heating element inside jug boils the water. Hot water is pushed up the stem by small pockets of steam. Hot water falls on to ground coffee inside perforated basket, trickles through and soluble extracts in coffee are dissolved. Coffee drips back into jug. The strength of the coffee increases throughout process. A second heating element keeps the coffee warm, or a thermostat reduces the temperature of a single element	• Energy saving • The coffee never boils • Leaves heating units on hob free for cooking • Can be used in rooms other than kitchen	• Takes up work surface space • Fiddly to clean
Filter coffee makers Drip tube — Reservoir Filter Jug Valve Heating element Heating tube	Water in the reservoir flows into the heating tube. The heating element around the tube boils the water. Steam forms, rises up the tube, condenses and drips from the drip tube on to the ground coffee in the filter. Soluble extracts in the coffee are dissolved and coffee drips into the jug where it keeps hot	As for coffee percolators, but easier to clean due to filter papers. Less likely to overheat	• Expensive to buy and to run due to cost of filter papers • Takes up more space than percolators

Type and design	Operation	Advantages	Disadvantages

Portable cooking appliances

Multi-cookers

Handle — Pan — Lid Heating element — Base Electricity supply and thermostat	The heating element moulded into base of the aluminium alloy pan heats appliance to temperature set. Controlled by a thermostat	• Energy saving • Useful when space does not permit conventional oven • Can be used in rooms other than kitchen • Can be used to roast, bake, fry, braise, casserole and steam as a *bain-marie*, a slow-cooker, double boiler and warmer	• Need working surface space. The appliance is bulky and requires clearance

Slow-cooking pots

Lid — Casserole Handle Socket — Base Heating elements	Heating elements in the sides of the pot heat appliance. The lower element operates at low and high settings and upper one at high settings only. Small cooking pots operate on one setting; others usually work on 'high' and 'low'. Not usually controlled by a thermostat	• Food can be left to cook • Can be used for batch cooking • Useful for people eating at different times • Energy saving for cooking • Can be used for casseroles, ratatouille, risotto, baked custards, tea breads and cakes, jams, chutneys and for heating garlic and herb breads	• Misuse, such as continual peeping when stewing meat can be dangerous in microbiological terms • Bulky and take up work surface space

Contact grills and sandwich toasters

Sealing device Hinge Heating elements — Heating plates	Heating elements positioned behind 2 hinged plates heat the plates. Temperature is controlled by a thermostat. In sandwich toasters shape of sections on plates ensures an efficient seal for sandwiches	• Energy and time-saving • Useful when space is at a premium • Can be used in different parts of the house • Sandwich toasters seal sandwiches efficiently • Contact grills can be used to toast sandwiches, grill meat, cook casseroles, bake scones and cakes and cook frozen meats	• Can be fiddly to clean • Take up extra space if an addition to a conventional grill

Type and design	Operation	Advantages	Disadvantages

Portable cooking appliances (continued)

Deep-fat fryer

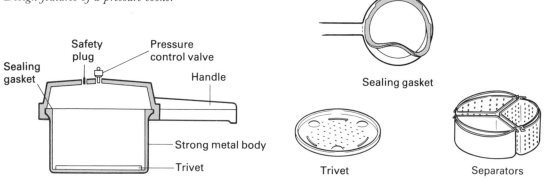

Lid   Handle

Outer cover

Electricity supply

Heating element at base of aluminium bowl

Heating elements sealed in the base heat the appliance. Temperature is controlled by a thermostat. In some types a charcoal filter absorbs cooking smells

- Food less likely to burn due to thermostatic control
- Over-filling less likely because of indicator on side
- Charcoal filter reduces cooking smells
- Easy to clean if with special filter mechanism
- Can be used to blanch vegetables, to cook soups and stews

- Large and take up storage and work surface space

Pressure cookers

Pressure cookers (Fig. 23.9) are designed to cook any food that is suitable for boiling, stewing or steaming.

Fig. 23.9
Design features of a pressure cooker

Safety plug

Pressure control valve

Sealing gasket

Handle

Strong metal body

Trivet

Sealing gasket

Trivet

Separators

Principles of pressure cooking

When the pressure cooker is in operation the lid is locked on. When the water inside the pan boils, it fills with steam most of which cannot escape, so pressure builds up inside. The boiling point of the water is increased due to the pressure. The pressure may be fixed, but in most cases the cooker will operate at low, medium and high pressure (Table 23.8).

The sealing gasket between the lid and base prevents the steam from escaping. A controlled amount can escape by way of the steam vent. The pressure weight or rotating valve determines this. Should the pressure inside the cooker build up too much (for example, if the steam vent gets blocked, or liquid in the pressure cooker boils dry), the safety device in the lid allows steam to be released automatically. The metal pin in the device melts if the pressure is excessive.

Table 23.8
Pressure, weight and temperature relationships

Type of pressure	Weight (kg)	Temperature (°C)
Low	2.26	109
Medium	4.53	115
High	6.79	121

Guidelines for using a pressure cooker

1 Consult the instruction book for step-by-step instructions on use and to check the required pressure. Low pressure is used for steaming puddings with chemical raising agents included in the ingredients. Medium pressure is recommended for blanching vegetables for freezing and for jam making. High pressure is suitable for foods such as pulses, risotto and meat stews.
2 Preliminary frying may be done in the pressure pan without the lid.
3 Avoid thickening liquids at the outset of cooking. Thicken later, using blended cornflour or the *beurre manié* method.
4 It is recommended that the pan should not be filled beyond two-thirds with solid food or one-half with liquids.
5 If the indicator-type weight is used or the rotating weight, it should be positioned on the steam vent, then the hot plate of the cooker or the burner underneath the pan turned on. If screw-type ring weights are used, wait for the steam to flow steadily from the steam vent before positioning the weight on the vent.
6 Time the cooking and lower the heat when the pressure is reached.
7 When the cooking time is up, reduce the pressure. Consult the instruction book for guidelines.
8 Should the safety device come into operation, let the pressure cooker cool down at room temperature. *Do not try to cool the pressure cooker quickly using cold water.* When the lid has cooled completely, the safety device should be replaced with a new one.
9 Check the manufacturer's instructions for maintenance. Periodically check that the sealing gasket has not perished, otherwise steam will escape and may cause burns.

Advantages of a pressure cooker

1 It saves time and energy, for example, oxtail stew can be cooked in 40 minutes instead of hours.
2 A complete meal can be cooked in the cooker using the separators, saving washing up.
3 Cooking smells and condensation are reduced.
4 Pressure-cooked vegetables retain more vitamin C than boiled ones due to using less water and speed of cooking process.
5 Flavour and colour are conserved.

Disadvantages of a pressure cooker

1 It takes up storage space.
2 It is only suitable for moist methods of cooking.
3 Timing is critical if over-cooking is to be prevented.
4 It needs to be maintained carefully, for example, replacing sealing gasket.
5 Money needed for initial outlay.

Consumer choice of pressure cookers

Considerations include: size, a 4.5-litre model is suitable for 2 to 3 people; colour; shape, either high- or low-domed; non-stick interior; handles, one or two; type of pressure weights and autotimers.

Food preparation machines

Food preparation machines are labour-saving and are designed to carry out specific food preparation tasks (Table 23.9).

Table 23.9
Food preparation machines

Machine	Operation	Uses	Advantages	Disadvantages
				Money needed for initial outlay and repairs
Blenders Goblet— Blades— Spindle— —Cooling fan —Motor Base	Cutting blades rotate, up to 15 000 revolutions per minute. Movement causes the mixture to move up the sides of the goblet and then to fall into the centre, on to the blades	To make purées, batters, breadcrumbs. To grind nuts; some have coffee-grinding attachment	• Saves food preparation time • Some can heat up foods such as sauces, soups and purées	• Not designed to cope with large quantities
Handmixers Beater ejector Motor Gear drive Spindle Beater— Cooling fan	Beaters rotate in opposite directions, so food being mixed is drawn between them	To mix, whisk or beat small quantities	• Can be used in different mixing vessels • Speedy compared with conventional procedures	• Not designed to cope with large quantities • Hand-held
Table mixers Drive belt Motor Bowl Whisk Spindle ■ Position for attachments	Either the mixing head rotates around the bowl or the beater is positioned off centre and the bowl rotates	To whisk, cream and knead large quantities. To blend mixtures. To carry out specialised functions using attachments, e.g., potato peeler, juice extractor and mincer	• Can deal with large quantities • Convenience of integral bowl and stand • Speedy compared wih conventional procedures • Has specialised functions according to attachments	• Cumbersome and bulky • Attachments add to the basic cost • Awkward using blender on base unit

Machine	Operation	Uses	Advantages	Disadvantages
Food processors 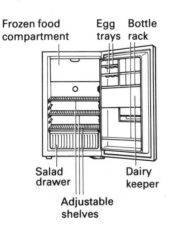	Cutting blades or discs fitted to the central spindle move rapidly. The result depends on the type of blade or disc fitted	To chop, liquidise, pulverise, grate and slice. Depending on design and attachments may whip, whisk, knead, etc.	• Much faster than table mixer • May carry out specialised functions	• Usually heavy to move • Not recommended for whisking egg white • Timing is critical if food is not to be over-processed • Can not cope with as large quantities as table mixers

Refrigerators

Refrigerators (Fig. 23.10) are designed to keep foods cool, clean and fresh. The cabinet and door are made up of two panels of sheet steel with an insulating material between; the finish on the steel is enamel. The seal between the door and cabinet may be a plastic or magnetic strip. In most refrigerators the evaporator is positioned at the top of the unit; this is the coldest part. The warmest part is at the base of the cabinet. The temperature inside the cabinet should range from 4°C to 7°C. Air circulation is by convection, and a fan may be included to help this.

Fig. 23.10
Types of refrigerator

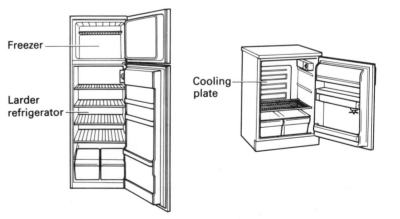

Fig. 23.11
Freezer symbol

1 *Conventional refrigerators* have a freezer compartment which forms the evaporator. This can be used to store frozen foods (Table 23.10) or to make ice cubes.
2 *Fridge-freezers* can be used to freeze foods as well. Look for the freezer symbol (Fig. 23.11).
3 *Larder refrigerators* do not have a freezer compartment.

Table 23.10
Star markings on refrigerators

Marking	Temperature (°C)	Storage time for frozen food
*	− 6	1 week
**	−12	1 month
***	−18	3 months

How a refrigerator works

There are two main types of refrigerator. Most are *compression refrigerators* which are operated by electricity. Absorption refrigerators are less common and usually run by gas.

Compression refrigerator (Fig. 23.12)
In the evaporator, which is inside the refrigerator, the refrigerant takes up heat from the air surrounding it and turns from liquid to vapour. The vapour formed is then pumped from the evaporator through pipes by an electrically driven compressor until it reaches the condenser, which is outside the cabinet; there the vapour cools to a liquid again, losing its heat to the outside air. The cooled liquid returns to the evaporator where the process begins again. The thermostat keeps a check on the internal temperature, and stops and starts the electric motor which drives the compressor as required.

Fig. 23.12
Cycle in a compression refrigerator

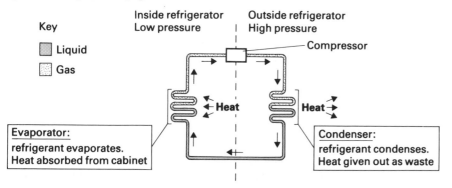

Consumer choice of refrigerators

Considerations for choice of refrigerators include: needs, it is usual to allow 43 litres per person; space (for example, table models or slim ones are recommended when floor space is limited); economics; personal preferences; and finish.

Guidelines for using a refrigerator

1 Check that the temperature inside the cabinet is correct.
2 Defrost regularly if manual or semi-automatic as required. If ice is allowed to build up round the evaporator running costs will increase.
3 When putting foods in the cabinet or removing them *do not leave the door open* as warm air will enter the cabinet and cold air will be lost.
4 Ensure that food put in the cabinet is *not hot* as it will raise the internal temperature of the cabinet.

5 Foods should be covered to prevent drying out and to prevent odours tainting other foods.
6 Store foods in the recommended parts of the cabinet (Table 23.11).
7 Refer to manufacturer's instructions for maintenance.

Table 23.11
Food storage in a refrigerator

Part	Food
Freezer compartment	Frozen food, ice
Cabinet – top shelf	Meat, poultry, offal, fish
main section	Cooked food, fats, cheese
racks	Milk, eggs, butter, drinks
vegetable drawer	Salad, fruit, vegetables

Defrosting
Defrosting may be carried out automatically. If not, carry out the operation about once every 2 weeks or when the ice in the evaporator is approximately 5 mm thick.

1 *Manual defrosting* requires the refrigerator to be switched off and the food removed and stored in a cool place. Frozen foods may be wrapped in newspaper or packed in an insulated bag. The ice around the evaporator melts and collects in a drip tray positioned directly underneath the ice box. To speed up the process a shallow vessel of hot water may be put inside the ice box. When all the ice has melted the cabinet should be wiped down to ensure that it is dry. The refrigerator is switched on and the foods returned.
2 *Semi-automatic defrosting* demands that the consumer either pushes a button or turns a switch. The drip tray may be emptied manually, or the melted ice may drain into containers positioned outside the refrigerator, where it is left to evaporate. When the semi-automatic defrosting is over, the refrigerator automatically starts up.
3 *Automatic defrosting* is usually associated with larder refrigerators and the main compartment of fridge-freezers. Defrosting is carried out when the compressor switches off and the melted ice drains away. The defrosting of the frozen food compartment of the fridge-freezer should be carried out manually at least twice a year.

Freezers

There are 3 main types of freezer: chest type, upright and fridge-freezer (Fig. 23.13). In Britain nearly 50% of households possess a freezer. There are a number of advantages in having a freezer:

1 Bulk buying is possible, and this can be an economical way to buy food.
2 Consumers who have ready access to home-grown produce can freeze foods and enjoy them at other times of the year.
3 Meals can be prepared in bulk or on the basis of 'eat-one-freeze-two'.
4 Unexpected situations, such as unannounced visitors, can be catered for if the freezer is well stocked, especially if it is used with a microwave oven.

Fig. 23.13
Types of freezer (see Fig. 23.10 for fridge freezer)

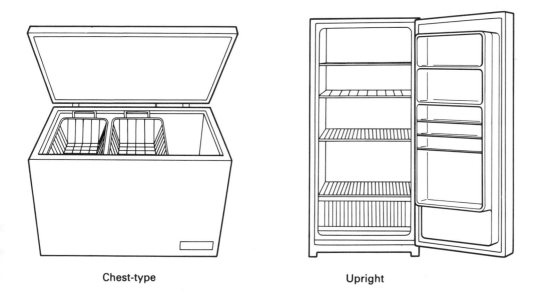

Chest-type   Upright

How a freezer works

Freezers are designed to ensure an internal temperature within the cabinet of −18°C or below. A freezer is like a compressor refrigerator in its mode of operation (p. 249).

Consumer choice of freezers

Allow 56 litres per person plus an extra 56 litres. Chest freezers are not as expensive as upright models; they are cheaper to run and can accommodate large items, and also keep colder during power cuts. Upright freezers take up less space than chest models and are easier to use as the door is simply opened without the user needing to bend. Fridge-freezers have the same advantages as upright freezers and take up even less total space. Design and finish are important considerations.

Guidelines for using a freezer

These are the same as for a refrigerator (p. 249).

Defrosting

Defrosting is necessary when the build-up of ice is about 5 mm thick. This usually happens after 12 months in a chest freezer and after 4–6 months in an upright model.

Turn the fast-freeze switch on about 6 hours before defrosting to ensure that the frozen food is as cold as possible. The food should be stored in a cool place while the freezer is being defrosted. Turn the switch off and disconnect the appliance; leave the door open, or put bowls of hot water inside and leave the door or lid shut. Collect the melted ice. While the ice is melting the process can be speeded up by using a plastic scraper. If the hot-water method is used the water will need to be changed periodically. Once all the ice has melted and been collected, the inside of the cabinet should be wiped dry.

If the cabinet has any odour, wipe the inside using a solution of bicarbonate of soda (1 × 5 ml tsp to 1 litre of water).

Small equipment

There is an enormous range of small equipment available.
Table 23.12

Equipment	Description	Uses	Consumer choice
Cutting tools			
Cooks' knives	Strong, pointed, sharp blades. From the handle, the blade is straight and half-way it gently curves upwards towards the point of the blade	Peeling vegetables, slicing, cubing and chopping	Useful to have a selection of sharp cooks' knives
Paring knives	Small knives, blades usually about 75 mm long with pointed ends	Peeling, trimming and cutting eyes out of vegetables	The shapes of the blades vary. Choice depends on personal taste
Palette knives	Wide, blunt edged blades, slightly flexible	Mixing, folding, scraping, turning pancakes	Those which bend at the end of handle easier to use
Grapefruit knives	Curved blades serrated on both sides; blades are slightly flexible with pointed tips	Segmenting grapefruit and oranges	
Potato peelers	V-shaped blades with sharpened slot down centre for peeling; the points of the blades are sharp for picking out blemishes	Peeling fruit and vegetables, making chocolate curls	Some are designed for left or right handed use; they can incorporate an apple corer; the swivel action type peels thinly and has a round handle
Graters	The surface punctured with rows of small holes, the size of the holes determines the degree of fineness of grated food; most include a slicing blade	Breaking food, e.g., cheese, apple, into a variety of shapes and sizes	It should have fine, medium and coarse sections; boxed graters are sturdy and rigid; flat graters are easier to store and clean
Kitchen scissors	Those with one plain and one serrated edge are popular	Cutting rind off bacon, chopping or cutting herbs, making patterns on pastry	Should be heavy; plastic handles can chip and paint comes off painted ones; all stainless steel without trimmings recommended
Pastry cutters	Range of sizes, plain or fluted	Cutting pastry, scones and biscuits, poaching eggs, cooking crumpets	Plastic cannot be used for cooking
Spoons, lifters and turners			
Wooden spoons	Various shapes and sizes	Creaming, beating, shaping a cottage loaf	Some are angled, which is useful when bowls and pans have crevices; ensure that the wood is smooth
Slotted spoons	Long handles, and the bowl of the spoon is perforated to allow liquid to pass through	Lifting food from pans, serving food, removing scum from stock	All stainless steel more durable than those with wooden or plastic handles

Equipment	Description	Uses	Consumer choice
Spoons, lifters and turners (continued)			
Spatulas/scrapers	Flexible with rubber or plastic blades	Scraping mixture from mixing vessels, folding and blending light aerated mixtures	Plastic bladed spatulas are cheaper but not as flexible as rubber ones
Lifters and turners	Various shapes and materials	Turning foods during cooking, serving foods such as flans	Nylon is useful for non-stick pans
Tools to break, crush and purée			
Potato mashers	Sturdy, perforated metal base attached by two metal arms to a single upright wooden handle	Mashing cooked potatoes and other root vegetables	Limited choice
Pestle and mortar	A pestle has a rounded head for pounding food; a mortar is a basin with rounded sides	Crushing foods to a paste or powder	Wooden pestles and mortars absorb flavours and colours; glass or porcelain ones are easier to clean
Tools for separating			
Colanders	Perforated basin shape with holes small enough to allow only liquids to pass through; has pedestal base and handles	Draining vegetables and pasta, washing and rinsing fruit and vegetables, as steamer over a pan of boiling water	Aluminium is durable; plastic is unsuitable for steaming and enamelled metal chips easily
Sieves	Mesh allows separation of fine particles from coarse ones and separation of solids and liquids	Drum and bowl-shaped sieves for sifting solids and liquids; conical sieves for liquids	Nylon and stainless steel prevent food discoloration
Tools for shaping and moulding			
Rolling-pins	Elongated with rounded edge, like a thick pole or broomstick	Rolling out pastry into flan tin, crushing biscuits, bashing meat	Rolling pins made of hardwood, well-sanded and rubbed smooth, are economical, durable and versatile. Rolling-pins made of china, marble and glass are cool and suitable for rolling pastry but are fragile and expensive
Forcing bags	Large, medium and small. Nozzles fit into cone	Large sizes for mashed potatoes, meringues, choux pastry; medium for whipped cream; and small for icing	Nylon bags are more durable than plastic ones; look for double stitching on seams and hemming on the top, and reinforcement around nozzle
Pastry brushes	Wide range of shapes, sizes and materials; hogs' bristles or nylon bristles; flat or rounded heads	Applying glazes, e.g., milk, egg and syrup to doughs, pastries and cakes	Nylon bristles can melt, and are harder than bristle brushes, leaving marks on soft pastry

Equipment	Description	Uses	Consumer choice
Whisks			
Balloon whisk	Metal wires in bulbous shape, particularly useful for whisking air into egg whites	Introducing air into mixtures, e.g., soufflés, whipped cream, meringues; beating sauces smooth	Personal taste will determine choice
Rotary whisk	Have 2 handles, 1 for holding whisk and 1 for turning blades		
Boards	Vary in size, shape and material; thick one for chopping; thinner one for pastry	Chopping, rolling out pastry and carving meat	Useful to have selection of boards for different uses
Bowls			
Mixing bowls	Yellow earthenware and glass both popular	Mixing ingredients together, e.g., batters, cakes, pastry and bread	Ensure earthenware bowls are not cracked; if tapped with a pencil resonant ring should be heard
Pudding basins	Pyrex, earthenware, aluminium and polypropylene can withstand steaming; aluminium and polypropylene basins may come with clip-on lids	Mixing ingredients together, cooking steamed puddings, e.g., steak and kidney pudding	Useful to have a selection; basins made of aluminium can discolour foods; basins made of polypropylene discolour with frequent use
Plates and dishes			
Pie plates	Pyrex, aluminium, stainless steel and enamelled metal; slightly deeper than dinner plates	Making tarts (e.g., apple), for steaming foods (e.g., fish)	Useful to have a variety of sizes; enamel chips easily
Pie dishes	Pyrex, stoneware, earthenware and enamelled steel; various shapes and sizes	Cooking pies, crumbles, cauliflower *au gratin*	Useful to have a variety of sizes; enamel chips; Pyrex is useful because food being cooked can be seen through the sides and base of dish
Baking tins			
Baking sheets	Various shapes and sizes, may have sloping rims or one edge with upright rim	Baking biscuits, meringues, bread rolls; round ones can be used for pizzas and as bases for flan rings	Heavy baking sheets do not buckle
Bread tins	Described according to weight of bread they hold	Baking bread, cooking patés and meat loaves	Non-stick aluminium tins are useful
Deep cake tins	Different shapes and sizes; some have removable bases	Baking rich cake mixtures, e.g., Dundee cake, fruit cake	Heavier tins are best. Those with removable bases are convenient

Equipment	Description	Uses	Consumer choice
Baking tins (continued)			
Shallow cake tins	Various shapes and sizes; some have clasp-fastened sides that are removable	Sandwich tins for sponges and Victoria sandwich mixtures; Swiss roll tins for Swiss rolls	An assortment is useful
Bun tins	Trays with sections in various shapes; the number of sections varies	Baking small cakes, pies, batters, éclairs and tartlets	Look for heavy tins
Flan rings	Various sizes; can be plain or fluted, round or rectangular	Making flans and quiches	Fluted tins get clogged up with pastry
Roasting pans	Various sizes, some have handles	Roasting joints and vegetables	Metal pans versatile
Saucepans, kettles and casseroles			
Saucepans	Various sizes, designs and materials; consist of a pan with 1 or 2 handles and a lid	Boiling and simmering foods	Ensure handles are comfortable to hold and firmly attached; also lids should fit well. Choose heavy pans for even heat distribution and to prevent sticking
Milk pan	Various sizes and materials; non-stick useful; have lipped rims for pouring and most have sloping sides	Heating milk	Check handle is comfortable and firmly attached; if non-stick check coating is not scratched
Kettles	Various shapes, sizes and materials; some have a whistle mechanism	Boiling water	Cannot fail owing to mechanical problems; choose one suitable for hob unit in question
Casseroles	Various shapes, sizes and materials	Stewing and casseroling	Useful to have a selection of different shapes and sizes
Frying-pans			
Shallow	Can have straight or curved sides; different sizes and materials; some have lips for easy pouring	Cooking pan-cakes, omelets, fried eggs	Non-stick shallow pans use less fat
Deep	Like saucepans but have lids with vents and incorporate a frying basket	Cooking chips, Scotch eggs or batter-coated fish	Some deep pans have a deodoriser included in lid.
Woks	Chinese origin; deep, round, sloping sides; 1 or 2 handles and lid; some have non-stick surface	Stir frying, e.g., sliced vegetables, meat or fish. Food is fried and steamed in a wok	Useful for quick cooking; flavours and textures are not spoilt and natural juices are not lost

Equipment	Description	Uses	Consumer choice
Measuring equipment			
Scales	Different types, e.g., balance, spring, beam and electronic	Measuring weight	Spring scales are least accurate but easy to operate
Measuring spoons	Range of sizes: 1.25, 2.5, 5 and 15 ml; held together by a ring or fit inside one another	Measuring volume of small quantities	Stainless steel durable; plastic breaks easily
Measuring cups	Range of sizes: $\frac{1}{4}$, $\frac{1}{3}$, $\frac{1}{2}$ and 1 cup. Held together by a ring or inside one another	Measuring volume	As for measuring spoons
Liquid and dry measurers	Jugs, beakers and conical beakers on base; different capacities, e.g., 500 ml, 1 litre	Measuring volume	Choose according to capacity and materials, e.g., toughened glass, aluminium and polypropylene
Thermometers	Different types, e.g., oven, frying, sugar, meat and freezer	Measuring temperature	Choice will depend on needs

Safety in the kitchen

Most of the accidents in the home are *falls*, *burns* and *scalds* and 40% of these accidents take place during the time meals are prepared, served or eaten. The majority of accidents are associated with cookers, electrical installations and out-of-reach storage.

Some guidelines for kitchen safety

1 Position pan handles so that they do not stick outwards. Pan guards are useful if children are around.
2 Stand back when opening the oven or using the grill.
3 Use an oven cloth or gloves to lift hot pans.
4 Follow manufacturers' instructions for using electrical equipment carefully.
5 Turn appliances off immediately after use.
6 Ensure that electric plugs are wired correctly and that the right fuse is fitted.
7 Ensure hands are dry when handling electric plugs.
8 Keep flexes to size required and check that they are not frayed or broken.
9 Keep flexes away from direct heat or water.
10 Socket covers are useful if children are around.
11 Store frequently-used items on lower shelves and less frequently-used items on upper shelves.
12 Keep heavy items within easy reach.
13 Stack items so they will not topple over.
14 Use a step ladder to reach items stored high up.
15 Treat sharp items such as knives, blades and graters with caution.
16 Locks on refrigerator and freezer doors are recommended if children are around.
17 Avoid tablecloths which overhang deeply. Keep hot foods and drinks away from the edge of the table.
18 Stack dishes safely and organise the washing up sequence methodically.
19 Clean up any spillages of food or breakages of equipment when they occur.

Part 2

Part 2 consists entirely of recipes, all of which have been tested and written in a standardised format. The recipes have been arranged in chapters which comply with *The National Food Guide: The Balance of Good Health*. Part 2 has been designed to accommodate healthy meal planning and investigative work.

Meal planning

The modified recipes are in the framework of *The Health of the Nation* targets and COMA DRVs and are recommended in the formulation of healthy meals. Each recipe has a code indicating any dietary modifications that have been made: *Fibre +* = increase in dietary fibre (NSP); *Fat –* = reduction in total fat; *Fat unsat* = reduction in saturated fat; *Sugar –* = reduction in non-milk extrinsic sugars; *Salt –* = reduction in sodium and chloride.

Investigative work

The standard recipes have been formatted to make them suitable for use as controls in experimental work. They may be used as controls in a number of ways.

Recipe balance/ratio
To find out what happens when the balance of a recipe is altered, it is necessary to have a control recipe against which experimental variations may be compared. Recipe balance is critical to the production of a 'quality' food product (see flour mixtures p. 73). An example of this would be to take the standard recipe for scones (p. 329) and change the ratio of baking powder to plain flour. The control and experimental variations could be assessed for shape, surface features, volume, texture, colour and flavour.

Preparation techniques
To find out what happens if standard food preparation techniques are altered, it is necessary to have a control recipe against which experimental variations may be compared. An example of this would be to take the standard recipe for short pastry (p. 277) and change the kneading times. The control and experimental variations could be assessed for shape, surface features, shortness, flakiness, colour and flavour.

Recipe modification
The Health of the Nation targets and COMA's DRVs need to be translated into foods that we are used to eating. The modified recipes are intended to fulfil this role and spark off ideas in this respect. An example of modifying a standard recipe could be to take the recipe for Glamorgan sausages (p. 320) and change the type of bread used with the aim of increasing the dietary fibre (NSP) content. The control and experimental variations could be assessed for shape, colour, flavour, texture and dietary fibre content.

Which brand?
The standard recipes may be made up and compared with manufactured counterparts. For example the recipe for coleslaw (p. 300) could be the control and could be compared with two different brands of the same product. The control and branded products could be assessed for preparation time, cost, colour, texture and flavour.

24 Soups, dips and spreads

Soups

Watercress soup

4 servings

Cooking time 35 minutes

Standard	Modified Fat⁻ Fatᵘⁿˢᵃᵗ Salt⁻
2 bunches of watercress	
2 large onions	
2 medium-sized potatoes	
50 g butter or margarine	use polyunsaturated margarine
500 ml chicken stock	
300 ml milk	use skimmed milk
salt and pepper	omit salt

1 Wash watercress, cut away coarse stalks. Keep 2 or 3 sprigs for garnishing. Chop remaining leaves and stalks.

2 Peel and finely slice onions (Fig. 30.2).

3 Scrub, peel and dice potatoes.

4 Add fat to a pan and put on gentle heat.

5 Add chopped watercress, sliced onions and diced potatoes. Leave over low heat with lid on for 15 minutes.

6 Add stock, pepper, and salt if used, and simmer for 15 minutes.

7 Liquidise soup in a blender

8 Pour soup back into a clean pan, add milk and additional seasoning if required. Bring to simmering point and serve garnished with watercress.

Carrot and orange soup

4 servings

Standard	Modified Fat⁻ Fatᵘⁿˢᵃᵗ Salt⁻
500 g carrots	
1 small onion	
1 large orange	
500 ml vegetable stock	
2 tablespoons vegetable oil	use 1 tablespoon sunflower or corn oil

Standard	Modified Fat⁻ Fat^unsat Salt⁻
1 tablespoon freshly chopped coriander*	use 2 tablespoons coriander
½ teaspoon paprika	
pinch of nutmeg	
salt and pepper	omit salt

Cooking time 50 minutes

*fresh parsley may be used in place of coriander

1 Scrape or peel if necessary and dice carrots.
2 Peel and dice onion (Fig. 30.2).
3 Wash the orange, remove zest, cut it in half and squeeze juice out.
4 Pour oil into a large pan. Add diced onion and fry for 5 minutes.
5 Add diced carrots and continue cooking over gentle heat for 5 minutes.
6 Add stock, juice and zest of orange, half the fresh coriander, paprika, nutmeg, pepper, and salt if used. Bring mixture to the boil and leave to simmer for 40 minutes.
7 Liquidise soup in a blender.
8 Pour soup back into a clean pan, add extra flavouring if necessary and bring to simmering point.
9 Serve sprinkled with fresh coriander.

French onion soup

4 servings

Standard	Modified Fibre⁺ Fat⁻ Fat^unsat Salt⁻ Sugar⁻
500 g onions	
1 tablespoon vegetable oil	use 1 teaspoon sunflower or corn oil
25 g butter or margarine	use polyunsaturated margarine
600 ml beef stock	
1 clove of garlic	
1 bay leaf	
1 bouquet garni	
¼ teaspoon granulated sugar	omit sugar
salt and pepper	omit salt
Topping:	
4 slices French bread	use 2 large slices wholewheat bread
100 g Cheddar cheese	use Edam cheese
2 teaspoons French mustard	

Cooking time 1 hour

1 Peel and slice onions finely (Fig. 30.2).

2 Skin and crush garlic.

3 Melt fat in a heavy-based pan, add onions, crushed garlic, and sugar if used. Fry for 25 minutes until onions are evenly browned.

4 Add beef stock, bay leaf, bouquet garni, pepper and salt if used. Simmer for 30 minutes.

5 Toast bread, spread with French mustard and arrange on the bottom of a flame-proof soup tureen.

6 Grate cheese.

7 Remove bouquet garni and bay leaf and adjust seasoning as necessary.

8 Pour soup into the tureen. When toast floats to surface sprinkle with grated cheese.

9 Put dish under a pre-heated grill for 3 to 5 minutes.

Gazpacho

4 servings

Standard	*Modified* Fat⁻ Fat^unsat Salt⁻
500 g tomatoes	
$\frac{1}{2}$ a cucumber	
1 large green pepper	
4 spring onions	
1 clove of garlic	
2 heaped teaspoons fresh chopped parsley	
300 ml cold water	
2 tablespoons vegetable oil	use 1 tablespoon sunflower or corn oil
1 tablespoon wine vinegar	
salt and pepper	omit salt

1 Skin (Fig. 30.3) and de-seed tomatoes or simply wash them. Chop roughly.

2 Wash cucumber and peel or leave skin on. Take half and chop roughly. Finely dice the other half.

3 Wash green pepper, remove seeds and divide it into two. Cut half up coarsely and finely dice other half (Fig. 31.2).

4 Wash spring onions. Cut 2 of them roughly and finely chop the other 2.

5 Put roughly chopped vegetables into a blender.

6 Skin and crush garlic, add to mixture and add oil, vinegar, 1 tablespoon chopped parsley, pepper, and salt if used.

7 Blend mixture until smooth.

8 Pour mixture into a bowl; add cold water. Adjust seasoning if necessary and chill.

9 Mix together finely chopped vegetables and remaining parsley.

10 Sprinkle on to chilled soup and serve.

Dips and spreads

Hummus

4 servings

Standard	Modified Fat⁻ Fatᵘⁿˢᵃᵗ Salt⁻ ᵐˢ
200 g chickpeas cooked or canned	
100 ml cooking liquid or water	
150 ml tahini	
juice of 1 large lemon	
2 cloves of garlic	
2 tablespoons olive oil	use 1 tablespoon sunflower oil
salt	omit salt
cayenne pepper	
2 heaped teaspoons fresh chopped parsley	

1 Crush garlic and drop into blender goblet.

2 Add drained chickpeas, oil, tahini, lemon juice, cayenne pepper, salt if used and cooking liquid or water.

3 Blend mixture until it looks like mayonnaise.

4 Pour mixture into a serving dish, sprinkle with freshly chopped parsley.

5 Serve with warm pitta bread or chunky wholewheat bread.

Vegan cheese

4 servings

Cooking time 2–3 minutes

Standard	Modified Fatᵘⁿˢᵃᵗ
100 g soya flour	
100 g Tomor or Trex	use polyunsaturated margarine
1 level teaspoon yeast extract	

1 Melt fat in a pan.

2 Add soya flour; stir, using a wooden spoon.

3 Add yeast extract and beat mixture.

4 Put the mixture into a heat-proof dish.

5 Leave to cool, and then chill.

Note: This cheese can be used as cheese or in cooking.

Peanut dip

4 servings

Standard	*Modified* Fibre⁺ Fat⁻ Salt⁻
200 g roasted peanuts*	
2 ripe bananas	
$\frac{1}{4}$ of a small onion	
juice and zest of 1 small lemon	
1 level tablespoon tomato purée	
150 ml plain yogurt	use low-fat yogurt
50 g fresh white breadcrumbs	use wholewheat breadcrumbs
salt and pepper	omit salt

* If salted peanuts are used simply wash off salt.

1 Grind peanuts in a blender and put into a large mixing bowl.

2 Peel and slice onion (Fig. 30.2) and put into the blender.

3 Peel and slice bananas and put into the blender with onion.

4 Add lemon juice, zest, tomato purée, yogurt, pepper, and salt if used. Liquidise and pour into the mixing bowl with peanuts.

5 Add breadcrumbs, and mix together.

6 Serve in 1 main dish or divide mixture to fill 4 individual dishes.

7 Chill for 1 hour. This dip goes well with fresh raw celery, carrot, green pepper or apple slices, or it may be used as a spread.

25 Savoury sauces and stuffings

Sauces

The amount of sauce to serve

Coating sauce: 250 ml to coat 4 helpings of fish or vegetable

Pouring sauce: ⎫
⎬ 250 ml for 4 to 6 helpings
Gravy: ⎭

Savoury white sauces: basic recipe

Standard			Modified	Fibre⁺ Fat⁻ Fat^unsat Salt⁻
	margarine or butter	flour	use polyunsaturated margarine	
Pouring	15 g	15 g	use wholewheat flour	
Coating	25 g	25 g		
Panada	50 g	50 g		
250 ml milk or 125 ml milk and 125 ml meat, fish or vegetable liquor			use skimmed milk	
¼ level teaspoon salt			omit salt	
pepper				

Method 1: roux

1 Make a *roux* with fat and flour; that is, melt fat, stir flour into it over low heat for 1 to 2 minutes.

2 Remove the pan from the heat, gradually stir in half the liquid, beat it smooth, then stir in remaining liquid.

3 When the uncooked sauce is smooth, return the pan to the heat, bring sauce slowly to boiling point, stirring vigorously.

4 Season, and taste sauce.

Method 2: beurre manié

1 Soften fat in a basin with a wooden spoon, then work flour into it to form a paste.

2 Bring the liquid almost to boiling point, remove the pan from the heat and whisk a little of the flour–fat paste at a time into the hot liquid.

3 When sauce is smoothly whisked return the pan to the heat, and with a wooden spoon stir till it boils.

4 Season and taste sauce.

Method 3: 'all-in-one'

1 Put all ingredients in a pan.

2 Put the pan over a moderate heat, stirring continuously with a wooden spoon.

3 After boiling point is reached continue cooking and stirring for 2–3 minutes.

4 Season and taste sauce.

Variations to the basic recipe are given in Table 25.1.

Table 25.1
Variations of white sauce

Sauce	Additions to basic recipe	Variation of method
Cheese sauce	Use all milk 2 heaped tablespoons dry, grated cheese $\frac{1}{4}$ teaspoon made mustard small shake of cayenne pepper	A cheese coating sauce is generally sprinkled with 1 to 2 tablespoons extra cheese and 1 teaspoon fresh crumbs, then browned under the grill
Egg sauce	1 hard-boiled egg, chopped	Add chopped egg to the hot sauce and re-heat it; season well
Mushroom sauce	50 g mushrooms 1 teaspoon lemon juice $\frac{1}{4}$ teaspoon Marmite	Wipe and chop mushrooms finely, cook them gently in margarine for 10 minutes
Onion sauce	1 Spanish or 2 English or French onions, boiled and chopped *A quick method*: chop onion finely and cook it in fat until soft in 10–15 minutes, make the *roux*, add all milk or $\frac{1}{2}$ milk, $\frac{1}{2}$ stock	Boil onion and use the liquid with milk for the sauce
Parsley sauce	$\frac{1}{2}$ tablespoon finely chopped parsley	Add parsley to boiling sauce and cook for 1 minute

Brown sauces: basic recipe

Standard	*Modified* Fibre⁺ Fatᵘⁿˢᵃᵗ Salt⁻
$1\frac{1}{2}$ tablespoons flour	use wholewheat flour
$1\frac{1}{2}$ tablespoons dripping	use sunflower oil
1 small onion	
1 small carrot	
250 ml stock	
$\frac{1}{2}$ teaspoon meat extract, yeast extract or savoury sauce	

	Standard	Modified	Fibre⁺ Fat^unsat Salt⁻

| | Standard | Modified | Fibre+   Fatunsat   Salt- |

| *Cooking time 25–35 minutes* | ½ teaspoon salt
a few shakes of pepper | omit salt | |

1 Peel and slice onion (Fig. 30.2)

2 Peel or scrape if necessary and slice carrot.

3 Melt fat, add onion and carrot and fry until golden-brown.

4 Stir in flour and fry slowly until it has darkened.

5 Add liquid and stir until it boils. Add other ingredients and simmer sauce gently for 20–30 minutes.

6 Strain sauce, taste and season. If necessary, colour with a few drops of gravy-browning.

Variations to the basic recipe are given in Table 25.2.

Table 25.2
Variations of brown sauce

Sauce	Additions to recipe	Variation of method
Italian sauce	1 extra onion or shallot peeled and chopped 25 g lean bacon, chopped 2 tomatoes, fresh or canned 25 g mushrooms, whole, wiped 2 teaspoons chopped parsley 1 teaspoon vinegar	Fry bacon with carrot and onion; add whole mushrooms and tomatoes with stock and simmer until mushrooms are soft, strain sauce, lift out mushrooms; chop and return to sauce; add vinegar and chopped parsley last
Mushroom sauce brown	50 g mushrooms, wiped ¼ teaspoon Marmite 1 teaspoon lemon juice	Cook mushrooms whole in sauce; strain sauce; when mushrooms are tender lift out, chop and return to sauce; add Marmite and lemon juice

Thin gravy

	Standard	Modified Salt⁻
4 servings	Sediment left in tin after roasting	
	250 ml vegetable liquor or stock	
Cooking time 5–10 minutes	salt and pepper	omit salt

1 Pour or spoon fat out of the pan.

2 Loosen crusty pieces in the pan using a wooden spoon. Put the pan over the heat.

3 Add vegetable liquor or stock and stir vigorously.

4 Boil briskly for 3–5 minutes.

5 Season and taste gravy. Strain if it is not smooth, and remove any visible surface fat using absorbent paper.

Thick gravy

	Standard	*Modified* Fibre+ Salt⁻
4 servings	Sediment left in tin after roasting	
	1 tablespoon fat from cooked meat	
	1 level tablespoon flour	use wholewheat flour
	250 ml vegetable liquor or stock	
Cooking time 5–10 minutes	Salt and pepper	omit salt

1 Leave sediment and fat in the roasting tin.

2 Loosen crusty pieces in the pan using a wooden spoon. Put the pan over a gentle heat.

3 Add flour to sizzling fat and work mixture together using a wooden spoon, making circular movements.

4 When flour has darkened and a smooth paste has formed, add liquid gradually and continue stirring vigorously.

5 Cook and continue stirring for 3–5 minutes.

6 Season and taste gravy. Strain and remove visible fat as for thin gravy.

Apple sauce

	Standard	*Modified* Fat⁻ Sugar⁻
	500 g cooking apples	
	a thin strip of lemon rind	
	2 tablespoons water	
	25 g sugar	omit sugar
Cooking time 10–15 minutes	1 tablespoon butter or margarine	omit fat

1 Peel, quarter, core and slice apples roughly.

2 Stew in water, and fat if used, and add lemon rind.

3 When apples are soft, lift out rind and beat apple pulp smooth with a wooden spoon or liquidise in a blender.

4 Add sugar to taste if desired.

Curry sauce

4 servings

Standard   *Modified* Fat⁻ Fatᵘⁿˢᵃᵗ Salt⁻

250 g canned tomatoes

100 g onions

50 g ghee, butter or margarine   use 25 g polyunsaturated margarine

2 cloves of garlic

10 g fresh peeled ginger

½ level teaspoon chilli powder

½ level teaspoon dried coriander

½ level teaspoon turmeric

½ level teaspoon salt   omit salt

Cooking time 30 minutes   3 tablespoons water

1 Peel and slice onions (Fig. 30.2).

2 Peel and crush garlic.

3 Wash and finely chop ginger.

4 Heat fat in a large pan over a moderate heat, add onion, garlic and ginger. Fry for 5 minutes.

5 Add chilli powder, dried coriander, turmeric, and salt if used. Continue frying for a further 5 minutes.

6 Add tomatoes and water, and continue cooking over a low heat for a further 20 minutes.

Note: This sauce can be used to make different types of curries: meat, fish, egg and vegetable.

Mint sauce

Standard   *Modified* Sugar⁻

2 rounded tablespoons finely chopped mint

1 tablespoon castor sugar   use 1 teaspoon castor sugar

2 tablespoons vinegar

2 tablespoons boiling water

1 Chop mint very finely.

2 Put it with sugar in a small sauce-boat.

3 Add boiling water and leave it to cool.

4 Add vinegar last.

Bread sauce

Standard	Modified Fibre⁺ Fat⁻ Salt⁻

Standard	Modified Fibre⁺ Fat⁻ Salt⁻
50 g stale white breadcrumbs	use wholewheat breadcrumbs
250 ml milk	use skimmed milk
1 onion	
1 blade of mace	
1 bay leaf	
4 peppercorns	
2 cloves	
salt to taste	omit salt
1 tablespoon butter or margarine or 1 tablespoon cream	omit butter, margarine and cream

Cooking time 45 minutes

1 Put peeled onion and spices in a pan with milk. Bring milk slowly to boiling point. Cover the pan and keep it in a warm place for ½ hour.

2 Strain milk, return it to the pan and add breadcrumbs.

3 Soak bread in hot milk for 15 minutes; re-heat sauce and stir using a wooden spoon.

4 Taste and season sauce, and stir in butter or cream if desired.

Barbecue sauce

4 servings

Standard	Modified Fat⁻ Fat^{unsat} Salt⁻ Sugar⁻
50 g butter or margarine	use 15 g polyunsaturated margarine
1 medium onion	
1 level teaspoon tomato purée	
2 tablespoons vinegar	
2 level tablespoons brown sugar	use 1 tablespoon brown sugar
2 level teaspoons dry mustard	
1 teaspoon Worcester sauce	
150 ml water	
salt and pepper	omit salt

Cooking time 20–25 minutes

1 Peel and dice onion (Fig. 30.2).

2 Heat fat in a pan, add onion and fry for 5 minutes until onion has softened.

3 Add tomato purée and stir thoroughly.

4 Blend together water, vinegar, sugar, mustard, Worcester sauce, pepper, and salt if used.

5 Add the blend to the pan and stir over the heat until mixture boils.

6 Simmer for 10 to 15 minutes with the lid off the pan.

Tomato sauce

4 servings

Cooking time 35 minutes

Standard	*Modified* Fat⁻ Fat^{unsat} Salt⁻
500 g tomatoes	
1 medium onion	
1 clove of garlic	
1 heaped teaspoon tomato purée	
2 level teaspoons freshly chopped basil or 1 level teaspoon dried basil	
1 tablespoon vegetable oil	use 1 teaspoon corn oil
salt and pepper	omit salt

1 Wash tomatoes, skin (Fig. 30.3) if desired. Chop flesh roughly.

2 Heat oil in a large pan.

3 Peel and slice onion (Fig. 30.2) and crush garlic. Add to hot oil. Cook for 5 minutes to soften them.

4 Add tomatoes, tomato purée, basil, pepper and salt if used. Stir thoroughly and simmer for 15 minutes with the lid on the pan.

5 Remove lid and simmer for a further 15 minutes.

6 Serve chunky or liquidised.

Horseradish sauce

Standard	*Modified* Fat⁻ Sugar⁻
2 tablespoons grated horseradish	
4 tablespoons single cream	use low-fat plain yogurt
2 teaspoons vinegar	
1 teaspoon lemon juice	
$\frac{1}{2}$ teaspoon sugar	omit sugar

1 Grate horseradish.

2 Mix all ingredients together in a small basin.

Cranberry sauce

Standard	Modified Sugar⁻
250 g cranberries	
150 ml water	
50–100 g sugar	omit sugar
¼ teaspoon lemon juice	

Cooking time 10–20 minutes

1 Stew cranberries in water with lemon juice until they 'pop'; add more water if necessary.

2 Liquidise if a smooth sauce is required.

3 Sweeten if desired and re-heat sauce.

Salad dressings

French dressing

Standard	Modified Fat^unsat Salt⁻ Sugar⁻
2 tablespoons vegetable oil	use sunflower or corn oil
1 tablespoon vinegar or lemon juice	
½ level teaspoon dry mustard	
pinch of sugar	omit sugar
salt and pepper	omit salt

1 The easiest way to make this dressing is to measure and mix it in a graduated medicine bottle, but any small, clean bottle can be used.

2 Shake ingredients until oil is emulsified, giving the dressing a cloudy look.

3 Serve at once, as the emulsion is only temporary.

Note: Other ingredients may be added to give exciting flavours, for example, 1 crushed clove of garlic; sprig of French tarragon; 1 level teaspoon freshly chopped parsley.

Mayonnaise

| Standard | Modified | Fat^{unsat} Salt[−] Sugar[−] |

Standard	Modified Fat^{unsat} Salt[−] Sugar[−]
125 ml vegetable oil	use corn oil or sunflower oil
1 to 2 tablespoons vinegar or lemon juice	
1 egg yolk	
$\frac{1}{4}$ teaspoon dry mustard	
$\frac{1}{4}$ teaspoon salt	omit salt
1 teaspoon castor sugar	omit sugar
a little pepper	

Optional: a few drops of Worcester sauce

1 Have oil and yolk cold but not just out of the refrigerator.

2 Using a small egg whisk or a rotary beater and a small basin, beat the dry seasonings into yolk.

3 Put oil in a small jug or in a bottle with two grooves in the cork and trickle it, drop by drop, into yolk, at the same time beating it vigorously; if a rotary beater is used add 1 dessertspoon oil at a time.

4 Once the emulsion begins to thicken, pour oil in a thin continuous trickle and keep up vigorous beating.

5 When the emulsion is too thick to beat easily, thin it by adding a little vinegar, drop by drop.

6 Beat in remaining oil, thinning emulsion with vinegar as needed. The finished mayonnaise should be as thick as double cream.

7 Taste and adjust the seasoning.

Note: With an electric blender, use whole egg and add vinegar with seasonings, then pour in oil in a steady stream with blender running.

Yogurt dressing

Standard	Modified Fat[−] Salt[−] Sugar[−]
150 ml plain yogurt	use low-fat yogurt
$\frac{1}{4}$ level teaspoon dry mustard	
$\frac{1}{4}$ level teaspoon castor sugar	omit sugar
salt and pepper	omit salt

Mix ingredients together in small basin.

Note: Other ingredients may be added – for example, 1 clove of crushed garlic; 1 level tablespoon of freshly chopped chives; 1 level tablespoon of freshly chopped mint, zest and juice from 1 small orange or lemon.

Stuffings

Stuffing is used mainly to add flavour to meat, fish or vegetables, but it may also make these foods a little more substantial or filling and it may make a significant contribution to the intake of certain nutrients.

Basic recipe

4 servings

Standard	*Modified* Fibre⁺ Fat⁻ Fatᵘⁿˢᵃᵗ Salt⁻
100 g white breadcrumbs or 100 g cooked white rice	use wholewheat breadcrumbs or brown rice
50 g margarine or chopped suet	use 25 g polyunsaturated margarine
½ to 1 beaten egg	
pepper and salt	omit salt
flavouring additions	

1 Crumb bread, soak in beaten egg, and when soft mash it smooth with a fork.

2 Chop shredded suet finely or mash margarine into bread or rice with a fork.

3 Mix all ingredients together, flavour, season and taste the mixture.

Variations to the basic recipe are given in Table 25.3.

Table 25.3
Variations of stuffings

Stuffing	Additions to basic recipe	Variation of method
Veal stuffing for chicken, veal or any purpose	1 tablespoon chopped parsley ½ teaspoon mixed chopped herbs grated zest of ½ lemon	
Sage and onion for pork and goose	1 large onion, chopped 2 teaspoons chopped sage	Cook onion sliced thickly in boiling water for 30 minutes and chop
Prune, for chicken, veal, pork, duck or goose	6 to 8 large soaked prunes 1 small cooking apple 1/16 teaspoon spice (nutmeg or cinnamon) 25 g chopped nuts grated zest and juice ½ lemon	Stone and chop prunes, chop or mill nuts, chop apple
Raisin and nut, for any meat or vegetable	50 g seedless raisins 50 g chopped nuts 1 teaspoon chopped parsley	

26 Breads and savoury scones

Short-time bread

*2 standard loaves
or 16 rolls*

*Oven 230 °C Gas No. 8
Baking time 30–35 minutes
for loaves; 15–20 minutes
for rolls*

*Fig. 26.1
Kneading bread dough*

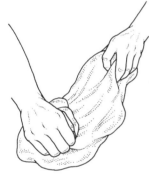

*Fig. 26.2
Shaping loaves*

For bread tin

Standard	*Modified* Fibre⁺ fatᵘⁿˢᵃᵗ Salt⁻
500 g strong flour	use brown or wholewheat flour
2 level teaspoons salt	omit salt
15 g lard or vegetable fat	use polyunsaturated margarine
20 g fresh yeast	
25 mg vitamin C tablet	
300 ml water	

1 Lightly grease tins and flour them or use non-stick tins.

2 Sift flour and salt into a large mixing bowl. Tip any bran in sieve into bowl.

3 Add fat and rub into flour using finger tips.

4 Boil $\frac{1}{3}$ of water and add to remaining cold water.

5 Put fresh yeast into basin and mix with 2 teaspoons liquid to soften it; stir in remaining liquid.

6 Add vitamin C tablet to liquid and crush, using back of tablespoon.

7 Make deep hole or 'well' in flour and add liquid mixture.

8 Mix thoroughly using hand with a clawing movement for 3 minutes until dough leaves fingers.

9 Turn dough on to lightly floured surface and knead (Fig. 26.1) until smooth and elastic (about 10 minutes).

10 Shape dough (Figs. 26.2 and 26.3) and leave to rise covered with greased polythene. Loaves take about 45 minutes and rolls about 25 minutes.

11 Brush surface with beaten egg or dust with flour. Bake in a hot oven until golden brown. When cooked, the bread or rolls sound hollow if the base is tapped.

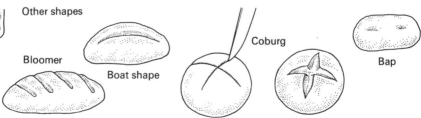

Other shapes

Bloomer

Boat shape

Coburg

Bap

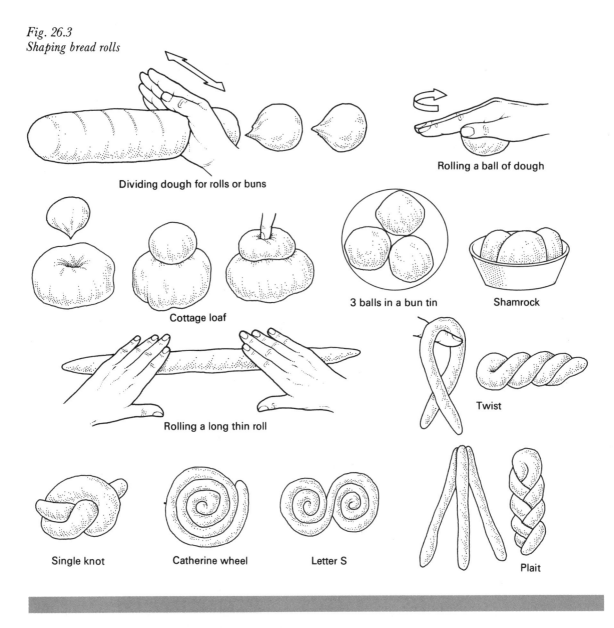

Fig. 26.3
Shaping bread rolls

Dividing dough for rolls or buns

Rolling a ball of dough

Cottage loaf

3 balls in a bun tin

Shamrock

Rolling a long thin roll

Twist

Single knot

Catherine wheel

Letter S

Plait

Pitta bread	*Standard*	*Modified* Fibre[+] Fat[unsat] Salt[−]
4 servings (8 pittas)	500 g strong white flour	use half wholewheat flour and half strong white flour
	250 ml water	
	3 level teaspoons dried yeast	
	2 level teaspoons sugar	
Oven 230 °C Gas No. 8	1 level teaspoon salt	omit salt
Baking time 15 minutes	3 tablespoons vegetable oil	use corn oil or sunflower oil

Fig. 26.4
Shaping pitta bread

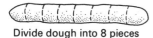

Divide dough into 8 pieces

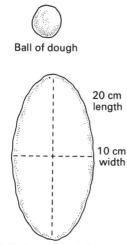

Ball of dough

20 cm length

10 cm width

Rolled out to oval shape

1 Put dried yeast, sugar and $\frac{1}{3}$ of the flour in a large mixing bowl.

2 Put water in a saucepan and bring to blood heat.

3 Add warm water to dry ingredients in the mixing bowl. Mix together, using a wooden spoon. Leave batter to stand for 20 minutes.

4 Add remaining $\frac{2}{3}$ of flour, salt if used, and oil. Mix ingredients together, using fingers. When mixture holds together as a firm dough put on to a lightly oiled work surface.

5 Knead dough for 5 minutes (Fig. 26.1).

6 Put dough into the mixing bowl, cover with a damp cloth or cling film and leave to stand in a warm place for 20 minutes.

7 Divide dough into 8 pieces and shape each piece into a ball (Fig. 26.4).

8 Lightly flour work surface and roll each ball into an oval shape (Fig. 26.4).

9 Lightly flour 2 baking sheets and put pittas on to them. Cover with a sheet of polythene and leave to keep warm for 10 minutes.

10 Lightly sprinkle surface of pittas with flour.

11 Bake for 15 minutes in a pre-heated oven on the top shelf or immediately below it. During cooking pitta bread usually puffs up to twice its original thickness.

12 Serve hot or cold, slit to take chosen filling, for example, sliced tomatoes, green salad or kebabs.

Basic recipe for scones

12 scones

Oven 230 °C Gas No. 8
Baking time 7–10 minutes

Standard		*Modified*	Fibre[+] Fat[−] Fat[unsat] Salt[−]
200 g plain flour 2½ to 3 level teaspoons baking powder	} with fresh milk	use wholewheat flour	
or 200 g plain flour 1 level teaspoon bicarbonate of soda 1 level teaspoon cream of tartar	} with sour milk or butter milk	use wholewheat flour	
or 200 g self-raising flour		use self-raising wholewheat flour	
½ level teaspoon salt		omit salt	
25 to 50 g butter or margarine		use 25 g polyunsaturated margarine	
125 ml milk		use skimmed milk	

1 Heat the oven.

2 Sift flour with other powder ingredients into a large mixing bowl. Tip in bran remaining in sieve.

3 Rub in fat, aerating flour at same time.

4 Make a deep 'well' in the flour, pour in almost all liquid and mix to a soft dough with a palette knife. Add remaining liquid if required.

5 On a floured surface, knead dough very lightly until it is just smooth. Divide dough into 2 and lightly shape each piece to a ball; flatten each to 20 mm thick and cut each round into 6 triangles or roll mixture to 20 mm thick and cut into rounds using a 5-cm plain cutter.

6 Heat the baking tray in the oven.

7 Brush scones with beaten egg for a glossy crust or with flour for a soft one.

8 If possible leave scones to rest for 10–15 minutes before baking.

9 Bake scones on heated baking tray at the top of the hot oven until well-risen and brown.

Variations to the basic recipe are given in Table 26.1.

Table 26.1
Types of savoury scones

Scone	Variations to basic recipe
Cheese	Add $\frac{1}{2}$ level teaspoon dry mustard to flour before sifting; add 50 g Cheddar cheese (or Edam) grated finely to fat and flour mixture
Bacon	Add 50 g diced cooked lean bacon to fat and flour mixture
Peanut butter	Add 2 level tablespoons crunchy peanut butter to fat and flour mixture
Sage and onion	Add 1 level teaspoon dried sage, 1 diced small onion, to fat and flour mixture
Apple	Add 1 grated eating apple to fat and flour mixture

27 Pastry and batter

Pastry

Short pastry: traditional method

Yield 200 g pastry

Standard	*Modified* Fibre⁺ Salt⁻
200 g plain flour	use brown or wholewheat flour
100 g fat ⎰ 50 g margarine or butter / 50 g lard or vegetable fat	
Pinch of salt	omit salt
About 8 teaspoons cold water	

Fig. 27.1
Kneading short pastry

Turn edges of pastry to the middle

With fingertips rock the pastry firmly

Turn the pastry round and repeat the rocking

1 Sift flour with salt (if used) into a large mixing bowl, tipping any bran in sieve into the bowl.

2 Drop fat into flour and cut it into small pieces.

3 Using finger tips rub fat into flour until the mixture looks like fine breadcrumbs.

4 Measure in most of the water and mix with a round-ended knife. When pastry begins to hold together finish mixing with 2 fingers and a thumb to get the 'feel' of the pastry to find if it needs the rest of the water and to draw it together into a firm ball.

5 Knead pastry until smooth and evenly mixed (Fig. 27.1) to shape required. Leave to rest while filling is prepared.

6 On a lightly floured board, with a floured rolling-pin press pastry to the shape required and roll with short, light movements of the rolling-pin, away from the worker. Turn pastry, not the rolling-pin, to alter the shape, so that equal pressure is exerted on each end of the rolling-pin. Roll pastry to required thickness.

Short pastry: all-in-one method

Yield 225 g

Standard	*Modified* Fibre+ Fat^unsat Salt-
225 g plain flour	use brown or wholewheat flour
150 g soft margarine	use polyunsaturated margarine
pinch of salt	omit salt
2 tablespoons cold water	

1 Sift flour, and salt if used, on to a plate including any bran in sieve.

2 Put fat, water and ⅓ flour into large mixing bowl. Cream mixture together for 30 seconds using a fork.

3 Add remaining flour and stir to form a soft dough.

4 Turn mixture out on to a floured surface and lightly knead to form a smooth, pliable mass.

5 Chill, then roll out as required.

Short pastry: food processor method

Yield 225 g

Standard	*Modified* Fibre+ Salt-
225 g plain flour	use brown or wholewheat flour
50 g butter or margarine	
50 g lard or vegetable fat	
pinch of salt	omit salt
2 tablespoons cold water	

1 Put flour, and salt if used, into the bowl of the processor.

2 Cut fat into small pieces and add to flour.

3 Put the lid on the processor and mix for a few seconds until mixture looks like fine breadcrumbs.

4 Add water and switch the processor on until a smooth dough is formed.

5 Roll out and use as required.

Samosa pastry

Yield 200 g pastry

Standard	*Modified* Fibre+ Fat^unsat Salt-
200 g plain white flour	use half wholewheat and half white flour
½ level teaspoon salt	omit salt

50 g ghee or margarine   use polyunsaturated margarine

75 ml water

---

1 Sift flour, and salt if used, into a large mixing bowl, tipping any bran in sieve into bowl.

2 Rub ghee or block margarine into flour; if soft margarine is used, mix using pastry blender. The mixture should look like fine breadcrumbs.

3 Boil the water and add to flour mixture. Mix together using a wooden spoon; when cool, knead mixture to form a smooth dough.

4 Leave mixture covered in the bowl with cling film or put inside a polythene bag until required.

Suet pastry

Yield 200 g pastry

Standard	*Modified* Fibre+ Salt-
200 g plain or self-raising flour*	use brown or wholewheat flour
$2\frac{1}{2}$ level teaspoons baking powder if plain flour is used	
100 g shredded suet or vegetable suet	
$\frac{1}{2}$ level teaspoon salt	omit salt
125 ml water	

---

* For a very light, pliable result, 50 g flour may be replaced by 50 g fresh, fine breadcrumbs, either white or brown.

1 Sift flour, baking powder, and salt if used, into a large mixing bowl, tipping any bran in sieve into the bowl.

2 Mix the suet into the flour.

3 Pour in most of the water and mix pastry to a soft, elastic but not sticky dough, adding the rest of the water if needed.

4 Turn ball of dough on to a floured board or work surface; it should leave the basin clean.

5 Using floured finger tips knead pastry lightly until evenly mixed and quite smooth; knead it to the required shape.

6 Press and roll it to the required size and shape.

Flaky and rough-puff pastry

Yield 200 g pastry

Standard	*Modified* Fibre⁺ Salt⁻
200 g strong flour	use 100 g strong flour and 100 g wholewheat flour
150 g fat $\left\{\begin{array}{l}\text{25 to 50 g lard or vegetable fat}\\\text{125 to 100 g margarine or butter}\end{array}\right.$	
¼ teaspoon salt	omit salt
2 teaspoons lemon juice	
Approximately 125 ml cold water	

Fig. 27.2
Method for flaky pastry

rub in ¹/₄ fat

Divide ³/₄ fat into 3

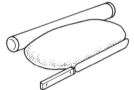

Press dough to a rectangle and roll it to a strip

Put fat on ²/₃ dough in small pats

Fold and roll twice more, adding fat at folds

Method for flaky pastry (Fig. 27.2)

1 Sift flour, and salt if used, into a large mixing bowl, tipping any bran remaining in sieve into the bowl.

2 Rub in ¼ of total fat, using all or most of the lard or vegetable fat.

3 Add lemon juice and most of the cold water and make a soft, pliable, but not sticky dough, using a palette knife for mixing. Add remaining water if necessary.

4 Turn dough on to a lightly floured board and knead very lightly, to mix it thoroughly. Wrap it in foil.

5 Leave dough to relax in a cool place for 20 minutes, if time allows.

6 Cut firm, cold fat into 3 and cut ⅓ of it into small, flat pieces.

7 Press and roll cooled dough to a long, narrow strip, under 5 mm thick. Use as little flour as possible on board and rolling-pin; straighten the edges of dough with the knife and the rolling-pin, pull the corners square and do all this very gently, with as little fingering as possible.

8 Mark the strip of dough into thirds, arrange little pats (⅓ of the remaining fat) over ⅔ of the strip. Fold the strip in three, with the plain section inside.

9 Turn folded pastry a quarter turn, so that the fold is to the left. Seal the open edges with the rolling-pin and straighten the edges so that they fit. Press and roll once more gently. Use just enough flour to keep pastry from sticking. If it should stick underneath, lift it on the rolling-pin. Scrape the board clear, and lightly re-flour it. If it sticks to the rolling-pin, scrape this clear, re-flour it and also lightly flour the sticky patch on the pastry.

10 Repeat addition of fat, folding and rolling twice more, then fold pastry once more and leave to relax before rolling it to shape (4 rollings in all).

Method for rough-puff pastry

1 Sift flour, and salt if used, into a large mixing bowl, tipping any bran remaining in sieve into the bowl.

2 Cut the cold, firm fat into 2-cm cubes and drop into sifted flour.

3 Add lemon juice and most of the water, and with a palette knife press mixture gently together, taking care not to break the pieces of fat.

4 When the whole is just bound together in a rough mass, with the addition of the remaining water if necessary, turn it on to a lightly floured board and press into a brick shape with palette knife and rolling-pin.

5 Press pastry gently into a long strip, using palette knife and rolling-pin to straighten edges.

6 Fold the strip in 3 and roll it exactly as for flaky pastry except that there is no more fat to add; repeat the folding and rolling 3 times more (4 rollings in all).

Batter

Yorkshire pudding or pancake batter

Standard	Modified Fibre⁺ Fat⁻ Salt⁻
100 g flour	use brown flour
1 to 2 eggs	
250 ml milk	use skimmed milk
¼ teaspoon salt	omit salt

Method of mixing

1 Sift flour, and salt if used, into a deep mixing bowl, tipping any bran in sieve into mixing bowl.

2 Using the back of a wooden spoon make a deep hole or 'well' in the flour by pushing it up the sides of the basin.

3 Drop egg into the well. Add half the milk and begin mixing.

4 Beat egg and milk so that the mixture washes around the sides of the 'well' and gradually draws flour into the liquid. Beat rapidly until all is mixed; it should be a smooth, thick cream.

5 Lightly beat in the rest of the milk.

Yorkshire pudding for roast beef

6 servings

Oven 200°C to 220°C Gas No. 6–7
Baking time 45 minutes for large; 20 minutes for small

Standard	*Modified*	Fibre⁺ Fat⁻ Fatᵘⁿˢᵃᵗ Salt⁻
250 ml batter	use modified batter	
25 g dripping	use corn oil	

1 Put fat into a wide, ovenware dish about 225 × 175 mm, or 6 to 8 large, deep bun tins.

2 Heat fat in the oven.

3 Pour batter into hot fat.

4 Bake it in the upper part of the oven until well risen, brown and crisp.

5 Serve at once.

Pancakes

4 servings

Standard	*Modified*	Fibre⁺ Fat⁻ Fatᵘⁿˢᵃᵗ Salt⁻
250 ml batter	use modified batter	
lard for frying	use corn oil	

1 To fry the pancakes, put a small piece of lard or a few drops of oil into the frying-pan. Heat it. Stir batter, and pour enough into the pan to cover it thinly. Cook pancake over moderate heat until it can be shaken free in the pan and is golden underneath.

2 To toss pancakes, hold the handle of the frying-pan comfortably with the thumb on top, toss pancake forward and up and catch it in the pan, cooked side up.

3 Cook the second side till it puffs up off the pan.

4 Turn pancake out upside down on to absorbent paper.

Rice

Boiled rice

4 servings

Cooking time: standard 15 minutes; modified 40 minutes

Standard	*Modified* Fibre⁺ Salt⁻
200 g Patna rice	use brown rice
600 ml water	
1 level teaspoon salt	omit salt

1 Bring the water to the boil in a large pan.
2 Add salt if desired.
3 Add rice and stir until the liquid boils to prevent clumping of grains.
4 Reduce heat and simmer, with the lid on, until rice is just cooked or *al dente* (firm with a bite).
5 Remove from the heat and fluff up rice using a fork or skewer.

Risotto: basic recipe

4 servings

Cooking time: standard 20 minutes; modified 45 minutes

Standard	*Modified* Fibre⁺ Fat⁻ Fat^unsat Salt⁻
200 g Patna rice	use brown rice
1 large onion	
25 g butter or margarine	use 15 g polyunsaturated margarine
salt and pepper	omit salt
600 ml water	
1 chicken stock cube	
1 bay leaf	
1 level teaspoon dried oregano	

1 Peel and slice onion (Fig. 30.2).
2 Melt fat in a large pan and gently fry onions to soften them.
3 Add rice; mix well to ensure grains are lightly coated with fat.
4 Prepare stock by crumbling cube into the boiling water.
5 Add stock; stir, using a wooden spoon.

6 Bring to the boil and add bay leaf, oregano, pepper, and salt if used.

7 Simmer gently with the lid on the pan until rice is cooked. Stir occasionally to stop mixture sticking to the base of the pan.

8 Cook for 15 minutes for white rice and 40 minutes for brown.

9 Add additional ingredients and cook for further 5 minutes. Remove bay leaf before serving.

Variations to the basic recipe are given in Table 28.1.

Table 28.1
Variations to basic recipe for risotto

Risotto	*Variations to basic recipe*
Chicken	Add 200 g diced cooked chicken
Ham	Add 200 g diced cooked ham
Tuna fish	Add 200 g flaked tuna fish
Cheese	Add 200 g grated Cheddar or Edam cheese; omit chicken stock cube and use vegetable stock cube in its place
Tofu	Add 200 g tofu cut into 1 cm cubes; omit chicken stock cube and use vegetable stock cube in its place
Vegetable	Add 50 g diced green pepper, 50 g diced red pepper, 50 g sweetcorn kernels and 50 g sliced mushrooms all previously stir-fried, and use a vegetable stock cube in place of chicken stock cube

Pilau rice

	Standard	*Modified* Fibre[+] Fat[-] Fat[unsat] Salt[-]
4 servings	200 g Patna rice	use brown rice
	25 g butter or margarine	use 15 g polyunsaturated margarine
	1 medium onion	
	1 bay leaf	
	2.5 cm stick of cinnamon	
	½ level teaspoon crushed cumin seeds	
	1 cardamom pod (crushed)	
Cooking time: standard 20 minutes; modified 45 minutes	salt	omit salt
	600 ml water	

1 Peel and slice onion (Fig. 30.2)

2 Melt fat in a large pan and gently fry onion to soften it.

3 Add rice, stir thoroughly and add flavourings.

4 Add water and bring to boiling point.

5 Simmer gently with the lid on for 15 minutes for white rice and 40 minutes for brown rice.

6 Remove cinnamon and bay leaf.

7 Lightly fluff up with a fork or skewer and serve at once.

Pasta

Boiled pasta

4 servings

Cooking time: read labels to check, varies according to type and size

Standard	*Modified* Fibre+ Salt–
200 g pasta	use brown pasta
1 litre water	
1 level teaspoon salt	omit salt
1 teaspoon vegetable oil	

1 Bring the water to boiling point in a large pan.

2 Add salt, if desired, and oil. The oil will stop the water from boiling over and reduce the risk of the pasta sticking together.

3 Add pasta. If long spaghetti is used, coil pasta into the boiling water.

4 While the water returns to boiling point, stir pasta, using a long fork, to prevent sticking.

5 Keep the water at a rolling boil and cook pasta for the appropriate time with the lid off the pan. The pasta should be just cooked or *al dente* (firm with a bite).

6 Drain pasta in a colander.

Other cereals

Muesli

1 serving

Standard	*Modified* Fat⁻ Sugar⁻
2 level tablespoons rolled oats	
1 tablespoon chopped nuts	
50 g chopped, stoned dates or sultanas	
50 g grated apple	
1 teaspoon honey	omit honey
2 tablespoons yogurt	use low-fat yogurt

Mix ingredients together and serve cold.

Porridge

2–3 servings

Cooking time 10 minutes

Standard	*Modified* Fat⁻ Salt⁻
1 cup rolled oats	
2½ cups milk, water or milk and water	use skimmed milk
1 level teaspoon salt	omit salt

1 Boil liquid, sprinkle in rolled oats and stir until mixture begins to thicken, then simmer for 10 minutes.

2 Serve porridge very hot.

29 Potato dishes

Preparation of potatoes

1 Scrub if muddy.

2 When possible cook potatoes and sweet potatoes in their skins. Peel the skin off yams.

3 Rinse and cook at once.

Boiled potatoes

1 Choose even-sized potatoes or sweet potatoes and prepare as described. Cut peeled yams into 25 mm pieces. Put on kettle of water.

2 Put the vegetable into a pan which it half fills.

3 Pour on boiling water not quite to cover the vegetable.

4 Simmer with the lid on for 15–20 minutes or until tender.

5 Drain water away.

6 Return pan to low heat and gently shake it to drive off steam.

Cooking time 15–20 minutes   7 Serve sprinkled with freshly chopped parsley.

Mashed potatoes

2–3 servings

Cooking time: as for boiling + 5 minutes

Standard	*Modified* Fat⁻ Salt⁻
500 g potatoes or sweet potatoes or yams	
1 tablespoon margarine	omit margarine
2–3 tablespoons milk	use 3 tablespoons skimmed milk
pepper, salt	omit salt
a little grated nutmeg	

1 Boil and dry the chosen vegetable.

2 Mash in saucepan, breaking up all lumps.

3 Draw the vegetable to one side of the pan, heat fat if used, add milk in empty space.

4 Add seasoning, then mash with hot liquid, adding more milk if needed until fluffy.

5 Pile in a hot dish; neaten with a knife or fork.

Duchesse potatoes

1–2 servings

Oven 200 °C Gas No. 6

Cooking time: 30–40 minutes

Standard	*Modified* Fat⁻ Fatᵘⁿˢᵃᵗ Salt⁻
250 g potatoes	
1 tablespoon margarine	use 1 teaspoon polyunsaturated margarine
1 egg yolk or ½ beaten egg	
1 tablespoon cream	use 1 tablespoon low-fat yogurt
pepper, salt	omit salt
grated nutmeg to taste	

Fig. 29.1
Piping duchesse potatoes

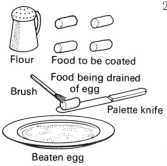

1 Boil, thoroughly dry and mash the potatoes.

2 In the pan melt margarine. Beat potatoes into it and season.

3 Add egg and beat in smoothly. Add a little cream or yogurt if mixture is dry.

4 Put potato mixture into a piping-bag with a large star pipe and pipe on to a greased oven tray (Fig. 29.1).

5 Bake for 15 minutes.

Stars   Coil

Potato croquettes

1–2 servings

Cooking time: 25–30 minutes

Standard	*Modified* Fibre⁺ Fat⁻ Fatᵘⁿˢᵃᵗ Salt⁻
Duchesse potato mixture (*above recipe*)	use modified recipe
To coat: egg and crumbs	use wholewheat breadcrumbs
To fry: shallow or deep fat	use corn oil or sunflower oil

Fig. 29.2
Coating with egg and crumbs

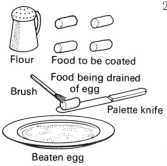

Flour   Food to be coated

Food being drained
of egg
Brush
Palette knife

Beaten egg

1 Make duchesse mixture, keeping it firm.

2 Divide into walnut-size pieces, dredge with flour, roll into balls or sausage shapes, and coat with egg and crumbs (Fig. 29.2). Fry in deep fat at 195°C or in shallow fat that will brown bread in 15 seconds or grill under a moderate grill for 5 minutes, turning to ensure even cooking.

Pile of crumbs on paper

Coated pieces

Tray for draining food

Baked potatoes

Oven 200 °C–220 °C Gas No. 6–7
Cooking time 10 minutes to boil; 40–45 minutes to bake

1 Choose equal size potatoes or sweet potatoes about size of a large egg and cut yams to size.

2 Boil gently for 10 minutes; drain and dry.

3 Have ready a baking tin with hot fat in. (To lower fat intake use a non-stick baking tin and 1 tablespoon corn oil.) Alternatively cook around joint.

4 Roll the vegetable in fat and baste.

5 Bake in moderately hot oven; turn and baste after 20 minutes.

Chips

Standard

1 Choose waxy potatoes of medium size. Peel them.

2 Slice them 5–10 mm thick, cut slices in 5- to 10-mm thick strips (Fig. 29.3).

3 Fold strips in a clean cloth or thick absorbent paper, to dry them.

4 Heat deep fat to 175°C or until it browns bread in 40 seconds.

5 Put a few chips at a time into fat, using a basket with deep fat; when the pan is half full add no more. Keep chips moving gently with a draining spoon until soft but not brown; lift them out and fry next half-panful in same way.

6 Heat fat to 190°C (or to brown bread in 15 seconds) and re-fry them for 2 or 3 minutes until crisp and golden. Drain on absorbent paper.

7 Serve at once, with salt if desired.

Fig. 29.3
Cutting chips

Slice lengthways

Modified   Fat⁻   Fat^unsat   Salt⁻

As above but with following variations:

1 Cut to thicker size to lower surface area for fat absorption.

2 In place of stages 4 and 5, soften potatoes by boiling for 5 minutes, allowing just enough water to cover them. Dry well on absorbent paper.

3 Use corn oil or sunflower oil for frying.

4 Omit sprinkling with salt.

Turn and slice at right angles

Jacket potatoes

Oven 200°C Gas No.6

Cooking time 50 minutes–1¼ hours

1 Choose large potatoes of equal size.

2 Score potatoes all around with the point of a knife, or pierce with a fork to let out steam.

3 Put on open oven shelves and then light the oven. Bake until soft. To save time cook in a microwave oven.

4 To serve, pile them in a wooden bowl or in a table napkin on a serving dish. Serve butter, margarine or low-fat spread with them or a sauce such as soured cream with chives or yogurt with chives.

Jacket potatoes with fillings

2 servings

Standard	Modified
2 large even potatoes	
fillings (see below)	use modified fillings

1 Score potatoes. Bake as above, cut in half by scoring line.

2 Scoop out cooked potato, leaving skin unbroken.

3 Mash potato in a bowl and beat in other ingredients. Taste and season.

Fillings for jacket potatoes

Chicken with yogurt

2 servings

Standard	Modified Fat⁻ Salt⁻
100 g cooked chicken	use flesh only
2 tablespoons plain yogurt	use low-fat yogurt
25 g sultanas	
salt and pepper	omit salt
1 tablespoon freshly chopped parsley	

1 Dice cooked chicken.

2 Add chicken, yogurt, sultanas, pepper, and salt if used, to potato flesh and mix well.

3 Pile mixture into potato skins.

4 Return to the oven for a further 10 minutes.

5 Garnish with parsley.

Tuna and spring onion

Standard	*Modified* Fat⁻ Salt⁻
100 g tuna fish	
4 spring onions	
2 tablespoons mayonnaise	use low-fat yogurt
salt and pepper	omit salt

1 Drain brine or oil from tuna fish.
2 Trim, wash and chop spring onions.
3 Add fish, onions, mayonnaise or yogurt, pepper, and salt if used, to potato flesh. Beat ingredients together.
4 Pile filling into potato skins.
5 Return to the oven for a further 10 minutes.

Cheese and pickle

Standard	*Modified* Fat⁻ Salt⁻
100 g Cheddar cheese	use Edam cheese
2 tablespoons piccalilli	
salt and pepper	omit salt

1 Grate cheese finely.
2 Add 75 g grated cheese, piccalilli, pepper, and salt if used, to potato flesh. Mix well.
3 Pile filling into potato skins and sprinkle remaining cheese on the surface.
4 Return to the oven for a further 10 minutes.

30 Vegetable dishes

Preparation of vegetables

A summary of vegetable preparation is given in Table 30.1. The addition of salt to the liquid in which vegetables are cooked is not recommended as this practice contradicts the dietary goal to reduce salt intake. If salt is added it is customary to add 5 ml per 500 ml of water. The glazing of cooked vegetables with butter or margarine is not recommended in the light of the dietary goal to reduce fat intake.

Table 30.1
Preparation of vegetables

Vegetable		Preparation technique	Time (mins) for boiling
Artichokes			
Globe		Cut off upper leaves and stem; rinse	15 to 20
Jerusalem		Scrape under water; add 10 ml lemon juice per 50 g	15 to 20
Aubergines		Trim off top, wash under running water, slice, sprinkle with salt and leave for ½ hour to extract bitter juices; rinse and dry	Usually fried in oil for use in recipes
Beans			
Broad	young	Remove stalk and tip and strip off string at the side; rinse	15 to 20
	old	Shell if mature	15 to 20
French		Remove stalk and tip and any string that can be stripped off; rinse	8 to 12
Runner	young	As for French beans	8 to 12
	old	Remove stalk and tip and strip off string at each side; snap into short lengths or cut diagonally; rinse	5 to 12
Beetroot (quick method)		Peel and slice thinly; after cooking drain off ½ the liquid and add vinegar to remaining half; cool beetroot in this liquid	20 to 30
Brussels sprouts		Remove damaged leaves; cut large sprouts in half; slit stalks of all sprouts; rinse	8 to 10
Cabbage		Remove damaged leaves; cut in half, remove stalk (Fig. 30.1), cut into quarters open out leaves, wash under running water; shred leaves	5 to 10

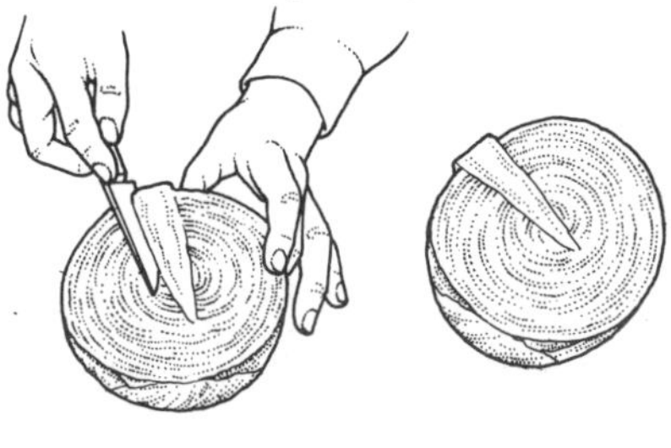

Fig. 30.1
Cutting the stalk out of cabbage

Vegetable	Preparation technique	Time (mins) for boiling
Spring cabbage or spring greens	Remove damaged leaves and tough fibrous stalks; open out leaves, wash under running water and shred; cook shredded stalks 4 minutes before leaves	7 to 10
Carrots young	Scrape if necessary, leave whole; rinse	10 to 15
old	Peel, slice in lengths or rounds; rinse	10 to 15
Cauliflower	Remove damaged parts and tough fibrous stalks; wash under running water; break into sprigs and slice stalk, or hollow stalk and leave head whole	8 to 10 (sprigs) 15 to 20 (whole)
Celery	Remove green leaves, broken or tough sticks; scrub under running water, scrape off brown patches; cut sticks into equal lengths and tie in bundles	15 to 20
Chinese leaves	Remove damaged leaves, separate leaves; wash under running water and shred	3 to 5
Courgettes	Rinse; trim ends; cut into slices 10 mm thick	7 to 10
Curly kale	Discard tough stalks and damaged leaves, wash under running water; shred usable stalks and large leaves, keep small inner leaves whole; cook shredded stalks 4 minutes before leaves	7 to 10
Kohlrabi	Trim off leaves and stalks. Peel thickly to remove hard fibrous skin; leave whole or slice; rinse	30 to 45
Leeks	Cut off roots, remove one outer layer and dark green tops; split leeks to 10 mm from root, turn leaves back and wash under running water; tie in bundles	10 to 15
Marrow	Peel, cut in half lengthways, scoop out seeds; cut into 25 mm squares	12 to 15
Okra	Remove top and tail; cut into slices or quarters; rinse	15 to 20
Onions	Peel off papery skin; leave whole; onions may be sliced or diced (Fig. 30.2) for use in recipes	20 to 30

Fig. 30.2
Cutting onion into dice

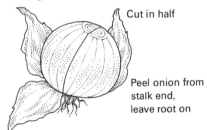

Cut in half

Peel onion from stalk end, leave root on

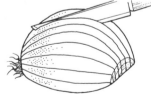

Cut onion in half and slice it, leaving root whole

Cut slices across

Parsnips	Scrape or peel; rinse; cut into thick chunks	15 to 20
Peas	Shell; add sprig of mint for flavour	8 to 12
Mangetouts	Remove top and tail and stringy spine; rinse	5 to 10

Vegetable	Preparation technique	Time (mins) for boiling
Plantain	Peel the banana-type skin off with a sharp knife; leave whole or cut into chunks	10 to 15
Pumpkin	Cut in half, remove seeds and fibres; cut into chunks and peel	12 to 15
Spinach	Wash leaves in at least 3 changes of water; strip off fibrous stalks and any tough mid-ribs; pack leaves firmly into pan; heat gently, drain and roughly chop	5 to 10
Sprouting broccoli	Remove damaged parts; wash under running water; keep all flower sprays whole	10 to 15
Swede	Peel thickly to remove hard fibrous skin; rinse; cut into cubes	15 to 20
Tomatoes	Remove skin if desired (Fig. 30.3) for use in recipes; to *grill* leave whole and pierce with skewer or cut in half at right angle to stalk	To grill 3 to 5

Fig. 30.3
Skinning tomatoes

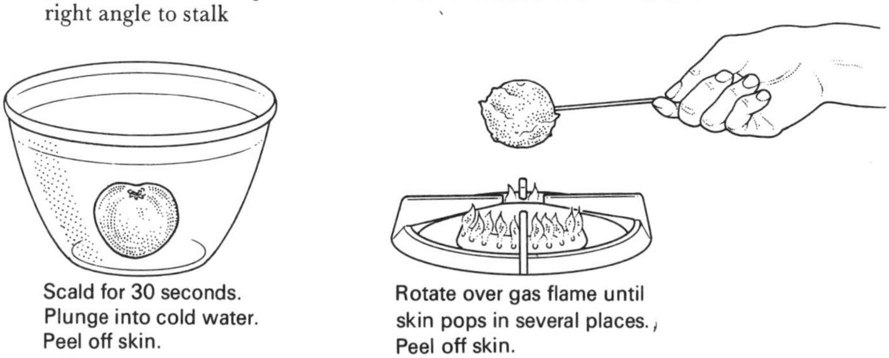

Scald for 30 seconds.
Plunge into cold water.
Peel off skin.

Rotate over gas flame until
skin pops in several places.
Peel off skin.

| Turnip | As for swede | 15 to 20 |

Boiling green vegetables

1 Use a pan just large enough to hold the vegetable and quarter fill it with boiling water.

2 Add the vegetable, boil steadily until stalks are tender when pierced with a skewer (Table 30.1).

3 Drain in a colander and keep the water for use in gravy, sauce or soup.

4 Serve the vegetable at once.

Boiling root, bulb and stem vegetables

1 Put the vegetable into the saucepan and pour on boiling water, not quite to cover.

2 Simmer gently until tender when pierced with a skewer (Table 30.1).

3 Drain in a colander and keep the water for use in gravy, sauce or soup.

4 The cooked vegetable may be coated with sauce.

5 Sprinkle with freshly chopped parsley.

Sweet-sour red cabbage

4 servings

	Standard	Modified	Fat⁻	Fat^unsat	Salt⁻	Sugar⁻
	500 g red cabbage					
	1 small onion					
	2 small or 1 large cooking apple					
	25 g margarine	use 15 g polyunsaturated margarine				
	1 tablespoon brown sugar	use 1 teaspoon brown sugar				
	1 to 2 tablespoons vinegar					
	2 teaspoons lemon juice					
Cooking time 1 hour	salt and pepper	omit salt				

1 Peel and chop onion finely (Fig. 30.2) and fry gently until soft, in the margarine.

2 Shred cabbage and shake it in the fat with the onion for a few minutes.

3 Peel and chop apple and add with sugar to pan over low heat for 10 minutes until juice is running from apple and cabbage.

4 Add lemon juice, vinegar and seasoning, and simmer gently until tender.

Ratatouille

4 servings

	Standard	Modified	Fat⁻	Fat^unsat	Salt⁻
	4 large tomatoes				
	2 large aubergines				
	1 large onion				
	1 large green pepper				
	4 medium-sized courgettes				
	2 cloves of garlic				
	4 tablespoons vegetable oil	use 2 tablespoons sunflower or corn oil			
	1 level teaspoon dried basil				
Cooking time 1 hour	salt and pepper	omit salt			

1 Either skin tomatoes (Fig. 30.3) or just wash and slice.

2 Prepare aubergines as described in Table 30.1.

3 Peel and slice onion (Fig. 30.2).

4 Wash, de-seed and slice green pepper (Fig. 31.2).

5 Wash and slice courgettes 2.5 cm thick.

6 Skin and crush garlic.

7 Take a flameproof casserole and pour in oil. Warm over a hot plate.

8 Add vegetables and add pepper, basil, and salt if used.

9 Stir the mixture thoroughly using a wooden spoon, and after 10 minutes put the lid on the pan and simmer for 50 minutes.

10 Ratatouille may be served hot or cold.

Vegetables *au gratin* (with cheese)

4 servings

Cooking time 30–35 minutes

Suitable vegetables: celery, cauliflower, leeks, onions, vegetable marrow or potatoes, or a mixture of root vegetables including potatoes.

Standard	*Modified*	Fibre⁺ Fat⁻ Fatunsat Salt⁻

Standard	*Modified*
500 g vegetables	
300 ml cheese sauce (p. 264)	use modified cheese sauce (p. 263)
2 tablespoons extra grated cheese	use Edam cheese
2 teaspoons breadcrumbs	use wholewheat breadcrumbs

1 Boil vegetable until tender (Table 30.1), drain and keep hot in shallow oven-proof dish. Make the surface of the vegetable smooth.

2 Make sauce with 150 ml vegetable water and 150 ml milk. Season, add cheese and taste.

3 Coat hot vegetable with cheese sauce.

4 Mix extra grated cheese with crumbs and sprinkle this over the sauce.

5 Brown under a moderate grill.

Stuffed sweet peppers

3 servings

Oven 170 °C–180 °C Gas No. 3–4

Cooking time 40–45 minutes

Standard	*Modified*	Fibre⁺ Fat⁻ Fatunsat Salt⁻

Standard	*Modified*
3 large green peppers	
Filling for 3 peppers:	
raisin and nut stuffing using rice instead of breadcrumbs (p. 272)	use modified raisin and nut stuffing recipe and brown rice in place of breadcrumbs
a little olive oil	use corn oil or sunflower oil

1 Scald peppers, leaving them for 3–5 minutes in near-boiling water. With a sharp-pointed knife cut all around base of stalk (Fig. 31.2).

2 Draw out stalk and core, and wash all seeds out. Stuff peppers and brush with oil.

3 Pack into an ovenproof dish or casserole that just fits them. Cover with foil or a lid.

4 Bake until soft.

31 Salads

Table 31.1
Preparation of salad plants

Plant	Preparation technique
Avocado pear	Wipe, cut lengthways around stone, twist halves to separate, remove stone; peel thinly and slice or cube flesh (Fig. 31.1); brush with lemon juice to prevent discolouration

Fig. 31.1
Slicing and cubing avocado pear

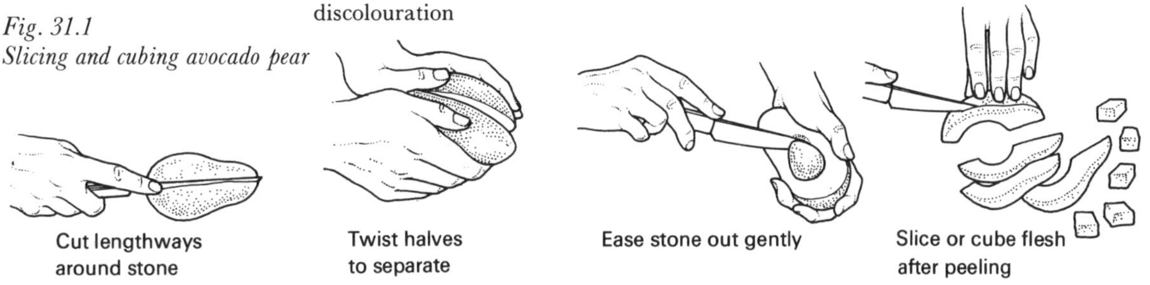

Cut lengthways around stone

Twist halves to separate

Ease stone out gently

Slice or cube flesh after peeling

Plant	Preparation technique
Chicory	Strip off damaged leaves, separate inner leaves, wash and shake dry
Cucumber	Wash, peel if desired, slice thinly
Endive	Remove coarse outer leaves, separate, wash under running water, drain and shake dry
Fennel	Wash, trim top and base, cut into slices
Lettuce	As for endive
Mustard and cress	Hold tiny leaves in small bundles and cut stalks. Wash in bundles, avoid tangling
Peppers	Cut in half lengthways; remove core, seeds and pith; slice or dice (Fig. 31.2)

Fig. 31.2
Preparation of sweet peppers

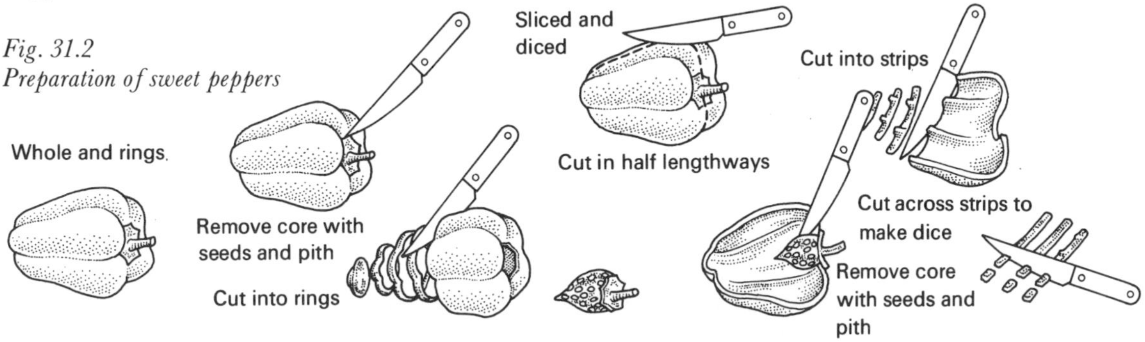

Sliced and diced

Cut into strips

Whole and rings.

Cut in half lengthways

Remove core with seeds and pith

Cut into rings

Cut across strips to make dice

Remove core with seeds and pith

Plant	Preparation technique
Radishes	Trim off leaf-stalks and roots; rub skins clean with kitchen paper
Spring onions	Cut off roots and tough dark tops, remove outer layer, wash; use whole or slice
Tomatoes	Wash, skin (Fig. 30.3) if desired; cut into slices or sections; cherry tomatoes may be left whole
Watercress	Remove damaged leaves, coarse stalks and rootlets; wash

Potato salad

4 servings

Standard	*Modified* Fat⁻ Salt⁻ Sugar⁻
350 g new potatoes	
1 to 2 spring onions *or* 2 teaspoons chopped chives	
150 ml mayonnaise (p. 271)	use modified yogurt dressing (p. 271)
1 tablespoon wine vinegar	
2 tablespoons chopped parsley	
1 teaspoon chopped mint	

1 Boil potatoes (p. 287).

2 While warm cut in 10 mm dice and baste with vinegar.

3 Chop onions or chives, parsley and mint and lightly mix these with cooled potatoes (leaving aside some parsley to garnish).

4 Make dressing. Add this to the potato mixture and mix well.

5 Pile mixture into a serving dish and sprinkle with remaining parsley.

Rice salad

4 servings

Standard	*Modified* Fibre⁺ Fat^unsat Salt⁻ Sugar⁻
200 g long grain rice	use brown rice
100 g tomatoes	
1 small red pepper	
1 small green pepper	
50 g raisins	
50 g walnut pieces	
50 ml French dressing (p. 270)	use modified French dressing

1 Cook rice (p. 283) and allow to cool.

2 Wash and chop tomatoes.

3 Wash, de-seed and dice peppers (Fig. 31.2).

4 Put rice, tomatoes, peppers, raisins, walnut pieces and dressing into a large mixing bowl. Gently fold ingredients together.

5 Pile into a serving dish and serve at once.

Minty green salad

4 servings

Standard	*Modified* Fat^unsat Salt⁻ Sugar⁻
½ an iceberg lettuce	
1 bunch of watercress	
1 green pepper	

1 tablespoon freshly chopped mint

50 ml French dressing (p. 270)   use modified French dressing

1 Wash lettuce and tear leaves into small pieces.

2 Wash and trim watercress.

3 Wash, de-seed and cut pepper into rings (Fig. 31.2).

4 Put lettuce, watercress, pepper and dressing into a large mixing bowl and gently fold ingredients together.

5 Pile up salad in a serving dish and sprinkle with chopped mint.

Tomato salad

4 servings

Standard	*Modified* Fat^{unsat} Salt$^-$ Sugar$^-$
200 g tomatoes	
1 medium onion	
50 ml French dressing (p. 270)	use modified dressing
2 tablespoons freshly chopped basil or parsley	

1 Wash tomatoes. Skin (Fig. 30.3) if desired, and slice thinly.

2 Peel and finely dice onion (Fig. 30.2).

3 Arrange tomatoes in a serving dish; sprinkle with diced onion.

4 Pour on dressing and serve sprinkled with chopped basil or parsley.

Carrot and orange salad

4 servings

Standard	*Modified* Fat$^-$
200 g carrots	
2 oranges	
50 g sultanas	
1 tablespoon fresh, chopped parsley	
100 ml plain yogurt	use low-fat yogurt

1 Scrub, peel or scrape if necessary and grate carrots.

2 Remove zest from oranges; remove pith and segment flesh (Fig. 37.1).

3 Put carrot, oranges, zest, sultanas and yogurt into a mixing bowl and fold together gently.

4 Heap salad into a serving dish and sprinkle with parsley.

Coleslaw

4 servings

Standard	*Modified* Fat⁻ Salt⁻ Sugar⁻

Standard	*Modified* Fat⁻ Salt⁻ Sugar⁻
200 g white cabbage	
1 medium carrot	
2 sticks celery	
1 red-skinned eating apple	
50 g sultanas	
100 ml mayonnaise (p. 271)	use modified yogurt dressing (p. 271)

1 Wash and shred cabbage.

2 Peel or scrape if necessary and grate carrot.

3 Wash and chop celery.

4 Wash and core apple and cut into dice.

5 Put cabbage, carrot, celery and apple into a large mixing bowl.

6 Add sultanas and dressing and gently fold mixture together.

7 Pile the mixture into a serving dish.

Sweetcorn and pepper salad

4 servings

Standard	*Modified* Fat^unsat Salt⁻
400 g sweetcorn kernels, cooked or canned	
1 small onion	
1 small red pepper	
1 small green pepper	
50 g sultanas	
2 tablespoons vegetable oil	use corn oil
1 tablespoon wine vinegar	
1 tablespoon tomato ketchup	
dash Worcester sauce	
salt and pepper	omit salt

1 Peel and dice onion (Fig. 30.2).

2 Wash, de-seed and dice peppers (Fig. 31.2).

3 Drain sweetcorn kernels; cool if cooked.

4 Pour oil into a mixing bowl. Add vinegar, ketchup, Worcester sauce, salt if used, and pepper and mix well.

5 Add onion, peppers, sweetcorn and sultanas and fold mixture together.

6 Leave for 1 hour before serving. Keep chilled.

Sambals (side dishes for curries)

Raita

4 servings

Standard	Modified Fat⁻
½ a cucumber	
150 ml plain yogurt	use low-fat yogurt

1 Wash cucumber, peel if desired and cut into dice.
2 Put yogurt and diced cucumber in a basin. Stir thoroughly.
3 Chill for ½ an hour.

Tomato bhurtha

4 servings

Standard	Modified Salt⁻
1 small onion	
4 medium tomatoes	
1 small green chilli	
salt	omit salt

1 Peel and dice onion (Fig. 30.2).
2 Wash tomatoes, skin if desired (Fig. 30.3), and chop into small pieces.
3 Wash, de-seed and finely chop green chilli.
4 Put onion, tomato, chilli, and salt if used, in a basin. Stir with a fork.
5 Leave mixture to chill for ½ an hour.

Prunes with yogurt

4 servings

Standard	Modified Fat⁻
100 g dried prunes soaked overnight	
150 ml plain yogurt	use low-fat yogurt

1 Drain prunes and chop into small pieces.
2 Put yogurt and chopped prunes in a mixing bowl. Stir with a fork.
3 Chill for ½ an hour.

32 Pulses, nut and myco-protein dishes

Tofu burgers

4 servings

	Standard	Modified	Fibre+ Fat⁻ Fatᵘⁿˢᵃᵗ Salt⁻

	Standard	*Modified*	Fibre⁺ Fat⁻ Fatᵘⁿˢᵃᵗ Salt⁻
	200 g firm tofu		
	100 g carrots		
	100 g breadcrumbs	use wholewheat breadcrumbs	
	1 small onion		
	1 level teaspoon dried mixed herbs		
	1 level teaspoon yeast extract		
	1 size 4 egg		
	salt and pepper	omit salt	
	For frying		
	3 tablespoons vegetable oil	use 2 tablespoons sunflower oil	

Cooking time 8–10 minutes

1 Peel or scrape carrots if necessary and grate.

2 Peel and dice onion (Fig. 30.2).

3 Grate tofu.

4 Put carrot, onion, tofu, breadcrumbs, herbs, yeast extract, salt if used, pepper and egg into a large mixing bowl. Mix well.

5 Divide mixture into rounds (Fig. 32.1).

6 Heat oil in pan until it browns bread in 15 seconds (use non-stick pan if lower amount of fat is used). Cook burgers 4–5 minutes on each side.

7 Drain on absorbent paper. Serve hot with salad.

Bean and okra stew

4 servings

	Standard	*Modified*	Fat⁻ Fatᵘⁿˢᵃᵗ Salt⁻
	500 g okra		
	200 g haricot beans cooked or canned		
	1 medium onion		
	1 medium green pepper		
	1 green chilli		

	4 large tomatoes	
	2 cloves of garlic	
	2 heaped tablespoons tomato purée	
	2 tablespoons fresh chopped parsley	
	4 tablespoons vegetable oil	use 1 tablespoon sunflower or corn oil
Oven 180 °C Gas No. 4	300 ml water	
Cooking time 40 minutes	salt and pepper	omit salt

1 Top and tail okra, cut in quarters and rinse.

2 Peel and slice onion (Fig. 30.2).

3 Wash, de-seed and slice green pepper (Fig. 31.2).

4 Wash, de-seed and slice chilli.

5 Wash tomatoes, skin (Fig. 30.3) and de-seed if desired and roughly chop.

6 Skin and crush garlic.

7 In a shallow frying-pan or wok heat oil over a moderate heat.

8 Add okra and sliced onions and fry for 5 minutes. Turn to ensure even cooking.

9 Add green pepper, chilli, tomatoes, garlic, tomato purée, parsley, pepper, and salt if used. Stir mixture thoroughly.

10 Add water and bring mixture to simmering point. Simmer for 20 minutes.

11 Add cooked haricot beans and simmer for a further 10 minutes.

Lentil curry

	Standard	Modified Fat⁻ Fatᵘⁿˢᵃᵗ Salt⁻
4 servings	150 g lentils	
	2 medium onions	
	2 cloves of garlic	
	2 tablespoons vegetable oil	use 1 tablespoon corn oil or sunflower oil
	600 ml water	
	3 bay leaves	
	$\frac{1}{2}$ level teaspoon salt	omit salt
	2 level teaspoons chilli powder	
Cooking time 35 minutes	$\frac{1}{2}$ level teaspoon cumin	

1   Peel and finely slice onions (Fig. 30.2).

2   Peel and crush garlic.

3   Put lentils, half the sliced onion, garlic, water, and salt if used, in a large pan, bring to simmering point and simmer for 30 minutes.

4   Put fat in a shallow frying-pan over a moderate heat. Add remaining onion, bay leaves, chilli powder and cumin and fry for 5 minutes.

5   Add contents of frying pan to cooked lentils and stir thoroughly with a wooden spoon.

6   Remove bay leaves and serve hot. This dish goes well with rice or chapatis and sambals.

Lentil croquettes

4 servings

Cooking time 20–25 minutes

Fig. 32.1
Shaping croquette mixtures

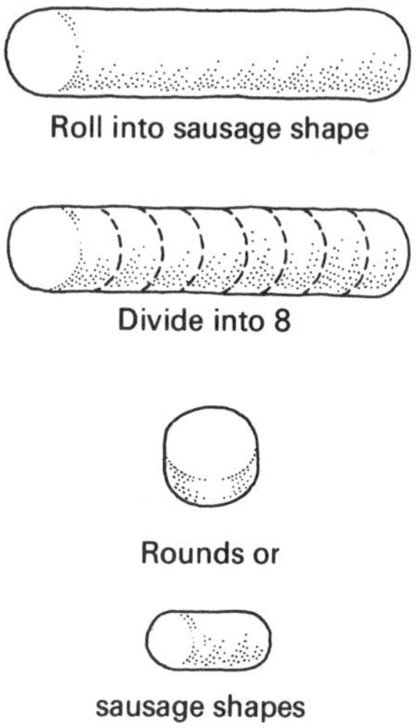

Roll into sausage shape

Divide into 8

Rounds or

sausage shapes

Standard	*Modified* Fibre⁺ Fat⁻ Fatᵘⁿˢᵃᵗ Salt⁻
100 g lentils	
25 g grated cheese	use Edam cheese
50 g breadcrumbs	use wholewheat breadcrumbs
1 tablespoon margarine or vegetable fat	omit fat
½ an egg	
1 teaspoon freshly chopped parsley	use 2 heaped teaspoons chopped parsley
½ teaspoon dried mixed herbs	
salt and pepper	omit salt
To coat: beaten egg and breadcrumbs	use wholewheat breadcrumbs
To fry: vegetable frying oil	use corn oil or sunflower oil
To serve: tomato sauce (p. 269) or cheese sauce (p. 264)	use modified tomato sauce

1   Cook lentils until tender; drain excess liquid and liquidise.

2   Add fat if used, herbs, cheese, seasoning and beadcrumbs. Beat in ½ an egg and, if necessary, a little cooking-water to give a moist paste that is stiff enough to shape into croquettes. Taste and season.

3   Shape into 8 sausage shapes or flat cakes (Fig. 32.1) with a little flour and coat (Fig. 29.2). Fry in shallow fat that will brown bread in 20 seconds. Drain on absorbent paper.

4   Serve hot.

Quorn Jambalaya

4 servings

*Cooking time
standard, 30 minutes
modified, 55 minutes*

Standard	Modified	Fibre[+] Fat[−]	Fat[unsat]	Salt[−]
350 g Quorn pieces				
2 tablespoons lime juice				
$\frac{1}{4}$ teaspoon cayenne pepper				
2 large cloves of garlic				
1 large onion				
2 sticks celery				
1 medium green pepper				
1 medium yellow pepper				
100 g okra				
50 g butter	use 25 g polyunsaturated margarine			
$\frac{1}{4}$ teaspoon ground ginger				
$\frac{1}{4}$ teaspoon chilli powder				
2 large tomatoes				
450 ml vegetable stock				
150 g patna rice	use brown rice			
1 ripe pawpaw				
175 g canned red kidney beans				
salt and pepper	omit salt			

1 Mix Quorn with $\frac{1}{2}$ the lime juice and the cayenne pepper and leave to marinate for $\frac{1}{2}$ an hour.
2 Peel and crush garlic. Peel and dice onion (Fig. 30.2).
3 Clean and remove unwanted parts from celery and peppers (Fig. 31.2) and chop.
4 Wash and trim okra.
5 Heat fat in heavy pan. Add onion and fry gently for 3 minutes. Add garlic, celery, peppers, ground ginger and chilli powder and cook for 2 more minutes.
6 Skin (Fig. 30.3) and roughly chop tomatoes and add to pan with Quorn and stock. Bring to boiling point and add rice and okra. Cover and simmer for 15 minutes for white rice and 40 minutes for brown rice.
7 Peel and slice pawpaw and add to pan with red kidney beans, seasoning and remaining lime juice. Stir gently for 2 minutes and serve.

33 Meat dishes

Bolognese sauce.

4 servings

Standard	Modified Fat⁻ Fatᵘⁿˢᵃᵗ Salt⁻
250 g minced beef	use lean mince or ground beef
2 rashers streaky bacon	use lean bacon
1 tablespoon vegetable oil	use 1 teaspoon sunflower oil or corn oil
1 small onion	
1 small green pepper	
50 g mushrooms	
2 heaped tablespoons tomato purée	
225 g canned tomatoes	
1 clove of garlic	
1 bay leaf	
1 level teaspoon dried oregano	
salt and pepper	omit salt

Cooking time 1 hour

1 Remove rind, rust and gristle from bacon and cut into dice.
2 Peel and dice onion (Fig. 30.2).
3 Wash, de-seed and dice green pepper (Fig. 31.2).
4 Wipe mushrooms and dice finely.
5 Skin and crush garlic.
6 Heat oil in a heavy-based pan over a gentle heat.
7 Add diced onion, crushed garlic and diced bacon and fry for 5 minutes.
8 Add diced mushrooms and green peppers and cook for 5 minutes.
9 Add minced or ground beef and stir, using a wooden spoon. Brown meat evenly, and continue frying until it no longer looks wet.
10 Add tomatoes, tomato purée, bay leaf, oregano, pepper, and salt if used.
11 Put the lid on the pan and leave mixture to simmer for 30 minutes.
12 Remove lid from the pan and continue simmering for 20 minutes.
13 Adjust seasoning if necessary and remove bay leaf.
14 Serve with boiled pasta as spaghetti bolognese, or use as fillings for savoury pancakes or baked potatoes, or top with mashed potato for bolognese pie.

Chilli con carne

4 servings

Cooking time 1 hour 20 minutes

Standard	*Modified* Fat⁻ Salt⁻
250 g minced beef	use lean mince or ground beef
1 large onion	
1 large green pepper	
425 g canned tomatoes	
425 g canned red kidney beans	
2 heaped tablespoons tomato purée	
1 tablespoon dripping	omit dripping
1 large clove of garlic	
1 level tablespoon chilli powder	
salt and pepper	omit salt

1 Put heavy-based pan on hot plate; add fat if used. Add beef, and fry until meat is lightly browned all over and not wet-looking.

2 Crush garlic and add to meat.

3 Peel and dice onion (Fig. 30.2), and add to meat.

4 Wash, core and dice green pepper (Fig. 31.2) and add to meat; continue cooking for 5 minutes.

5 Add chilli powder, pepper, salt if used, tomato purée and tomatoes. Stir mixture using a wooden spoon.

6 Put lid on the pan and leave to simmer for 1 hour.

7 Drain liquid away from kidney beans and add to meat mixture 10 minutes before serving.

8 Serve with boiled rice or jacket potatoes, or hearty chunks of bread and raita.

Meat ball curry (Kofta curry)

4 servings

Standard	*Modified* Fibre⁺ Fat⁻ Fatᵘⁿˢᵃᵗ Salt⁻
curry sauce (p. 267)	use modified curry sauce
Meat balls:	
250 g minced beef	use lean mince or ground beef
50 g fresh white breadcrumbs	use wholewheat breadcrumbs
50 g sultanas	
50 g plain yogurt	use low-fat yogurt
1 level teaspoon garam masala	
For frying:	
3 tablespoons vegetable oil	use 1 tablespoon corn oil or sunflower oil

To finish:

150 g natural yogurt	use low-fat yogurt

2 level tablespoons cottage cheese

2 heaped teaspoons finely chopped coriander leaves or parsley

Cooking time 1 hour 10 minutes

1 Put meat, breadcrumbs, sultanas, plain yogurt and garam masala in a large mixing bowl. Thoroughly mix ingredients together.

2 Shape mixture, using hands, into little balls about the size of walnuts.

3 Heat oil in a shallow frying-pan over a moderate heat.

4 Fry meat balls: allow 5 minutes for each batch. Drain on absorbent paper.

5 Pour curry sauce into a large pan and add meat balls. Put the pan over a moderate heat and simmer for 30 minutes.

6 Mix yogurt and cottage cheese together in a small basin. Add mixture to meat balls and curry sauce. Cook for further $\frac{1}{2}$ hour.

7 When served, sprinkle chopped coriander leaves or parsley over top.

8 Kofta curry goes well with rice or chapatis and sambals.

Hamburgers

4 hamburgers

Cooking time 15 minutes

Standard	*Modified* Fibre⁺ Fat⁻ Salt⁻
250 g minced beef	use lean mince or ground beef
1 small onion	
salt and pepper	omit salt
$\frac{1}{2}$ an egg	
To fry: dripping or vegetable fat or oil	grill, using no added fat
To serve: soft white bap	serve in wholewheat bun

1 Peel and grate onion.

2 Mix minced meat with other ingredients, beating it smooth and pressing it well together.

3 Divide mixture into 4 and, with a lightly floured hand and a palette knife, shape pieces into round cakes 20 mm thick. Press cakes firmly into shape. A hamburger press is recommended for shaping.

4 If frying, heat about 5 mm fat in a frying-pan until it will brown a piece of bread in 15 seconds, or use a non-stick pan, put in hamburgers one at a time and fry for 2 minutes each side, reduce heat and fry gently for a

further 10 minutes or until firm. If grilling, put hamburgers under a pre-heated hot grill. Cook for 2 minutes on each side, reduce heat and cook on each side for a further 5 minutes.

5 Hamburgers may be served in hot, toasted buns and with barbecue sauce.

Meat in pastry

Cornish pasties

3–4 servings

Oven 200 °C or Gas No. 6

Cooking time 50 minutes

Fig. 33.1
Shaping Cornish pasties

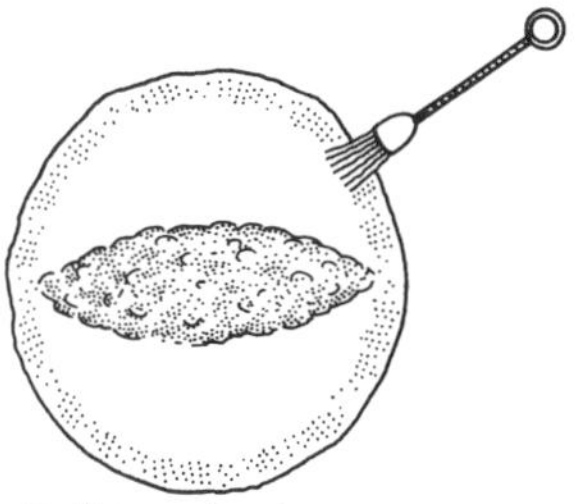

Roll rounds of pastry, put filling across middle, damp edges

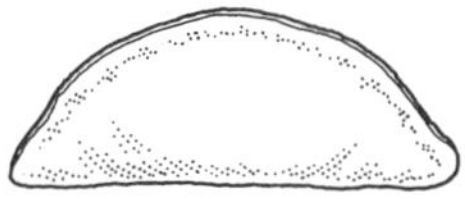

Seal edges and flute them

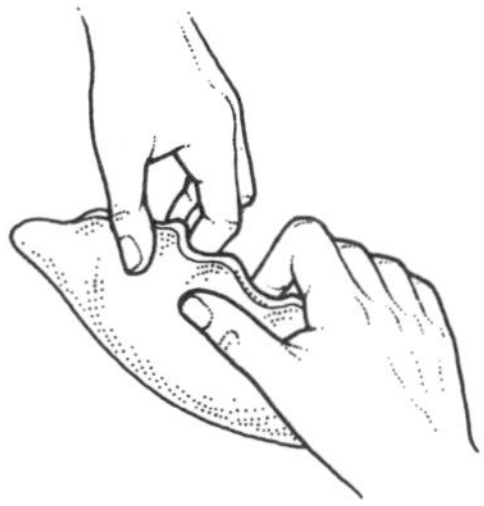

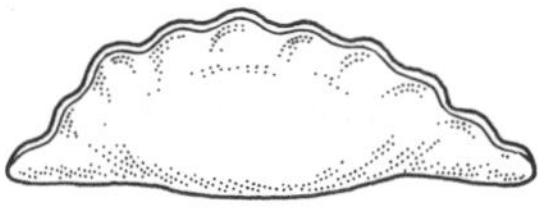

Standard	*Modified* Fibre⁺ Salt⁻
200 g short pastry (p. 277)	use modified short pastry
175 g chuck steak	
50 g kidney or liver	
100 g potato	
$\frac{1}{2}$ very small swede or turnip (optional but a really Cornish addition)	
1 small onion	
1 tablespoon water	
pepper and salt	omit salt

1 Make pastry, divide into four and roll each piece to a round about 150 mm across.

2 Cut meat into 10 mm thick strips, liver or kidney into small pieces; scrub the root vegetables; then peel and dice potatoes and turnip; and peel and chop onion finely.

3 Mix filling, add seasoning and water.

4 Pile $\frac{1}{4}$ mixture on to each round of pastry, damp edges, fold pastry in half and press edges firmly together, knock up edge (Fig. 33.1).

5 To shape pasties as in north Cornwall, set pasty on edge with join on top. Flute this edge with the thumb and fingers. With a skewer make a hole in the fluting to allow steam to escape. To shape pasties as in south Cornwall, fold the cut edge neatly back on to pasty and flute it with a spoon handle or the back of a knife.

6 Brush pasties with beaten egg or milk.

7 Bake for 20 minutes at 200°C Gas No. 6, and at 160 °C Gas No. 2 for the remaining $\frac{1}{2}$ hour to cook meat without overcooking the pastry.

North Cornish

South Cornish

Samosas with meat filling

4 servings

Standard	*Modified*	Fibre⁺ Fat⁻ Fatᵘⁿˢᵃᵗ Salt⁻

Standard	*Modified*
Samosa pastry (p. 278)	use modified samosa pastry
150 g minced beef	use lean mince or ground beef
1 tablespoon vegetable oil	use 1 teaspoon corn oil or sunflower oil
1 small onion	
1 clove of garlic	
1 level teaspoon ground coriander	
$\frac{1}{2}$ level teaspoon chilli powder	
$\frac{1}{2}$ level teaspoon garam masala	
$\frac{1}{4}$ level teaspoon ground ginger	
salt	omit salt
1 tablespoon water	

For deep fat frying:

Cooking time 45 minutes

Vegetable oil	use corn oil or sunflower oil

1 Peel and dice onion (Fig. 30.2).

2 Peel and crush garlic.

3 Heat oil in a shallow frying-pan over a moderate heat.

4 Add diced onion and garlic, and fry until golden brown.

5 Add meat, coriander, chilli powder, garam masala, ginger, and salt if used. Continue frying for 5 minutes.

6 Put lid on pan and continue cooking over a gentle heat for 30 minutes. If mixture looks dry add the tablespoon of water.

7 Leave mixture to cool. Shape samosa dough (Fig. 33.2) into a sausage shape and divide into 16 pieces. Shape each piece of dough into a ball and roll out to form a round, 13 cm in diameter. Cut each round in half, add filling and fold to make a cone, sealing with water.

8 Heat fat to 190°C and fry until golden brown. Drain on absorbent paper.

9 Serve hot or at room temperature with wedges of lemon.

Fig. 33.2
Shaping samosa pastry

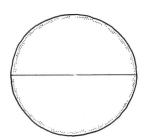

Cut circle in half

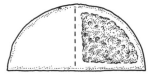

Arrange filling on one side of semi-circle

Fold and seal edges

Sausage rolls

8 large or 12 small rolls

Oven 200 °C Gas No. 6 for short pastry; 220 °C Gas No. 7 for flaky pastry

Cooking time ½ hour

Standard	*Modified* Fibre⁺ Fat⁻ Salt⁻

Standard *Modified* Fibre⁺ Fat⁻ Salt⁻

200 g short pastry (p. 277) or flaky or rough-puff pastry (p. 280) — use modified pastry

250 g sausages or sausage meat — use low-fat sausages

1 Make pastry.

2 Skin sausages and roll on a floured board to 2 long rolls.

3 Roll pastry to an oblong about 180 mm wide and 5 mm thick.

4 Cut oblong into 2 strips lengthways; put a roll of sausage on each.

5 Damp one edge of each strip (Fig. 33.3).

With short pastry

Roll the dry edge of the strip of pastry over sausage to overlap damp edge, press join firmly under the roll (Fig. 33.3).

With flaky or rough-puff pastry

1 Fold pastry in half lengthways, sausage inside. Press cut edges together at the side of the roll (Fig. 33.3).

2 Brush pastry with beaten egg, cut into suitable lengths and cut tops of rolls with a sharp knife or scissors:

3 Bake rolls at 200°C Gas No.6 for short pastry, 220°C Gas No.7 for flaky and rough-puff pastry, for the first ¼ hour; then at 170°C–180°C Gas No. 2–3 for second ¼ hour.

Fig. 33.3
Shaping sausage rolls

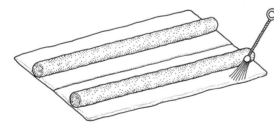

Roll pastry to rectangle, cut 2 strips
Roll sausage to long rolls
Brush edge of pastry with water

Flaky pastry

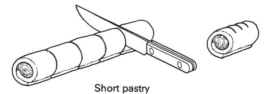

Short pastry

Meat in batter

'Toad in a hole'
(sausages in batter)

3 servings

Oven 220°C Gas No.7

Cooking time 50 minutes

Standard	Modified Fibre⁺ Fat⁻ Salt⁻
250 ml pancake batter (p. 281)	use modified batter
250 g sausages	use fat-reduced sausages

1 Heat the oven.

2 If sausages have skins soak in cold water for 5 minutes to soften skins; slit skins lengthwise with a sharp knife or scissors and, holding one edge of skin, shake and roll sausage out of its skin.

3 Put sausages in an ovenproof dish and bake for 5 minutes until fat runs from them and the dish is hot.

4 Make batter and pour over hot sausages.

5 Bake for 45 minutes until batter is well risen, brown and crisp.

6 Serve at once.

Individual toads in the hole or sausage puffs

Recipe as above, using 4 deep patty tins 100 mm across or 8 to 12 smaller ones.

1 Prepare oven, sausages and batter as above.

2 Divide sausages between the tins, heat them as above, pour an equal amount of batter into each tin.

3 Bake for 30 minutes.

34 Fish dishes

Poached fish

1 Clean, dry and season fish. Sprinkle with lemon juice and fold fillets in 3 or roll them.

2 Have enough boiling fish stock, milk, salted water or water to come half-way up fish in a shallow pan.

3 Remove the pan from the heat, put fish in and baste with the hot liquid; cover fish with greased paper and a lid.

4 Simmer fish gently, allowing liquid to bubble slowly at 1 side of the pan, for 10–15 minutes for small, thin fillets or for 10 minutes to each 500 g and 10 minutes over for large pieces.

5 Use all the liquid in a coating sauce. Keep fish hot while sauce is being made; coat and garnish fish.

Fish pie

3 servings

Standard	*Modified* Fibre[+] Fat[−] Fat[unsat] Salt[−]
250–500 g cooked, raw or canned fish	use white fish
125 ml white coating sauce (p. 263)	use modified white coating sauce
2 teaspoons chopped parsley	use 4 teaspoons parsley
salt and pepper	omit salt
lemon juice	
Topping: 500 g potatoes	
1 level tablespoon margarine	omit margarine
a little milk	use skimmed milk
salt and pepper	omit salt
a little nutmeg	
a little beaten egg to brush	

Oven 220 °C Gas No. 7

Cooking time 30–45 minutes

Optional extras:
1 hard-boiled egg or 1 or 2 tomatoes skinned (Fig. 30.3)

1 Take a 550 ml pie dish. Lightly grease unless non-stick dish is used.

2 Scrub, peel and boil potatoes; drain thoroughly. Add seasoning, fat if used and milk if necessary and mash.

3 Flake cooked or raw fish; include skin and bones of canned fish.

4 Slice egg or tomato and line the sides of the dish with either.

5 Mix fish and sauce, season and add parsley and lemon juice to taste.

6 Put fish mixture in the pie dish, cover it with potato and smooth the top with a wet knife. Mark the top neatly with the tip of the knife or fork and brush with egg if desired.

7 Bake for 30 minutes if cooked fish is used, 45 minutes if raw fish; turn down heat when top is brown.

Fish cakes

	Standard	Modified	Fibre⁺ Fat⁻ Fatᵘⁿˢᵃᵗ Salt⁻

4 servings, 8 fish cakes

Standard	Modified
250 g cooked fish or canned herrings, salmon, pilchards, or tuna fish	use white fish
250 g cooked potato	
1 level tablespoon margarine	omit margarine
2 teaspoons chopped parsley	use 4 teaspoons parsley
salt and pepper	omit salt
lemon juice	
a little white sauce or beaten egg oil for shallow frying	use corn or sunflower oil
Coating: beaten egg breadcrumbs	use wholewheat breadcrumbs

Cooking time 4–6 minutes

1 Remove bones and skin from cooked fish but not from tinned fish.

2 Flake and mash fish.

3 Melt margarine in a pan if fat is used. Add potato and mash; add fish and beat mixture smooth.

4 Season and add lemon juice and parsley, then add just enough sauce or beaten egg to shape mixture.

5 On a floured surface form mixture into a long roll and cut 8 cakes (Fig. 32.1).

6 Coat with egg and crumbs (Fig. 29.2).

7 Fry in fat that browns bread in 20 seconds and drain on absorbent paper. Alternatively, grill under a pre-heated moderate grill allowing 2–3 minutes on each side.

Kedgeree

3 servings

Cooking time 30–60 minutes

Standard	Modified	Fibre+ Fat⁻ Fat^unsat Salt⁻
250 g smoked haddock		
100 g Patna rice	use brown rice	
25 g margarine	use 15 g polyunsaturated margarine	
½ teaspoon chopped parsley		
1 teaspoon curry powder		
a little grated nutmeg		
salt, pepper (cayenne if liked)	omit salt	
To garnish: 1 hard-boiled egg		

1 Poach haddock (p. 313), drain and flake, removing bones and skin.

2 Boil rice (p. 283).

3 Melt margarine and in it re-heat rice and haddock, shaking and tossing. Season to taste.

4 Slice egg, pile kedgeree high and loosely in a hot dish. Arrange egg around it and sprinkle with chopped parsley.

Soused herrings or mackerel

2 servings

Oven 150°C–170°C Gas No. 2

Cooking time 1 hour

Standard	Modified	Salt⁻
2 herrings or mackerel		
equal measures of vinegar and water to cover them		
2 teaspoons salt	omit salt	
12 peppercorns		
2 bay leaves		
4 cloves		
2 sliced onions		

1 Clean and bone fish, roll them from head to tail and pack into a deep ovenproof dish, closely, with tails up.

2 Half-fill the dish with vinegar, then fill up with water to cover fish.

3 Put in spices, salt, if used, and onion, and cover the dish with a lid or foil.

4 Bake for 1 hour in a slow oven.

5 Leave fish to cool in liquid.

Fish curry (molee)

4 servings

Cooking time 35 minutes

Standard	Modified Fat⁻ Fatⁿˢᵃᵗ Salt⁻
500 g white fish fillets	
1 large onion	
1 large tomato	
2 green chillies	
1 small bunch of coriander or parsley	
25 g cashew nuts	
2 tablespoons vegetable oil	use 1 tablespoon corn oil or sunflower oil
2 level teaspoons salt	omit salt
1 level teaspoon ground ginger	
1 level teaspoon ground coriander	
1 level teaspoon turmeric	
$\frac{1}{2}$ level teaspoon ground fenugreek	
2 cloves of garlic	
300 ml water	

1 Wash coriander leaves or parsley and chop finely.

2 Warm the water in a pan and add chopped coriander or parsley, ground coriander, ground fenugreek, ground ginger and turmeric. Leave mixture for $\frac{1}{2}$ hour.

3 Remove skin from fish fillets and cut fish into small pieces. If salt is used, sprinkle over fish.

4 Peel and slice onion (Fig. 30.2).

5 Peel and crush garlic.

6 Wash, split and de-seed green chillies.

7 Heat oil in a large pan over moderate heat. Add sliced onion, crushed garlic and chillies. Fry for 5 minutes until onion begins to brown.

8 Add fish and continue frying for 5 minutes.

9 Wash tomato and skin (Fig. 30.3) if desired. Cut into chunky pieces and add to fish mixture.

10 Strain liquid containing flavourings and add to larger pan with fish and tomatoes.

11 Chop cashew nuts finely and add to the pan.

12 When mixture simmers, time cooking for 25 minutes. Leave pan lid off. This dish goes well with boiled rice or chapatis and sambals.

35 Egg dishes

Scrambled eggs

1 serving

Cooking time 10 minutes

Standard	Modified	Fibre[+] Fat[−]	Fat[unsat]	Salt[−]
1 egg				
1 tablespoon milk	use skimmed milk			
1 tablespoon butter, margarine or frying oil	use polyunsaturated margarine			
salt and pepper to taste	omit salt			
For dishing:				
a slice of buttered toast	use wholewheat toast without butter			

1 Make toast, butter it if desired and keep warm in the serving dish.

2 Beat egg with milk and seasoning.

3 Melt fat over moderate heat, pour in egg mixture and cook quickly, stirring and scraping off the bottom of the pan until set firmly. Pile on toast and serve immediately.

4 One tablespoon of any of the following may be added: grated cheese; cooked, flaked, smoked haddock; cooked, chopped bacon or ham. These may be added to the raw egg mixture.

Eggs with cheese sauce

(eggs *au gratin* or eggs mornay)

2–4 servings

Oven 220 °C Gas No. 7 or grill

Cooking time 3–5 minutes

Standard	Moderate	Fibre[+] Fat[−]	Fat[unsat]	Salt[−]
4 eggs				
250 ml white coating sauce (p. 263)	use modified white coating sauce			
50–75 g grated cheese	use Edam cheese			
1 tablespoon fresh crumbs	use wholewheat breadcrumbs			
$\frac{1}{8}$ teaspoon cayenne or mustard				
pepper and salt	omit salt			

1 Lightly grease ovenproof baking dish of 200 mm diameter or 4 individual baking cups, and heat in an oven or under a moderate grill.

2 Make white sauce and keep hot.

3 Break eggs and slide into the hot dish.

4 Stir all but 2 tablespoons of cheese into hot sauce, taste and season.

5 Coat eggs with hot sauce, sprinkle remaining cheese, mixed with crumbs, evenly over the top.

6 Brown the top in a hot oven, 220°C Gas No.7, for 3 minutes, or under a moderate grill.

Scotch eggs

1 serving

Cooking time 20 minutes

Fig. 35.1
Wrapping egg in sausage meat

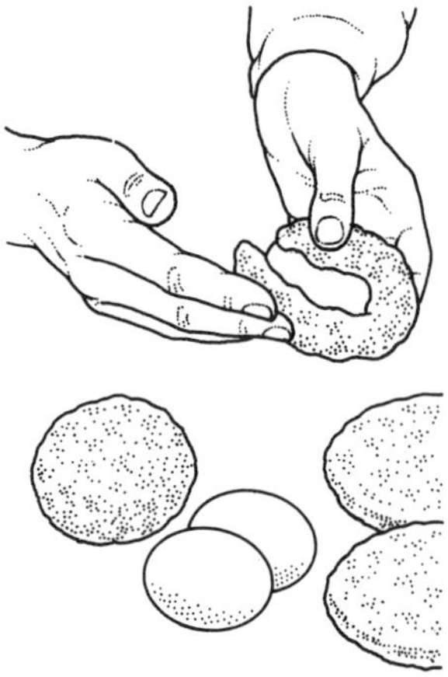

Standard	Modified Fibre⁺ Fat⁻ Fatᵘⁿˢᵃᵗ
1 egg	
1 sausage or 50 g sausage meat	use fat-reduced sausages
To coat: beaten egg and crumbs	use wholewheat crumbs
To fry: shallow or deep fat	use corn oil or sunflower oil

1 Hard boil, cool and shell egg, dust lightly with flour.

2 Skin sausage and shape into flat, round cake.

3 Wrap egg in sausage meat, pressing out all cracks and keeping meat to an even thickness (Fig. 35.1).

4 Coat with egg and crumbs, twice if possible (Fig. 29.2).

5 Heat fat: shallow fat to come half-way up egg, until it browns bread in 50 seconds; or deep fat to 170°C.

6 Fry egg over moderate heat for 7–10 minutes until raw sausage is cooked. Drain on absorbent paper.

7 Cut egg in half with a sharp knife and serve cold or hot.

Savoury or French omelet

1–2 servings

For a 170–180-mm omelet or frying-pan

Standard	Modified Fat⁻ Fatᵘⁿˢᵃᵗ Salt⁻
3 eggs	
salt and pepper	omit salt
1½ tablespoons cooking fat or clarified butter *or* 3 teaspoons olive oil or cooking oil	½ tablespoon corn oil or sunflower oil

Keep a pan for omelets; never wash it but clean it with dry salt and soft, clean paper, wiping out all the salt.

1 Beat eggs slightly and season.

Fig. 35.2
Loosening omelet around edge of pan

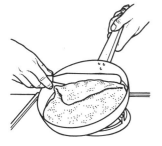

2 Have ready a hot serving dish and palette knife.

3 Heat fat or oil until tiny ripples can be seen on the surface; keep pan over strong heat.

4 Pour eggs slowly into hot fat: as it touches the fat it should set. Lift off the bottom of the pan constantly with the palette knife so that more liquid flows into the hot fat.

5 When the whole mixture is firmly set loosen it around the edge (Fig. 35.2), take the pan off the heat and tilt it sharply so that omelet rolls down it to fold in 3. Press it into a crescent shape with the palette knife. Invert omelet on to the hot dish and serve it at once.

Egg curry

4 servings

Cooking time 30–35 minutes

Standard	*Modified* Fat⁻ Fat^unsat Salt⁻
4 eggs	
50 g ghee	use 25 g polyunsaturated margarine
150 g plain yogurt	use low-fat yogurt
1 medium-sized onion	
2 cloves of garlic	
6 peppercorns	
4 cloves	
1 level teaspoon ground coriander	
1 level teaspoon ground ginger	
½ level teaspoon chilli powder	
½ level teaspoon garam masala	
½ level teaspoon salt	omit salt
pinch of ground cumin	

1 Hard-boil eggs and remove shells.

2 Peel and slice onion (Fig. 30.2); peel and crush garlic.

3 Heat fat in a large pan over a moderate heat, and add onion and garlic. Fry for 5 minutes until onion browns.

4 Add coriander, ginger, chilli powder, turmeric, garam masala, cumin, and salt if used. Continue frying for 5 minutes.

5 Add yogurt, cloves and peppercorns. Continue cooking for 10–15 minutes.

6 Add hard-boiled eggs and leave mixture over a gentle heat for 3 minutes. This dish goes well with rice or chapatis and sambals.

36 Cheese dishes

Welsh rarebit

2 servings

Standard	Modified Fibre⁺ Fat⁻ Salt⁻

Standard	Modified Fibre⁺ Fat⁻ Salt⁻
75 g grated cheese	use Edam cheese
1 tablespoon melted butter or margarine	use 1 teaspoon low-fat spread
1 to 2 tablespoons milk	use skimmed milk
$\frac{1}{4}$ teaspoon made mustard	
salt and cayenne pepper	omit salt
2 fairly large slices of buttered toast	use wholewheat toast without butter

Grilling time 5–7 minutes

1 Make toast; butter it if desired. Keep hot.

2 Melt fat, stir into it cheese, seasonings and enough liquid to make a soft paste.

3 Spread on toast, make it smooth and grill slowly until golden brown. Serve at once.

Glamorgan sausages

4 servings

Standard	Modified	Fibre⁺ Fat⁻	Fat^unsat	Salt⁻
125 g fresh white breadcrumbs	use wholewheat breadcrumbs			
100 g mature Cheddar cheese	use Edam cheese			
1 small onion				
1 egg				
1 level teaspoon dried mixed herbs				
$\frac{1}{2}$ teaspoon mustard powder				
salt and pepper	omit salt			
Coating: 1 egg				
25 g white breadcrumbs	use wholewheat breadcrumbs			
oil for frying	use sunflower oil			

Cooking time 5 minutes

1 Grate cheese. Peel and grate onion.

2 Put cheese, onion, breadcrumbs, dried mixed herbs, mustard powder, pepper, and salt if used, into a large mixing bowl.

3 Pour egg into the mixing bowl with dry ingredients.

4 Stir mixture together, using a fork. When it holds together, divide mixture into 12 sausage shapes (Fig. 32.1).

5 Dip sausages into egg and coat with breadcrumbs (Fig. 29.2).

6 Take a shallow frying-pan and pour in around 6 mm oil. Put over a moderate heat until fat browns bread in 20 seconds and fry sausages for 5 minutes. Turn to ensure even cooking.

7 Remove sausages from the pan using a slotted spoon, and drain on absorbent paper. Serve hot or cold with salad.

Cheese and vegetable loaf

6 servings

Oven 190 °C Gas No. 5

Baking time 1 hour

Standard	Modified	Fibre⁺ Fat⁻ Fatᵘⁿˢᵃᵗ Salt⁻
1 medium green pepper		
1 medium red pepper		
1 medium onion		
350 g mushrooms		
3 sticks celery		
225 g white breadcrumbs	use wholewheat breadcrumbs	
150 g Cheddar cheese	use Edam cheese	
1 size 1 egg		
3 tablespoons oil	use sunflower oil	
salt and pepper	omit salt	

1 Lightly grease a 900 g loaf tin.

2 Peel and dice onion (Fig. 30.2).

3 Remove core, seeds and pith from peppers, rinse and dice (Fig. 31.2).

4 Wipe and chop mushrooms finely.

5 Wash and dice celery.

6 Grate cheese.

7 Heat oil in a large pan, add pepper and onion; cook for 5 minutes.

8 Add mushrooms and celery; continue cooking for a further 5 minutes.

9 Remove pan from heat, stir in 200 g breadcrumbs and 100 g cheese.

10 Beat egg with seasonings and add to mixture in pan, stir to mix thoroughly.

11 Pour mixture into prepared tin, level the surface and sprinkle with remaining breadcrumbs and cheese. Bake for 1 hour.

12 Serve hot or cold with salad.

Cheesy potato pizza

4 servings

Oven 200 °C Gas No. 6

Cooking time 1 hour

Standard	*Modified*	Fibre[+] Fat[−]	Fat[unsat]	Salt[−]

Topping:

Standard	*Modified*
150 g Cheddar cheese	use Edam cheese
200 g onions	
100 g mushrooms	
1 medium red pepper	
1 clove garlic	
1 tablespoon vegetable oil	use 2 teaspoons sunflower oil
2 tablespoons tomato purée	
½ level teaspoon dried oregano	
salt and pepper	omit salt

Base:

Standard	*Modified*
200 g potatoes	
50 g butter or margarine	use polyunsaturated margarine
100 g self-raising flour	use self-raising wholewheat flour
salt and pepper	omit salt

1 Lightly grease a baking sheet.

2 Boil potatoes (p. 287), mash with margarine, add flour, salt if used and pepper. Mix to form a dough and knead lightly.

3 Roll dough to a 25 cm round and put on the baking sheet.

4 Peel and slice onion finely (Fig. 30.2).

5 Peel and crush garlic.

6 Remove core, seeds and pith from pepper, rinse and dice thinly (Fig. 31.2).

7 Wipe mushrooms and slice thinly.

8 Heat oil in pan, add onions, garlic and pepper. Fry for 5 minutes. Add mushrooms, oregano, salt if used, and pepper.

9 Grate cheese.

10 Spread tomato purée on pizza base, top with vegetable mixture and cover with grated cheese.

11 Bake for 30 to 40 minutes.

12 Serve hot or cold with salad.

Cheese flan or quiche Lorraine

4–6 servings

Oven 190 °C Gas No. 5

Baking time 35–40 minutes

Standard	Modified	Fibre[+] Fat[-] Fat[unsat] Salt[-]
100–125 g short pastry (p. 277)	use modified short pastry	
Filling: 1 small onion		
2 rashers of streaky bacon	use lean bacon	
200 ml milk	use skimmed milk	
2 eggs		
1 tablespoon margarine	use 1 teaspoon polyunsaturated margarine	
50 g grated cheese	use Edam cheese	
pepper and salt	omit salt	

*Fig. 36.1
Lining a flan ring*

1 Make pastry and line a deep 170-mm sandwich tin, flan ring or a 500-ml, deep ovenproof pie plate (Fig. 36.1).

2 Peel and chop onion finely.

3 Remove rind, rust and gristle from bacon and cut into dice.

4 Fry bacon and onion gently in margarine until tender; turn them into the pastry case.

5 Beat egg, stir in milk, seasoning and most of the cheese, pour mixture into the case and sprinkle the top with the rest of the cheese.

6 Bake flan until just set and golden brown on top.

37 Sweet dishes

Fruity kebabs

4 servings

	Standard	Modified Sugar⁻
	200 g canned pineapple chunks	use fresh pineapple or fruit canned in natural juice
	2 peaches	
	2 eating apples	
	2 bananas	
	2 tablespoons lemon juice	
	1 orange	
	3 tablespoons clear honey	use 1 tablespoon honey
Cooking time 5 minutes	¼ level teaspoon dried ginger	

1 Wash peaches. Peel; stone and cut into chunks.

2 Wash, core and chunk apples. Brush with lemon juice.

3 Peel and cut bananas into 25-mm pieces. Brush with lemon juice.

4 Drain pineapple from juice or peel and chunk (Fig. 37.2).

5 Mix all the fruit together in a large mixing bowl with the remaining lemon juice.

6 Remove zest from orange using a grater or zester.

7 Squeeze juice from orange and add to fruit.

8 Thread fruit on to 4 kebab skewers. Brush with honey and cook under a moderate grill for 5 minutes, turning frequently throughout.

9 Sprinkle orange zest and ground ginger over kebabs and serve at once.

Fruit salad

4 servings

	Standard	Modified Sugar⁻
	500 g mixture of fruit in season	
	250 ml water with 100 g sugar	omit sugar syrup and use unsweetened orange, pineapple or apple juice
Cooking time 5 minutes	juice of ½ to 1 lemon	

1 Choose a mixture of fruit with a variety of colours, textures and flavours.

2 Prepare fresh fruit (Table 37.1).

3 For sugar syrup, put sugar and water in a pan, add any apple or pear peelings, stones, inner skin of oranges and a few strips of orange or lemon rind, removed with a vegetable peeler. Bring syrup to boiling point, put on the lid and leave to infuse for 20 minutes. Strain and cool.

4 Put fruit in a mixing bowl and add syrup or fruit juice. Leave covered. Serve in 1 bowl or in individual glasses.

Note: Soft berries and bananas lose colour and become pulpy, and should be added just before serving.

Table 37.1
Preparation of fruit for fresh fruit salad

Name	Preparation technique
Apples	Wash, either peel thinly or leave skin on, quarter and remove cores, cut into slices; rub with lemon juice
Apricots	Wash, remove stalks, cut in half and remove stones
Bananas	Peel, strip off 'strings', cut into slices and rub with lemon juice
Cherries	Wash, remove stalks–remove stones using a cherry-stoner or skewer
Grapefruit	Remove rind and pith and slit segments from skin (Fig. 37.1); remove any pips using a skewer

Fig. 37.1
Cutting orange or grapefruit segments

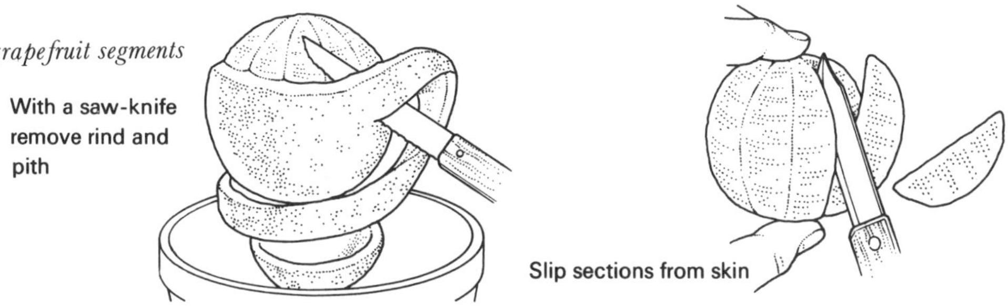

With a saw-knife remove rind and pith

Slip sections from skin

Grapes	Wash, remove stalks and prise out pips using a sharp knife
Kiwi fruit	Peel thinly and cut into slices
Mango	Slit around fruit horizontally, remove flesh from stone, peel and cut into slices
Melon	Slice, remove seeds, then either peel thickly and cut into dice or make melon balls
Nectarines	Wash, halve, remove stones and cut into slices
Oranges	As for grapefruit
Peach	Scrape off skin with the back of a knife or scald for 30 seconds in boiling water, immediately cooling in cold water and peel the skin away; cut in half, remove stone and slice
Pear	As for apples

Name	Preparation technique
Pineapple	Cut off top and bottom, cut pineapple into thick slices; remove thick rind and eyes; remove woody core and cut into cubes (Fig. 37.2)

Fig. 37.2
Cutting pineapple cubes

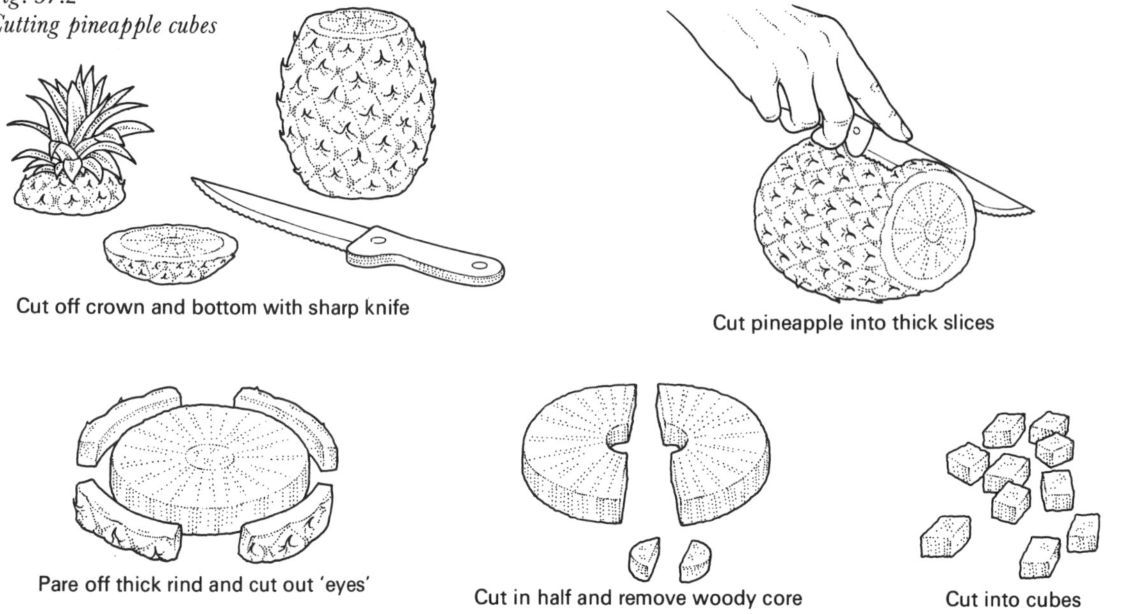

Cut off crown and bottom with sharp knife

Cut pineapple into thick slices

Pare off thick rind and cut out 'eyes'

Cut in half and remove woody core

Cut into cubes

Plums	As for apricots
Raspberries	Remove any leaves and grubs; put into a colander and dip into cold water; drain on absorbent paper
Strawberries	As for raspberries but cut into halves or quarters if large

Tofu banana pudding

4 servings

Standard	*Modified* Sugar⁻
200 g tofu	
4 bananas	
vanilla essence to taste	
2 tablespoons of clear honey	use 1 tablespoon clear honey
50 g dried bananas	

1 Peel and slice bananas; roughly chop tofu.

2 Put bananas and tofu in a blender with honey and vanilla essence.

3 Liquidise to a smooth mixture and chill in individual serving dishes.

4 Chop dried bananas and sprinkle over chilled mixture.

Bread and butter pudding

3–4 servings

Oven 180°C Gas No.4

Baking time 30–40 minutes

Standard	*Modified*	Fibre⁺ Fat⁻	Fatᵘⁿˢᵃᵗ Sugar⁻
4 thin slices bread from medium loaf	use brown bread		
30 g butter	use 15 g polyunsaturated margarine		
250 ml milk	use skimmed milk		
1 egg			
1 tablespoon sugar	omit sugar and add extra 50 g sultanas		
1 tablespoon currants or sultanas			

1 Spread bread with fat and cut into squares or triangles.

2 Arrange half pieces of bread and fat on the bottom of a 425-ml pie dish, put dried fruit on top and then a layer of bread and fat on top.

3 Beat egg with 2 tablespoons milk and sugar if used.

4 Heat the rest of the milk until it steams; stir into egg mixture.

5 Strain custard over bread mixture.

6 Bake in a roasting tin with hot water surrounding the pie dish.

Brown bread ice-cream

4 servings

Oven temperature 190 °C Gas No. 5

Cooking time 10 minutes

Standard	*Modified*	Fibre⁺ Fat⁻ Sugar⁻
75 g brown breadcrumbs	use wholewheat breadcrumbs	
75 g demerara sugar		
1 tablespoon honey	omit honey	
400 ml double cream	use whipping cream	
2 eggs		

1 Mix breadcrumbs and sugar and spread evenly on a baking sheet. Bake in a pre-heated oven for 10 minutes.

2 Cool mixture thoroughly.

3 Separate egg whites from yolks.

4 To yolks add honey (if used), and beat well.

5 Whip cream.

6 Whisk egg whites until light and fluffy.

7 Fold egg yolk and caramelised breadcrumbs into whipped cream.

8 Fold egg whites into cream mixture.

9 Freeze mixture in a swiss roll tin for 2 hours and put in the refrigerator for about 20 minutes before serving.

Vegan ice-cream

4 servings

Standard	*Modified* Sugar⁻
4 large ripe bananas	
100 g cashew nuts	
100 g strawberries or raspberries or peaches	
50 g brown sugar	omit sugar

1 Wash strawberries or raspberries, or peel, stone and slice peaches.

2 Peel and chop bananas.

3 Put banana, selected fruit, cashew nuts and sugar if used, in a blender; blend mixture until smooth.

4 Spread mixture in a swiss roll tin and freeze for about 3 hours.

5 To serve, scoop ice-cream into a large bowl or into individual serving dishes.

Buns: yeast mixture

Currant buns

8 buns

Oven 220 °C Gas No. 7

Baking time 20 minutes

Standard	*Modified* Fibre⁺ Salt⁻ Fat⁻ Fat^unsat Sugar⁻
250 g strong plain flour	use 125 g strong white flour and 125 g wholewheat flour
50 g currants	
½ level teaspoon salt	
25 g sugar	use 15 g sugar
20 g fresh yeast	
25 g margarine	use 15 g polyunsaturated margarine
1 egg	
scant 125 ml milk	use skimmed milk
½ level teaspoon mixed spice	
25 mg vitamin C tablet	

1 Lightly grease a tin unless a non-stick tin is used.

2 Sift flour, salt if used, and mixed spice into a large mixing bowl. Tip bran in the sieve into the bowl.

3 Add margarine; rub this into flour until the mixture looks like fine breadcrumbs. Add sugar.

4 Boil $\frac{1}{3}$ of milk and add to remaining cold milk.

5 Put fresh yeast into a basin and mix with 2 teaspoons of liquid to soften it. Stir in remaining liquid.

6 Add vitamin C tablet to liquid and crush it, using the back of a tablespoon.

7 Make a deep 'well' in the flour and add liquid mixture.

8 Mix thoroughly, using the hand, for about 3 minutes until dough leaves the fingers.

9 Turn dough on to a lightly floured surface and knead (Fig. 26.1) until smooth and elastic (10 minutes).

10 Knead in currants and shape dough into 8 balls. Leave to rise on a baking sheet and cover with greased polythene.

11 Bake and glaze with milk and sugar.

Scones: rubbing in method

Sweet scones: basic recipe

12 scones

Oven 230 °C Gas No. 8

Baking time 7–10 minutes

Standard		*Modified* Fibre^{+} Salt^{-} Fat^{-} Fat^{unsat} Sugar^{-}
200 g plain flour 2½–3 level teaspoons baking powder	with fresh milk	use brown or wholewheat flour
or		
200 g plain flour 1 level teaspoon bicarbonate of soda 1 level teaspoon cream of tartar	with sour milk or butter-milk	use brown or wholewheat flour
or		
200 g self-raising flour		use self-raising brown or wholewheat flour
½ level teaspoon salt		omit salt
25–50 g butter or margarine		use 25 g polyunsaturated margarine
25–50 g sugar		use 25 g sugar
125 ml milk		use skimmed milk

1 Heat the oven.

2 Sift flour with other powder ingredients. Tip bran in sieve into mixing bowl.

3 Rub in fat, aerating flour at the same time.

4 Add sugar.

5 Make a 'well' in flour mixture and add milk. Mix to a soft, spongy dough with a palette knife.

6 On a floured surface, knead dough lightly until smooth. Divide in 2 and lightly knead each piece to a ball. Flatten each to 20 mm thick and cut each round into 6 triangles, or roll mixture to 20 mm thick and cut into rounds using a 5-cm fluted cutter.

7 Heat the baking tray in oven.

8 Brush scones with beaten egg for a glossy crust or with flour for a soft one.

9 If possible, leave scones to rest for 10–15 minutes before baking.

10 Bake scones at the top of the hot oven until they are well risen and brown.

Variations to the basic recipe are given in Table 37.2.

Table 37.2
Types of sweet scones

Scone	Variation of basic recipe
Mixed fruit	Add 50 g mixed dried fruit to dry ingredients
Date	Add 50 g stoned dried dates, finely chopped, to dry ingredients
Apple	Add 50 g grated apple to dry ingredients
Carrot	Add 50 g grated carrot to dry ingredients

Cakes: rubbing in method

Rock buns

	Standard	Modified	Fibre[+] Fat[unsat]	Sugar[-]	Salt[-]
	200 g plain flour and 2–2½ level teaspoons baking powder *or* 200 g self-raising flour	use wholewheat flour with baking powder *or* self-raising wholewheat flour			
	75 g granulated or brown sugar	use 50 g granulated or brown sugar			
	75 g margarine	use 75 g polyunsaturated margarine			

	Standard	Modified	Fibre⁺ Fat^unsat	Sugar⁻	Salt⁻
	75 g currants and sultanas				
	25 g candied peel				
Oven 190°C Gas No.5	¼ teaspoon mixed spice				
Baking time 15–20 minutes	½ level teaspoon salt	omit salt			
	1 egg				
	a little milk	use skimmed milk			

1 Heat oven. Lightly grease a baking tray, unless non-stick.

2 Sift together all powdered ingredients and flour. Tip any bran in sieve into mixing bowl. Add sugar.

3 Rub in fat with fingertips, aerating flour at the same time.

4 Add fruit and candied peel.

5 Beat egg lightly.

6 Make a deep hole or 'well' in flour. Pour in egg and mix smoothly, adding milk if needed. Rubbed-in cakes should be of a more or less stiff consistency.

7 Using a spoon and fork, divide dough into 12 pieces and shape into a 'rocky' cone on the baking tray.

8 Bake until well risen and brown.

Cakes: creaming method

Queencakes

24 cakes

	Standard	Modified	Fibre⁺ Fat⁻	Fat^unsat	Sugar⁻
	200 g self-raising flour *or* 200 g plain flour and 2 level teaspoons baking powder	use 100 g plain flour and 100 g wholewheat flour with baking powder			
	100–150 g castor sugar	use 100 g sugar			
	100 g butter or margarine	use polyunsaturated margarine			
	100 g currants and sultanas				
	zest of ½ a lemon				
Oven 180 °C Gas No. 4	2 eggs				
Baking time 20 minutes	2–4 tablespoons milk	use skimmed milk			

1 Heat the oven. Line bun tins with paper cases.

2 Sift flour with powdered ingredients, tipping in any bran in sieve. Beat eggs slightly.

3 Cream fat and sugar together by working them vigorously around the bowl with the back of a wooden spoon or use an electric hand whisk. From time to time scrape mixture down sides of bowl. Continue creaming until mixture is white and fluffy and passes the aeration test (Fig. 16.4).

4 Beat in equivalent of 1 beaten egg at a time, continuing to beat after each addition until mixture is smooth and has stiffened.

5 Stir in fruit and lemon zest.

6 Sift half flour once more, this time directly into mixture and fold in lightly.

7 When flour is folded in add milk.

8 Sift and fold in other half of flour.

9 Spread mixture evenly into prepared tins and bake.

Cakes: all-in-one method

Sandwich cake

Standard	Modified Fibre+ Sugar−
125 g self-raising flour	use self-raising brown flour
1 level teaspoon of baking powder	
2 size 2 eggs	
125 g castor sugar	use 75 g castor sugar and 50 g grated carrot
125 g soft margarine	
Filling:	
3 tablespoons of jam	use low-sugar jam or fruit spread

Oven 160 °C Gas No. 3

Baking time 25–35 minutes

1 Heat the oven and lightly grease and line the bases of 2 18-cm sandwich tins or use non-stick tins.

2 Put all ingredients into a large mixture bowl and beat well, using a wooden spoon, for 3–4 minutes.

3 Pour mixture evenly into the tins. Smooth the surface mixture with a spatula.

4 Put the tins on the middle shelf of the oven and bake for 25–35 minutes.

5 Allow cakes to cool for 10 minutes in the tin, then turn out on to a cooling wire rack.

6 Sandwich cakes together with filling.

Cakes: melting method

Ginger bread

Standard	Modified	Fibre[+] Fat[-] Fat[unsat] Sugar[-]
200 g plain flour	use wholewheat flour	
1 level teaspoon bicarbonate of soda		
1½ level teaspoons ground ginger		
75 g margarine	use 50 g polyunsaturated margarine	
50 g brown sugar	use 25 g sugar	
75 g black treacle	use 50 g treacle	
75 g golden syrup	use 50 g syrup	
1 large egg		
4–5 tablespoons milk	use skimmed milk	

Oven 150 °C Gas No. 2

Baking time 1–1¼ hours

1 Heat the oven, prepare the tin (Fig. 37.3): for 200-g size use a 200-mm round tin or an oblong tin about 240 × 150 mm.

2 In a pan gently warm fat and sugar, syrup and treacle until fat and syrup are just melted: do not boil or the gingerbread will be hard. Cool syrup mixture.

3 Sift powdered ingredients into a mixing bowl, tipping in any bran.

4 Make a 'well' in the dry mixture. Mix egg with half milk, and pour this and cooled liquid syrup mixture into it.

5 Mix all ingredients to a smooth, thick batter, adding more milk if necessary. Pour mixture into the tin and bake for 1–1¼ hours for 200-g size.

6 Gingerbread is improved by storing it in a tin for at least a week, when the crust gets soft and the whole texture moist and spongy.

Fig. 37.3
Lining cake tins

Square tin

Pencil all around tin

Cut — Cut — Cut

Crease just inside all lines

Fold along creases and slip paper 'box' into tin

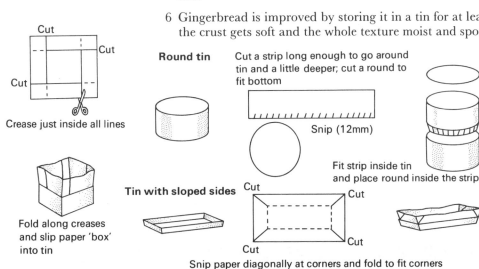

Round tin   Cut a strip long enough to go around tin and a little deeper; cut a round to fit bottom

Snip (12mm)

Fit strip inside tin and place round inside the strip

Tin with sloped sides   Cut — Cut — Cut — Cut

Snip paper diagonally at corners and fold to fit corners

Cakes: whisking method

Swiss roll

Standard	Modified Fibre⁺ Sugar⁻
2 size 2 eggs	
75 g castor sugar	
50 g flour	use brown flour
$\frac{1}{4}$ teaspoon vanilla essence	
1 tablespoon warm water	
Filling:	
2–3 tablespoons jam	use low-sugar jam or fruit spread

Oven 200 °C–220 °C Gas No. 6–7

Baking time 7–8 minutes

1 Prepare and line a baking tray 270 mm × 180 mm (Fig. 37.3).

2 Heat the oven. Warm the flour.

3 Whisk eggs and sugar until thick and light in colour (p. 82), and fold in flour as for sponge cake, adding water and vanilla as the last flour is folded in.

4 Spread mixture in the tin, pushing it well into the corners.

5 Bake roll at top of the oven.

6 While it is baking, warm the filling in a basin over boiling water. Dredge a sheet of paper with castor sugar *or* wring a cloth tightly out of cold water.

7 When the roll is cooked turn it upside down on to the cloth or paper (Fig. 37.4); with a finger dipped in water damp the edges of the paper and peel it off.

8 Trim the crisp edges off cake, spread with warm filling, leaving 20-mm margins on 3 sides (Fig. 37.4).

9 Mark 22 mm from the near, short end with the back of a knife, to begin the roll, and, holding the paper or cloth, roll cake as tightly as possible away from you (Fig. 37.4). Hold the roll in shape for a second or two, then remove the paper or cloth and dredge the roll with castor sugar.

Fig. 37.4
Rolling a swiss roll

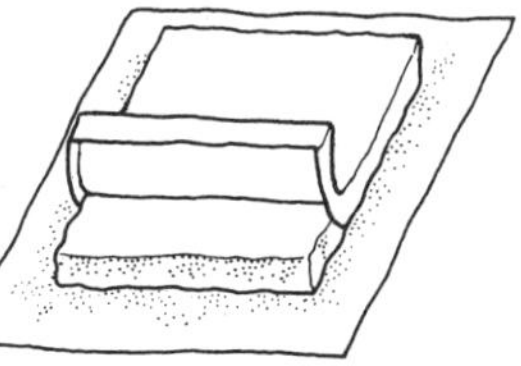

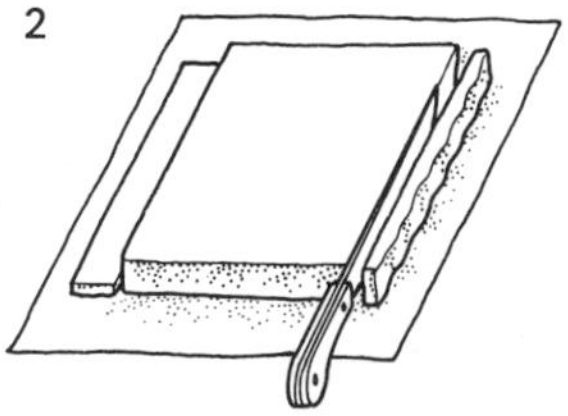

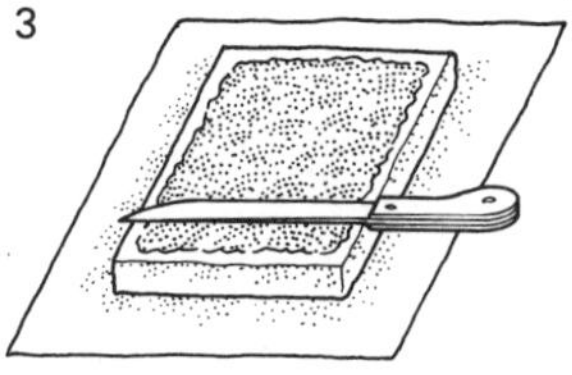

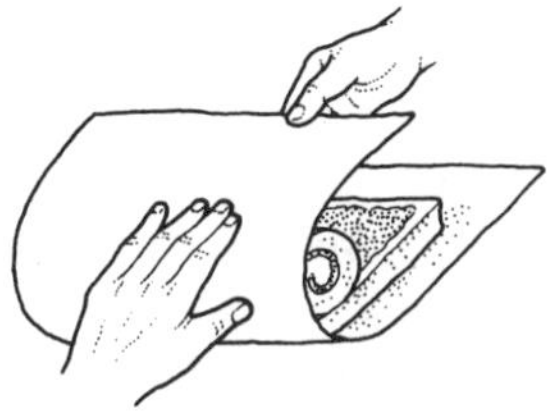

Cakes: dried fruit based

Fruit and All-Bran loaf

Oven 180 °C Gas No. 4

Baking time 1 hour

Standard	Modified Fibre⁺ Fat⁻ Sugar⁻
275 g mixed dried fruit	
100 g All-Bran	
100 g self-raising flour	use self-raising brown flour
150 g castor sugar	use 75 g castor sugar and 75 g chopped dates
300 ml milk	use skimmed milk

1 Put dried fruit, All-Bran, sugar and milk into a mixing bowl.

2 Mix well and leave to stand for 30 minutes.

3 Add flour by passing it through a sieve. If brown flour is used, tip the bran remaining in the sieve into the mixture. Mix thoroughly.

4 Pour mixture into a lightly greased or non-stick 900-g loaf tin.

5 Bake for about 1 hour.

Date cake

Oven 180 °C Gas No. 4

Baking time 1 hour

Standard	Modified Fibre⁺
250 g plain flour	use wholewheat flour
2 level teaspoons baking powder	
300 g stoned dried dates	
100 ml corn oil	
200 ml water	

1 Sift flour and baking powder into a large mixing bowl. Tip bran remaining in the sieve into the bowl.

2 Chop dates into small pieces.

3 Place ⅔ of dates in with dry ingredients.

4 Place remaining ⅓ of dates in a blender with oil and water. Blend thoroughly.

5 Pour liquid mixture in with dry ingredients and mix thoroughly.

6 Pour cake mixture into a lightly greased or non-stick 150-mm round cake tin or into a 900 g loaf tin.

7 Cook on the middle shelf of the oven for about 1 hour.

Apricot bites

4 servings

Standard	*Modified* Fibre⁺ Sugar⁻
100 g dried apricots	
75 g desiccated coconut	
2 teaspoons orange juice	
½ level teaspoon orange zest	
½ level teaspoon lemon zest	
25 g castor sugar (for rolling)	use 25 g desiccated coconut

1 Put apricots in a bowl and pour boiling water to cover them. Leave for 10 minutes.

2 Drain water away; mince apricots or chop finely.

3 Put apricots into a mixing bowl and add coconut, orange juice and orange and lemon zests.

4 Knead mixture to blend thoroughly.

5 Shape mixture into balls 25 mm in diameter.

6 Roll balls in sugar or desiccated coconut and serve chilled.

Biscuits: rubbing-in method

Shortbread

Oven 170 °C Gas No. 3

Baking time ¾ hour for 1 cake; 15 minutes for fingers

Standard	*Modified* Fibre⁺ Sugar⁻ Salt⁻
100 g flour	use wholewheat flour
50 g cornflour	
100 g butter	
50 g castor sugar	use 30 g sugar
⅛ teaspoon salt	omit salt

1 Lightly grease a baking tray unless a non-stick tray is used.

2 Sift flours (include bran left in sieve) into a large mixing bowl with salt if used.

3 Add sugar and fat. Cut fat into small pieces in the flour, using a palette knife.

4 Rub fat into flour, using fingertips.

5 Knead dry dough until ingredients hold together as in pastry.

6 *To shape a large shortbread:*
   (a) Knead dough to a smooth ball, gently press and roll it to a round 18 mm thick and keep the edges smooth.
   (b) Lift carefully on to a square of greaseproof paper on the underside of a baking tray to make it easy to slide off when baked.
   (c) Neatly pinch edge or mark it with a spoon handle and pierce shortbread all over in a neat pattern.
   (d) In warm weather cool before baking.
   (e) Bake until firm and light golden-fawn in colour; if shortbread colours before it is set, move it to a cooler shelf or cover with foil.

A wooden shortbread mould may be used: Dust it with flour, make sure that the dough is cool and firm, knead into a smooth ball and lightly press into the mould with a rolling-pin or the hand. Knock it out of the mould on to paper as above and pierce it.

Shortbread fingers or shapes

1 Roll dough 5 mm thick for fingers or 10 mm thick for shapes.

2 Cut fingers 25 × 50 mm, or small fancy shapes with cutters about 25 mm across.

3 Pierce them.

4 Bake until set and pale golden brown.

38　Beverages

Orange and apricot drink

4 servings
Cooking time 10 minutes

Standard	*Modified*　Sugar⁻
100 g dried apricots	
600 ml sweetened orange juice	use unsweetened orange juice

1　Soak apricots for 1 hour in orange juice.
2　Bring mixture to boiling point and simmer for 10 minutes.
3　Liquidise mixture and strain if desired.
4　Chill before serving.

Banana milk shake

4 servings

Standard	*Modified*　Fat⁻
600 ml milk	use skimmed milk
2 bananas	
pinch of nutmeg	

1　Peel and roughly chop banana.
2　Put banana, milk and nutmeg into a blender and liquidise until smooth.
3　Leave to chill and then serve.

Tea

1 level teaspoon or 1 teabag for each person	allowing at least 125 ml water for each person
1 level teaspoon 'for the pot'	

1　Fill the kettle with freshly drawn cold water and just before it boils scald the teapot and empty it.
2　Measure tea into the heated teapot.
3　As soon as the water boils take the teapot to the kettle and fill it with boiling water.

4 Infuse small-leaf tea for 3 minutes, china tea and other large-leaf teas for 5 minutes. Have ready more boiling water, in a jug, to refill the teapot for second cups.

5 Serve tea with milk, preferably skimmed milk, or thin slices of lemon.

Coffee – filter method

1 measure of filter coffee per cup

water for the requisite number of cups

1 Fill the water holder or jug to the desired level with water.

2 Put a coffee filter paper in the filter holder.

3 Add the required number of measures of filter coffee.

4 Switch the machine on.

5 Serve coffee when all the water in the holder has passed through the coffee into the jug.

6 Coffee may be served with hot or cold milk or cream and sugar. In the interest of health choose skimmed milk and avoid sugar.

Coffee – percolator method

2–3 servings

4 level tablespoons ground coffee

500 ml water

1 Put measured coffee into the perforated holder. The coffee should only half fill the holder because it swells when the water reaches it and it may overflow.

2 Pour the water into the pot.

3 Position the perforated holder, with its perforated lid on, inside the pot.

4 Put the lid on the pot and heat it gently on the hot plate, or turn on electricity if using an electric percolator.

5 Percolate until the indicator light on the electric percolator shows coffee is ready, or for 10 minutes after the sound or sight of coffee beating against the lid when using a hot plate.

6 Serve as for filter coffee.

Cocoa

Standard	*Modified* Fat⁻ Sugar⁻
To each breakfast cup of milk or milk and water:	use skimmed milk
2 level teaspoons of cocoa	
1 level teaspoon sugar	omit sugar altogether or use less

1 Put cocoa, sugar if used, and 2 teaspoons of measured liquid into a mug or cup.

2 Blend together using a teaspoon.

3 Put remaining liquid on to boil. Whisk continuously to prevent skin formation.

4 Pour boiled liquid on to blended mixture, stirring continuously.

Index

Italicised page numbers refer to recipes

Pearson Education Limited
Edinburgh Gate
Harlow
Essex
CM20 2JE
England and Associated Companies throughout the World.

First published 1963
Second edition 1974
Third edition 1988
Fourth edition 1997
Fifth impression 2000

ISBN 0582 30573 X

Illustrations by Gecko Limited, John Woodcock and Tony Richardson.
Cover illustration by FMS

Printed in Singapore (COS)

Acknowledgements

The author would like to thank Marie Davies and Linda Betiku for their assistance
in the preparation of the manuscript.

We are indebted to the Controller of Her Majesty's Stationery Office for
permission to reproduce extracts from The Food Labelling Regulations (1996)
and The Health of the Nation (1992) Crown copyright.

We are grateful to the following for permission to reproduce photographs:
Allinson Wholemeal Bread Education Service, page 63; Camilla Jessel, page 51; Dr
D. S. Mclaren, pages 29, 38; National Diary Council, pages 153, 162; Oxfam, page
31; RHM, page 64; St. Bartholomew's Hospital, London, page 27.